Sir Amias Poulet, John Morris

The Letter-Books of Sir Amias Poulet

Sir Amias Poulet, John Morris

The Letter-Books of Sir Amias Poulet

ISBN/EAN: 9783744713863

Printed in Europe, USA, Canada, Australia, Japan

Cover: Foto ©ninafisch / pixelio.de

More available books at **www.hansebooks.com**

THE LETTER-BOOKS OF

SIR AMIAS POULET

Keeper of Mary Queen of Scots.

EDITED BY

JOHN MORRIS,

Priest of the Society of Jesus.

LONDON:

BURNS AND OATES, PORTMAN STREET

AND PATERNOSTER ROW.

———

1874.

INTRODUCTION.

THE present volume does not pretend to be a complete history of that portion of the captivity of the Queen of Scots of which it treats. It gives no account of the greatest event of that captivity, Mary's trial at Fotheringay, nor of the tragedy that brought the long imprisonment to an end. The reader is forewarned lest he should be disappointed.

Neither is it a systematic defence of the innocence of the captive and martyred Queen. The substance of the book is from the pen of one of her bitterest enemies, and if his words are accompanied with some comment, the spirit in which that comment is written is certainly not that of blind partizanship. The remarks elicited by the letters of Sir Amias Poulet are everywhere kept within very moderate compass, and are intended solely to enable the reader to form a just and intelligent judgment on the materials of history now placed before him.

It happens certainly that the narrative of a popular writer has been very frequently placed in juxtaposition with the sources of information as to facts, fidelity to which constitutes the difference between a history and a romance. The examination of Mr. Froude's historical inaccuracy has, however, been carried no further than strictly belonged to the work in hand. Unhappily a single chapter of that gentleman's *History of England* has sufficed to furnish a number of unfounded statements, the parallel of which it would be difficult to find in any one claiming to occupy the judicial position of a historian.

This book has been undertaken, then, not as a defence of Queen Mary, nor as a reply to her assailants, but only because, by a piece of singular literary good fortune, letters unpublished and unknown concerning the last months of the life of the Queen of Scots came into the Editor's hands through the kindness of his friend, Dr. Blackett. The reader is the judge whether their interest does not justify their publication. Elsewhere the kindness of that friend is acknowledged, but the Editor cannot fail in this place to repeat the recognition of the obligation.

There is another friend by whom the comments that accompany the letters have been carefully revised, and for the help thus kindly given the Editor finds it very difficult adequately to express his gratitude. To the same hand the Editor and the reader are alike indebted for the interesting extracts from the Paris letters of Sir Amias Poulet, and for the prefatory remarks by which they are introduced.

The Editor is further bound to express his obligations to the Rev. H. O. Coxe, Bodley's

Librarian, who, after the Manuscripts had been purchased by the Library, kindly permitted them to remain in the Editor's hands until the Press had been corrected from them. If it were necessary to give any proof of the authenticity of these documents, it would be afforded by the fact of their purchase by the Curators of the Bodleian on the recommendation of their experienced Librarian. It is, however, unnecessary, for they speak for themselves. And besides, many original letters exist in the British Museum and among our Public Records, the copies of which are found in these letter-books.[1] For the books in question are the clerk's copies, taken at the time, of the letters written by Sir Amias Poulet. They occupy in all forty-two folios, and are parts of three different letter-books, the handwriting of each book being different from that of the others. One was written at Tutbury, the second at Chartley, and the last at Fotheringay.

The portion surviving of the Tutbury letter-book contains twelve letters to Lord Burghley, of which six were already known; fifteen letters and a considerable fragment of a letter to Sir Francis Walsingham, of which thirteen letters were known; two letters to the Earl of Leicester, and one to Sir John Perrot. This is the concluding part of the letter-book, and thus the letter with which it

---

[1] As these letters have been passing through the press, the Editor has come to the knowledge of the existence of some originals, of which he was not aware when the first sheets were printed. The letters that are new to the public are thirty-eight in number, besides fragments, so that the statement made below (p. 4) needs correction.

ends is perfect. The dates of these letters are from the latter end of May to August 19, 1585. In this book there are seventeen folios.

The portion of the letter-book written at Chartley commences and ends with fragments of letters to Lord Burghley, to whom there are besides eight letters, all new. This letter-book further contains twenty-four letters to Walsingham, of which four only are new; one letter to the Justices of Stafford, one to M. Arnault, and one to Lord Howard of Effingham, the Lord Admiral. The earliest date in this letter-book is November 7, 1585, and the latest May 25, 1586. There are fourteen folios in this book.

The last fragmentary letter-book begins with four lines of a letter to Queen Elizabeth, and contains one letter to Earl Buckhurst, one to Mr. Stallenge, one to the Earl of Leicester, one to Sir John Perrot, five to Lord Burghley, of which one is in the British Museum, five to Sir Francis Walsingham, two of which are in the Record Office, and nine, with a portion of a tenth, to Secretary Davison. This book begins at the latter end of November, 1586, and the closing letter is dated February 2, 1586-7. The letter-book contains eleven folios.

It will be seen that it is to this last book that we owe most of the letters hitherto unknown. But though the letters preserved in the Public Record Office and the British Museum have been hitherto accessible, the interesting matter contained in them is far from being exhausted, and they have largely

· contributed to complete the series of letters now placed before the reader.

One liberty the Editor has unwillingly and hesitatingly ventured to take with the letters. The spelling is modernized throughout. The phrases and the words are otherwise unaltered ; but to have left the difficulty presented to most readers by the uncouth and irregular spelling of the time would have been to deter many from perusing the book. An apology is due to the antiquarian, for whose contentment the letters quoted in the Preface are given spelled as they are in the Manuscript.

There remains one duty, appropriate to this place, and this is to show how Sir Amias Poulet came to be chosen for the charge of the Queen of Scots. For this appointment the letters written by him when English Ambassador at Paris fully account. They are now placed before the reader, together with the Preface already mentioned, to the writer of which the Editor renews his acknowledgments and thanks.

J. M.

St. Beuno's College, St. Asaph,
April 25, 1874.

PREFACE.

THE appointment of the Captain of Jersey to succeed the Earl of Shrewsbury in the charge of Mary Stuart was matter both of surprise and speculation among contemporaries. Men were asking why, when others were to be had, the Queen should go to the West of England "to pick out Poulet?"[1] Apart from the fact that neither his rank nor fortune justified the choice, Poulet's health was so completely broken, that Somers, then acting under Sir Ralph Sadler, Mary's temporary keeper, strongly urged the substitution of some fitter person.[2] Meanwhile Mary herself, evidently anxious, sent repeated

---

[1] *Infra*, p. 19.

[2] *Infra*, p. 4. Sadler also indirectly expostulated by writing letters after he had received notice of Poulet's appointment, ignoring it completely, and recommending other persons, notably Sir John Zouch, who had assisted the Earl of Shrewsbury during his illness in 1569. Both Sadler and Somers wrote under the impression that he was chosen only to assist Lord St. John of Bletso. Poulet, it was well known, was heart and soul of Leicester's party, and for years Leicester had covertly worked to have the Queen of Scots removed from Shrewsbury's keeping into that of some man devoted to his policy. It was a change which Mary had all along anticipated with dread as the prelude to disaster. Nine years earlier she had written, "Je sçay que Leicester tasche par tous moyens de m'oster d'entre les mains de Shrewsbury, pour me tenir en la garde de quelqu'un qui soit a sa dévotion, et en lieu où il ayt puissance" (Mary to Glasgow, February 20, 1576; Labanoff, tom. iv., p. 298). Shrewsbury himself points significantly to the repeated efforts of Mary's enemies to get her out of his hands when, in the storm raised against him on his step-daughter's marriage to Lord Charles Stuart, he tells Burghley that "this great ado" is to be set down neither to the marriage nor personal ill-will towards himself; "it is a greater matter, which I leave to conjecture, not doubting but your lordship's wisdom hath foreseen it" (Lodge ii., p. 126).

remonstrances to Elizabeth on the score that Poulet during his embassy to Paris had shown himself her enemy. The Queen wrote reassuringly, vindicating Poulet's "dealings" while in France, and insisting that her captive might every way feel herself safe in the hands of a man of strict honour, who being what he was, never could "do anything unworthy of himself."[1] Walsingham and his mistress together having made the choice, naturally all objections raised went for nothing, and in April, 1585, just one month after the famous bond of association had been embodied in an Act of Parliament, Sir Amias went down to Tutbury.[2]

Now keeping in view both the ground of Mary's objection and the date of Poulet's entrance upon his office, it may be worth while to look back to the period of his embassy, and pass in review a few specimens of his diplomatic correspondence which, considering that through the very letters before us Walsingham must have gained special insight into

---

[1] *Infra.*, p. 6.

[2] Robertson, and a train of writers after him, assign as motive for the change of Mary's guardian, that Elizabeth, considering that the Earl treated his prisoner with over courtesy and indulgence, purposely placed her under a man of inferior rank, who would be likely, with an eye to future favour or preferment, to be severely vigilant in his charge (*Hist. Scotland*, ii., p. 124). An early biographer of the Queen of Scots, Strangvage, quoted by Mr. Ogle, expounds the opinion current in his day. After giving as the reason alleged by Elizabeth's Government for removing the prisoner, that a plot was on foot for her escape, he goes on, "Moreover, there were letters shown as if they had been intercepted in the which the friends of that Queen complained that all their hopes were quite cut off, if she were but put into the custody of the Puritans. Under this colour she was taken from Shrewsbury, and that of purpose (as some thinke) that being driven into desperation she might be more apt to take abrupt counsels, and more easie to be trapped. For Shrewsbury, in all that fifteen yeeres, had so providently kept her, that there was no place left of plots, for her or against her" (Strangvage, *Life of Mary*, p. 158. See Shrewsbury to Elizabeth, December 29, 1573, Murdin, p. 272).

the views, aims, and character of the Puritan envoy, do, we think, throw a cross light on his appointment at a particular juncture as keeper to the Queen of Scots.

At the date of Poulet's Embassy (September, 1576) the course of events was shaping Elizabeth's policy into open and active interference in the Netherlands, a circumstance which probably in some degree accounts for his being sent into France. For Jersey had during his government served as sanctuary to French Huguenots, and its Captain, widely known for a thorough-going partisan of "the religion," was exactly the man to be trusted by the chiefs of that party in Flanders.

Poulet's official correspondence, as contained in the well known *Rawlinson MS.*,[1] and its companion volume, only lately brought to light, covers the period from the end of May, 1577, up to August 29, 1578.[2] It supplies interesting details respecting advances made by the States to Elizabeth through her envoy at Paris, and throws strong light on the views and interests of both Courts, French and English, in the Low Countries, and especially on the action of the Queen-Mother, who busily scheming for d'Alençon, contrives from first to last by means of Poulet, a willing instrument, to stimulate Elizabeth's fears and jealousy of Spain and of Don John. And the handling of these and other matters affords details of Catharine's secret

---

[1] *Vide infra*, p. 3.

[2] *Rawlinson MS.*, A. 331; May 22, 1577—January 10, 158⅞. *Bodleian Addl. MSS.*, vii., C. 12. January 12, 157⅞—August 29, 1578.

working against Mary Stuart, all pointing to the fact that during the after course of events, she it was whose strong hand kept back Henry III. from active interference on behalf of his kinswoman.

Resolutely passing over much tempting matter directly or indirectly bearing upon the history of Mary Stuart, we choose as a sample of Catharine's earlier workings for her favourite project, the joint action of France and England against Spain, as well as of Poulet's personal views and diplomatic talents, part of a single despatch to the Secretaries. It reports successive conversations with Mazzini Delbena, an Italian hanger-on of the Queen-Mother, into whose dexterous hands she seems to have put the manipulation of the Ambassador.

" He [Delbena] tolde me of the great preparacions made, by the Kings of Spaine and Portugall of xl. or l. gallyes which should be sent into these narowe seas, of the good successe of Don John in the Lowe Countreys, of lykelihode of newe troubles in Scotlande, of some things sounding to the dishonour of the Duke of Guyse, of the arryvall of an Iryshe Bysshopp,[1] and hereuppon long speche passed betwene him and me, wherin I tooke a contrary course to his expectacion, and, in dede, would not seme to perceave wherunto he tendyd, onlie I sayd that the greatnes of Don John in the Lowe Countreys ought to be more suspected, and might be more daungerous to France then to Englande, which had the sea for his ramparte betwene yt and the Spaniarde, wheras Fraunce

---

[1] The Franciscan Bishop of Killaloe, Cornelius O'Mullrain.

had the Spaniard and his alyes his next neighbours of everie syde."

Delbena next, skilfully shifting his ground to the vulnerable points of England, her sister countries, expatiates on the arrival at Court of the Irish Bishop, come for the alleged purpose of demanding Henry's justice on Breton pirates by whom he had been robbed on his voyage from Lisbon. Upon which, says Poulet :

" I told him that this Irishe Bysshopp sholde do well to aunswere to the roberyes which himself hathe don of late upon some Englishe men, and that yf justice were to be had in Fraunce against Iryshe rebells or Irishe theves, I would not fayle to bestowe this Irishe Byshopp where he shoulde be forthe comyng. Then he asked me what I herde out of Scotland. I aunsweryd that I was advertised of some treating betwene them to dysmysse the Regent, and to put the whole Government into the Kings handes. We saye here (sayeth he) that there [is] likelyhode of troubles among them, and that Veracq, karver to Quene-Mother, or Manderville,[1] a gentleman of Normandye shalbe sent thither shortlye, and that the motyon of mariage betwene the Scottishe King and the Princes of. Lorrayne shalbe renewed.[2] Do youe thinke (quod I) that Q. Mother wilbe a dealer

---

[1] Mary to Glasgow, May 9, 1578. Labanoff, tom. v., p. 35. Both de Vérac and Mandreville, Catharine's Intendant of the Household, had previously been sent into Scotland as agents of the French Government. Mandreville's instructions for a special mission, dated May, 1578, a month later than the conversation between Poulet and Delbena, are printed in Teulet.

[2] Mary to Glasgow, September 15, 1578. Labanoff, tom. v., p. 58.

in these matters? He aunswerid that Q. Mother was greatlie affectyd to the Princesse, and was so vehement in her affections, as she woulde some tymes forgett her self in matters of greatest consequence as sone as anye other, as had appeared in the King that now ys whom contrarye to lawe and reason, only because she loved him without measure, she made him Lieftennant generall, and (yf he might so call him) King of this realme, when his brother yet lyved."

The talk then fell again upon the Low Countries, Delbena trying, says Poulet, "to feel my opinion touching the Spaniard." That opinion was given frankly enough. Close union between France and England, always a thing comfortable and profitable, Sir Amias said, had in these days become a vital necessity to both sides. Don John's ascendancy in the Low Countries threatened danger to all his neighbours, but, beyond all others, danger to France. For, lying full open to the Spaniard, it behoved her to beware lest she should be the first to fall "under the tyranny of that barbarous nation." United, France and England would be strong enough to beat off the threatened peril, to drive Don John and his Spaniards out of Flanders, to restore that country to its ancient rights, and make it, instead of being, as now, the battle-ground of nations, what it had been in old times, the market-place of Western Europe. But—here perhaps the Puritan envoy was carried away beyond Elizabeth's instructions—but only in France and by Henry's own hand, could the foundations of this most wholesome amity be laid.

For how could England join hands with France while her King persecuted the religion professed by the Queen of England? As a thing essential to a solid friendship between the two countries, Henry must at once make a lasting peace with his Protestant subjects on such terms as "woulde make yt to appeare unto the worlde that he did not hate their religyon, and dyd admytt the same in his realmes and domynions frankly, and with his good will. I sayed experience had showyd that this religion had taken suche roote in the harts of this people, as the same was not to be removyd by fyre, sworde, or anye other vyolence whatsoever, and that the successe of things from tyme to tyme contrarye to the opynion of all men dyd wytnesse plainely that God had decreyd to plant his gospell in this countrie, and woulde mainteyn yt against all worldly power whatsoever."

On this matter Sir Amias protested that he had spoken his mind as a good Christian, a loyal Englishman, and a sincere friend and well-wisher to France; he cared not if all the Kings and Queens in Europe heard his words, and he bade Delbena carry them back to those who had sent him. The words were heart-felt, spoken too with a fearless honesty from which it is impossible to withhold respect; yet we do not forget the while that the speaker set geographical limits to the virtue of tolerance. Across the Channel Poulet could preach up its duties to Catharine de Medicis. At home, ever insatiate even over the full measure of fine, prison, rack and gibbet, dealt out by Elizabeth to those of her subjects professing the same faith as Henry III., it was with him perpetual cause of bitter complaint that "her Highness doth so dandle the Catholics." Finally, Sir Amias, looking back to real business, let Catharine's agent know that if there were to be friendship with France the marriage scheme between James and a Princess of Lorraine must be quashed, and that, for the future, "Scottish matters" must be left entirely in Elizabeth's hands. Going straight from Poulet to Catharine, Delbena reported the conference. The Queen-Mother, ignoring the sermon on tolerance altogether, returned as her answer that she was willing to strike a bargain with Elizabeth. Only let the latter make a league offensive and defensive with Henry in view of their joint action in the Netherlands, and from that day forward "Scotland shoulde be lefte to the disposycion of her Highnes, and that nothing shoulde be done from hence to the contrarie. . . . Also he usyd many arguments, and made a long *recytall of many things paste to perswade me that Quene-Mother never loved the Scottishe Quene*, which I canne be easlelie inducyd to beleve, and would have beleved hym herein the rather yf he had not sayed the lyke of the King of Spaine. But the truthe ys that she lovethe and hatythe as makethe most for her profytt. . . . As this woman canne make. her profytt of tymes and occasyons, and perchaunce sekethe to serve her tourne without respecte to the right or the wrong. So I truste her Majestie will not refuse in juste and honorable causes to make oportunytes when they are profered,

b

which being plainely ment will serve to represse the insolencie of the Spaniarde, to discover the suttelties of the Scott, and to assure those of the religyon here in suche sorte as yf they be wyse they will not be easelie removed herafter."[1]

Among other topics of these letters, Poulet's comments on the civil war raging in France during the first year of his embassy,[2] may be next mentioned as exhibiting him in the combined character of dogmatist and statesman, and as offering at the same time some curious illustrations of his code of political morals.[3] It was a bitter and a bloody struggle. Sismondi, the Protestant historian, gives a melancholy description, not only of the miseries entailed upon France through the long series of religious wars, but of the frightful demoralization of the Huguenot army during the campaign of 1577. Their early religious enthusiasm dying out had, he says, given place to a fierce spirit of vengeance, and moreover that living at free quarters in the country,

---

[1] To the Secretaries, April 2, 1578.

[2] The sixth religious war, which broke out January, 1577, and was ended by the peace of Bergerac in the following September.

[3] It belonged to Poulet's official duties during the war to endeavour to blind Henry as to the covert aid Elizabeth was sending to his revolted subjects. Whenever this subject is discussed, the dialogue between himself and the King or Queen-Mother invariably exhibits a personal trait in the Puritan envoy. While equal to a fair amount of shuffling and evasion, Sir Amias cannot command himself to tell a direct falsehood. Where this is imperative, he gets over the difficulty by becoming a mere mouthpiece for his mistress : "I told him (Henry) that your Majesty had commanded me to assure him of your innocency in these things," &c. The thing, a trifle in itself, invites comparison with the dialogue of the Fotheringay letter-book, where Poulet holding, by Elizabeth's order, talk with Mary Stuart for the sole purpose of extorting some admission of her guilt, can yet never bring himself to charge her simply and directly with her imputed crime (*infra*, p. 330).

"c'est à dire par un vrai brigandage," the troops had come to rival their former companions-in-arms, the Reiters, in brutality and licence.[1] Now all that Sismondi describes, Elizabeth's envoy, following in the wake of the Court through the disturbed provinces, saw with his own eyes. Nor, as many of the despatches bear him honourable witness, was he a man who could unmoved contemplate the widespread popular misery. Take as example, one letter where Sir Amias, the human heart within him quickening his prolix English into force and terseness, paints the situation in a few graphic sentences.

" God longe preserve you in peace and quietnes, if it be His good pleasure, and deliver you and your contrey from the myseries and calamities of this poore realme, which are such and so great as a Cristian enymie shalbe movid to have pittie of them ; and many do thinke the same have not growne of anie one cause more then of the particular quarrells of some great personages, which often tymes have their begening of nothing, and for nothinge, being neclected as thinges of nothinge, growe afterwardes to be somwhatt, and many tymes ireconcyliable. You woulde thinke that the oppressions which this realme hath enduirde within these fower monethes were inoughe to destroye a mightie kingdome. One armye in Poictou and Guyenn, the other before La Charité, the third in the borders for doubte of the Reistres, Bussy d'Amboise in Anjou with great companies. I

[1] *Histoire des Français*, tom. xix., p. 447.

spake nothinge of those of the religion, who are forcyd by necessytie to comitt spoyles daylye; *le bon homme* is eaten to the bone, and is manye tymes beaten, hurt, and kylled because he will not geve that which he hath not."[1]

But how strangely in contrast with the tone of feeling which marks the above letter is that of an official despatch, written not a month afterwards. In view of the preliminaries then going forward for the peace of Bergerac, Poulet is urging his mistress to prolong hostilities by once again bringing Casimir and his Reiters upon the country.

"Manie here of good judgment are perswadyd that the suerty and safty of the Protestants dependeth altogether of the coming or not coming of the Reistres, and that the K[ing] is incensyd with such furye against the trewe relygion as he will never condescend to anie reasonable condicions of peace untill he shalbe constrayned by the sworde, which cannot be expected of the French sworde, the odds being of the King's syde without comparison. . . . Manie other circomstances may seme worthy to be consydered, and espetiallie that if this tract of tyme may be anie waye profittable unto the Protestants which are nowe the weaker, how much may it be more profittable unto the Papists which are now the stronger, who maketh his profitt of the presente tyme and will provide to be the lyke for the tyme to come. I have hard saye that the defence ys as just where an offence is expectid as where the offence is given allready, so as the defence doe not

---

[1] Poulet to Sir George Speke, Tours, May, 1577.

proceed of needlesse feare or maliceous covetousnes. And if this rule be trewe, yt shalbe meete for
Christian princes to consider in tyme yf they be not
already dryven to thys necessytie, as eyther must
offer violence in season or suffer violence out of
season. If religion were not a sworne quarrell,
whoe can looke that when the Protestants here
shalbe underfoote, that these their army wilbe ydle
att home? Yf att other tymes yt hath bene⎪received for a maxime that Fraunce must alwayes
have some warre in hande, how much more now
when they have ben unsetled as they cannott
abyde to lyve in peace? God graunt the end of
these things to redounde to the glorye of God,
to the honor of your Majestie, and of all other
trew Christian princes, and to the comfort of the
poore afflycted Church of Christ."[1]

Poulet's eloquence fell dead, for Elizabeth at
the time having other schemes on hand, showed
no disposition to repeat her notorious breaches of
the treaty of Blois. Peace was concluded, and
Sir Amias finds his only consolation in bewailing
to Secretary Wilson that—

" Our enemies are manie, craftie, and malicious,
and resolute to do us all the hurt that they may;
our frindes are few, or non at all. Our selfes so
full of conscience that our conscience will not serve
to defend ourselves from knowen and manifest
daungers."[2]

These maxims, that where offence is expected

---

[1] To the Queen, Tours, June 22, 1577.
[2] To Dr. Wilson, November, 1577.

defence is as lawful as where the offence has been given, that conscience is not to be allowed to stand in the way of important issues, with kindred axioms flowing from the teaching that all means used towards a good end become lawful, find frequent expression under various forms in the letters. Here we have before us the evil doctrine, which, falsely charged against the Jesuits, did in truth govern the counsels of Elizabethan statesmen, and which received its fullest illustration in their action against Mary Stuart. Light burden of conscience to Poulet and his chiefs could be the deepest personal wrong, provided only that the private wrong served the great interests of the common-wealth and of "the religion."[1]

Sent into France under Leicester's patronage, Poulet, as might be expected, shows himself an active enemy of the Queen of Scots. About that time a restlessness in Ireland, the state of parties in Scotland, and the irritation of the oppressed Catholics at home, all seemed to be opening the way to some united movement of the Catholic Powers for the rescue of Elizabeth's prisoner, and considerable apprehension was felt on the subject

---

[1] Burghley's declaration that he bore no ill-will to the Queen of Scots, but that he only "did intend principally the service and honour of God, and jointly with it, the surety and quietness of my sovereign lady, the Queen's Majesty (*Strype*, ii., c. xxxvi, p. 385); Poulet's asseveration over the pillage at Chartley, "I renounce my part of the joys of Heaven if in anything I have said, written, or done, I have had any other respect than the furtherance of her Majesty's service" (*infra*, p. 291); and the well-known evasion with which Walsingham rose to his feet when charged face to face by Mary, on the Fotheringay trial, with having used forgeries to compass her destruction; these may one and all be mentioned as entirely supporting the above conclusion.

by the English Government, an uneasiness heightened by the circumstance that Mary, despairing of help from Henry and Catharine de Medicis, had then openly thrown herself upon the protection of Spain, and was, also, negotiating the removal of her young son from Scotland into France, to be brought up by her kinsmen of the house of Lorraine. And while she was working to carry out her plans, the situation received fresh complications through collateral intrigues, of which she had, without her sanction, become the object. Don John, Philip's half-brother, appointed governor of the Netherlands in 1576, was looking forward, after the settlement of the Provinces, to a raid upon England for the purpose of giving Mary her freedom, and of claiming her hand as its price. These are topics upon which Sir Amias never grows weary of ringing the changes. Parts of the correspondence indeed strike us as written for the express purpose of agitating Elizabeth's mind. Warnings of domestic conspiracy, rumours current in France that Don John had already peremptorily demanded the hand of the Queen of Scots,[1] that having broken prison, she was in the field at the head of English forces, while the whole Catholic confederacy was arming to set her on her rival's throne; France and Spain in league to crush England; Don John arriving on the eastern coast,

---

[1] Here and elsewhere we get sight of a hand sowing the rumours. "Twoo such as I knowe to be spyes for Q[ueen] Mother have tould me within these twoe dayes that *Don John hath sent to your Majestie to requier the Queen of Scoots for his wife,* and because this tale cometh from suspected men, I doubt it hath some further meaning" (To the Queen, August, 1577).

Spain and the Guise behind him, while simultane-
ously Westmoreland and Fitzmaurice seize Ireland :
these and the like alarms are perpetually iterated,
and well besprinkled with dark sayings, which read
in the light of the Fotheringay letter-book become
palpably clear.

Poulet's despatches did their work. Mary's
enemies drew occasion from them to put the Queen
into a paroxysm of fear and suspicion. Mary was
straitened in her prison, and intrigues were renewed
for removing her from Shrewsbury's guardianship
into "surer keeping."[1] They did their work in that
day,—they have come down to our own an indis-
putable proof that, as a preliminary to Walsingham's
contrivances against her, the captive was knowingly
and deliberately put into the hands of a declared
enemy.

We find Poulet at his first interview with his
prisoner after arriving at Tutbury, frankly admitting
that while Ambassador at Paris, he had been "careful and curious over Morgan's doings."[2] Now it
happens that the Paris despatches reveal the secrets
of this surveillance, presenting a story so curious
in itself, so illustrative both of Walsingham's tactics,
and of Poulet's personal character, and withal, so
deeply significant when viewed in connection with
his after appointment, that it will be worth while to
let Sir Amias tell it for us in his own words.

The following is part of a letter from him to

[1] Burghley to Shrewsbury, September 7, 1577. Lodge ii., p. 163. *Public
Record Office MSS., Mary Queen of Scots*, vol. xi., nn. 2, 3, 4, 5.
[2] *Infra.*, p. 8.

Sir Francis Walsingham, dated January 8, 1577-8, and is the only one in the series taken from the Rawlinson Manuscript. The others have, we believe, been hitherto unknown.

"Yt may please your honor to be advertised that the xxvijth of the last, M. D.[1] resorted to my lodginge, where he declared unto mee that after many meetinges and conferences with J. B., the said J. had now at the last assured hym that he was accquainted with all the particularyties of the D[uke] of N[orfolk] his treason, as also with all that was practised by the Pope and the K[ing] of Spaine by the negotiation of Radolpho,[2] and that uppon assurance of consideration worthy of a service of this ymportance, he woulde reveale all his knowledge. And further, whereas M[organ] now beinge in this Towne, ys not ignorant of the bottom of all the latter conspiracies betwene the Queene of Scotts and her confederats, under pretence to goe with the said M[organ] to Rome, he woulde deliver hym into the handes of soche as her Majestie woulde appoint at Caseluther[3] or Heddberge.[4] The said D. protesting that he woulde not be the instrument to effectuat this devise onleast he might receave her Majesties promise that the said M[organ] shoulde not be touched in his lyfe, which beinge saved, he referred hym in all other thinges to the consideracion of her Highnes. He added that he woulde be contented that J. B. shoulde also be aprehended and sent into England with the other, uppon promise

---

[1] Mazzini Delbena.   [2] Ridolfi.   [3] Kaiserlautern.   [4] Heidelberg.

that he shoulde not be yll used; as indeede (saythe
he) beinge the meane of the aprehension of
M[organ], he doethe deserve good intertainement.
He concluded that theis thinges could not be
performed onleast yt woulde please her Majestie,
or you, Mr. Walsingham, in her behalfe, to assure
hym by two or three wordes that J. should be
well recompensed, who woulde do nothinge untill
he might see his letres of warrant for his assurance.

"I asked hym yf J. coulde not be perswaded
to acept my worde and promise for his satisfaction,
and to be contente to make presente declaracion
of his knowledge in theis thinges, because I coulde
not tell if the same might be soche as woulde abide
no delay. He said (as before) that B. woulde do
nothinge onlesse he had his warrant out of England.
I toulde hym I doubted not but that he did already
understand all that M[organ] did know, and therefore shoulde do well to reveale the same, with
his owne knowledge in the other thinges before
specified, which might serve to good purpose,
although M[organ] were aprehended. He answered
that yt was not possible to get any thinge from
M[organ], wherin B. had don all that he coulde,
but in vayne, and that if the saide J. shoulde presse
M[organ] herein, he woulde not only repulse hym,
but also conceave an yll opinion of hym, and woulde
wryte to the frindes of the said J. in Englande to
his discredyt. But (quoth I) where will you fynde
that Prince in Cristendom, and specially in Germany,
where they make great accompte of theire privi-
ledges, and dare not doe any thinge that shalbe to

the derogacion of the same, yf for no other cause then to avoyd the displeasure of the other Princes theire neighbours, that will deliver a straunger into the hands of any Prince whatsoever[?] That ys no parte (saythe he) yt ys you that must looke to that. Yt is a matter that must be considered, quod I. D[uke] C[asimir], saithe he, will not refuse the Q[ueen] your mistres, no more then the P. of S. hathe done already for J. I toulde [him] J. was never delivered. In deede you say truly, sayeth he, but yt shalbe ynoughe for the Q[ueen] your mistres, yf he be examyned upon tortures or otherwise, at her pleasure, which [no] prince that ys frinde to her Majestie will deny. And I dare take yt upon me (saythe he), that this shalbe don at Seddan.[1] I concluded that when a man coulde not do as he woulde, he must be content to do as he could. And because D. made no mencion of any consideracion to be used towardes hymselfe, I thought good to use soch speaches as might serve to assure hym that he should not finde her Majestie ungratefull."

Next day the Queen-Mother's agent again visits Poulet for the purpose of sounding him as to the intentions of his mistress towards the Archduke Matthias, and proposes that England and France should conjointly erect the Netherlands into an independent sovereignty, with a view to use it as a lever against the power of Philip in Europe. After detailing the dialogue, Poulet pronounces his opinion.

---

[1] The Duke de Bouillon was sovereign of Sedan.

"The firste matter hath ben handled with great dexteritie; these twoe honest men employing all theire conninge, that D. ys not ignorant of all that J. knoweth. But the prodigalytie of J. coulde not be maintayned, nor his necessitie relived yf D. should utter his knowledg in this matter without the helpe of the other. Also yt is not for nothing that this matter hath ben defered untill this presente. Wherin he knewe as much twoe monethes paste as nowe, and dyd then put me in great hope that he woulde revele his knowledg unto me without delaye, and therefore there is some other mysterie in this tract of tyme. I am not ignorant that ther is great and straight frindship between J. and M[organ], and ame more then halfe perswaded that he [is] acquainted with all that M[organ] knowethe, and theirfore this pretty conveighans is also to be consedered. These men are not unknowne [to *erased*], and therfor [it] shalbe mete to deale warely with them, so as, yf there conning have a further reache, the same may fall uppon theire owne pates. Touching the second pointe, I take it to be most certain that this man came not unto me of himself, but was sent by great personages, wherin manie things maye be devined which are without the compase of my charge, and therfore leave them to your wysdomes. He is no doubt a faithfull servant to Q. Mother, and therfore I dealt as warely as I could with him, and yt seameth worthie to be notted that he shewed himself very yll content that I would not allowe his proposition, wherin, no doubte, as in all other of this question, he sheweth great treachery. Yf this matter shalbe followed, yt may please your honor to send Mr. Beale or some suche other sufficient man hether unto me, as well for my assystance herin, as also to serve for a wittnes of my doinges, because these things may touche I cannot tell whom."

John Blackbourne, the non-juring Bishop, has printed this letter in the collection prefixed to his edition of Bacon's works, fol. Lond., 1730.[1] Blackbourne says, as Mr. Ogle has pointed out in his Preface,[2] that it "lays the scene" of the Queen of Scots much deeper than any other intelligence, and also that it "accounts for the reason why the Queen of Scots was afterwards committed to the custody of Sir Amyas Powlett, since he seems to have made the first discovery of her practices and to have been master of the whole secret."[3]

In the next letter, J. B. appears in person. He bargains for a round sum down from Elizabeth— the amount he will leave to her Majesty's generosity. In return he promises information respecting the Duke of Norfolk's affair and "certain practises" of La Mothe Fénelon while ambassador in London. Also "he hath renewed his former promise touching Morgan." Beyond this he offers, for a pension, to live at the French Court as Poulet's spy, "affirming that he hath great credit with the Cardinal of

---

[1] Macray's *Catalogue of Rawlinson MSS.*, A. 331.
[2] *Poulet's Letters*, Roxburghe Club, 1866.   [3] Vol. i., p. 36.

Guise. I knowe not," the letter goes on, "howe importante his service maye be in these olde matters, but I take yt to be most certaine that in the occurrents of this presente tyme he is able to doe great and singuler service, having good credytt with the Frenche and Spanishe of better sorte. I am unworthie to geve councell in a matter of this waight, and woulde be as sorie to encrease her Majesties charge as anie other. But considering the state of this presente tyme, I wyshe him to be intertained, yea, liberallye intertaynede. The burden is not contynuall, and may be shaken of when yt shall please her Majestie, but the profytt of one howers service maye be tasted manie yeares her-after, to the comforte of her Majestie, and all her trew subjects; and the best service in these badd dayes ys comonlye don by the worst men. . . . A wyse man and well affected to religion hath tolde me of late that we are too good in Englande; and that yf Morgan had bene well handeled, he woulde have dyscoverid manie thinges which are nowe secret, and then coulde not have don the hurte which he now doythe; and that Guarras[1] is ac-quainted with great practises, and ought to be intreated to reveale them.[2]

Allusions to men of this stamp, "hired Papists" Poulet calls them, who traded in the secrets of the

---

[1] Antonio de Guaras, Spanish factor at London, at that time in the Tower for writing to the Queen of Scots.

[2] Poulet to the Secretaries, January 24, 1578. Bodleian Library, *Additional MSS.*, vii., C. 12. Under this reference the subsequent letters will also be found.

Catholic party with Walsingham, are frequent in the correspondence. In his more respectable character of spy and informer, the fellow was hired on the spot. Poulet forwards intelligence and stolen letters procured by "my new acquaintance," the "matter of recompense" meanwhile waiting her Majesty's pleasure. J. B. was a well born English scoundrel, of the same type as Edward Woodshawe, who three years before had offered his services as spy and poisoner, to Burghley. Burghley had not scrupled in 1575 to hire Woodshawe to entrap the Earl of Westmoreland on his way from Flanders into France,[1] and "carry him dead or alive to England;" and now Walsingham was equally ready to hire J. B. to perform the same good offices for Morgan. But his answer coming somewhat slowly, Sir Amias, feverish under the delay, writes some weeks afterwards to Beale, whom he had asked Walsingham to send out, in case Delbena's proposals were to be entertained.

"Suche ys the malyce of this wycked tyme wherein good things go slowlye forwardes, and evyll practyses want no furtherance. I wrote my opynyon to Mr. Walsingham long sythens of the badd felowe, and nowe of late I have wryten no lesse to Doctour Boutteryshe, intending to do the lyke to Duke Cazymir. This man hathe done greate hurte alreadie, and groweth in abyllite and credytt to do more and more. . . . You wyshe some good occasyon to bring you hether, and I

---

[1] Mr. Froude tells the story; *History of England*, vol. x., p. 347.

cannot expresse how much I desyre to see youe here."[1]

Two days later, Walsingham's messenger had come. Elizabeth sent a hundred crowns, with promise of future reward. The spy was furious that so paltry a price should be set upon services which, as he said, put his very life in risk. " I cannot expresse unto youe howe J. B. stormed and raged, as well in wordes as in contenance," wrote Poulet, . . . "he sayed that he marvelled verie muche that her Majestie made no better accompte of his service, which he knewe could assure her person and State from manie daungers, that he estemed lytell of [the] crownes, that he was not ignorant of the dealinge of Princes of this tyme, that they would make theire profyt of all men, that when their tourne was served they had litle care of the instrument; that he had profered his service to her Majestie, viij yeres paste. . . That he had alreadie made good demonstracione of his good affection towards her Majesties service, that he received nothing againe from her Majestie, her present gyftes being of 'no valewe, and her rewarde to come uncertaine, and therfore with manie thanks for my good wyll and greate protestacion of his greate affection towardes me, tolde me that he woulde deale no further therin." Upon this threat, both argument and persuasion were tried with B. Among other things Poulet told him—" That he had great cause to thinke well of

[1] To Beale, March 11, 1578.

her Majesties profer, that her acceptance of his servyce, and promise of reward was signified unto him under the signe and seale of one of her Councellors, and by the mouth of her Ambassador . . . that her Highnes had promysed to consider him liberallie, that she would performe yt."[1]

Relenting under iterated assurances of this kind, B., for whose crafty wits his patron's slow brain proved a poor match, at last agreed to continue his service as spy, but was resolved "to deal no further in this matter." That was to be his last word. Later on, however, he contrived to let the Ambassador know that a higher bid might shake even his resolution, and finally Poulet was able to report in triumph that "now J. hath given himself to her Majesty, and doth promise to send me something in writing very secretly." Poulet was all eagerness and self-importance. Clearly Heaven had destined him as the man whose wisdom should unravel every clew and winding of conspiracy, and above and beyond all else, provide the swift "occasion" for applying Cecil's "remedy." The "something in writing" he seems to forward in this letter as a foretaste of what might be forthcoming if only Royalty could be prevailed with to be openhanded.

"Yt maye please your honors to be advertised of the occasyon of this despatche by these coppies inclosyd, not doubting but my letres to her Majestie wilbe impartyd unto youe, and maye suffice to acquainte youe with my symple

---

[1] Poulet to the Secretaries, March 13, 1578.

opynyon herein. . . I referre these other copies inclosed to the consyderacion of your wysedomes, wyshing rather that .these faultes be dyssembled for a season then to enter into anye actyon that maye bewraye the meane of discoverie, *which may hinder a better service* in matters of greater import- ance. There ys great hope or rather yt is most certaine that great things wilbe discoveryd by this instrument, and therefore yt weare a great faulte in my symple opynion yf he shoulde not be lyberallie intertaynde, wherein I will wryte more particularlie unto your honors by my nexte messenger."[1]

On the same day, he writes to Walsingham. "Although I have addressyd my other letres joyntlie unto your honor and Mr. Wylson, which coulde not but be don otherwyse in my opynion, yet I have comandyd this bearer my servant yf he doe not finde youe att Grenewyche, wherof I have willed him to make secrett inquyrie, to seke you at London or els where, and to deliver these letres firste unto your honor, in the which youe shall finde inclosyde the copie of my letres to her Majestie, as knowythe the Almightie, who alwayes preserve your honor."[2]

The letter inclosed, of the 19th, to the Queen, except a few lines at the end, is wanting.

.On the 25th, Walsingham still keeping silence, Sir Amias took it upon himself to appeal to the Queen. He encloses, he says, a copy of "a dis-

---

[1] To the Secretaries, March 19, 1578.
[2] To Walsingham, March 19, 1578.

course delyverid unto me of late by one that professeth all fideletie and service to your Highnes," and "because this sayd wrytinge makythe mencyon of a great personage, I am bolde to imparte the same onlie to your [Majestie]." The rest of this folio has been cut out of the book, but the next shows Poulet deep in argument for an offer of higher terms to "B." "Corrupted instruments," and especially such as have credit with the English rebels and other enemies are not easy to be found, and therefore they that may be obtained ought not to be refused for the price. Money so spent in good time will spare the fitting out of fleets and armies afterwards, and "that penny is well laid out that saveth the spending of many pounds." Merchants are willing to make ventures, and so must sovereigns, and rewards and pensions are the merchandise of princes. Pardon he craves for boldness, but how can loyalty suffer him to keep silence while "your honorable and most happie State ys envyed and threatened of everie syde, and subjecte to present daunger if present remedy be not applyed. . . . I have dispatched this bearer with the more dilligence douting least the Spanishe Ambassador might have so muche credytt with your Majestie to procure the delyverance of Guarace before the receipt of these letres, and indede I might perceave by his owne speche when he was yet here, that this matter was especiallie recomendyd unto hym. Yt maye please your Majestie to consider yf yt shall more further your service that this

Morgan be apprehendyd, or that he contynewe here so longe as youe are provided of an other that is inward with hym that maye discover his secretts. I finde the humour of this instrument, and do feede ytt as well as I canne, having alreadie receaved some promyses of hym to reveale his whole knowledge unto me, and to referre his recompense to your Highnes pleasure, but when he comyth to the executyon he recant-ethe, doubting least when he hathe saide what he canne, he shalbe shaken of without rewarde." [1]

This letter to Walsingham despatched the same day may count among the curiosities of diplomatic literature.

" I have no other refuge in my necessyties then in your good friendshipp, and therfore do nowe most humblie praie your honor to geve me leave to deale boldlie with youe, and to referre myself to your good advice, beinge not ignorante that your wysedome and experiens will easelie consider what maye be most expedyent to be done herein.

" Youe maye perceave by these copies inclosed what I have wryten to the Quene, and yf youe shall thinke good to delyver my letres to her Majestie then yt maye please youe not to be knowen that youe have receyved these copies, and maye tell Mr. Wylson that youe founde the Quenes letres in the pacquet. But if youe shall finde suche imper-fection in my letres as youe shall thinke that *they will not be agreable to her Majestie*, then I shall

[1] To the Queen, March 25, 1578.

moste humblye praye youe to detaine them, and to delyver onlie the copie inclosyd, bering her Highnes in hande that youe have receyved the said copie in your paquet. I am perswaded that before I am six dayes older, the partie will tell me all that he knowyth, althoughe yt shall not be mete that youe take any knowledge that I am in this hope, and therfore yt maye please your honor to geve me your advice by your next dispatche in what order I shall make advertisement therof. Yf in ciphre, yf by the reporte of my sonne, yf by letres onlie to her Majestie, and of suche other cyrcomstances appertaining. I am not ignorant of your great wante of leasure, and yet I shall most humblie praie youe to spare me some fewe lynes for my satisfaction herein. Yf I were worthie to geve her Majestie councell, a present shoulde be made to this partie of 300 crownes, and a promyse of a pension of the lyke some by the yeare. He hath refused the hundred crownes, as you maye understande by my former letres, and yet he hath borowed of me sythens that tyme 130 crownes at one tyme, and 80 crownes at an other tyme, and I thinke yt well bestowed, yf I should paye yt x. tymes of my owne purse. I cannot perswade hym to make anye demaunde, reffering hym selfe wholie to her Majesties goodnes. Yt is easie to see that he dealethe plainelie and franklie. I write openlie unto you, but I have taken suche order with the messangers, as I trust my letres shall come safelie unto youe. Thus your honor seeth how boldly I deale with youe, as one that presumeth of your favour. Yf my opynion of the yerlie pension be thought to great, lett the rewarde in hand be the more libe-rall. Yt is not reason that any man shoulde be caryed awaye with bare promyses where there is questyon of lyving and lyf. We stumbell at strawes, and leape over blockes. And thus, &c."[1]

Walsingham must have seen that his friend's zeal, overriding his natural caution, was putting him into the hands of a practised and greedy scoundrel. He suppressed the letter to Elizabeth, and probably sent a warning. But Poulet, though he answers humbly, thanking the Secretary for saving his credit and "hiding my [great *erased*] faults from her Majesty and the Council,"[2] held like a sleuth-hound to his scheme for striking through Morgan at Morgan's mistress. Here is the epi-logue to the story.

"I cannot expresse unto your honor howe sorie I was to receave your letres sent by Tupper, and I praye God this pinching sparing be not repentid when spending will not helppe ytt, wherin yf I were worthie to geve councell I woulde her Majestie to spare no charge to knowe all the treasons of all tymes and ages, and woulde perchaunce be of opynion that when these treasons are knowen they shoulde never be discoveryd. These matters do not depende of my consideracion, and therfore I leave them to the better judgement of my supperyours, being not a lyttell satisfied with the testymonie of my conscyence that I have done my

<hr>

[1] To Walsingham, March 25, 1578.   [2] To Walsingham, April 15, 1578.

dewtie. But yf these greate and older things maye be forborne, yet who would loose the service · of suche an instrument for the discoverie of the presente doings of this deceytfull tyme. He hathe geven good testymoney that he hath good creditt with a great number of our principall adversaries, Romysshe, Scottishe, and Englishe, and nowe the newe Nuntio ys expected after twoe or three daies with whom he is famylliarye acquainted. None more likelye to fall dangerouslye then those which have eyes and cannot see. We see our daungers, but we will not avoide them, or rather we canne not, because God hathe desired our punishement. Yt maye please youe to have care of my revoca- tion as tyme and occasyon will serve youe. I am, wheresoever I am, at your commandement, as knoweth the Almightie whoe alwayes preserve your honor. From Paris, the xxiiij of Aprill, 1578."

Comment would be wasted upon this episode of Poulet's embassy. Enough to say that it reveals the strong fact that Walsingham, when he sent Sir Amias down to Tutbury, knew him from past experience for a man who would be found willing to connect himself with "instruments" like Gifford and Phelippes, and who would, keeping the end in view, approve and abet the worst intrigues against Mary Stuart. Elizabeth's knowledge of the plot against Morgan also goes some way to explain her anger and disappointment when Poulet refused to act upon her instigation for secretly cutting off his prisoner.

SIR AMIAS POULET'S LETTERS.

SIR AMIAS POULET,

KEEPER OF MARY QUEEN OF SCOTS.

———◆———

SIR AMIAS POULET,[1] of Hinton St. George, in Somersetshire,
from whom the present Earl Poulett is descended, was the head
of the family of which the Marquisses of Winchester, afterwards
Dukes of Bolton, were a younger branch.   His father, Sir Hugh
Poulet, was Captain of the Isle of Jersey, to which office he
succeeded on his father's death in 1571.   Long previous to this
time, Sir Hugh Poulet had ceased to reside in the island, having
been appointed Vice-president of Wales, and Amias was made
Lieutenant of Jersey, April 25, 1559.   Letters from him between
that date and 1569 are preserved amongst the State Papers in
the Public Record Office.[2]

Sir Amias Poulet was knighted in 1576, and soon after he
was sent to France as Ambassador.   On September 25, 1576,
he wrote a letter from Calais to his friend Lord Burghley,[3] the
Lord High Treasurer, from which the following extract is taken.
Francis Bacon, Lord Burghley's nephew, then about sixteen, was
probably one of those who accompanied him to Paris.   He was
certainly with him there in the following year.

I must confess that in this little journey between
London and Dover, I already find your lordship's words

---

[1] The name is now, and always has been, spelled in various ways.
Sir Amias signed his letters "A. Poulet," and this form is here followed.
The inscription on his tombstone is "Amitio Pouletto," and as he wrote his
Christian name "Amice," it was probably so pronounced.   At the present
time, his direct descendant the earl spells the surname Poulett; the Marquis
of Winchester Paulet, while the Duke of Cleveland, as heir to the Duke of
Bolton, has assumed the name of Powlett.

[2] *Domestic, Addenda, Elizabeth,* vol. ix., n. 20; vol. xiv., n. 63.

[3] *Ibid.,* vol. xxiv., n. 92.

B

true, and do feel the weight of my heavy train, and shall feel it more deeply before my coming to Paris, being accompanied with an extraordinary number, whereof some have been recommended unto me by the Queen, some by other noble men, only until their coming to Paris. . . . I do not use these many words so much to excuse my follies, which are too many, as well herein as in all my other doings, as thereby to entreat your good lordship to use your reasonable favour towards me in my allowance for my transportation, my charges (no doubt) being much increased by these extraordinary occasions, and yet I will ask nothing unreasonable. If I ever pass again into France, I will seek my passage at some other port, the haven of Dover being in such utter ruin, as the passage thereby is utterly decayed. The Queen's ships, as likewise the other barks appointed for me and my horses, were forced to seek their surety at Sandwich, when the wind did serve to have passed into France. It were to be wished, for her Majesty's service, that Dover were provided of a better harbour.

Poulet was succeeded by Sir Henry Cobham as Ambassador to France, in November, 1579. He was appointed a Privy Councillor, early in 1585, and sent by Elizabeth to Tutbury, as keeper of Mary Queen of Scots, in the place of Sir Ralph Sadler. In that charge he continued at Tutbury, Chartley, and Fotheringay, till Mary's execution relieved him of his captive. The Queen of Scots was executed February 8, 158$\frac{6}{7}$, and Poulet soon followed his prisoner to the grave. He was made Chancellor of the Garter on the Eve of St. George, 1587, in succession to Walsingham, and Sir John Wolley succeeded him on the feast in the year following.[1] He died[2] September 26, 1588.

By his wife Catherine, daughter and heir of Anthony Harvey, of Columb John, in Devonshire, he had three sons, Hugh, who died in infancy, Sir Anthony, his lieutenant and successor in

---

[1] Ashmole's *Order of the Garter*, p. 521.
[2] Collins, following the inquisition taken January 15, 158$\frac{8}{9}$.

the government of Jersey, and George, who, by marriage with a distant cousin, became the possessor of the old family seat of Gothurst, in Somersetshire; and three daughters, Joan, who married Robert Heyden of Bowood, Devon, Sarah, who married Sir Francis Vincent of Stoke Dabernon, Surrey, and Elizabeth, who died unmarried. The last is probably the "little jewel," Lord Burghley's goddaughter, born while her father had charge of Queen Mary, mentioned in his letter to Lord Burghley of May 12, 1586. His grandson, John Poulet, was made a baron, June 23, 1627; and the fourth Lord Poulet was created Viscount Hinton St. George and Earl Poulet, December 29, 1706.

A very large number of the letters of Sir Amias Poulet are in existence. A volume of his letter-book, containing his letters when Ambassador in France, the first dated from Tours, May 26, 1577, and the last from Paris, January 10, 157⅞, is in the Bodleian Library.[1] It was edited, in 1866, for the Roxburghe Club by Mr. Ogle.

The continuation of this letter-book, beginning January 12, 157⅞, and ending August 29, 1578, was kindly placed in the hands of the present Editor by Dr. Blackett, of 28, Green Street, London. It has now, together with those next to be mentioned, become by purchase the property of the Bodleian Library.

Together with this, were three portions of a still more valuable letter-book, in which were entered copies of such letters, written by Poulet when keeper of the Queen of Scots, as might meet the eyes of his secretary.

In the Public Record Office there are preserved the originals of more than one hundred letters,[2] addressed by him to Sir Francis Walsingham during that period. At a glance it is plain that many of the later letters of this series are missing, and that they were purposely withdrawn from the collection is shown by the significant erasure of the item, "A bundle of letters from Sir Amias Paulett, succeeding Sir Ralph Sadler, 1585 and 1586," in "A note of papers concerning the Queen of Scotland."[3] The

[1] *Rawlinson MSS.*, A., 331.

[2] State Papers, *Mary Queen of Scots*; calendared by Mr. Thorpe. The volumes mentioned in the following notes refer to these State Papers.

[3] Vol. xxi., n. 43.

B 2

portions of the letter-book for the use of which the Editor is
indebted to Dr. Blackett contain more than fifty letters written
by Sir Amias Poulet at that most interesting period, the originals
of which are not to be found in the Public Record Office.   All
these are here printed at length, transcribed in everything but the
spelling, from the letter-book.   The State Papers have long been
accessible to students of history; they are therefore only used
in the following pages sufficiently to link together and render
intelligible the historical material now first published.

The first mention of Poulet in connection with the Queen of
Scots is in a letter in the State Papers,[1] dated January 4, 158⅘,
in which Lord Burghley informs Sir Francis Walsingham that
Lord St. John of Bletso has refused to take charge of Mary, at
which Elizabeth was much displeased, and that she had commanded Burghley "to write to Rycott[2] for Sir Amyes Paulett."
Mr. John Somer, Sir Ralph Sadler's assistant, wrote at once,[3] on
the 13th of January, the very day of their transfer from the
Earl of Shrewsbury's, at Wingfield, to Tutbury, though he
was under the impression that Poulet was coming to assist
Lord St. John, to propose the substitution of other fit persons
instead of Sir Amias Poulet.   "Your good judgment of the
weak state of his body, and the distance of his dwelling, I
think," he says, "are to be allowed for a sufficient *supersedeas*
in this matter."

Sadler naturally was delighted that any man could be found
to relieve him of a position that he disliked extremely.   He
wrote thus to Lord Burghley,[4] in reply to the news of Poulet's
appointment : " I perceive by your lordship's letter, brought to me
by John Danet, that my Lord St. John being excused from this
charge upon such considerable causes as your lordship allegeth,

---

[1] Vol. xv., n. 5.

[2] Rycote, near Thame, where, in Queen Mary's time, Elizabeth was Lord
Williams' prisoner, was now the property of Lord Norreys, whose only
daughter, Catherine, was married to Poulet's eldest son in 1583.

[3] Vol. xv., n. 20.   The draft of this letter is printed in the *State Papers
and Letters of Sir Ralph Sadler*, vol. ii., p. 482.   Edited by Arthur Clifford.
Edinburgh, 1809.

[4] Sadler's *State Papers*, vol. ii., p. 501.

Sir Amyas Pawlet, now worthily one of her Majesty's Privy Council, is appointed, and hath willingly consented to take it upon him, whereof I am right glad, but gladder that your lordship trusteth I shall not tarry here many days ; and for my further comfort, that you will hasten him to the best speed you can. I heartily thank her Majesty and your good lordship for these good tidings." This letter is dated February 5, 158⅘. On the 18th of February,[1] Somer wrote to Walsingham, to express the fear that Mary entertained of her coming keeper, whom "she hath heard of when he was Ambassador in France." On the same day,[2] Walsingham informs Sir Ralph Sadler that Sir Amias Poulet was to set out "on Monday come sevenight." As this letter answers Mary's request for a Priest to attend her, a subject on which we shall have much information in the sequel, an extract from it will not be out of place here.

For that Queen's request, if she shall not greatly insist for a present answer, you may tell her that she shall receive the same by the gentleman that is to succeed you ; but otherwise, if she shall require to have the same soon, you may then let her understand, first, for the Priest, that her Majesty, misliking the like motion heretofore made unto her, my Lord Treasurer and I durst not now renew the same again, knowing that it would both be in vain, and besides offensive to her Majesty.

Sir Amias did not start so soon as the 1st of March, as Sir Francis Walsingham expected, nor, indeed, for two months after. His instructions[3] are dated March 4. They were, apparently, not precise enough for Poulet, who requests Elizabeth's commands respecting the amount of liberty he was to allow his charge.[4] The answers to these requests are not amongst the State Papers, but the instructions, after providing for her strict custody and against the "secret conveyance of letters and other like practices," contain the following clause in Walsingham's handwriting.

[1] Vol. xv., n. 36.   [2] *Ibid.*, n. 38.   [3] *Ibid.*, n. 50.   [4] *Ibid.*, n. 59.

You shall order that she shall not, in taking the air, pass through any towns, nor suffer the people to be in the way where she shall pass, appointing some always to go before to make them to withdraw themselves, for that heretofore, under colour of giving of alms and other extraordinary courses used by her, she hath won the hearts of the people that habit about those places where she hath heretofore lain.

Meanwhile Sir Ralph Sadler and Mr. Somer wrote frequently,[1] showing Mary's great anxiety respecting her new keeper, and Elizabeth herself undertook his defence,[2] in a letter to Mary, in accordance with a suggestion made by Mr. Somer.

And as for Poulet, against whom you seem to take exceptions, in respect of his dealings (as you say) against you at such time as he had the charge of our Ambassade in France, the question is whether the cause grew from himself or from you and your Ministers there. If he did but advertise us truly of such things as he heard were practised both by yourself and them against us, therein he did but discharge his duty. And if you still hold the rule which you have heretofore professed, that you love and esteem best those who serve us most faithfully, then have you more cause to like than to dislike him, for we repute him to be towards God religious, towards us most faithful, of calling honourable, by birth, in respect of the antiquity of his house, most noble. And therefore, if we should see hereafter cause to use him in Sadler's place, you need not to doubt that a man that reverenceth God, loveth his Prince, and is no less by calling honourable than by birth noble, will ever do anything unworthy of himself.

Sir Ralph Sadler was writing most urgent letters to procure his deliverance from that charge, which overwhelmed him with

[1] Vol. xv., nn. 41, 48, 49.   [2] *Ibid.*, n. 57.

care and grief,[1] and at the same time defending himself from complaints of having allowed his prisoner too much liberty. Elizabeth accepted his explanations,[2] but required the Queen of Scots to be more strictly looked to. Elizabeth's complaint against Sir Ralph was that he had allowed the Queen of Scots to go hawking with him, some distance from the castle.[3] It is a curious contrast that Poulet's first letters after taking charge,[4] should be written in self-defence, against complaints made against him for undue rigour in his first week of authority.

This letter, and the joint letter[5] written by him and Sir Ralph Sadler to announce his arrival, are subjoined.

Sir Ralph Sadler and Sir Amias Poulet to Queen Elizabeth.

It may please your most excellent Majesty to be advertised that I, Amice Poulet, arrived here the seventeenth of this present in the evening, and spending that night and the next morning in conference with me, Ralph Sadler, after dinner we signified unto this lady that we were desirous to have access unto her, which being granted, I, Amice Poulet, delivered unto her your Majesty's letters, which she seemed to receive very gladly, and after she had perused them, desired to be informed of the state of your health, which was answered to be very good and perfect, thanks be to God for it.

Then this Queen said unto me, Amice Poulet, that indeed she had been informed that I had been ill affected towards her, and that I complained of her kinsmen and Ministers when I was Ambassador in France, and that she was not to be blamed if she desired to be committed to the custody of such as did bear her no ill will, thinking that she had enemies in England, and did not know if I were of that number.

I answered that I was very glad to hear that her challenge had no better ground than that I had served your Majesty truly and faithfully, and did confess that

---

[1] Vol. xv., n. 69.   [2] *Ibid.*, n. 63.   [3] *Ibid.*, nn. 58, 60.
[4] *Ibid.*, n. 74.   [5] *Ibid.*, n. 84.

being employed in France as a public Minister, I was
content to make it known that I did not like with some of
her kinsmen and Ministers, because I was not ignorant
that they sought the disturbance of the quiet of this realm,
and especially Morgan, your Majesty's subject and her
professed Minister, whose doings I was careful and curious
to observe. I told her that this conceit would soon be
removed, if she would be content to judge of my actions
with that measure which was due to all subjects. I asked
her if, when she reigned in Scotland as absolute Queen, she
would have liked of that subject that would have shaken
hands or had intelligence with any Prince abroad or subject
at home, that had maintained her rebels and fugitives, had
allured her subjects to renounce their obedience, or had
attempted the subversion of her estate and dignity. I
prayed her to have like consideration of my duty towards
her [your] Majesty, promising to honour her kinsmen
when they shall be your good neighbours and friends,
and to love her Ministers when they shall leave their bad
practices.

She said that she could not but allow of all subjects to
be obedient to their sovereigns, but that she had heard
that I did not love her, as she would tell me further at
some other time, but that of late she had heard so well of
me as she was now better satisfied, and did trust that I
would give her no cause to the contrary.

After this talk between this Queen and me, Amice
Poulet, she uttered how grievously she took it that . . . she
had not yet received any full answer to the special points
of her offers and motions to your Majesty, . . . but instead
thereof, after a long time, she had received now lately a
letter from your Majesty to the contrary. . . . Thereunto I
answered, . . . that she hath not a better friend in Christendom than your Majesty is to her, all things considered. She
acknowledged that indeed your Majesty was so, but yet
her long prison, said she, these seventeen years, with loss

of health and limbs, and little effect of all her offers, and the remembrance of your Majesty's late letter, breaking off her whole hope, made her mistrust the worst, and therefore must rest in patience. . . .

"And now, Madame," quoth I, "it may please you to give me leave to say something unto you concerning myself, and do trust that being sent hither in such sort and for such purpose as hath appeared unto you, it will not mislike you, and will stand best with the discharge of my duty in many respects, if at my first entrance into this place, I declare unto you in plain terms what I desire to find at your hands, and at the hands of all those belonging unto you, and what you may expect from me, because plain dealing is always best."

"It is a thing that I love well," said she, and promised to deal as plainly with me. I told her that I was bound by duty of allegiance to serve your Majesty truly and faithfully, and would not fail to employ all my endeavours to acquit myself of that duty, neither would be diverted from it for hope of gain, for fear of loss, or for any other respect whatsoever. Your Highness' commandment and service being first observed, I did assure her that your pleasure was that I should do her all the good offices, and show her all the courtesy that might seem convenient, wherein there should be no fault on my part.

And to the intent that this course might have his continuance without let or interruption, to her satisfaction and to the better discharge of my duty, I prayed her to have care of my poor honesty and credit, a thing more precious unto me than living or life, and that nothing might be done directly or indirectly by her or her servants, that might procure me blame, or suspicion of blame at your Majesty's hands, having no worldly thing in so great reputation as your service and contentment. And therefore, if occasion did move her to send any letters or remembrances to London or any other place, I desired that they might be delivered unto me, and I would see them safely conveyed and would procure an answer, if so it pleased her.

"Indeed," saith she, "the time was that being deprived of all open means to send to my friends, and to hear again from them, as it is natural for all persons to seek to help themselves, I did not spare to seek some extraordinary helps to convey my letters, which, sithence I entered into good terms with the Queen, my good sister, I have utterly forborne," assuring me that I should have no blame for any of her doings, and asked me, Ralph Sadler, if she had used any such practices during my attendance on her. . . .

I, Ralph Sadler, departing from hence this present day, Mr. Somer remaineth here with me, Amice Poulet, for some short time, according to your Majesty's direction, for my better instruction in all things belonging to this charge, wherein both he and I will employ our uttermost endeavours, and do trust that all things shall be ordered to your Highness' good contentment. And, thus, not having wherewith else to trouble your Majesty, we both do pray to God, as we are most bounden, to preserve your Majesty in health and all felicity long to reign over us, our most gracious Queen and Sovereign.

From Tutbury, the 19th of April, 1585.

Your Majesty's most obedient and faithful subjects,

R. SADLEIR,
A. POULET.

To the Queen's most excellent Majesty.

Sir Amias Poulet to Sir Francis Walsingham.

Sir,—I fear lest my calm beginning here will have a rough proceeding. And doubting lest some complaint may be made, I have thought good to prepare you to answer. Mr. Somer hath been charged by one of this Queen's retinue that rigours and alterations have been used of late in this house, and that he is the author of them. I must confess that I have no commission to show any rigours; and therefore, if I have exceeded my commission, it is reasonable that I answer it at my peril. But I trust these rigours shall be found nothing else than dutiful service, and besides that, my dealings have been far from rigour in substance. I may affirm, and Mr. Somer will bear me witness, that the manner of my proceedings hath had no taste of rigour, but hath been as plausible and as quiet as was possible, and yet so tempered as they might perceive that their cavilling and quarrelling could not divert me from my duty. And indeed there may be no yielding to this people, but being assured to require nothing but that which is meet, to stand stiffly to it.

The rigours are these. First, I restrained Sharp, this lady's coachman, from riding abroad without my privity, and yet with this condition that he should be permitted to breathe his horses as often as he would, in giving me knowledge of his intention, so as some of my servants might ride with him. This was found hard, because he had not been restrained in times past, as they said.

The second rigour was this. I found at my arrival here in the great chamber where Sir Ralph Sadler did usually dine and sup, a cloth of Estate for this Queen, representing by letters the names of her father and mother, and furnished with the arms of Scotland in the midst, and the same quartered with the arms of Lorraine of every side. Sir Ralph Sadler told me at my first entering into the said chamber, that this cloth of Estate was set up at the first coming hither of this Queen, upon a meaning that she should dine and sup ordinarily in that chamber, referring the standing or taking down of the same to my discretion.

Wherein I have considered that, in my simple opinion, her Majesty's subjects may not with their duties allow in

this realm of any more cloths of Estate than that which is
due to her Highness. And therefore this chamber being
applied to the use of the governor here, and so employed
in all this time, I could not but resolve with myself that
the same was now to be accounted as Her Majesty's side,
as they call it commonly in the Court, and therefore no
cloth of Estate representing any foreign Prince to be
allowed in the said chamber.

Whereunto may be added that this Queen had not
dined or supped there more than one only night, shortly
after her coming hither, at which time Sir Ralph Sadler
supped also at the lower end of the said chamber, as my
Lord of Shrewsbury did the like at Sheffield, and I must
do as much if the use of this chamber be allowed unto
her, which would breed a dangerous familiarity between
these two families.

Upon this opinion I resolved to move this matter,
wherein I had this farther argument to induce them to
yield to my motion, that this Queen is now entered into
a diet, and will not come out of her chamber these six
weeks.

But willing to deal herein in as plausible manner as
I might with the discharge of my duty, I prayed her
secretary, Nau, to come unto me, where, in the presence
of Mr. Somer, I delivered unto him my opinion at good
length, touching this cloth of Estate. And as the same has
served his mistress to no use in all this time, neither could
do during the keeping of her chamber by reason of her
diet ; so I might worthily be condemned of want of
judgment, or rather of loyalty, to endure it to stand in
that place which served for my ordinary use to dine and
sup in. And therefore required him to move his mistress
herein, which, as I told him, I thought would like her
better than if the motion were delivered unto her by
myself, referring to her pleasure to set up the said cloth
in her own dining-room, if she thought good.

I received answer from this Queen the next day by Nau that she desired to know if I had in commandment from the Queen's Majesty to take down this cloth or no; and if I had no such direction, that then I would write to her Highness, before I proceeded farther.

I answered that I had received no such commandment from her Majesty, affirming that to my knowledge or thinking, her Highness had never been advertised of any part of this matter. And to write, I said I should condemn myself of want of discretion, and should forget the duty of my place, if in plain and open causes I should be troublesome to her Majesty with my letters.

Then he told me that his mistress doubted lest the taking down of this cloth of Estate did threaten a diminution of her estate, which she believed the rather for three causes. The first, the late motions in the Parliament against her; the second, the strange and unnatural dealing of her son; the third, that she was not ignorant that some great personages in England had assured her son that he should be the next successor to this crown, and that she should be deprived of her title. So as, these things concurring together, he said she had just cause to conceive that this matter of the cloth of Estate was but an entrance into greater innovations. He concluded that I had promised this Queen in my first speech to deal plainly with her, and therefore prayed me that if I had in commandment to make any alterations of importance, I would signify the same rather at one word than to minister new griefs from day to day.

I told him that I had no commandment, neither did I see cause to make any such innovations as should breed dislike, and having already, with the assent of his mistress, forbidden the cocher to ride abroad without my privity, there remained only one thing to be redressed, which for his better satisfaction I was content to tell him at that present. I said, I misliked greatly that those of this Queen's retinue were seen often walking upon the walls, where they overlooked the gate and ward, and took a full view of all comers and goers, a thing very offensive to all the neighbours, and not meet to be endured in reason and judgment.

He said it was not done with any evil intent, and that those which did so, had no other meaning than to take the open air, which was not without need for such as were shut up in this castle. I answered they should not, neither had been, denied to walk abroad in convenient sort when they did require it, and therefore this excuse was of small effect.

He did not insist in the defence of it, but yielded that it should be reformed. And concluded that the cloth of Estate should be taken down, trusting that upon request made in that behalf by the Queen his mistress, I would not refuse to write in her favour, that after her diet ended the cloth might be restored, and she admitted to dine and sup in that chamber.

These are three of the rigours. The fourth and last is as frivolous as the former, by the which I ordered that Sharp, this Queen's cocher, having accustomed to dine and sup with Sir Ralph Sadler's men, as he had in time past with those belonging to the Earl of Shrewsbury, should not dine and sup with my servants, a familiarity too dangerous in my simple opinion, considering the quality of the man, but should be bestowed among his fellows of the Scottish train.

These are the rigours which I have showed, whereof Mr. Somer beareth the blame in words, but the grudge and displeasure is against me. And now I refer to your consideration if there be any rigour in them; or rather, as I was bound in duty to require the observation of them, if this people ought not in reason to grant them without contradiction, as matters importing them nothing at all.

It is not to be doubted but that Sir Ralph Sadler, attending here during the treaty between her Majesty and this lady, can show good cause why he was not curious in these trifles, and perchance, by this occasion was the more inward with her, and did gather the more from her. And, therefore, I shall earnestly pray you so to temper this advertisement as his doings may not be brought in question.

I learn by Mr. Somer that there is no other way to do good to this people than to begin roundly with them, and that whatsover liberty or anything else is once granted unto them cannot be drawn back again without great exclamation.

I find the gentlemen servants to this Queen very well satisfied in appearance, and so I presume I shall find herself at my next access to her, which hath been forborne these four or five days, by reason of her physic to prepare her body for the diet.

Because these cavilling matters require no great haste, I send these letters by one of my own servants, who hath to do at London at this time.

The three posts between Tutbury and Stamford were agreed for by Sir Ralph Sadler at 3*s.* 4*d.* by the day, amounting to 23*s.* 4*d.* by the week, which may be reduced to 15*s.* by the week, praying you to take order how the same shall be paid. And thus I leave to trouble you, committing you to the merciful protection of the Almighty.

From Tutbury, the 27th of April, 1585.

Your assured poor friend,

A. POULET.

I had just occasion in my last speech with this Queen to tell her, according to your direction, that it was not enough that some of her Ministers had not long sithence practised most execrably the utter ruin of her Majesty, but that now also, very lately, the Duc d'Aumale had rifled one of her Highness' servants,[1] in his return out of France, of all his letters and papers, which must be said to have been done either by her assent or for her sake, and that it could not be but that these bad offices falling out daily in this sort, must breed jealousy and mistrust in the Queen my mistress.

She protested that she knew nothing of it, adding that this Duke was a mere stranger unto her, and that she had never seen him.   I answered that he knew her to be his kinswoman, and was content to give testimony of his good affection towards her by doing wrong to the Queen's Majesty.

She spareth not to bewray her hard opinion of you, whereupon I told her that I remembered to have seen a letter written by Sir Ralph Sadler, wherein he maketh mention that Nau, her secretary, acknowledged himself very well used generally by all the lords of the Council, but especially by you, and Nau being present, I asked him if it were not so, which he confessed.

"Yea, in words," saith she, "but I know what I know, and am able to prove that which I say."

I answered that this conceit could have no other ground than the report of some busybody, advising her not to be hasty upon so slender foundations to conceive so hard impressions of any of her Majesty's Council, which could not be honourable or profitable unto her.   The residue of her talk is not worthy of the writing.   It may be that this motion was the cause that I heard nothing of the rigours.

The foregoing letter is dated from Tutbury, April 27, 1585. Some portion of the next also deserves transcription.[2]   Its date is May 2nd.

---

[1] From the next letter we learn that this was William Waad or Wade, clerk of the Privy Council, afterwards knighted by James I., and made lieutenant of the Tower of London. His journey to France was to try to obtain the extradition of Morgan.

[2] Vol. xv., n. 84.

Sir,—I had forgotten in my letters of the 28th of the last, to thank you for yours of the 18th of the same, advertising the stay of the Earl of Arundel, and the hard usage offered to Mr. Wade in his return out of France. I have also received your letters sent by Mr. Darrell, and therewith some heads of the French occurrents, wherein I think myself beholden unto you. And, indeed, it may stand me in stead to be acquainted with some part of the French and Scottish doings, which will minister good occasion of talk between this lady and me, whereby somewhat, perchance, may be drawn from her, when she is in her angry mood.

And now, this last evening, at six of the clock, I received your letters of the 28th of the last, trusting that before this time you have received mine of the 27th of the same. The post having his pay, whether he work or play, I thought good to make this short despatch, thereby to advertise you that it is found strange here that the French Ambassador hath sent to this Queen by Mr. Darrell so good store of money, and hath written nothing mentioning the same, which was excused by answering that indeed Mr. Darrell received letters for her, but delivered them unto you, and not speaking with you at his departure the same remain in your hands, which he thought you would send hither by the next passage, and now this last packet being arrived, whereof they cannot be ignorant, because the post, after his accustomed order (although out of order, and shall not be done hereafter), sounded his horn at his approaching towards the gate. There is no doubt but that they will mistrust false measure when they shall hear that no letters are come for them. It may, therefore, please you to consider what I shall do with the packet which I have received from you for this Queen, being very sorry that the same was not opened there, because this tickle[1] time doth seem to require that it be perused before it be delivered.

[1] *Tickle*, uncertain.

C

The 30th of the last, this Queen sent her Secretary Nau to pray me to come to her chamber, where she told me that having spent some days in taking of physic, and being now entered into her diet, she was willing to spend half an hour with me, more to pass the time than for any serious matter that she had to say. . . .

The plate which she desired was brought and delivered unto her: the hangings for her chamber were sent, and being unlined, through the negligence of some inferior officer, order was taken for the lining of them out of hand. Only the three Turkey carpets for the compassing of her bed were forgotten, which should be remembered by my next letters.

Somer's application for the carpets ran thus :[1]

Certain Turkey carpets to lie about the Queen's bed. One under her feet in her dining-chamber, and one like in her bed-chamber, as she eateth there when she is not well. In all, five or six. She hath the best of the old long ends to walk on in her chamber, which is matted, but yet too hard for her sore foot. The dining-chamber floor is plaster, very cold, though strewed with rushes.

Poulet's letter also contains this paragraph, the importance of which will be afterwards seen.

I had forgotten to write unto you in my last letters, that besides the cloth of Estate which hath been taken down, there is another always standing in the chamber where she dineth and suppeth.

And now, with Poulet's letters before us, we are in a position to judge of the accuracy and trustworthiness of Mr. Froude's assertion, that, "notwithstanding his forbidding creed, Mary Stuart tried her enchantments upon him."[2] "She hinted," he

<hr />

[1] Vol. xv., n. 48, I.   [2] *History of England,* 12mo., 1870, vol. xi., p. 376.

says, "by the advice of Morgan, that if ever she came to the crown, 'he might have another manner of assurance of that island [Jersey] than ever was given to an English subject.'" What authority has Mr. Froude for putting such words into Mary's mouth? Any reader would think that Poulet was the authority. "He understood her perfectly," he adds: that is, Poulet understood those words when uttered by Mary. But it is clear that she never uttered them, nor was in the mood to utter them to Poulet, as his letters plainly show. And "he replied," says Mr. Froude, to the hint respecting the island of Jersey, that he could not be "diverted from his duty for hope of gain, for fear of loss, or for any other respect whatsoever." This, Poulet tells us, was uttered by him in the presence of Sir Ralph Sadler. Was Mary's offer of a bribe made before him too?

But Mr. Froude's inaccuracy may be still more plainly shown, for we know from Mary herself[1] that Morgan's letter, in which the advice was contained, had not reached her at that time. This letter formed one of the packet of eight that she received just a twelvemonth afterwards. "Her enchantments" were tried on Poulet in April, 1585, and the letter that contained the advice on which, according to Mr. Froude, she acted, reached her at Chartley, in April, 1586.

Morgan's letter,[2] from which Mr. Froude drew the words, is interesting; and though, having been printed by Murdin,[3] it is far from new, the passage relating to Poulet is well worthy of insertion here. We are dependent on Thomas Phelippes for the decipher of the letter. It is dated from the Bastile, where Morgan had been recently imprisoned, and where he remained for at least five years. He says that he fears that this will be the last letter he will ever be able to address to her.

I understand that Sir Amias Poulet is appointed to wait upon your Majesty. He is a gentleman of an honourable family, a Puritan in religion, and very ambitious, of which

---

[1] Vol. xvii., n. 80; Labanoff, tom. vi., p. 325.
[2] Vol. xv., nn. 64, 65.
[3] *State Papers*, London, 1759, p. 443.

C 2

humour you may take hold.   He is courteous, and I hope
will know his duty towards your Majesty.   But he will
be very curious and watchful about your Majesty and
your people, and respecteth Secretary Walsingham above
all the rest of the men in the service of that State, and
I believe Walsingham was the procurer of him to that
charge.

The said Poulet was, within this twelvemonth, far out
of liking with Leicester, and I pray God the matter be
not altered between them.   The said Poulet is Governor
of the Isle of Jersey, belonging to that crown, which is
worth to him 1,000*l.* by the year at the least.   The hope
he may conceive of your Majesty's favour towards him
and his house, and that they may continue in that charge
and receive some advancement otherwise, may bring him
with time to be careful and tender of your Majesty, far
contrary to the expectation that is conceived of him.
They that serve that State desire nothing else but commodity present, and advancement which your Majesty
may assure him, and make him and his house for his
good service another manner of assurance of the said
island than ever was given to subject of that realm of a
thing of like state and nature.   For you [may] give him
the said island for many years, or in fee if he deserve it,
where he hath the same at this time but for term of life
to himself and his son at the most.

He may dispend in lands of his own 1,000*l.* by year.
His son and heir is married to the daughter of the
Lord Norris, a Protestant, and out with Leicester, unless
they be lately reconciled.   The wife of the said Poulet
is a plain gentlewoman, and was the daughter of one
Mr. Anthony Harvye, a Catholic gentleman of the west
country of England ; but he is dead a good while
sithence,[1] whereof I am the more sorry as the case now

---

[1] Anthony Hervey died May 23, 1564, 6 Eliz., when his daughter and heir
Margaret, wife of Amias Poulet, was 28 years of age. *Collins.*

falleth out; and the wife of the said Poulet was a Catholic during her father's life.

I do think of all the means I can to find out amongst Poulet his friends and followers some to serve your turn, which God will send you. There is one Hotman, a Frenchman, that much haunteth the said Poulet, whose children he brought up both here and in England. The said Hotman is a great Huguenot, and much addicted to Leicester as far as I perceive. The said Hotman is a kinsman to Hotman that serveth your Majesty in your council here : whereof upon these occasions I will give instructions to the Bishop of Glasgow to deal with old Hotman, and to see whether the other may be made an honest man and an instrument to serve your Majesty, which he might do without all suspicion. . . .

There is a discreet lady called the Lady Pope, who was married to the aforesaid Poulet his father. She is a Catholic, by whose means it may be that you shall draw some service of Poulet and some of his. . . . It should seem to me that all the noble and gentle men of the north part of England, from London to Berwick, do receive a great check, in that the Queen went to the west parts of the realm to pick out Poulet to attend upon your Majesty, and could not find any of the nobility and gentlemen between London and Berwick to take that charge ; and as it is a check to all the north parts, as I would have them take it, so is it also a great argument of the diffidence which the State hath of the north parts, though it be yet to your honour, as I have alleged and written, as soon as I heard of the resolution that Poulet should wait upon your Majesty.

I think it shall not be amiss for the service of your own turn, that you cause some of your friends of those parts to visit Poulet, and to do him some courtesy, which will breed some amity between them which may turn to your service ; whereas, if Poulet be left there alone like a stranger, it will break occasions of repair to the place of your continuance, which, the more it be, the more will serve for your turn, which I desire, as God knoweth. . . .

Written in the Bastile, where I am prisoner, this 9th of April [March 30, O.S.] 1585.

> Your Majesty's most humble and faithful
>
> servant to the death,
>
> THO. MORGAN.

Godfrey Foljambe in March wrote to Gilbert Curle, one of Mary's secretaries.[1]

I hear Sir Amias Poulet shall have the custody of her, whereupon I have inquired what men towards him are fit to be dealt with for her Majesty's service. I have learned the names. Mr. Heydon, his son-in-law and his wife, Hugh Brice or his son, one called M'Roe. All will serve, thought reasonable men and likely to be dealt with all.

Sir Ralph Sadler wrote to Walsingham of the neighbourhood of Tutbury, February 28, 158⅘:[2] "Surely, sir, this is a perilous country, for both men and women of all degrees are almost all Papists." Two he thinks worthy of especial mention. Of these Sir Thomas Gerard was prevented from "lurking" in his own house, by being sent to the Tower, August 23, 1586.

I need not to tell you what an obstinate Papist Langford is, and Sir Thomas Gerard as ill as he, which both do lurk here in their houses, the furthest not past four miles from this castle. Neither of them both, their wives nor families, come to the church, nor yet have our common prayers or service said in their houses, but do nourish certain Massing Priests which do haunt their

---

[1] Vol. xv., n. 67.
[2] Vol. xv., n. 44; Sadler's *State Papers*, vol. ii., p. 525.

houses, where it is thought they have their Masses secretly, but so closely and cunningly used as it will be hard to take them with the manner. These surely be dangerous persons, if they had power according to their will, and therefore would be looked unto. I would to God there were no more in this country, where I hear of very few good. It seemeth that the Bishop of the diocese is not so diligent and careful of his charge as he ought to be, and therefore would be quickened and admonished from her Majesty to look better to his flock, so as they may be induced to come to the church according to the law, or else that they feel the smart of the same.

It may be well here to correct an inaccuracy that is found in more than one writer. Robertson says that " Elizabeth resolved to take Mary out of the hands of the Earl of Shrewsbury, and to appoint Sir Amias Paulet and Sir Drue Drury to be her keepers."[1] Birch, in like manner, " The Queen of Scots was removed from the custody of George, Earl of Shrewsbury, into that of Sir Drew Drury and Sir Amias Paulet."[2] Miss Strickland is not quite so incorrect, but she says that " her comparatively humane keeper, Sir Ralph Sadler, was superseded by Sir Amias Poulet and Sir Drew Drury, two rigid Puritans."[3] Mr. Froude also is inaccurate in saying that " Sir Drew Drury had remained at Fotheringay to share his charge with him."[4] The arrival of Sir Drew Drury at Fotheringay is announced by Poulet to Walsingham on the 15th November, 1586, a month after Mary's trial. He came for no other purpose but to share Poulet's charge; it is therefore not easy to see the meaning of Mr. Froude's "*had remained.*" From April, 1585, to November, 1586, Sir Amias Poulet was Mary's sole keeper, unless the assistance he received from Mr. Richard Bagot[5] entitles that gentleman to share with him the unenviable designation.

[1] *History of Scotland*, London, 1794, vol. ii., p. 124.
[2] *Memoirs of the reign of Elizabeth*, 1754, vol. i., p. 49.
[3] *Lives of the Queens of England*, 1864, vol. iii., p. 366.
[4] *History of England*, 1870, vol. xii., p. 238.
[5] Vol. xvi., n. 36.

We now proceed to our letter-book, which opens in the midst of a letter to Walsingham, written in May, 1585. The book has been thus defective from a very early time, for the folios are marked in a contemporary hand, and folio 1 begins in the middle of a sentence. There are two more letters in the Record Office that precede this, dated respectively the 2nd and 15th of May. The true date of our fragment is probably the 28th of May, on which day Poulet wrote the letter to Lord Burghley that we subjoin.

In this fragment we come upon the first mention by Poulet of Mary's *aumonier*, Camille du Préau. When he was first admitted amongst her retinue we have no means of ascertaining. He is mentioned [1] by Sir Ralph Sadler as in Mary's service at Wingfield, November 5, 1584, but he does not seem to have suspected that he was a Priest.[2] We shall now be able to trace Du Préau through the letters to the very end. As far back as November 22, 1571, Mary wrote from Sheffield to M. de la Mothe Fénélon,[3] "J'avoy demandé ung prestre pour m' administrer le Sainct Sacrement, et en l'estat où je suis, me renger du tout ce qui peult nuire à ma conscience," but the only answer to this was that she received "en lieu de consolation ung livre diffamatoire par ung athée Buccanan."

And in the beautiful letter [4] which Mary addressed to Elizabeth from Sheffield, November 8, 1582, she thus asks for the exercise of her religion: "Deux choses enfin ay-je principallement à requérir: l'une, que proche comme je suis de partir de ce monde, je puisse avoir près de moy pour ma consolation quelque honorable homme d'église, affin de me ramantevoir journellement le chemin que j'ay à paraschever, et m'instruire à le parfaire selon ma religion, où je suis fermemant résolue de vivre et mourir. C'est un dernier debvoir qu'au plus chétif et misérable qui vive ne se pourroit desnier; c'est une liberté que vous donnez à tous les ambassadeurs estrangers, comme aussi

---

[1] Sadler's *State Papers*, vol. ii., p. 437.

[2] In 1578 Mary Stuart recommends Ninian Winzet her confessor to the Duke of Bavaria. Vol. xi., nn. 8, 10. He probably was her confessor previous to her captivity.

[3] Vol. vii., n. 66; Labanoff, tom. iv., p. 4.

[4] *Cotton. MSS.*, Calig., C. vii., f. 51; Labanoff, tom. v., p. 332.

tous aultres Roys Chatoliques donnent aux vostres exercice de leur religion. Et moy-mesmes, ay-je forcé mes propres subjectz à aulcune chose contraire à leur religion, ores que j'eusse tout pouvoir et aucthorité sur eulx? Et que je fusse en ceste extresmité privé de telle licence, vous ne le pouvez justement faire. Quel advantage vous reviendrat-il quand vous me le desnirez? J'espère que Dieu m'excusera si, par vous de ceste façon oppressée, je ne laisse de lui randre se debvoir qu'en mon cœur il me sera permis. Mais vous donnerez très mauvais exemple aux aultres princes de la Chrestienté d'user, vers leurs subjectz et parentz, la mesme rigueur que vous me tiendrez, royne souveraine, et vostre plus proche parente, comme je suis, et seray tant que je vivray, en despit de mes ennemys." Mary wrote to M. de Mauvissière (Dec. 3, 1582):[1] "Mon intention n'estant d'avoir l'exercice de ma religion que privément, entre les miens, où nul des serviteurs du dit comte ne hante," that is of the Earl of Shrewsbury, to whom she had spoken on the subject.

The whole of the following fragment is interesting. Poulet's mention of the prayer-book as "dangerous" is characteristic of the man. It may be well to add that M. de Mauvissière was the French Ambassador at this time. He left England in September, and was succeeded by M. de l'Aubespine de Châteauneuf.

A few further words explanatory of the position of the Queen of Scots are needed to render the letter thoroughly intelligible, and it is not possible to avoid making a few remarks on Mr. Froude by the way.

For some time past the policy of the young King of Scotland had been watched with deep anxiety by the English Government. Early in 1584 James had written to the Pope, professing himself to be Catholic at heart; he had cooperated with the Duke of Guise in his project of an invasion of England from Scotland, and had openly proclaimed his purpose of delivering his mother and associating her with himself in the government. Accordingly it became apparent to Burghley and Walsingham that James must, at any cost, be brought over to the interests of England. No time was lost in opening successive intrigues at the Court of Holyrood, with results which showed that, in spite of all

---

[1] *Cotton. MSS.,* Calig., C. vii., f. 64; Labanoff, tom. v., p. 343.

promises, James would, were the bribe high enough, be found ready at once to sacrifice his mother, and to throw the whole power of Scotland in the balance on the side of Elizabeth and the Protestant interest. Mary Stuart, on her part, was actively treating with Elizabeth for her release. She had offered every security, and was willing to make all concessions, even to the point of absolutely renouncing the crown of Scotland, and succession to that of England, in her son's favour. Broken in health as in spirits, for herself she desired nothing beyond freedom and quiet for the rest of her life.[1] Such was the position in October, 1584, when the Master of Gray came up to London to negotiate on the part of his sovereign with Elizabeth. Mary Stuart was to be associated with her son in the projected treaty, and she sent up her French secretary, Nau, as her representative. At this crisis, as Mr. Froude justly remarks, "had James resolutely identified himself with his mother, and demanded, at the side of France, a general treaty between the three nations of which her release was to be a condition, Elizabeth had engaged herself so deeply that she could not have refused." [2] But Gray, who professed himself devoted to the Queen of Scots, was prepared to betray her cause and sell his services to the English Government, and it soon became clear to the mind of the French Ambassador that James himself was willing to make good terms with Elizabeth, by separating from his mother.[3] The upshot of this miserable business was that, by the spring of 1585, James had concluded his bargain, agreeing finally to leave his mother to the tender mercies of Elizabeth, in consideration of the paltry bribe of a dozen bloodhounds, an annual pension of five thousand pounds, and vague promises of succession to the English crown.

The year 1585 opened ominously for Mary Stuart. Abandoned by her son she fell more entirely under the power of the Queen of England. Her pleadings for liberty were met by prevarications and evasions. She was committed to closer imprisonment, and

---

[1] *Articles from Mary Stuart*, Labanoff, tom. vi., p. 59 ; and her subsequent letters.

[2] *History*, vol. xi., p. 526.

[3] Mauvissière to the King, November $\frac{15}{25}$. *Teulet.*

treated with marked increase of rigour. Mr. Froude gives us an admirable description of her removal to Tutbury Castle, the dreariness of her new prison-house, the bitterness and desolation of the hapless captive as the fact slowly forced itself upon her mind of her desertion by the son who owed everything to his mother, and who ought in conscience as in honour to have stood by her had she been forsaken by the whole world besides. To Tutbury, in March, Elizabeth sent on a letter from James to Mary, in which he repudiated his formal association with her, and declared his final resolve to separate his interests from hers in most unfilial terms, even going the length of taunting his mother with her captivity. Mr. Froude certainly does not spare James, but then why should he labour to turn even this bitter episode of Mary's long captivity to her discredit, by seizing the occasion to show her up as violent and implacable? "She cursed the Master of Gray; she cursed her son; she swore that sooner than he should enjoy her right in England, as he had already usurped her actual crown, she would disinherit him as a false, treacherous, and ungrateful child, and would bequeath her claims, whatever they might be, to the worst enemy that he had."[1] This statement Mr. Froude supports by a quotation from Mary's letter to Mauvissière. Now, turning to his reference, we find Mary writing that she is so cut to the heart by the impiety and ingratitude which her son has been compelled to commit in the letter which she believes to have been dictated to him by Gray, that "*si mon fils persiste en cela*"—you may tell the Justice Clerk in answer (Bellenden had brought up James' letter to London)—"*que* j'invoqueray la malédiction de Dieu sur luy, et luy donneray, non seullement la mienne, avec telles circonstances qu'il luy toucheront au vif, mais aussi le désériteray-je, et priveray, comme fils desnaturé, ingrat et perfide et désobéissant, de toute la grandeur qu'il peult jamais avoir de moy en ce monde; et, plustost, en tel cas, *donnerois-je* mon droit, quel qui soit, au plus grand ennemy qu'il aye, avant que jamais il en jouisse par usurpation, comme il faict, de ma couronne à laquelle il n'a aulcun droict, refusant le mien, comme je monstreray qu'il confesse de sa propre main."[2] In citing this passage in a

[1] *History*, vol. xi., p. 573.　　[2] Labanoff, tom. vi., p. 125.

footnote Mr. Froude has suppressed the *que*, has changed the conditional *donnerois* to the indicative *donneray*, and leaves out the close of the sentence. Had the quotation been honestly given it would not have been easy either to make the unqualified statement in the narrative, or to mention, as he does on the foregoing page, the association between James and his mother as one to which she had pretended that he had consented.

Fragment of a letter to Sir Francis Walsingham [May 28?], 1585.

. . . . from any other than from her. And yet the Ambassador writeth faintly in his defence, fearing to justify him too far, as it seemeth, but in perusing these letters Nau told me that he was not to be trusted, and that he knew there was intelligence between him and Gray.

In this packet or in the last he made mention of one Clearke,[1] lately arrived out of Scotland, affirming that he would by no means see him or speak with him, and was credibly advertised that he utterly refused to come to this Queen, and would not come if he had been commanded by the Queen's Majesty.

In the third packet, Mauvissière, writing to this Queen, calleth the King of Scots by the name of her son, saying that, following her commandment,[2] he will no more give him the title of King, and yet will take the advice of the King his master therein. Then he entereth into a long discourse of Archibald Douglas,[3] with whom he met as he walked for his recreation by the river side, and there the said Archibald pressed to speak with him, desiring to know what he had heard from the Scottish Queen.

---

[1] Sir Lewis Bellenden. "1585, Justice Clerk in England for border causes." *Burghley's Notes, in* Murdin, p. 782. Labanoff, tom. vi., p. 123. When Hunsdon in 1584 was sent to Scotland to gain Arran over to the interests of Elizabeth, the pretext for his coming was also a settlement of border affairs. Labanoff, tom. vi., p. 4.

[2] Labanoff, tom. vi., p. 143.

[3] Archibald Douglas, cousin to the Earl of Morton, on whose imprisonment in 1581 he fled to England, where, in May, 1586, he was James' Ambassador.

He told him for news that which this Queen had written unto him with her own hand, which was the distrust she had of his overgreat familiarity with the Master of Gray, of whom she rested ill satisfied because he had done her ill service, and had deceived her greatly; that she little regarded his credit with her son, that she cared little for all his drifts and practices, that she feared him not and all the rest as little that gave her son ill counsel, and that she had charged the said Ambassador not to make or meddle with them any way, and to deal roundly with him (as he termed it). He concluded in this Queen's behalf that, if he did not give open testimony of his faithful service and fidelity towards her, according to his former promise and profession, she did renounce his service and refuse him for her subject, and would carry this opinion of him, that he had such credit in Scotland as he thought he had no need of her favour.

Archibald would not believe that this message came from the Queen, but the Ambassador assuring him of it, and that she made no account of him, and thereupon bidding him farewell, Archibald answered that this Queen had good reason not to account of him, and not to think him to be her faithful subject and servant. The Ambassador, not listening to his speeches, took his way towards his house, and the other took his way.

But Archibald had not gone thirty paces before he returned, praying to speak two words more with him. And then told him that he would write to this Queen himself, if he thought his letters would be acceptable unto her; but prayed him to write unto her by the next, that he was ready to declare himself her faithful servant and subject, in what terms and in what order it would please her to command him, affirming his fidelity by oath, and that his actions should show his sincere affection towards her, although it should cost him his life within eight days after; and that he would not seek wealth, honour, or favour in Scotland, or credit with her son, but by her means, calling the Ambassador to witness of his plain and direct dealing, and if he had not foretold all the mischiefs that have ensued, which the Ambassador in his letter avouched to be true, and that he had told him that the only cause of his stay in this realm after his imprisonment was for this Queen's service, by the said Ambassador's commandment, delivered unto him in her behalf, &c.

The Ambassador, falling from this purpose, thus con-cludeth his letter. That this Queen hath just occasion to be greatly grieved to be so little regarded of her son, in whom she had reposed her only trust ; but she hopeth that her son will know himself, and that she will stretch forth her hand to raise him up, as otherwise she can expect no other thing in this world than displeasure, and that this unkindness would grow and increase to both their destructions, if they fall not speedily to some good reconciliation.

In one of these letters mention was made of a book of prayers sent to this Queen from one belonging to the Scottish Ambassador in France. I asked Nau for this book. He answered that it was delivered in Mr. Somer's time, and that Mr. Somer had seen it. These books are dangerous.

The Ambassador maketh mention in all his letters of the civil wars in France, wherein he carrieth himself so evenly as he neither offendeth the King his master nor the Duke of Guise. He is of opinion, by his last letters,. that there is little hope of composition, and that these troubles are like to prove more dangerous to that State than any that hath been these last twenty-four years. He writeth that her Majesty hath offered all assistance to the French King.

I pray you consider that I perused these letters super-ficially and in haste, and therefore can deliver you no more than my short memory could carry away. Only I dare affirm that I have omitted no matter of moment. Although I am not ignorant that these affairs are of small importance, yet it is good to know the humours of the world.

I hear that the Ambassador of France is required to make complaint to her Majesty in the behalf of this Queen, that she is restrained to give her alms; wherein the abuse hath been so great in times past, as, if I were not warranted by mine instructions, I could do no less in reason and judgment than to redress it. The distributor of this alms is one that beareth the name to be a reader unto this Queen, but I am much deceived if he be not a Massing Priest. His meaning was to have gone from house to house as in time past, and to have bestowed the alms by discretion. Their alms are very liberal, which will easily win the hearts of this poor people, if rather they be not won already. And thus leaving to trouble you, I commit you to the mercy of the Almighty.

From Tutbury, &c.

Thomas, the second Lord Paget, was a fugitive on the Continent, having left England on the arrest of Francis Throgmorton in 1584. His property was thus at Elizabeth's mercy. He was attainted by Parliament, together with his brother Charles, in 1586.[1] His houses at Burton and Beaudesert were stripped, and his " household stuff and other things,"[2] were sent to Tutbury. In the following letter we have the first mention of the Burton brewer, who was one of the chief agents in the treachery by which Mary was betrayed, and that he should have been put by Walsingham into Lord Paget's empty house, seems to show that the scheme of her betrayal was already sketched out.

[1] He died at Brussels in 1589, leaving one son William, who was knighted before the expedition to Cadiz under the Earl of Essex, in which he took part, and in the first Parliament after the accession of James his honours and lands were restored.

[2] Vol. xiv., n. 51.

To my Lord Treasurer, 28 Maii, 1585.

My very good Lord,—Besides the grounds and tithings mentioned in my former letters to belong to the manor of Burton, and thought meet to be reserved for the service of this house, I find in the end of the survey one other tithing, called Michleover, lying in a good corn country, and not distant from hence above four miles, which it may please your lordship to stay to that purpose. These tithings will provide wheat for the pantry, and oats and straw for the stable, which, being delivered here by the several farmers, will be both profitable and commodious. Presuming upon your lordship's favour, and being forced to make a large provision of beefs and muttons for the fretting[1] of our grounds, I have been so bold as to pray Mr. Bagot to defray 200*l.* for the service of this house, to which purpose I had already delivered to Mr. Darrell 100*l.* out of my little store, trusting that your lordship will take order that the residue of the money resting in Mr. Bagot's hands may be also employed to this use.

After the signing and sealing of this certificate upon the Commission lately directed hither for the survey of the Lord Paget's lands, Mr. Baynham moved me in a matter which was far from my thoughts, and yet finding the same, besides his friendly meaning towards me, to be grounded upon some reasonable considerations, I would not refuse to harken unto it, so far forth as to advertise your lordship thereof. The motion tended to this effect, that forasmuch as I was placed in this charge, and might, perchance, continue some time therein, although he doubted not but that I was sufficiently authorized to command the neighbours adjoining upon all occasions concerning her Majesty's service, yet he wished me to be a suitor for the stewardship of the Lord Paget's lands in these two shires of Stafford and Derby, whereby he said I should be better known to the said lord's tenants, and should find them the

---

[1] *Fretting*, grazing. Anglo-Saxon, *frĕtan.*

more willing to depend of me, which he thought to be needful, as well in respect of their near neighbourhood, as also that the Lord Paget's lands are able to furnish a thousand able men. And now, referring myself herein to your lordship's favour and better judgment, and forbearing to desire it otherwise than as you shall think it to be meet for me, I will say no more, but that if your lordship shall think good [to bestow] it on me, I trust to see it discharged by one of my own servants to your contentation, and to the good liking of the tenants.

The brewer that serveth this house with .beer, breweth his beer in the Lord Paget's house at Burton, where he is lodged with his wife and family, and therefore I think, in my simple opinion, your lordship shall do well to forbear during this service here to grant the keeping of the house to any other, because inconveniences may grow between the two families, and the house being utterly naked, the brewer may seem sufficient to have charge of it. And thus resting at your lordship's commandment, &c.

The next letter to Walsingham being amongst the State Papers,[1] a long abstract made by Poulet of the contents of the letters of the French Ambassador to Mary is here omitted. It must be remarked that Walsingham's letter of the 28th of May,[2] to which this is an answer, not only desires Poulet to open the packets addressed to the Queen of Scots, but also directs that her almsgiving was to be restrained.

To Sir Francis Walsingham, 4 Junii, 1585.

Sir,—I have received your letters of the 28th of the last, together with two packets for this Queen, and two notes of advertisements out of the Low Countries, where their ill success seemeth to require a more diligence in their commissioners expected here, whose overlate help may perchance be little profitable unto them, and will not

---

[1] Vol. xv., n. 97.   [2] *Ibid.*, n. 96.

D

fail to be hurtful unto their neighbours. Whereas your leisure doth not suffer you to peruse this Queen's packets, and therefore do desire that the same may be done here by me, and to avoid the inconveniences which as you think I have conceived, are content that I shall tell this people that their letters have been opened by yourself directed thereunto by her Majesty, as a thing meet in this dangerous time. Following your direction, which I will be always willing to observe, I have opened and perused the said two packets, but because the same and the rest hereafter are to be delivered by me open, I shall never persuade them that I have not perused them, and therefore it shall not be amiss in my simple opinion to tell them plainly that I have opened them and perused them, which course I have followed in these packets, and I see no reason why they should mislike it, being all one to them to have them opened here or in another place. And for my part, I do not esteem it as an inconvenience that they should know I had perused their letters, which can be no way offensive unto them, and if it were, I account little of it in respect of her Majesty's service, as hath already and shall always appear in all my actions in this place. . . . In the end of his letters, he [the French Ambassador] telleth this Queen that he will visit you at Barne Elmes, and that you are a friendly furtherer of all her causes, affirming no less for Mr. Somer, wherein I think you both are more beholden unto him than you deserve.

It seemeth that the French Ambassador hath learned a new phrase of writing of the French troubles sithence his last letters, which may be profitable unto this Queen, and cannot be hurtful unto me, because it is likely I shall find her the more quiet.

This Queen is now towards the end of her diet, and trusteth to come out of her chamber this next week.

These letters containing no matter of weight, I have forborne to send them sooner, hoping to have found some other convenient messenger, whereby I might have spared the labour of the ordinary post, who deserveth his small wages dearly in my opinion, and yet for want of other opportunity, I have been forced to have recourse to his help herein. As knoweth the Almighty, who always preserve you.

From Tutbury, &c.

Then come two letters addressed to Lord Burghley. It is doubtful whether Poulet would have been so grateful for the stewardship of Lord Paget's estate, if he had known that he was not to have the appointment of his deputy, or that his own fee from it was to be 40s. a year.

To my Lord Treasurer, the 8th of Junii [sic], 1585.[1]

My very good Lord,—I have been more bound to your lordship sithence my coming hither for your courteous letters and liberal advertisements of the state of things at home and abroad, than to all the Court of England besides, and yet I have craved it shamefully (if I may say so) as a thing very necessary for my better service in this place. I know your lordship hath least leisure of all others, and therefore your favour towards me is the more evident, whereof I would not fail to be worthy if my ability were answerable to my poor goodwill, which shall be always ready at your lordship's commandment.

I was bold to write to your lordship touching the stewardship of the Lord Paget's lands, and yet surely I did it in fear, doubting how your lordship would take it, but I find by your letters that it pleaseth you not only to allow of my suit, but also to grant it, wherein I think myself greatly bound to your lordship. Thus your lordship heapeth your benefits upon me daily, and I trust it will suffice you that I acknowledge them with all dutiful thankfulness.

[1] The original is in the British Museum. *Harl. MSS.*, 6,993, f. 84, 85.

D 2

I was bold in my former letters to pray your lordship's favour towards me touching the opening of this Queen's packets, wherein what hath passed sithence between Mr. Secretary [Walsingham] and me, may appear by this minute inclosed, so as now I have yielded to peruse them when I shall be thereunto appointed, and I find that it is not misliked, that my plain, round, and sincere dealing (if it be lawful to say so well of myself) doth win me credit, because they find that as I [do] not fear to do the duty of my charge, so I do nothing maliciously or frowardly. And thus, with humble remembrance of my duty, I commit your good lordship to the merciful protection of the Almighty.

From Tutbury, &c.

To my Lord Treasurer, 10° Junii, 1585.

My very good Lord,—Considering that by occasion of the term now in hand, your lordship shall be absent sometimes from the Court, I am bold to trouble you with this copy inclosed, addressed herewith to Mr. Secretary, which I send to your lordship in respect only of this Queen's opinion touching the French troubles, and thus resting at your commandment, I commit your good lordship to the merciful protection, &c.

The letter to Walsingham here mentioned is worthy of insertion, though it is in the Record Office.[1]

To Sir Francis Walsingham, 10° Junii, 1585.

Sir,—The occasion of my writing from hence is always so slender as besides that I ought to make conscience to trouble the posts without just cause, I fear also to be troublesome unto you, and from hence it cometh that you hear not more often from me, and now I write rather for fashion sake than for any matter of substance.

[1] Vol. xv., n. 98 ; *Harl. MSS.*, 6,993, f. 87.

On Sunday, the 11th of this present, after dinner, this Queen sent Nau to my wife and me to come unto her, which we did and found her in her bed, but had left her diet that day, and did intend to leave her bed the next morrow, and in the end of the week to take the air abroad. After long speech of matters of nothing, she told me that she took it unkindly that in all this time of her diet, she had not been visited from the Queen's Majesty either by her letters or at the least by some message, a thing which she knew her Highness had vouchsafed to do often to the Earl of Shrewsbury, and to many other of baser quality, whereby she might perceive the little care was had of her, which appeared also in that she could have no answer of so many letters which she had sent to her Majesty, wherein of her part she would save labour hereafter, and would forbear to say or write any more, finding that she was kept to no other use than to serve a turn, when upon some new accident need might require it, and therefore was resolved to shake off all opinion of hope, and to refer herself and her causes to God's providence ; concluding that she would be glad her Majesty did know how unkindly she took it that she had not been visited from her in all this time of her diet.

I told her I would not do her so much wrong to be the messenger of so unkind a message, because I could not see that there was any ground of this hard conceit, being assured that her Majesty had not received any information at all of her sickness, but rather that she had been hunting and hawking at sundry times, and the day next before the departure of Sir Ralph Sadler had been walking in the garden. This manner of her diet being not esteemed in this country as a sickness, but rather a mean to prevent sickness that might come hereafter.

She answered that she had advertised her Majesty by her letters of her sickness and lameness, and had signified by the same that no receipt of physic could

so much further her health as the assurance of her
Highness' favour. I prayed her to believe constantly
that her Majesty had great care of her health and of
her good estate, affirming that I could speak it of my
own knowledge, as a thing which I had heard at her
Highness' own mouth.

Then glancing at her unhappiness in that she was
encountered every day with new occasions to the hindrance of her desires, which she understood by the
French Ambassador's letters to have had the slower
passage by reason of the French troubles, she asked
what I had heard of them. I said I had heard no more
than that which I had read in the French Ambassador's
letters directed unto her, which I had perused as she
did know.

She asked if I thought that the Queen's mother's
mediation would prevail. I answered that although I did
concur in opinion with the French Ambassador that the
French King might not endure with his honour that
arms should be taken in his country without his permission, and would never condescend to the outrageous
demands of controllers; yet I did think that this war
would be ended by composition of preferments in honours
and dignities, to be bestowed in some good measure upon
her kinsmen, which I doubted not they would gladly
accept, and the rather because they were abandoned
(which I said the French Ambassador's letters did import)
of a great number of the French nobility, whose assistance
they expected.

"You are deceived," quoth she; "these wars will be
drawn into great length;" and then, whispering me in
the ear, said that France would be cantoned after the
German fashion, as that Champaigne, Burgundy, Picardy,
Lyonnois, and some other parts adjoining to the Duke
of Savoy would take that course, and that the project
hereof was laid long since.

I was very willing to sound her farther upon this subject, and thereupon told her that I remembered when I was Ambassador in France her kinsman the Duke of Guise was the head and principal party in many leagues and associations which were made at that time in many parts of France; and although the same was pretended to be done with the King's good favour and assent, yet many of good judgment were of opinion that it carried a meaning of cantoning. "Yea," saith she, "this matter hath not slept, but hath been much laboured since that time, and when Monsieur went first to Cambray, Normandy had taken arms if her kinsman had not stayed it." She seemed unwilling to discourse farther of this matter, excusing her kinsmen so coldly as it might appear she was nothing glad of [their] enterprise.

It is now long since that this Queen was restrained to give her alms as I have heretofore written unto you, and yet in all this time I had heard nothing therein from her own mouth until this present, that bewraying with many words her discontented mind, she said she might easily see that no account was made of her. If any seemed willing to further [her] causes, or would be content to hear well of her, he was greatly misliked; if [any] spake ill of her, as some had spoken so ill as they could not speak worse, they were rather allowed than blamed. Yea, it was not thought meet that any should think there were virtue or goodness in her, "or else," saith she, "why did you restrain me to give any alms to the poor folks, who would perchance have prayed for my better health, which was all the hurt that could have ensued of my almsgiving?" And then she recited that, during her being at Buckstone [Buxton], she was moved in pity to give a smock to a poor naked woman, which was carried to her Majesty with great advantage, as if she had a purpose to win the hearts of the people by indirect means. "But shall I tell you," quoth she, "what will ensue hereof? You fear lest by giving alms I should win the favour of the people, but you ought rather to fear lest the restraining of my alms may animate the people against you."

I prayed her to give me leave to deliver my simple opinion unto her in all plainness, which was that giving of alms was a thing convenient in all estates and degrees, but not expedient in all times and all seasons, neither meet to be distributed by all kinds of people to all sorts of people without difference. If her giving of alms had no other meaning than to do the office of a Christian conscience, she might bestow her liberality by her Ministers in other countries, which would be no less acceptable before God than if she had given the same here with her own hands. The laws of this realm had provided so carefully for the relief of the poor as none could want, but either through their own lewdness, or by the negligence of the officers of several parishes, so as it was to be trusted that the people here had no need of her alms, and that it could not be denied but that, by what means I know not, she had gotten the hearts of some bad subjects in this realm, when in her favour they were content to take arms against their Prince and country.

"They were two earls,"[1] said she, "which were discontented upon private occasions." "But these two," quoth I, "carried great multitudes with them," wishing her to carry this constant opinion, that as no alms whatsoever could procure her any favour that might stand her in stead, so I feared nothing the danger that might come unto me by restraining her alms. "But," saith she, "when I am sick in body or troubled in mind, and would be glad to be assisted with the prayers of the poor people, I must say it is hard, or rather barbarous, to restrain me."

---

[1] The Earls of Northumberland and Westmoreland, the leaders of the insurrection of the north, in 1569.

Nau having before that time declared unto me that his mistress would complain to her Majesty of this rigour, as he termed it, I concluded that I doubted not but that she had or would give information of my doings herein, and by the answer she should know what opinion was conceived hereof in other places. Indeed, Mr. Somer hath written unto me that he hath seen this Queen's letters to the French Ambassador to this effect, terming the restraint a rigour.

If I might hear sometimes from you, of the French proceedings, I might deal the better with this Queen in many respects, and therefore I am bold to renew this suit again unto you.

Although, as I have before written in the first part of this letter, I told this Queen that I would not do her so much wrong to be her messenger of that unkind message to her Majesty, because she should not expect answer thereof, yet I have thought it agreeable with my duty to advertise the same.

Request was made unto me yesterday to permit Sharp to ride five miles hence to see certain horses, which I refused, whereupon Nau came unto me this last evening, and after a long and tedious discourse of the great promises of favour towards his mistress, which he had received from her Majesty at his last being at the Court, finding by late experience that she is more straitly used than in time past, and here rippeth up all the old rigour, as he called them, as also that she had heard nothing from her Highness in answer of her several letters, would needs draw it into a peremptory consequence that there was no meaning to treat farther with her, concluding that he spake it as of himself, not commanded by his mistress.

Surely you would have been merry to have heard the talk that followed between him and me,[1] wherein I think

---

[1] " He [Poulet] so little trusted his power to match such a diplomatist, that he dared not speak to Nau." Froude's *History*, vol. xi., p. 579.

I was more plain with him than his mistress durst to have been, and advising him to peruse with leisure and judgment the French Ambassador's late letters to his mistress, wherein he setteth down at good length the just and necessary causes of the stay of this treaty, and yet giveth great hope that as time and occasions shall change, the same may go forward with effect. I told him he should do well to follow the same course, and considering his great credit with his mistress, to beware to abuse it to her hurt by his distempered and violent counsels, wherein his haste might make more waste in one hour than he could recompense in all his life after. Yet [it] was easy to see that his necessary inferences in Princes' causes were uttered by direction, and did proceed from his mistress' own mouth, and so I took it, and therefore would forbear to answer him any farther therein, concluding that I was expressly commanded by her Majesty to intreat this Queen honourably, and to have singular and special care of her health, and of her safety against all dangers, and therefore, if I had done anything that deserved the name of rigour and straitness, I must submit myself to the censure of the Queen my mistress.

He would needs persuade me that I was wise and discreet, and that I had done nothing herein but by direction from above. I reported me therein to his own judgment, who knew very well that all my invocations had been very sudden, so as the fault being found in one day was redressed the next morrow, which could not be done by order from above, but it sufficeth me that my conscience told me I had done nothing herein frowardly or maliciously, and that I had no other respect than her Majesty's service, from the which I would never be diverted for any other respect whatsoever.

Although all these alterations seemed to have been buried, and as I think, had not been renewed but upon the occasion before recited touching Sharp, yet, no doubt, they are grieved amongst the rest with these things, especially that they are removed from walking on the walls; that Sharp may not ride abroad as in times past, alone at his pleasure; that he hath his lodgings within the house, which he had heretofore without the gate; that they cannot take their walks into the town; that none of my servants from the highest to the lowest, do eat, drink, talk, or confer with them; and finally, that this lady's alms are restrained; wherein I will say no more but that, if you were here in my place, I am much deceived if you would not say with me that the least of all these abuses might breed great and dangerous inconveniences. When flesh and blood hath done what it can, yet, as things are compassed here, all their treacherous means can never be avoided. And yet, reason commandeth to redress all open and known faults.

I know Nau better than I may make known by writing, and I know him so well as I would be glad with all my heart he were removed, and his place supplied with any two others whosoever, I care not out of what country or from whence they came.

Nau, in his long discourse, told me amongst other things, that Sir Ralph Sadler and also Mr. Somer were known to have said that no honest[1] Englishman would serve this Queen, and that they could not think them honest that would serve her; whereof he informed [me] that there was a meaning to make his mistress a mere stranger to all English subjects. This argueth their unthankfulness, which I can prove many ways in the cause of my predecessors, and therefore a yard and inch is a good measure for them, and it may be given with such temperance as it will be as thankworthy as if they had larger measure. I have troubled you too much, now I leave you to the fatherly keeping of the Almighty.

From Tutbury, &c.

[1] The word is used in the old sense of faithful, loyal.

The assertion in the following letter, that it "was sent by an honest man," is at first a little startling, as this is the way in which, when the plot for Mary's destruction was in progress, Poulet used to designate the brewer who was concerned in it. The phrase must however be simply a coincidence, for the plot was not yet hatched. Mr. Froude thinks that the brewer was so christened by Poulet in irony; but may it not simply mean a trustworthy agent? So Morgan, in his letter says, "the other may be made an honest man and an instrument to serve your Majesty;" and so, when Poulet told Mary that he was the servant of the Queen of England and would not fail to do the duty of his charge, she answered that she "could not blame his honesty."

To my Lord Treasurer, the 16th Januarii [June], 1585.

My very good Lord,—This bearer, my servant, being upon the point of his departure towards London for his necessary business, I received your lordship's most favourable letters, dated at Tibalds, the 14th of this present, for the which I most humbly thank your good lordship, and would not fail to acknowledge your favour with more plenty of words, if the messenger were not pressed to take his journey with speed, whereby I am forced to write in this short manner, which it may please your lordship to take in good part, as proceeding from one that would be loth to be found unthankful, although otherwise not able to do your lordship any service. The two letters which your lordship received last from me were diversely sent, the one with a packet to Mr. Secretary, tied to the same with a thread, the other being first in date, and containing some matter touching the opening of this Queen's packets, was sent by an honest man travelling towards London, who promised to deliver the said letters at your lordship's house on Saturday last, at night, and I think will not fail to perform his promise.

I think myself bound yet once again to thank your lordship most humbly for your liberal letters, written in a

time of so little leisure, when you expected her Majesty
the next day. Beseeching God to assist this honourable
assembly with His mercy and favour, and to bless and
prosper all your lordship's actions to His glory and your
increase of honour.

From Tutbury, &c.

In the letter to Sir Francis Walsingham, of June 22,[1] after
giving his opinion respecting foreign politics, and that "it
behoveth us to provide for our own safety by liberal support
of Protestant Princes abroad, and especially by the good amity
of Scotland," Poulet says a few words of his prisoner's health,
which are repeated word for word in the next letter to Lord
Burghley.

The Earl of Leicester was Master of the Queen's Horse, or
as Poulet calls it "her Majesty's Race," as well as Lord High
Steward of her Household. In the former capacity, he received
the following letter.

To my Lord of Leicester, 22° Junii, 1585.

My very good Lord,—I have received your lordship's
letters of the 5th of this present, by the which you require
my assent and furtherance in retaining of the little park
adjoining to this castle for the use of her Majesty's Race,
under your lordship's charge, as likewise that the provision
of firewood for this household, now taken in Castlehaye
Park, may be removed to some other place.

Touching the first, I wrote unto your lordship long
sithence, that forasmuch as the horses belonging to this
castle were to attend upon the Scottish Queen upon every
short warning, it was of necessity that either the horses
must have grass at hand, or else must be kept continually
at house, which would prove chargeable to her Majesty,
referring to your lordship's consideration, if the little
park might be spared to this use or no. But receiving
no answer from your lordship, I hired a ground of

---

[1] Vol. xv., n. 100.

Mr. Candishe [Cavendish], adjoining to the said park, at the price of forty marks by the year, which serveth very fitly to this purpose, and do think that Mr. Candishe will be entreated to spare the said ground during this service, so as there will be no cause to desire the park.

The wood in Castlehaye Park may not be spared without some loss to her Majesty in respect of the carriage, which is already discharged for one whole year, to be ended in February next, by the counties of Stafford, Derby, and Leicester, at the rate of 16*d.* for every load, with 2*d.* to be paid by her Highness; the greater part of this contribution being already levied, and no new composition can be made for this year, and it is not to be hoped that they will come to any larger contribution the next year.

Mr. Eton and Mr. Darrell, upon a view taken by them of that walk of Nedewood Forest, which is nearest adjoining to this castle (as, indeed, it is to no purpose to'speak of the other walks, in respect of their far distance), as also of Stockley Park, distant from hence less than two miles, do find that those two places will furnish this castle of firewood during the space of three years, or thereabouts.

One Alsopp, yeoman of her Majesty's Race, proffering to carry all the wood out of Stockley Park at 18*d.* the load, and out of all the forest walk of Nedewood at 2*s.* the load; so as the surcharge of the first is only 2*d.* in every load, and of the other 8*d.* in every load, the wood in Stockley Park being said to be sufficient for one year or two, in which time her Majesty's charge will be little increased.

Thus I have delivered unto your lordship the true state of the matter, referring the same to the better consideration of your lordship and others of her Majesty's Council, only I shall pray you to consider that the summer season is well spent, the ways hereabouts so foul, as there

is no means to carry wood after Michaelmas, and therefore, if it shall be resolved to remove this service out of
Castlehaye Park, it may please your lordship to procure
warrant for the taking of wood in Stockley Park, or
Nedewood, to be sent hither without delay. Thus, with
humble remembrance of my duty, I commit your good
lordship, &c.

To my Lord Treasurer, 22 Junii, 1585.

My very good Lord,—Mr. Candishe [Cavendish] his
house adjoining to the walks of this castlo, was so necessary for this service in many things this last winter, as it
might not have been spared by any means, and hereafter,
by reason of our provision of hay, corn, straw, and other
like household stores, besides some lodgings for servants,
will be more needful than at any time before.

Mr. Candishe hath belonging to this house no great
quantity of grounds, and yet they are such as may stand
us in great stead for the summering of our horses, for hay
for the stable, and for other profitable commodities.

There remaineth one other thing worthy of consideration, in my simple opinion, which is that Mr. Candishe,
and my lady his wife, being straitly lodged in a house
distant from this castle four miles or thereabouts, do, for
their recreation, make their often repair to this house,
a matter which may prove dangerous unto them, this
people being very willing to entertain such like old
acquaintance, whereof I have had some experience of
late, and therefore would be glad to avoid the occasion.
And the rather because I find Mr. Candishe well affected
to her Majesty's service, and for his liberal proffers to that
purpose have good cause to like well of him.

Upon the considerations (without making any mention
of this latter), I have conferred with Mr. Candishe, who is
well content to exchange the use of his whole house
(reserving a chamber or two for the keeping of his stuff)

for the use of Lord Paget's house at Burton, and his grounds here for other grounds to like value there, wherein he deserveth thanks in my simple opinion. And now, if it shall please your lordship to allow of this bargain, I trust to see him satisfied, and the service shall be greatly furthered.

I repent greatly that I have forgotten to pray your lordship to reserve the parks of Beaudesert and Bromley for the use of this house, which will serve to great purpose, as well for provision of venison as other ways, and shall be so husbanded, as her Majesty shall find her officers here profitable tenants.

It may please your lordship to do me that favour to peruse these copies inclosed of letters which I have received of late from my Lord of Leicester, and of my answer to the same.

This Queen took the air in the garden here the 18th of this present, and the next morrow went abroad in her coach, so as now I think I shall be driven henceforth to forget the gout, and stand to my limbs.

Thus, with humble remembrance of duty, I beseech God to preserve and keep your lordship in long life and good health.

From Tutbury, &c.

The threat, so broadly expressed in the following letter,[1] that in case of an attempt at rescue, the Queen of Scots should at once be killed, is not here made for the first time. Lord Shrewsbury had said the same, and Somer, when defending Sir Ralph Sadler for having permitted her to go out hawking, said that "if any danger had been offered, or doubts suspected, this Queen's body should first have tasted of the gall."[2]

To Sir Francis Walsingham, the 5th of July, 1585.

Sir,—Whereas it hath pleased her Majesty to commit unto me the charge, as well as of the safe keeping of this

---

[1] *Harl. MSS.,* 6,993, f. 94.   [2] Vol. xv., n. 60.

Queen, as of the restraining of her, and such as attend upon her, from secret conveyance of letters and other like practices, and for my better instruction and direction in that behalf, hath delivered unto me certain articles, commanding me to have a special care to see the same duly put in execution touching the safety and forthcoming of this Queen's person, I will never ask pardon if she depart out of my hands by any treacherous slight or cunning device, because I must confess that the same cannot come to pass without some gross negligence, or rather traitorous carelessness : and if I shall be assaulted with force at home or abroad, as I will not be beholden to traitors for my life, whereof I make little account in respect of my allegiance to the Queen my sovereign, so I will be assured by the grace of God that she shall die before me, so as I doubt not to perform this first point, and (as I may say) the substance of my charge, to the full discharge of my duty.

Concerning the other part of my instructions, by the which I am commanded to restrain this people from secret conveyance of letters and other like practices, my conscience beareth me witness, and my doing I hope shall testify for me, that as I have been very careful and curious to perform every syllable contained in my instructions with all preciseness and severity, so I have not been negligent to observe all the actions, as well of those of this family as of others abroad, and have done all my endeavour to make this people and their friends to know that if it were possible I would not be deceived by them.

I have (I thank God) reformed no small number of abuses of dangerous consequence, and experience doth inform me daily of other such new faults as might carry great peril, which I omit not to redress by little and little as I may, and do not doubt to reduce to some better order in time convenient ; and among these faults I

E

account this not the least, that upon due examination of the qualities of all her Majesty's under ministers in this house, from whence they came, and on whom they depended before their coming hither, I have just cause to suspect that divers of them were foisted in to serve turns which may not be imputed to Sir Ralph Sadler, who had no dealings therein, as likewise Mr. Cave,[1] being a stranger in these parts, could not know them or judge of them.

All these sores are nothing grievous unto me, because I have the remedy in my own power; but there is yet remaining one disorder, which is so foul, as it [is] easily seen, but not so easily redressed. And because the same is expressly mentioned in my instructions, I find myself the more nearly touched in honesty and credit to utter my simple opinion therein, and to pray her Majesty's direction for the reformation thereof.

It is set down in my instructions, amongst other things, that cochers [coachmen], laundresses and such like, have heretofore been used as principal instruments for the conveying of letters [and] messages, and therefore I am commanded to have special regard that a watchful eye be carried over them, and that their doings be so observed as the like inconvenience may not grow by them hereafter.

The cocher [Sharp] is so restrained, and so narrowly observed, as he can do no hurt, although no doubt he wanteth no goodwill to do all service possible to this Queen his mistress.

The laundresses are three in number, whereof the chiefest and the trustiest in treachery is sister to Sharp's wife, and one of the other two sister to Sharp. What fruits are to be expected from this people so nearly allied to Sharp I refer to your judgment. Mr. Somer had a good opinion of them, and commended them greatly to

---

[1] Bryan Cave preceded Marmaduke Darrell as Master of the Household.

me and my wife for their honesty and plain dealing. So as I found two of them unsworn at my coming hither, which since have received their oath,[1] Mr. Somer affirming that the third had been sworn at Sheffield. These women wash, eat and drink, and are lodged in a little house in the park adjoining to this castle, without the precinct of the said castle. They have by this means full liberty to go where they list by day or night. They may receive into their houses whom they will. The keeper of the said park, servant to Mr. Candishe [Cavendish], is their very near neighbour. They have access to this Queen and her gentlewomen for their clothes, and now, what is it that they may not carry and convey here and there at their pleasure? You will say they may be searched as they pass in and out. Indeed, all other laundresses which serve the gentlemen and other of the Scottish retinue are stayed at the gate, and their clothes are searched, received, and delivered, but this Queen's laundresses have been always allowed to go to her chamber, and it may be that these things do require sometimes such conference as were not meet to be uttered in the presence of soldiers. To make narrow search of these clothes at the gate, as it cannot be comely, so it will be as little profitable, unless the women be also stripped unto their smocks.

Although I had no certainty of any good success, yet when I have observed that this people hath been busy in writing a day or two, I have appointed some of my trustiest servants to watch about the laundry all night, taking order with them, that if any did approach the house, to permit him to pass quietly, and to stay him in his return, and if he did not return, then to enter the house in the morning and to arrest him there. But as I thought good to hazard this labour, so it hath been hazarded without profit, and in truth, when I consider the

---

[1] A copy of the soldiers' oath is in the *State Papers*, vol. xv., n. 28.

ready means which these laundresses have, either by this keeper, or by any other of their old acquaintance, whereof there is good store here at hand, I may easily see that they may do at high noon what they shall think meet, and need not to trouble themselves at unseasonable hours.

This service being so subject to so open and apparent means of treacherous devices, I have thought agreeable with my duty, and to stand best with my discharge against all events, to deliver them plainly and fully unto you, referring the same to the grave consideration of her Majesty. Only I will say that, in my simple opinion, there is no other remedy to redress this abuse but by removing of these women and placing others in their room, which being well chosen may in all likelihood prove honest and faithful, but the rather if they be taken out of some country far distant from this castle. This alteration will breed (no doubt) great storms and marvellous unkind-ness, which shall trouble me nothing at all if it shall be found to import her Majesty's service.

This Queen hath been thrice abroad in her coach, and hath been also at some other times in the garden, carried thither in a chair, but useth sometimes her feet, being sustained by two of her gentlemen, so as it seemeth that her legs are yet weak, and indeed are wrapped in gross manner, as hath appeared to my wife. It is greatly misliked that she is accompanied in her walking abroad with so many horsemen, all furnished with snaphaunces[1] or cases of pistols, and a good number of harquebuziers on foot with their matches lighted, attending on her coach. The first day it was thought to be done for fashion's sake, and not meant to be continued. The second day Nau was sick, and when he is absent all things are well taken. The third day Nau being present, it was secretly pretended that this Queen's person might be in danger, and that she

---

[1] *Snaphaunce,* a firelock. Dutch, *snaphaan.*

had more cause to fear her keeper than he had to be afraid
of foreign violence, and forsooth to keep her from harm,
Nau and Curle may not depart from her coach. This is
a secret which I must pray you most earnestly not to
discover to any other than to her Majesty. If I play not
the blab, I shall know more. It is thought she will try
how my harquebuziers on foot will hold out when she
rideth upon her horse, but I must tell her that soft riding
is best for her health. And indeed she shall be deceived,
if she hope to go beyond the limits of two miles prescribed
unto me,[1] although she shall never know by me how far
they extend.

I find by this little experience of her going abroad,
that I had some reason to restrain this Queen's alms,
which should have been distributed by one appointed to go
to that purpose from house to house, as by my former
letters hath been advertised, wherein she had been prodigal
in times past, as (no doubt) she hath gotten the hearts of
the whole town, a matter of no consequence because the
town is little and beggarly, but it is certain that the fame
thereof hath won her credit in other places. She hath
bestowed in this town little less than twenty marks in one
day, and if I should tell you what I have heard by credible
report of her liberality, as well within this castle as abroad,
and for the more part upon very slender occasions, you
would find it strange. Of this one thing I will assure you,
that none of my servants or soldiers shall be beholden unto
her or to any belonging unto her for one penny during
my service in this place. Serving-men and soldiers are
slippery fellows, and I may be deceived, but I dare
promise great things for these, and I think they will not
deceive me. I take strait order that this Queen is not
followed in her going by any others of any quality whatsoever than myself and my retinue, and yet I see she

---

[1] Poulet's instructions say two miles. The original draft of them said
three (Vol. xv., n. 50).

giveth daily upon light occasions, and in very liberal sort, and I am deceived if she be not sorry that she giveth not more than she doth give, as well in alms as in rewards otherwise.

They seek as much as they can to hide their gifts from me, but they find they have many eyes upon them. As I think it is not meant that they shall be restrained to give alms to a poor man meeting them upon the way, so I am of opinion that you will not allow that passing through a street they shall cast down their alms in good little sums to be taken up by them that list to stoop for it, and so to give they know not to whom, wherein is more ostentation in appearance than charity.

I have been informed that every chamber of the Scottish retinue here hath his case of pistols, and that some chambers have more, for the certain knowledge whereof I prayed them [a] fortnight since to permit Mr. Darrell to take an inventory of their several chambers, a thing very needful for his discharge and mine, which hath been delayed by Nau hitherunto, but is promised to be performed one day this week. I do not think that they will hide those things, because they are said to have had them now many years, and finding them I desire to know what I shall do therein. If they will be provided of pistols for their surety when by her Majesty's licence they shall take any journey, it may be permitted with this condition in my simple opinion, that they remain in the custody of the governor here until they shall have occasion to use them.

A Scottish pirate hath given out that he trusted to meet my son, Anthony Poulet, on his way towards Jersey, and would not fail to keep him for a pledge of my good behaviour towards this Queen; and, indeed, I am persuaded that my charge there carrieth the more danger in respect of [my] charge here, most humbly praying her Majesty, if any soldiers should be put in readiness for Guernsey, that the like may be done for Jersey. I have been so spare in asking, as one loth to put her Majesty to needless charges, that [I] assure you I have not one spare caliver[1] in that castle, and as little store of powder. It is true that I had this last year a supply of thirty calivers, half a last[2] of corn powder, and a last of serpentine powder, and this might suffice in a time of peace, but these threatening days do require a better store.

It may please you to take order for the conveyance of this letter inclosed to the Lord Deputy of Ireland, and thus referring all those things to your better consideration, I commit you to God, who prosper all your actions to His glory.

From Tutbury, &c.

Sir Ralph Sadler had heard that Poulet was willing to undertake this office. The next letter, which is addressed to Sir John Perrot, Lord Deputy of Ireland, shows signs of discontent. These steadily increase during the ensuing correspondence. Perrot's "service of great toil," was a war of extermination against the Catholics of Ireland. "The execution system," says Mr. Froude,[3] "notwithstanding the fair promises with which Sir John Perrot commenced his administration, was continued, which seemed intended to clear the south" of Ireland "of its remaining population."

To Sir John Perrot, Lord Deputy of Ireland, 5 *Julii,* 1585.

My good Lord and friend,—As your letters of April came slowly to my hands, so I answer them slowly, and yet as willingly as any letters have been answered these seven years. I trust not to live so long to be forgetful of an old acquaintance and so good a friend

---

[1] *Caliver,* a lighter weapon than a musket, and fired without a rest. *Latham.*

[2] *Last* of gunpowder, twenty-four barrels, each containing one hundred pounds. *Maculloch.*

[3] *History,* vol. xii., p. 89.

as is Sir John Perrot, and I pray you believe that Amice Poulet is towards you one and the same, and will so remain your assured to my little power.

I trusted to have written unto you by a messenger out of these parts, but being disappointed thereof, I send my letters to Mr. Secretary, who (I trust) will convey them unto you with the next.

You write that you are placed in a service of great toil and little thanks, wherein I am deceived if I be much behind you, being cast out into the north, where I want no care, and shall buy my thanks dearly if I have any. Let it suffice both you and me that as we [are] Christian subjects, so we are bound to obey, and accept of any standing or calling that shall be appointed unto us. God give us grace to do the duties of good and faithful servants, and then the same God will not fail to bless our labours ; and thus, with my most hearty commendations, I commit you to the Almighty, who prosper all your actions to His glory.

From my prison in Tutbury Castle, &c.

Elizabeth's closeness in money matters kept Poulet in continual straits. He now begins a series of complaints to the Lord Treasurer of the want of ready money which only end with his charge. The two "families" were numerous, and it is clear that Mr. Darrell held no sinecure. Sir Ralph Sadler has left on record the number of Mary's retinue, and the provision that was made for them in answer to "A note of certain points to be resolved by Sir R. Sadler,"[1] Wingfield, November 5, 1584.

"What number of persons the said Queen hath attending her?

"Forty-eight, viz., herself, five gentlemen, fourteen servitors, three cooks, four boys, three gentlemen's men, six gentlewomen, two wives, ten wenches and children.

"What number of chambers shall be thought meet to be furnished for the said Queen?

[1] Vol. xiv., n. 25 ; Sadler's *State Papers*, vol. ii., p. 437.

"She hath for herself two, and for her maids three, besides two for two women that have their husbands here, and eight for her gentlemen, officers, and men servants; in all, fifteen. Note, that the two secretaries, master of her household, her physician, and De Préau, have several chambers, and so always have had.

"What the Queen of Scots' ordinary diet is, both fish-days and flesh-days?

"About sixteen dishes at both courses, dressed after their own manner. Sometimes more or less, as the provision serveth.

"How many messes, besides her own diet, are served to the rest of her train; and in what sort the said messes are furnished, both fish-days and flesh-days?

"The two secretaries, master of her household, the physician, and De Préau, have a mess of seven or eight dishes, and do dine always before the Queen, and their own servants have their reversion; and the rest of her folk dine with the reversion of her meat. Also her gentlewomen and the two wives and other maids and children, being sixteen, have two messes of meat of nine dishes at both courses for the better sort, and five dishes for the meaner sort."

To my Lord Treasurer 5 *Julii,* 1585.[1]

My very good Lord,—I know I have many shrewd eyes fixed upon me, and that [it] behoveth me to eat with a long spoon; and therefore, fearing to be charged with remissness in the execution of the instructions received from her Majesty, I have thought good to write herewith to Mr. Secretary, to such effect as may appear by this copy inclosed, humbly praying your lordship to assist me there with your favourable opinion, if the contents of my said letters shall be called in question before your lordship. My purpose and meaning is, according to your lordship's grave and most friendly advice, to keep the broad highway in all my actions and doings, and will strive to be blameless, if it be possible, even in the judgment of those that would not be sorry for my blame, if any such be.

[1] *Harl. MSS.,* 6,993, f. 93.

It may please your lordship to receive herewith a view of this last month's expenses of household here, by the which I trust will appear that myself and Mr. Darrell have done our best endeavours to lessen her Majesty's charges, and surely it cannot be expected that the same can be reduced to a lower rate. I may say truly, that if this household were kept at my charge, I would not fail to spend many things which now are spared. My table is furnished with plenty of good meats (God and her Majesty be thanked for it), but without excess, or dishes of charge, little expense of wine, little expense of spices. Your lordship shall find that the charges are lessened every month by at the least two oxen and twenty sheep, three or four hogsheads of wine, and in all other things that are spent by me and mine after that rate. I received from your lordship, at my coming from London, 800*l.*, but it was all spent before my arrival here, and sithence I have had of Mr. Bagot 500*l.*, which by reason of our provision of beefs, muttons, and wines, besides the ordinary expenses of household, are also consumed, and Mr. Darrell in debt to me and some others, whereof it may [please] your lordship to have consideration.

Your lordship shall do me singular favour, and no less to Mr. Candishe, to rid him out of his house in this town; and thus, resting at your lordship's commandment, I commit you to the fatherly protection of the Almighty.

From Tutbury, &c.

The next letter relates to one of Walsingham's spies, an apostate, who was "very careful to entertain his credit with the Papists," that he might betray them. The letter was signed by Thomas Gresley as well as by Poulet, and this accounts for the way in which Poulet names himself in it, as in a previous letter which was written jointly by himself and Sir Ralph Sadler.

To Sir Francis Walsingham, 9 *Julii,* 1585.

Sir,—This bearer, naming himself Robert Woodward,[1] finding me, Amice Poulet, yesterday in the evening at the gate of this castle, delivered unto me this little paper book inclosed, upon the perusing whereof entering into further communication with him, I found that after he had served many masters in this realm, he roved beyond the seas, and there spent six or seven years in France and Italy, and being returned from thence two years past, or thereabouts, had been very careful to entertain his credit with the Papists of these parts, and to that purpose had travelled from one shire to another, to no other end, as he said, than to know them, that he might discover them, and among other things, told me that he was born within two miles of the Earl of Shrewsbury's house at Wingfield, and that his mother, yet living, and his elder brother, were tenants to the said earl.   Comparing these things together, I could not be persuaded to think well of this man, doubting lest his coming hither had been grounded upon some treachery, and that he had some practice in hand for this people under my charge, and therefore committing him, without pretence of suspicion, to a chamber of this castle, under the keeping of some of my servants, with promise to speak with him again this morning, I sent to Mr. Gresley to have his assistance in my proceeding herein.   Upon conference with him, he telleth us that indeed his desire was to have made his repair unto you, but doubting the goodness of his horse, came to me, Amice Poulet, and sayeth that at his first return out of France he was brought before you by John de Vigo, and having then uttered

---

[1] In the original letter in the Public Record Office (Vol. xvi., n. 5), "Robert Woodward" is erased, and instead is written, apparently by Walsingham, "Thomas Taylor of Warsington." In a spy's letter to Burghley, printed in Strype's *Annals*, vol. iii., App., p. 64, the passage occurs, "[Tither, in the Marshalsea] warned me to beware of one Robert Woodward, who served some time Dr. Wenden, in Rome.   They have great intelligence, and fear him much."

unto you the whole course of his life, in like sort as now unto us, was employed by you to discover the doings of the Papists, which he did in Norfolk and Suffolk, to the best of his power. We caused him to be searched, for our better satisfaction, and now finding no appearance that his coming hither was for any evil meaning, we thought good to advise him to make his repair unto you, which we did the more willingly because we find that he came to inform you touching one Daniel Morton, who intendeth to go shortly to the Court in Scotland, and willing to have the company of this man in his journey, as likewise he will advertise you of one James Harrison,[1] a Seminary Priest, and of John Bencroft, a coiner of money, affirming that these two pieces inclosed were made by him. And thus leaving to trouble you, we commit you to the mercy of the Almighty.

From Tutbury, &c.

The next letter to Walsingham, dated July 14, 1585, is also in the Record Office.[2] The following extract from it is about the Priest Du Préau, "*alias* Sir John," as Poulet calls him. His unwillingness to let the town of Tutbury see him and the Priest riding together is natural and amusing.

This Queen hath been discontented with me of late. The cause is this, that taking great pleasure in a greyhound which was given unto her before my coming hither, she desired to see him run at a deer, whereunto I assented, but prayed Curle, the messenger, to desire the Queen, his mistress, to take order that Du Préau (*alias* Sir John) might not ride with her in this hunting. He asked the cause. I said he ought to believe that I would not have moved it without causes. This hunting was appointed in

---

[1] Walsingham has underlined the name of "Harrison," and written in the margin, "Antō Babingtō." There was, however, a "James Harrison, a Seminary Priest," who was martyred at York, March 22, 1602.

[2] Vol. xvi., n. 10.

Stockley Park, distant from this castle one mile, and the only way thither is through this town. The man was left behind, and this Queen, having hunted, in her return called me unto her, and told me that she found my message sent [by] Curle, touching Du Préau, very strange. I prayed her to take it in good part, as a thing not desired without reason. She said she could not like that a servant should be forbidden to attend on her. I answered that all her gentlemen waited on her, and that I did not take Du Préau to be of that number. "I must be attended," saith she, "by others than gentlemen." "So you have, madam," quoth I, "one to carry your cloak, and if you will have more I will not let it." She said she did not like to be commanded in this sort. I told her I did not command her, but prayed her to give me leave to direct her servants. I was servant to the Queen of England, and would not fail to do the duty of my charge. I took no pleasure to offend her, and if she would give me leave to be an honest man I would not offend her. She said she could not blame my honest[y], but could not like of this restraint of her servants. I told her when she taketh the air in the meadows he should be permitted to wait on her, but the town of Tutbury should not hold him and me together. "Well," quoth she, "I find innovations every day." "I know none," quoth I, "but such as are reasonable." She said she would complain to the Queen her good sister, and that she knew these things came from above. I answered that indeed my duty, which was the ground of my doings, came from above; but she might well judge that her Majesty had no part in the matter then in question between her and me. She was now come to the park gate, which interrupted our speech, and sithence I have heard no more of it. This man hath been accustomed to distribute the alms of this Queen, and by that means is so well known in Tutbury town, as when he appeareth all the people resort unto him, because they have tasted of his liberality.

This Queen knoweth that the restraining of this man hath no other hand than to let her almsgiving, which I had rather she divined than I should signify so much unto her. To avoid this giving of alms, I am commanded by my instructions to remove the people from this Queen and her company, which would serve to little purpose unless I did also make fast the door, because they would cast their alms into every door.

To my Lord Treasurer, the 16th of July, 1585.

My very good Lord,—Having met this day by appointment with Mr. Harry Candishe at Burton for the view of the Lord Paget's house there, I have received his resolute answer, which is that I shall have grounds of him to the value of 60*l.* by the year or thereabouts, and will be content to take grounds at Burton in recompense, wherein he will refer himself to the judgment of two gentlemen to be indifferently chosen. Touching his house he prayeth that consideration may be had of the great loss which he shall sustain so many ways if he depart from it and dwell at Burton, where he hath no provision of wood or corn, which he hath in great plenty at Tutbury, and especially of corn, having the tithes of many parishes adjoining; he shall lose the services of his tenants; he shall amend and maintain another man's house, and impair his own; he shall dwell in a populous poor town, which will be chargeable unto him: besides the discontentment of his mind in many respects: and for these causes desireth a recompense of one hundred pounds by the year for the use of his house, or else, being indebted to the sum of three thousand pounds, that it may please her Majesty for so many years as his house and grounds shall be employed to this service, in full satisfaction of the one and the other, to lend him two thousand pounds upon sufficient sureties, whereof the Earl of Shrewsbury to be one, or upon assurance of a good portion of land. This is his final answer, and in my simple opinion is not much different from reason. A gentlemen of his calling cannot be removed in this sort without great hindrances and greater discommodities. It may be, although he doth not say it, he will be content with the loan of 1,500*l.* And thus resting at your commandment, I commit your good lordship to the favour and mercy of the Almighty.

From Tutbury, &c.

The next letter being in the Record Office,[1] an extract from it will here be sufficient. It is addressed to Sir Francis Walsingham, July 17, 1585.

This Queen hath made no mention at all of removing these six weeks or more, until yesterday late in the evening, having sent for me to tell me that her packet was ready, she complained of the coldness of her chamber, being subject to the wind in many places by reason the walls were not of stone, which she prayed to have amended, and to that purpose to be removed by the space of six weeks.

I told her I knew no house in this country fit for her, and to remove far off for so short a time was not possible, and that the faults in her chamber walls might be amended although she did not remove. She said she thought those faults would not so easily be repaired. I answered all should be done that was possible.

She said no more, but I am deceived if I cannot tell you rightly the ground of this motion. I have the promise of Mr. Candishe's house in this town, and this day he and I shall meet at Burton to deliver unto him in exchange the Lord Paget's house there. Mr. Candishe undiscreetly persuadeth himself that I take his house to serve for a

[1] Vol. xvi., n. 14.

removing place for this Queen, although I never said so much to him, and indeed would be ashamed to have made him so foul a lie. This matter by her laundresses or by some other such like mean is come to her ears, and now she prayeth to be removed. I know Mr. Candishe's house and this country so well, as I would not take upon me to keep her there for one week for more money than I shall spend these seven years. And thus I commit you to the mercy and favour of the Almighty.

From Tutbury, &c. ·

Autograph postscript in the original. Mr. Candishe and I have met at Burton, but we cannot agree upon the price.

The Henry Cavendish so frequently mentioned in these letters at this period, was the eldest son of Sir William Cavendish by his third wife, Bess of Hardwick, who married fourthly George, ninth Earl of Shrewsbury, keeper of Mary Queen of Scots from 1569 to 1584. The wife of Mr. Cavendish, who is spoken of by Poulet as "an old acquaintance of this Queen," was Lady Grace Talbot, daughter of the above-mentioned George Earl of Shrewsbury by his first wife, Lady Gertrude Manners. The mother of "young Pierrepont," whose friends Lord Leicester warned Poulet to look to, was Frances, wife of Sir Henry Pierrepont, Henry Cavendish's sister. The young lady was the companion from her childhood of the Queen of Scots. Writing to her, September 13, 1583,[1] Mary begins the letter, "Mignone," and addresses it, "To my well-beloved bedfellow, Bess Pierpont."

To my Lord of Leicester, . . . Julii [sic] 1585.

My very good Lord,—Your lordship's letters of the 26th of the last were delivered unto me by the ordinary post the 10th of this present after noon, so as it seemeth your letters were misdated, or else the post made no post

---

[1] *Cotton. MSS.*, Vesp., F. iii., f. 38 ; Labanoff, tom. v., p. 370.

haste, but rather is worthy of blame for his negligence. Your lordship promiseth to send hither shortly a warrant for taking wood for the necessary use of this house, which shall be very welcome.

I thank your lordship most humbly for your advertisement contained in the paper[1] inclosed in your said letters, whereof I have had especial care, as may appear by my letters written to Sir Francis Walsingham five days before the receipt of yours, and had already conferred with Mr. Candishe to redeem his house and grounds here in exchange for the Lord Paget's house at Burton and other grounds there to the value, thereby to avoid the occasion of resort hither, and having written herein to my Lord Treasurer, have now lately received direction from his lordship to conclude this bargain with Mr. Candishe, which I trust to do before many days pass.

I can assure your lordship that [no one] hath desired to speak with Pierrepont sithence my coming hither. They are too cunning to deal so grossly. And thus, with humble remembrance of my duty, I commit your good lordship to the mercy of the Almighty.

From Tutbury, &c.

Your lordship writeth in your minute that you know letters have passed. Praying your lordship to do me the favour to let me know your knowledge therein, because I can hardly believe it. If it be true, it will stead me greatly to know it; if it be untrue, your lordship shall know by whom you have been abused.

Poulet, when asking for the stewardship of Lord Paget's property, promised that it should be discharged by one of his own servants, "to the good liking of the tenants." How far it was to the good liking of the Catholic tenants we now see. Mr. Baynham, who wanted to be made his deputy, is the man

---

[1] The paper or minute is given after the following letter.

F

who suggested to him to make the application to Lord Burghley for the stewardship. It would appear from the letter of January 10, that Baynham was appointed deputy-steward after all.

To my Lord Treasurer, . . . Julii, 1585.

My very good Lord,—I think myself greatly bound unto your lordship for the stewardship of the Lord Paget's lands, and do thank you no less for the choice of Mr. Cradocke to serve as my deputy therein, of whom I cannot conceive but well, being recommended by your lordship, and have yielded gladly to your pleasure, which I have signified unto him.

Mr. Baynham hath desired it by his letters, but they came three days after yours. I was willing to have bestowed it upon one of my servants, a man of sufficient judgment and experience for this place, but it standeth better with my discharge to have a man of better learning, especially being well affected in religion, as Mr. Cradocke is reported to be, so as, I trust, by his good endeavour, joined with my assistance, so many recusants will not be found hereafter among the Lord Paget's tenants as are at this present. I thank your lordship once again for the office and for my deputy.

It may please your lordship to peruse this letter inclosed with the minute contained in the same ; by the date of which said letters it may seem that my last letters to Mr. Secretary were grounded upon the same minute. But the truth is, that it came not to my hands until the 10th of this present month, which was five days after the sending of my said letters. If his lordship's letters were not misdated upon some meaning touching the provision of wood for this house, it must be confessed that there was great negligence in the post, because they came to me by him.

I am not sorry that my letters to Mr. Secretary did concur so well with this advertisement. Your lordship seeth how much I presume upon your lordship's favour, forbearing to trouble you with the copy of my letters sent herewith to Mr. Secretary, for no other cause than that I fear to be over troublesome unto your lordship; but indeed do desire nothing more than that it may be lawful for me to acquaint your lordship with all my advertisements from hence which shall import her Majesty's service or my poor credit, as one desirous to submit all my doings to your lordship's censure. As knoweth the Almighty, who always preserve your good lordship.

From Tutbury, &c.

A copy of a Minute from my Lord of Leicester, 10° *Julii,* 1585.

I now begin to fear Scotland, and that there is great dissimulation by Arc.[1] there and his mistress. You had need look well to the servants of Ca. and his La.,[2] for they have intelligence in your house; and beware one look to such as desire to speak with the young Pierrepont there. I know that letters have passed that way, and I know also that Ha. [*probably* H. Ca.] and his La. make their abode thereabouts only to serve, &c. If good wait be laid, you will find it.

Answer to Mr. Secretary concerning this clause.

It may seem that my last letters were partly grounded upon this minute, but the truth is I did not receive it until the 10th of this present, which was five days after the date of my said letters unto you. My lord writeth that he knoweth letters have passed that way. Praying you to do me the favour to let me know his knowledge therein, because I can hardly believe it. If it be true, it will stead me greatly to know it; if it be untrue, his lordship shall know by whom he hath been abused.

[1] Probably Archibald Douglas.
[2] Henry and Lady Grace Cavendish.

The accusation against the Cavendishes was mortifying to Poulet, and it was still more mortifying that it should be supposed that he had allowed Bessie Pierrepont to be a channel of communication, especially as (if Morgan be right) he was "far out of liking with Leicester." He naturally tries to make the best of it, partly by showing that he had anticipated it in his negotiations, prompted solely by his own sagacity, for the removal of the Cavendish family and servants from close proximity to the castle, and partly by disbelieving it, which he might well do, as he had not long before praised Mr. Cavendish as "well affected to her Majesty's service." It is curious that the letter to Walsingham, from which the preceding passage sent to Burghley was taken, is not to be found either in the letterbook or at the Record Office.

The next letter to Lord Burghley is given by Strype,[1] with the remark, "The whole letter I reposit in the Appendix, knowing that these State letters are valuable and tend much to let into a true knowledge of matters transacted." It is a singular fact that Strype, who had access to Lord Burghley's papers, should have only this one to "reposit," out of the large number addressed to Burghley by Poulet.

To my Lord Treasurer, the 26th of July, 1585.

My very good Lord,—Although I have increased in health daily sithence the first day of my arrival here (I thank God for it), and do now find myself able to go strongly, and as speedily as at any time these two or three years last past, yet, being subject to the gout, and considering the nature of the disease, I must look for a fresh assault in the accustomed season, at which time the importance of this service will require the assistance of some honest and faithful gentleman, which no doubt may be easily found, both in the Court and in this country.

But because your resolutions at the Court are not always speedy, and that my assistant may be found

---

[1] *Annals of the Reformation*, London, 1728, vol. iii., p. 300; Appendix, p. 117.

wanting before he can come, presuming upon your lordship's favour towards me, I will be so bold to name a gentleman who I know will be content to come hither unto me, and to spend some long time here with me, and rabating[1] so many of my number as he and his servants will amount unto, which may be in all five or six, cannot be any way chargeable to her Majesty.

The gentleman is Mr. John Colls,[2] a man not unknown, I think, to your lordship for his good discretion, and so well known to me, as I will answer for his fidelity at my utmost peril. And I am deceived if he 'be not sufficient to take the charge of this service during my sickness, when God shall send it, and especially if, by living here with me, he may be trained[3] therein some little time before I shall be visited with sickness. I will stand always answerable for the charge. My supply shall be in house with me, ready upon every occasion ; her Majesty's charge shall not be increased of one penny, and I shall have the comfort of a very discreet[4] friend.

If your lordship shall find this motion reasonable and likely to have passage, it may please you to further it, and to do further[5] therein as you shall think good. If your lordship shall not allow of it, then I shall most humbly pray you that it may rest with you in secret. It may be that your lordship will not mislike it, but would not be a dealer therein, whereof being advertised I will not fail to seek it in such order and by such means as your lordship shall direct.

It may please your lordship to give me leave' to say plainly unto you, as to my special good lord, that I fear

---

[1] *Rabbate*, to abate. *Halliwell* quoting Palsgrave.
[2] Poulet made a similar request of Walsingham, August 27 (Vol. xvi., n. 33), then suggesting Mr. John Colls, Mr. Richard Bagot, or Sir John Zouch. Mr. Bagot was appointed (*Ibid.*, n. 36).
[3] Trusted. *Strype.*
[4] An honest, discreet friend. *Strype.*
[5] To proceed therein. *Strype.*

there will be some cunning in the choice of my supply, if he come from the Court. This one thing I may affirm, that Mr. John Colls honoureth and respecteth your lordship before all the noblemen in this land. I fear I have presumed too far, wherein I crave your lordship's pardon. And thus resting at your commandment, I commit your lordship to the protection of the Almighty.

From Tutbury [the 26th of July, 1585.

Your lordship's to command,

A. POULET,]

It seems a singular request to a Secretary of State, that he should send down a washerwoman from the Court. With this Poulet's letter to Walsingham of July 26[1] opens. He then says that "the last letters from the French Ambassador to this Queen have lifted the hearts of this people marvellously, and now they hold themselves assured that the exercise of religion is utterly abolished in France, and that the fire kindled there will be extended farther." Nau's brother had written of "the good disposition of the Scottish King towards this Queen," which Poulet recommended Mary to be slow to believe. After saying that the letter from Nau's brother being sealed, he had opened and perused it, according to his general practice, he concludes by asking that instructions may be sent to his son, Anthony Poulet, respecting the reception of French Protestant refugees in Jersey. The following appears in the Record Office as a separate letter.[2]

Ad eundem [Walsingham] *eodem die* [July 26, 1585].

Sir,—I had forgotten in my other letters to pray to be advertised from you if you have received any letters from me by the hands of one Robert Woodward, wherein it may please you to hold me excused. I have received even now letters from Sir John Zouch, by the which it appeareth that he hath travelled faithfully and carefully in seeking to discover the practices of Ralph Elweys,

---

[1] Vol. xvi., n. 22.   [2] *Ibid.*, n. 23.

according to your instructions in that behalf, but no good effect hath followed as yet. And thus once again I take my leave of you.

From Tutbury, &c.

To Sir Francis Walsingham, 2° Augusti [1585].

Sir,—Your letters [of] the 25th and 26th of the last came to my hand the 29th of the same, but the extracts of foreign proceedings mentioned in the said letters I did not receive. It is likely they were forgotten in the closing up of the letters.

Finding this Queen's packets sent with the said letters fast sealed, having received no countermandment from you, I opened and perused the same after my accustomed manner, wherein perchance I use double diligence, but I dare not do otherwise. Referring you for the substance of the said packet to this paper inclosed, which I send the more willingly because mention is made of the King's good affection to this Queen, and of a device to work a divorce between Arran and Gray.

We have so long lulled in a most dangerous security, that we are apt to take every light occasion to entertain the same, or rather it has now grown to an habit in us, so as we cannot shake it off in open show of imminent danger. God continue His mercy and favour towards us, and remove this bad humour from us. These letters requiring no haste, I have forborne to use the post, and do send the same by one of my own servants, who is abiding at London. And thus I commit you to the fatherly protection of the Almighty, who give us strength of mind and body to sustain the labours of this busy time.

From Tutbury, &c.

The original of the next letter is among the State Papers, and the copy sent by Poulet to Burghley is in the British Museum.[1]

[1] Vol. xvi., n. 30; *Harl. MSS.*, 6993, f. 98.

To Sir Francis Walsingham, 8° Augusti, 1585.

Sir,—I have received your letters of the 3rd of this present, and am heartily sorry for the loss of that good earl and his son,[1] partly for the particular interest I had in them both, but especially in respect of our Queen and country, who in these days of treachery and treason against God and His anointed, cannot be deprived of the faithful service of two such personages without singular damage.

Whereas you write this Queen hath desired that for the cleansing and sweetening of this house, she might remove to some other place for some short time, it is most certain that there is no house in these parts either sufficient and commodious for her and her train, or assured for the governor. The Lord Paget had only two houses in this country; the one at Burton,[2] distant three miles from this castle, a ruinous house, the buildings scattered, and adjoining to a very poor town, full of bad neighbours; the other at Beaudesert, distant twelve miles, a house of no strength, the buildings not finished, and both those houses naked and utterly unfurnished of all things belonging to household, so as the furniture of this remove must come altogether from this castle, which will be a matter of excessive charges and trouble, and almost impossible to be performed, this charge being such as the company may not be divided one day and night without peril.

If she should be removed for some short time, it is of necessity that it must be to some house furnished

---

[1] Francis Russell, second Earl of Bedford, died July 28, 1585. His third son, Francis, said by Collins to have been summoned to Parliament as Lord Russell, was killed in Scotland in an accidental fray, July 27, 1585.

[2] From this letter it would appear that Mr. Cavendish moved from his own house, but did not take possession of Burton, and the brewer was probably left in quiet possession. Lord Burghley's assent to the bargain which would have displaced the brewer renders it likely that he was not privy to the details of Walsingham's plot.

already, of which sort I know no other than Mr. Candishe's house, which being insufficiently furnished to receive this company, considering the nearness of this castle, the defects may be supplied from hence; but to say nothing of the weakness of the house, it is not capable of the Scottish train alone, and yet they must lodge divided in many pieces.

Mr. Candishe hath builded a little dining chamber, and a chamber or two adjoining. All the residue of the house is old and ruinous, the kitchen, and all other houses of office, being far less than sufficient to serve both these households. One thing I may add, that this country is so ill affected (a thing not unknown unto you), as I think no man of judgment would willingly take the charge of this Queen in any house in this shire out of this castle. No doubt this Queen was in some hope to have been removed to Mr. Candishe his house, as I have heretofore written unto you, which was the cause and ground of this motion, but finding in conference with me sithence the despatch of her last packet, that the house was not any way fit for her use, and promising to provide carpenters and other artificers to repair her lodgings in such sort as should be devised by her Ministers, Nau being present said that I could say no more, so as urging the matter of their remove no farther, it seemed to me that they were satisfied.

Notwithstanding, following your direction, and to the end this Queen might know her Majesty's favour towards her, I have given her to understand that her Highness is well pleased that she be removed so as any fit house might be found; and hereupon I have told her that I know only three vacant houses in these parts, viz., Mr. Candishe's house, and the Lord Paget's at Burton and Beaudesert, and have delivered unto her my opinion touching the said houses, which is that Mr. Candishe his house is less than sufficient to receive her own train; that

the house at Burton standeth so near to the river as it
will not stand with her health to remove thither, that
it is so ruinous as it will not be repaired in a short time,
that it is unfurnished of all implements belonging to
household, and is also too little to receive this great
company; that the house at Beaudesert is not yet
finished, and so unfurnished as it hath not so much as
one stool or bedstead in it, and that, considering the far
distance from hence, there is no possibility to remove all
the stuff of this house thither in convenient time. I have
added to these foresaid reasons that the weather here
hath been such of long time as there is little sign of
summer, and that when all diligence shall be used, before
this remove shall be performed, and that beer, wine,
wood, coal, and such necessaries shall be provided, winter
will be in his full strength. I said that Mr. Candishe's
house was already well known to her principal Ministers,
who could judge if I said truly or no, and the house at
Burton might be seen by any of her servants when she
would.

She replied very little, only that the Earl of Shrewsbury removed his stuff from one house to another, and
that if the house were too little, some part of her
company might be lodged in the town. I answered that
the Earl perchance removed some part of his best stuff,
but was not troubled with the carriage of his kitchen stuff,
bedsteads, table-boards, and such like, and that it were
very inconvenient that her train should be lodged far from
her. I prayed her to consider of it, which she said she
would do, so as I think I shall hear little of this matter.
If any new motion shall be made herein by the French
Ambassador, it may please you to take no knowledge of
that which hath passed between this Queen and me until
I shall receive her resolution.

I have received the three packets for this Queen and
have perused them with her good liking, because, having

passed over the first packet, I send it immediately unto her, and so one after another until all be delivered, which pleaseth her greatly. The French Ambassador, in his letters to this Queen, changeth not his style touching Archibald Douglas, saving that he adviseth her, considering his departure, to appoint the said Archibald to follow her causes about that Court. All other things mentioned in the said packets, and seeming worthy to be observed, are contained in this paper inclosed. It may be, and it is very likely, that I advertise many things that are needless, wherein I crave pardon, because I do not know what you know already; but of this I am sure, that I have omitted nothing that may concern our Queen or country, and have used such expedition therein, as I am deceived if this Queen think anything less than that I have taken any extracts of her letters.

It is likely that her Majesty will confer with my Lord Treasurer touching this remove, and therefore I have thought good to advertise his lordship of my proceedings herein with this Queen, and of my simple opinion of the vacant houses in these parts; and thus I commit you to the Almighty, who prosper all your actions to His glory.

From Tutbury, &c.

Postscript in the original, not in the letter-book. It were better, in my simple opinion, that the refusal of this remove proceeded from this Queen than that she were dissuaded from above.

The copy of this former letter to Mr. Secretary was written the said day, 8° Augusti, 1585, to my Lord Treasurer, with this exordium before it.[1]

My very good Lord,—I have grown so thrifty that, to save a little paper, I do not stick, instead of a just letter, to trouble your lordship with a copy of my letters to

[1] *Harl. MSS.*, 6993, f. 98.

Mr. Secretary as followeth, &c. [*In marg.* Lege autem quæ sequuntur]. And thus I leave to trouble your lordship any farther, resting always at your commandment, and so I do commit your good lordship to the mercy of the Highest.

From Tutbury, &c.

It is remarkable that Mary's proposal in the next letter that she should be removed to the house of Sir Thomas Gerard, is not accompanied by any remark on Poulet's part that Sir Thomas was one of her warmest friends. It was not until August of the following year, 1586, that Sir Thomas Gerard was sent to the Tower, but we are told by his son, Father John Gerard, in his autobiography,[1] that he had been previously imprisoned on Queen Mary's account. "When a child of five years of age," he says, " I was forced, together with my brother, who was also a child, to dwell among heretics under another roof, for that my father, with two other gentlemen, had been cast into the Tower of London, for having conspired to restore the Scottish Queen to liberty and to her kingdom. She was at that time confined in the county of Derby at two miles distance from us. Three years afterwards my father, having obtained his release by the payment of a large sum, brought us home, free however from any taint of heresy, as he had maintained a Catholic tutor over us." The price of this liberation is said to have been the transfer of the lordship of Gerards Bromley to his kinsman, Sir Gilbert Gerard, the Master of the Rolls, whose eldest son took his title from it when raised to the peerage. Father Gerard was wrong in thinking that Tutbury was in Derbyshire. It was close to the borders of that county, but in Staffordshire. Etwall in Derbyshire came to Sir Thomas Gerard by his marriage with Elizabeth, the eldest of the daughters and coheirs of Sir John Port, who died in 1557.[2] As Father Gerard was born in 1564, he is necessarily speaking of Mary's first imprisonment at Tutbury. She arrived there from Bolton under the charge of Lord Shrewsbury and Sir Francis Knollys, in February, 1569.[3] She

[1] *Condition of Catholics under James I.,* p. x. [2] *Ibid.,* p. ccliii.
[3] Vol. iii., n. 40.

was not there three months on that occasion, as she was transferred to Wingfield towards the end of April.[1] Mary says of Tutbury,[2] "Comme ce lieu a esté ma première prison et restrinction en ce royaulme, et où, du commencement, j'ay reçeu de très grands rigeurs, rudesses, et indignitez, aussi l'ay-je tousjours depuis tenue malheureuse et infortunée, comme dès l'hyver passé, avant qu'y venir, je feis remonstrer à ladicte Royne d'Angleterre." Her description of the place in the same letter shows that it must have been far from a pleasant residence for a sick person.

To Sir Francis Walsingham, 18th of August, 1585.[3]

Sir,—This Queen being grieved in one of her legs, and having kept her bed a day or two, prayed me to come unto her the 8th of this present, and then asked me what I thought of her remove. I told her that I had already delivered unto her my opinion touching the houses which I knew in these parts. "But," said she, "it is likely that the Queen hath houses in Nottingham and Coventry." I answered that I was a stranger in this country, so as I could say nothing therein. "I remember," quoth she, "as I came hitherwards from Derby, I saw a fair house not far from hence which was said to belong to a knight called Gerard, and as I hear he lieth not in it." I said I thought this house was too little for her use. She prayed me to cause it to be seen, which I promised to do.

On Tuesday, the 10th of this present, at eleven of the clock in the night I received your letters of the 8th of the same, with her Majesty's letters inclosed, addressed to this Queen, and because it was not convenient to pray access unto her in the morning, and being not ignorant that these letters would be very welcome unto her, I delivered them unto Nau the next morning.

The two or three days next following, she kept her bed by reason of the infirmity before-mentioned, and the

---

[1] Vol. iii., n. 72.   [2] Labanoff, tom. vi., p. 218.
[3] *Harl. MSS.*, 6993, f. 104.

15th of this present, being risen out of her bed, but not able to go, and therefore lying upon a pallet, she sent for me, and at my repair unto her told me that being at the point to take physic, at the very instant of the receipt of her Majesty's letters, she was so much comforted by the same, that she refused her physic and found herself more refreshed by this kindness from the Queen, her good sister, than she should have been by all the ministry of all the physic in the world.[1]

She prayed me to excuse her that she had not sent sooner for me, which she said proceeded partly of her infirmity, but especially that she was very willing to write unto her Majesty as soon as she could, and by that occasion to do the like to the French King and some others, wherein she had been busy a day or two. She said that she had always carried a firm and constant opinion of her Majesty's friendly and natural disposition towards her, that for her part she could not cease to honour and respect her as Queen of England, and to love her entirely as her elder sister and nearest ally, that this realm is more dear unto her than all other countries whatsoever.[2] And yet she can find no comfort in it, because if it be distressed, and feel or fear any calamity, she is also grieved as one that wisheth unto it all happy prosperity. If it flourish in security then she feareth the worse and is the less regarded that she had given herself wholly to her Majesty in all humbleness, in all faithfulness, in all sincerity, in all integrity (I use her own words), and had removed all foreign helps to please her Highness, and thereby to give her to know that she depended wholly of

---

[1] Mary had written the day before to M. de Mauvissière to the same effect. Labanoff, tom. vi., p. 212.

[2] "Et quoy qu'il advienne, je veulx vivre et mourir bonne Angloise, ayant plus d'esgard au bien de la dite Royne, ma bonne sœur, et au public du pays et de la nation, que non aux particulières factions de mes dits ennemys, ou aux maulx que j'ay receuz d'eulx en mon particulier." Mary to Mauvissière, August 17, 1585. Labanoff, tom. vi., p. 212.

her. That her words had no credit, she was not believed, and her proffers refused when they might have done good. That she hath proffered her heart and body to her Majesty: her body is taken and great care taken for the safe keeping of it, but her heart is refused. That when she sayeth if she were employed she might do good, and when she shall be required hereafter it will be too late, then she is said to boast. When she offereth herself and service with all humbleness, then she is said to flatter. That she felt the smart of every accident that happened to the danger of her Majesty's person or estate, although she were guiltless in heart and tongue. That if she had desired great liberty, her Majesty might instantly have been jealous of her, but she desired only reasonable liberty for her health. That if the treaty had proceeded between her Majesty and her, she knoweth France had now been quiet. That considering the indisposition of her body, she hath no hope of long life, and much less of a pleasant life, having lost the use of her limbs, and therefore is far from the humour of ambition, desiring only to be well accepted where she shall deserve well, and by that mean during her short days to carry a contented and satisfied mind. That it was not her calling to win fame by victories, but would think herself happy if, by her mediation, peace might be entertained in all countries generally, but especially in this realm. That if she had spoken with the King of Navarre his Ambassador at his being here this last winter, she thinketh there had been now good amity between his master and the house of Guise, and did not doubt to have done some good if she had been made acquainted with his last being here. That her son is a stranger unto her; but he should be possessed with ambition, he play of both hands and do bad office [*sic*]. That her son did reproach her in his letters that she was shut up in a desert, so as he could not send to her or hear from her, which was the cause that he did help

himself by other means the best he could, and was forced
so to do. Finally, that although she had been esteemed
as nobody, and have determined if her help were hereafter
required to be indeed as nobody, and so to answer, yet,
for the love that she beareth to her Majesty and this
realm, she will not refuse to employ her best means if it
shall please her Highness to use her service, which she
will do, not so much for her own particular as for her
Majesty's surety and benefit of this realm.

I omit her protestations of her sincere and upright
dealing with her Majesty, and her solemn oaths that she
hath not of long time given or received any intelligence to
or from any of her friends, because they are no new
things unto you. It seemed she could not satisfy herself
with speaking, and therefore I said the less, advising
her to comfort herself with her Majesty's favour, whereof
(no doubt) some good effect would ensue, if herself or her
friends did not give cause to the contrary. I know this
kind of matter is not new unto you, and perchance I
should have forborne in some other time to have reported
the same, but, considering the scope of her Majesty's
letters unto this Queen, I thought agreeable with my duty
to acquaint you with her speeches, and so do refer them to
your better consideration.

This Queen having thus uttered her griefs and
complaints with many words, asked me if I had sought
to inform myself of the houses which she mentioned unto
me. I answered that the houses at Nottingham and
Coventry (if her Majesty had any there) were so far
distant from hence as I had no mean in this short time
to learn the true state of them, and, touching Sir Thomas
Gerard's house, I told her that I had caused it to be
viewed, and did find that the house is newly builded,
and standeth as yet in two parts, and that the hall and
kitchen are yet wanting, which should tie those two parts
together, besides many other imperfections. Being satisfied

touching this house, she said indeed that she had made mention of the houses at Nottingham and Coventry unto me, not that she was curious to inform herself of her Majesty's houses, but that, upon question of her remove before her coming hither, she did remember that these two houses were named, and, as she was not affected to any house, so it stood her upon for the preservation of her health to be removed from hence, her body being reduced to that weakness as, although the open air abroad did not offend her, yet she could not endure the least air in the world in her chamber, whereunto she was much subject where she is now lodged, by reason of the thinness of the walls. I told her that, besides that might be done by carpenters and other artificers, she was now provided of double hangings for her chamber, which I thought might suffice to defend the cold air. She insisted to urge the remove with great earnestness, alleging that this late accident of grief so shortly after her diet did give her to understand that she was greatly subject to the rheum upon any cold, which caused a distillation into her legs, and now bereaved her of the use of them, so as it behoved her to have care of her health.

She hath been heretofore (as I hear) free from all grief during the summer season, but it seemeth that this humour hath possessed her, and that there is little hope that she shall recover her limbs hereafter. I told her that, besides the providing and furnishing of a house, and many things of necessary importance not easy to be provided, it was not possible in this little time which remained of summer to make a sufficient provision of wood and coal to serve for the whole winter, the expense whereof was so great in this great household, as, having the whole summer season before me, there was yet wanting the third part of winter's proportion.

All this and much more could not suffice to satisfy her, concluding that she would be a suitor to her Majesty

G

therein by her letters, and that she would desire to be removed only for three weeks, in which time her lodging here might be repaired and some new lodgings builded, to be joined to these which she hath already. A remove for this little space might be made to Mr. Candishe's house with little trouble and as little charge, if she might be kept there safely, a matter of great peril in my simple opinion, and therefore I durst not make any mention thereof to this Queen. [*In marg.* She asketh no more than to have her own lodgings plastered overhead, which cannot be done without a remove.]

This Queen hath here, in the number of her retinue, one Audrey, an embroiderer, with his wife and five children, being willing to discharge the said Audrey with his wife and four children, and hath prayed me to write for their passport, which I refer to your better consideration. Only I have thought good to put you in remembrance that this Audrey's wife, being a woman of judgment and understanding, which I know to be true, as well by this Queen's own report as otherways, may prove a dangerous messenger in this dangerous [time], although you were assured that she carried with you [her] no letters at all.

I was informed of Peter Bayte long before the receipt of your letters by Mr. Francis Hastings, and have taken order to see his doings observed. I cannot learn that Sir Randolfe Brewerton is in these parts. I have thought good to acquaint my Lord Treasurer, by my letters sent herewith, with that which hath passed between this Queen and me touching this remove.

Seeing that this Queen's letters come so slowly from her, I have thought good to send these unto you, to the end you may be the better prepared to answer hers when they come. And thus I commit you to the mercy of the Highest.

From Tutbury, &c.

To my Lord Treasurer, 18° Augusti, 1585.[1]

My very good Lord,—This Queen insisting to be removed with all earnestness, and not doubting but that your lordship's advice will be used therein, I am bold to trouble you with all that hath passed in that behalf between her and me, which shall appear in this copy inclosed of my letters sent herewith to Mr. Secretary, the same containing some other matter not worthy of your lordship, but my said letters might not be dismembered without some maim.

Her Majesty will be a great loser this year in the meadow grounds which were reserved for the use of this house by reason of the great floods, which have done great hurt in these parts; but I trust this loss shall be recompensed with usury in the rents which I have increased upon the tithes, and some other things which I have set. I doubt not to yield your lordship a very good reckoning of the parks and all other things which I have reserved, wherein I have been as careful as if the matter had concerned myself. And resting at your lordship's commandment, &c.

Postscript in the original. It may please your lordship to have this house in remembrance for a supply of money for our household affairs.

On the next day Mary's letters were ready. Poulet forwarded them to Walsingham with the following letter,[2] inclosing a copy of the letter to M. de Mauvissière, which he describes as "carrying a harder style" than the other. The inclosure is preserved in the Record Office.[3] Prince Labanoff prints it,[4] as well as the letter which is "short and very plausible."[5] Poulet does not remark that the first is dated August 12, before the receipt of Elizabeth's letter, and the other August 17, after she had received it. "Depuis mes encloses j'ay receu des lettres de la Royne

---

[1] *Harl. MSS.*, 6993, f. 102.   [2] Vol. xvi., n. 32.
[3] *Ibid.*, n. 32 I.   [4] Tom. vi., p. 195.   [5] *Ibid.*, p. 211.

d'Angleterre, madame ma bonne sœur, plaines de tant de cour-
toisies et démonstration de bonne volonté, qu'il fault que je
vous dye n'avoir, il y a quatre moys, ressenty plus de consolation
en tous mes maulx, tant d'esprit que du corps, que j'ay faict par
ceste souvenance qu'il m'apparoist qu'elle ha de moy et de mon
estat par deça."[1] Poulet's phrase would convey the impression
that Mary was writing two letters to the same person at the same
time in different sense. The fact is, that one was a postscript to
the other.

Mary's rejoicings over a letter from Elizabeth, "overflowing
with courtesy and demonstrations of good will," rouse both pity
and indignation in view of the scheme for her destruction arranged
between Walsingham and his mistress. This was the last letter
Mary was to receive from the Queen of England, until she was
bidden by her to plead for her life before the Commissioners at
Fotheringay.[2] Of Elizabeth's "enchantments" Mr. Froude has
not a word to say.

To Sir Francis Walsingham, 19° Augusti, 1585.

Sir,—I send you herewith this Queen's letters to her
Majesty, inclosed in her packets to the French Ambassador, with other letters to the French King, Queen
Mother, French Queen, Duke of Guise, Mauvissière, and
Chasteauneuf,[3] and divers other letters from Nau and
others of the Scottish train to their friends in London
and in France, all which letters I have perused and have
seen them sealed and made up in this packet, the same
containing no other matter worthy of advertisement than
may appear unto you in this paper inclosed.

This Queen's letters to the French contain no other
matter than ordinary compliments, saving that in her
letters to the Duke of Guise, she prayeth his friendly
assistance towards Mauvissière in his suit to the French

---

[1] A further extract has been previously given in a note.
[2] Vol. xx., n. 6.
[3] These letters may be seen in Labanoff, tom. vi., pp. 204, 206, 207, 209,
but the letter to Elizabeth of this date has not been preserved.

King for the bailiwick of Vitrye, which he hath given
him. She urgeth her remove from hence to the French
Ambassador with great earnestness, although both she
and Nau do know it to be impossible at this time.

The order which I take in perusing of these letters
is this. Nau bringeth all the letters unto me unsealed,
and after the reading of one or two of them, I tell him
that I am not accustomed to read many French letters,
and therefore do pray him to give me some time to peruse
them, and by this means I read them with leisure, and
write out anything which I think worthy.

This Queen writeth two several letters to the French
Ambassador, whereof the one is short and very plausible,
containing many good words of her devotion towards
her Majesty, which perchance shall be showed to you
and such others. The other letter carrieth a harder style.

And thus I leave to trouble you, and so do commit
you to the mercy of the Highest.

From, &c.

Postscript in the original. From this Queen to Chérelles
with her own hand.

Je vous mercie *des confitures seiches* [I suspect some
other meaning. *Poulet's note in the margin.*] que m'envoy-
asses le quaresme passé, les ayant trouvez fort belles.
Faites que celles dont la memoire vous ha esté dernie-
rement addressée, soyent aussi bien choysies.

Mary had great confidence in Chérelles, so that Poulet says,[1]
"I can assure you that Fontenay and Chérelles are expected
here with great devotion." But certainly there was no need for
Poulet to make himself anxious respecting anything that passed
between Mary and the French Ambassador. Chérelles, who was
secretary of the French Embassy to M. de Mauvissière and
M. de Châteauneuf successively, sent copies of Mary's letters
to Walsingham. Prince Labanoff[2] has printed these letters from

---

[1] Vol. xvi., n. 38.   [2] Tom. v., pp. 361, 430.

the copies in Chérelles' hand, now in Lord Salisbury's collection at Hatfield House, in the Public Record Office, and the British Museum. One of the latter[1] has the following disgraceful note to Walsingham, added to the letter he was betraying, written by Chérelles. "Je vous supplie bien humblement, monsieur, de tenir tout cy le plus secret qu'il sera possible, affin que monsieur l'ambassadeur ne s'en aperçoive d'aucune sorte, comme je sçay que vous sçaurez très bien faire : car je ne voudrois pour tout l'or du monde estre découvert pour la honte que je sçay que je recevrois, non seullement la honte, mais aussi la vye y perdrois ; de laquelle je ne me soucie point tant que de la dite honte que je pourrois recevoir, car toujours faut-il mourir." Here is the confession of one of those wretches whose sense of shame is entirely confined to being found out. For this singularly base piece of treachery Mr. Froude has no word of blame. All he has to say is, "Chérelles was bought to watch his master," and, again, of the whole plot against the Queen of Scots, "Walsingham had contrived an ingenious scheme to gain political information."[2] It was a base system that induced a man for money to betray the trust reposed in him, and no sympathy for the persons that were involved in it should induce us to excuse its baseness. Mary Stuart had no right to complain, for she was not free from its guilt. For instance, she speaks of Phelippes as one whom Morgan "dealt withal long ago to have served me, about Secretary Walsingham." There is, however, this difference between Mary and Walsingham, that the one was acting in self-defence, while the other was contriving the destruction of a helpless prisoner.

Mr. Froude bases his argument in defence of Walsingham's plot on the ground that, extensive and thorough-going as was Walsingham's system ofe spionage and bribery, yet, information procured by such means being anything but trustworthy, that acute-minded statesman at length "felt it imperatively necessary to obtain a clue to the Catholic secrets on which he knew he could depend."[3] But, in truth, the Secretary and his mistress, before they laid their snare for the Queen of Scots, had

---

[1] *Harl. MSS.*, 1582, f. 311.
[2] *History*, vol. xii., pp. 102, 147.   [3] *Ibid.*, p. 106.

furnished themselves with this clue by means of intercepted correspondence. Not only had Chérelles been bought over to rob his master's desk, and to forward Mary's secret correspondence regularly to Walsingham, but a letter[1] in Walsingham's hand addressed to Phelippes, dated November 30, 1585, while Mary was still at Tutbury, sufficiently demonstrates that the confidential correspondence both of Philip of Spain and of Mendoza by some secret treachery passed into Elizabeth's hands, and was deciphered by Phelippes.

I send you here inclosed another letter, written from the King of Spain unto some nobleman within this realm, which was delivered unto me by her Majesty, together with the other letter of Don Bernardino's [Mendoza] remaining in your hands, which, if it may be deciphered, will, I hope, lay open the treachery that reigneth here amongst us. Her Majesty hath promised to double your pension, and to be otherwise good unto you. And so I commit you to God.

At the Court, the 30th of November, 1585.

Your loving friend,

FRA. WALSINGHAM.

Mary tells the French Ambassador[2] that her having fallen sick again, "m'estant survenu principalement par les vents couliz, moisteur et froydeur, où ma chambre est subjecte, ainsi que mon medecin a témoisgné au sieur Paulet qui est icy." And, again,[3] "Je suis icy si mal-accommodée en ces deulx méchantes petites chambres, que je ne puis rester l'hyver sans très grand hazard de ma vye." Poulet's mention of the great floods in August bears out Mary's complaint of the unhealthiness of Tutbury.

The following is Poulet's letter sent at the same time to Lord Burghley, and with it the first letter-book ends.

---

[1] *Cotton. MSS.*, Calig., C. ix., f. 568.
[2] Labanoff, tom. vi., p. 198.   [3] *Ibid.*, p. 201.

To my Lord Treasurer, 19° *Augusti,* 1585.

My very good Lord,—After the signing and sealing
of this Queen's letters, sent herewith to her Majesty, Nau
had long speech with me touching the desired remove,
and after many arguments alleged by me of the impossi-
bility thereof at this season of the year, his last words
were that if there were any mean of remove he wished
and desired it greatly, but if the same were accompanied
with so great difficulty, then the sooner it were known
the better it were for the repairing of this Queen's lodgings
in this castle.

I have gone so far with this Queen and with Nau,
that I can assure your lordship they do not look to be
removed at this time, although this Queen desireth it
earnestly by her letters to her Majesty and to the French
Ambassador. I have told this Queen, and have said no
less to Nau, that the French Ambassador is worthy to
bear the blame of this matter, because having the same
in charge at the departure from Mr. Somer, he never
returned an answer until within these eight or ten days,
whereby it seemeth that he did either forget or neglect
to move it, and that now it was urged with great instance
when there was no possibility to perform it, winter at
hand, the ways for carriages as foul already as in winter,
her Majesty's houses being seldom used, likely to require
some good time to repair them, wood and coal not to
be had in sufficient quantity for any money, besides many
other provisions not easy to be recovered. I thought
agreeable with my duty to advertise your lordship of the
premises, referring the same to your better judgment;
and so do commit your good lordship to the mercy of
the Almighty, &c.

The next letter-book, or rather the portion of it that remains,
was entirely written at Chartley. It is written by another clerk,
and he has not added the name of the place to each letter, as

the clerk employed at Tutbury did. The book begins with the following fragment of a letter addressed to Lord Burghley.

. . . Secretary in any of these household causes or money matters until I shall be thereunto directed by your lordship, and yet I cannot tell if you would not think it some ease unto you that these money motions, which are not always pleasing, were sometimes made by some other than yourself, wherein I refer myself to your lordship's good pleasure. And so, &c.

In the interval between the date when one letter-book ends and the other begins many letters passed which remain among the State Papers. On these we draw sufficiently to link the two portions of our story together.

Poulet to Walsingham.[1]

I asked this Queen what she thought of her remove. " A goodly remove," saith she, "to Mr. Candishe's house." " Madam," quoth I, "the air is good, and you shall be well lodged for yourself, and the time of the year will not permit a further remove." She said it was not sufficient for her and me. I answered that a little room should serve my turn, and that she and her company should be provided. "As though," saith she, "by my remove thither, my lodgings here would be made fit for me." I said there should be as much done as herself would appoint. " No," saith she, "my lodgings will not be made fit without new buildings." I told her that her mind being known, all should be done that was possible. "It is too late," saith she, "for this year." Then I asked her if any other rooms in this house, besides those which she had already, would serve her turn, either in the state they were in, or by translating of them. She said she knew none, and that she was not unacquainted with my

[1] Vol. xvi., n. 38.

two lodgings, wherein she had been lodged before this time, and knew them to be very cold. I am deceived if she did speak herein as she thought, although indeed the lodgings are extremely cold, being leaded over head and unplastered, and the most distant from the ground nineteen foot, but she doubted that for some respects these lodgings would not be granted unto her, in which behalf I have thought good for my better discharge to deliver unto you the true state of the said lodgings, referring the same to your better consideration ; and, indeed, I may be lodged in the other end of the house, although not so fitly for the service of this castle, neither so commodiously for myself, yet well enough, I trust, to serve all turns.

The two chambers wherein I am lodged have their windows open upon the dykes, and are distant in height from the ground twenty-four foot. All such of this castle as will walk into the little park (the only place of recreation for this household), being forced to pass close by these windows, which give free liberty as well of conference, as of other conveyances, and, as I have been informed by gentlemen of good credit in these parts, have served to that purpose in time past. These windows overlook the town, and a good part of the country adjoining, and have their full prospect into the way which leadeth from the town to the castle, by means whereof it may be easy for the Scottish people to have intelligence with those abroad at their pleasure.

The danger of escape by these windows is also evident, if they be not watched day and night, which will require a greater number of soldiers, as also a new house to be builded to that purpose. There is belonging to these chambers a house of office, which is open at the foot, and was found to be of such danger when this Queen came first to this castle, that the Earl of Shrewsbury caused a hovel to be made at the foot of the wall for the succour of the soldiers appointed to watch in that place, but the truth is that it will be very hard, for many causes, to guard that place with a watch in any surety.

It seemeth worthy of consideration, that having these two chambers added to those which they have already, they have all their rooms several to themselves, so as they shall live by day and night all shut up from the view and sight of the governor and his company; whereas now my wife, myself, and those of my chamber, pass through the room wherein the Queen's gentlemen and gentlewomen do dine and sup, so as the whole company saving the Queen herself, and Pierrepont, are seen every day, a necessary matter in my simple opinion, and of good surety to the governor. This is the true state of these chambers, which I have thought good, for my better discharge, to deliver unto you. . . .

This Queen allegeth in one of her articles of request, that she hath been carried for her recreation ordinarily to a little park half a mile distant from this castle, but she hath forgotten to advertise that out of this little park she hath been carried three times at the least into another park not far distant from the said little park, where she hath coursed and hunted at every time of her being there, and when she was at the farthest of this walk, she was little less than two miles distant from this castle. I assure you that this is true, and therefore her advertisement in this point is the more strange. She hath also taken her recreation in other places of little less measure.

Poulet told Walsingham in the same letter, that when Mary received from him " the several answers to the several demands " she had made to Elizabeth, " she found herself so much grieved as she brake out forthwith into her accustomed complaints, declaring with many tears that being fed with feigned words as in all time past, so in these things now in question, the deeds did witness that the words were feigned, and that she found by long experience that to be true which the Countess of Shrewsbury always said unto her, which was that, do what she would, she should never be trusted, concluding that she would never accept of words again as long as she lived, and that she would see deeds hereafter before she would enlarge herself in word or deed.

"The cause of this great mislike groweth altogether upon the refusing of the Countess of Athol to attend upon her, that Fontenay his passport is not to be sent herewith, for whom she had written expressly by name, and therefore thinketh that the answer to that article doth import a denial of his coming unto her, and lastly, the excusing of Chérelles repair unto her at this time, but she is especially troubled with these two latter, touching Fontenay and Chérelles."

Poulet's explanation to her of the refusal was that "he wished her to have regard to times and seasons with wisdom and temperance, and laying apart all partiality and affection, to consider if in the greatest heat of this great flame which is kindled in France by her kinsmen, with a meaning, as may be supposed, that the coals should be extended into this realm, her Majesty.ought in reason and judgment to consider that Chérelles, coming so lately out of France, should have access unto her, or that Fontenay should be permitted to come from thence, until the troubles there were somewhat appeased."

Walsingham did not attempt to soften matters. His next letter was rougher, and went further than the former, for it ordered that she should have no direct communication with the new French Ambassador. He was known to be friendly to the Queen of Scots, and more willing to help her than his predecessor; and this is evidently the reason why Mary was required henceforward to send her letters for France through Walsingham. As Mary put it, Walsingham could not have "as good intelligence" with this Ambassador as he had with Mauvissière.

The following are "The heads of a letter unto Sir Amyas Poulet,"[1] and Poulet's answer shows that the letter was written and sent.

---

[1] Vol. xvi., n. 40.

That though the Queen his charge's unpassionate and unthankful manner of dealing deserveth little care or favour at her Majesty's hands, yet can she not whatsoever she deserveth, but do that which is fit for herself.

That therefore, doubting that the coldness of Tutbury Castle may increase her sickness, she thinketh meet that she should be removed to some other place, and hearing that Chartley, the Earl of Essex' house, is both large and strong, in respect that it is environed with water, she would have him to see it and certify how he liketh of it.

To let him understand that all the packets that she doth hereafter send into France must be directed unto me, and not unto the new French Ambassador, for that her Majesty's meaning is, that he shall not have anything to do with the conveyance of her letters into France, having also given order unto the B[ishop] of Glasgow, that such letters as he shall send from thence shall be delivered unto Mr. Stafford.

That there shall be shortly sent a letter from her Majesty to Mr. Bagot, to assist him in cases of necessity.

This was accompanied, or shortly followed, by a very severe letter[1] against Mary, addressed to Poulet by Elizabeth, showing her determination to control her communications with France. She says that she has "just cause to judge that the repair of those persons whose access she desireth carried some other meaning than the private use of them about her person, or the acquainting her with her particular affairs, having just cause so to judge when we either consider her former proceedings towards us, or the course that is now held by her kindred in France." She then alleges "that horrible and wicked practice and attempt against our own person, discovered to have been practised by Morgan, a principal and chief servant of hers, a matter that so grieved our subjects, as we had much ado to stay them in public Parliament to have called her in question for the same."

[1] Vol. xvi., n. 41.

The first of these two letters is indorsed September 13th. On the 21st Walsingham wrote thus :[1] " Her Majesty, considering now that the Earl of Essex' house will perhaps be misliked as unwholesome in respect of the water, hath thought upon Sir Walter Aston's house, a very fair house, and fit in any sort for that Queen, which is meant shall be borrowed of him, and Beauregard [Beaudesert], the Lord Paget's house, lent him to lie in. Wherefore her Majesty's pleasure is, you should view the said house with all convenient speed, for that in such indifferent things she is very careful to yield that lady any reasonable contentment."

Poulet, on the 23rd September,[2] answered Walsingham's letter of the 13th. First he reports favourably of Chartley, "distant from hence twelve miles, to pass by Utceter [Uttoxeter], which is the fairest way," which he had visited in company with Mr. Richard Bagot, "not doubting but that my wife and servants would yield me a good account of this charge, although my occasions should require my absence for a longer time." "The water which environeth this house is of such depth as may stand in stead of a strong wall, saving that it is narrow in some places, and therefore must be the better watched." "One commodity, sufficient in itself to recompense many incommodities," he found at Chartley, "which is, that by reason of the abundance of water adjoining to this house, this Queen's laundresses may be lodged and do all their business within the gates, whereof I am the more glad, because, having done my best endeavour to procure some faithful women out of Somersetshire, I can find none that will be entreated to come so far."

He discusses the lodging of the soldiers and the providing of hay, coal, and wood.

Mr. Bagot telleth me that one hundred loads of sea coal will be had from Beaudesert, and would be more favourable than three hundred loads of charcoal, the charge of every load whereof at the pit would be only 12*d.* to her Majesty, besides the carriage, a good part whereof will be performed without cost (as he thinketh) by the Lord Paget's tenants.

[1] Vol. xvi., n. 42.   [2] *Ibid.,* n. 43.

There is but one little kitchen at Chartley, which is so little as I marvel how it could suffice for so great a house, having but one range to roast and boil. This kitchen must serve for this Queen, and by Mr. Bagot's advice it is intended that a little charge shall be bestowed upon another little room, which then may serve her Majesty's household for a kitchen. It may please you to cause the Earl of Essex to be entreated not to remove his hangings or bedding, doubting lest our hangings will not be found fit for the chambers there, and I know we shall stand in need of his bedding. His hangings are only for five chambers, and as I learn he hath not above fourteen or fifteen beds. I will take upon me that the stuff shall take as little hurt as is possible.

Following your direction I signified to this Queen her Majesty's pleasure touching her packets coming from hence and to be sent hereafter into France, to be directed unto you, and not to the new French Ambassador, and that order was given that such letters as the Bishop of Glasgow should send out of France should be delivered unto her Majesty's Ambassador there.

I can hardly express unto you by writing how much she was moved with this message, and will forbear to utter the greater part of her angry speeches, because you have been accustomed unto them, so as I should trouble you with vain repetitions. She saith that the like was in question long sithence in Mauvissière's time, but took not his effect until now, when you above think that you cannot have so good intelligence with this Ambassador as you had with Mauvissière. Her letters must be showed by you, as in time past, to her enemies, the Countess of Shrewsbury and others. She would not be separated from her union with the King of France; he was her ally, and she was under his protection. His Ambassador was specially appointed to have care of her, and that she knew he would not like to hear that she might not use his Ministers as heretofore. She doubted not but that France, Spain, and other countries would have care of her. She might see plainly that her destruction was sought, and that her life shall be taken from her one of these days, and then it shall be said that she was sickly and that she died of some sickness.

She took it between her and her conscience that she believed it constantly, and would do her best that all others should also believe it; that when she was at the lowest, her heart was greatest, and therefore now looking for no other than all extremity, she would not fail to urge her enemies to do the worst they could.

I told her I could see no just cause why she should be so greatly troubled with this matter, being not forbidden to write into France as much and as often as she would, and her letters, both coming and going, being likely to find more free passage than in time past; that nothing was less intended hereby than to interrupt her amity with France, but I said she should do well to commit herself especially to her Majesty's protection, and not to abuse herself with a vain opinion of foreign Princes, who could do her no further good than as should please her Majesty to permit.

I told her that this order touching her packets might grow upon some new occasion of foreign causes or otherwise, which being hereafter taken away, the effect would also cease. "No," saith she, "I trust the occasion will not be taken away, and I pray God it may increase," meaning the enterprise of her kinsmen in France.

I used all reasonable arguments to dissuade her from her fond, or rather wicked, opinion of her intended destruction, which I told her was a foul and most manifest slander, and as therein she did wrong to many others, so if her impression were unfeigned, she might do no good to herself. I said this matter reached unto me, which she denied with many words, but said it might be done by others without my knowledge. The truth is, I could not satisfy her herein, and so I leave her until a more contented mood shall give her a better mind.

I think the care of my charge greatly increased by reason of this Queen's discontentment, because it is likely that now she will employ her best means to renew her practices, as well by letters as other ways. I can add nothing to my former diligence, only I will promise to continue therein, leaving the success to the Almighty.

The indisposition of this Queen's body, and the great infirmity of her legs, which is so desperate as herself doth not hope of any recovery, is no small advantage to her keeper, who shall not need to stand in great fear of her running away, if he can foresee that she be not taken from him by force.

And thus I leave to trouble you, beseeching God to bless your counsels and to give them a happy issue.

Tutbury, the 23rd of September, 1585.

Your most assured poor friend,

A. POULET.

I had some feeling of my gout at the very instant of my going to Chartley, so as I could not conveniently have repaired thither without the help of my coach, and therefore it may please you to procure that Mr. Bagot's letter of assistance may be sent by the next.

It is not easy to avoid some little satisfaction when Poulet's twinges of gout find their way into his letters, after reading the way in which he has just spoken of the sickness and lameness of his prisoner. The following is a sort of postscript to his former letter.

Sir,—I had almost forgotten to signify unto you that this Queen is so desirous to be removed, as she could not be satisfied until she had spoken with me after my

II

return from Chartley and, therefore, being lame in one of her legs, prayed me to come to her chamber this last evening, where I told her my opinion touching the house, wherewith she is greatly quieted. And, indeed, she shall be as well lodged as herself could desire, having a very fair great chamber, which may serve her to walk instead of a gallery, a very fair chamber for herself, a large cabinet, sufficient room for all her gentlewomen, with a brushing-room, all within her own chamber door, which is good for her, and no less good for me.

And thus I commit you once again to the tuition of the Almighty.

From Tutbury, the 23rd of September, 1585.

Your most assured poor friend,

A. POULET.

Walsingham, on the 26th September, wrote[1] to Poulet that the Earl of Essex begged that his wood might not " be felled for the household use of that Queen." " Besides, his lordship is also very loth to let the said Queen have the use of his house, who, as he saith, may very conveniently be lodged at the house of one Gifford of that country, a recusant, which you shall do well to cause to be viewed for that purpose, but specially that she should have the use of his house, doubting lest in respect of her mislike both of his father and of himself, those of her train should abuse, or rather spoil it."

Poulet's next two letters treat of the two houses he has been directed to visit; that of September 27th[2] describes Sir Walter Aston's house at Tixall, and that of October 3rd,[3] Mr. Gifford's. An extract from each will be interesting.

While acknowledging the fitness of Tixall for the purpose, Poulet supports Sir Walter Aston's entreaty that Mary may not be taken there, as "it will not stand with her Majesty's service to overthrow such a household as Sir Walter's is in this infected shire, as the world goeth at this present." " Sir Walter Aston saith that he hath upon the point of a hundred persons uprising

---

[1] Vol. xvi., n. 45.   [2] *Ibid.,* n. 46.   [3] *Ibid.,* n. 48.

and downlying in his house. He is sufficiently provided of corn, hay, grass, about his house, and of all other things necessary for so great a family. He hath three score milch kyne, three ploughs of oxen, and one of horses, whose labour must provide him of corn for the next year." This Sir Walter Aston, whom Poulet praises greatly for his being "well affected in religion," is the father of the first Lord Aston of Forfar, who became a Catholic when Ambassador in Spain in the time of James I.[1]

On the 3rd of October, Poulet reports[2] respecting Mr. Gifford's house, and the description gives us a good idea of the wealth and social position of the family. We should not have expected to find a country gentleman's house capable of lodging, however straitly, "both these families," and "furnished with many fair lodgings," fit for a captive Queen.

Immediately upon the receipt of your letters of the 26th of the last, I took order for the stay of felling of wood at Chartley, and being required by your said letters to cause a view to be taken of Mr. Gifford's house, I prayed Mr. Darrell to make his immediate repair thither, by whom I understand that the house is well seated, and is furnished with many fair lodgings, so as this Queen may be very well placed, with great chamber, gallery, cabinet, and lodgings for her gentlewomen, as likewise the governor, and her gentlemen, may be lodged in convenient sort. A fair orchard and garden walled about, great store of wood, Cankwood not far off for charcoal, and sea coal may be had with little charge. Two or three parks at hand, good pasture adjoining to the house, besides the dove house and other like commodities.

The discommodities are these. The house very strait to lodge both these families. The brewhouse and brewing vessels so little as will brew but one tun at a time, which is much less than sufficient, and no common brewhouse in any town adjoining, or in any other place of this shire that

---

[1] *Troubles of our Catholic Forefathers*, first series, p. 369.
[2] Vol. xvi., n. 48.

I can hear of. Stable room less than enough for twenty geldings, which may be enlarged to the number of eight or ten by means of a stall, and to a far greater number by the help of the barns, whereof there are three or four, if they were not full of corn; hay in the house twenty loads or thereabouts, a small store for so many horses as must follow this family, and little hay to be had in those parts for money, which may be holpen by the plenty of good straw, which by likelihood may be had out of these barns, and as the year hath fallen out, good straw is better than the best hay in all the parts of the shire.

I had almost forgotten to advertise you that the house is very well furnished, which may by no means be spared if this household shall remove thither, this castle being distant from thence twenty miles, so as it were a matter of extreme trouble and charge to remove all things from hence, when by reason of the late foul weather the ways be already as deep and foul as is possible.

I pray you consider effectually of the brewhouse, because it is a matter which importeth greatly, and it passeth my understanding to find a remedy for it.

To this letter Walsingham answered on the 10th of October.

Walsingham to Poulet.[1]

Sir,—I have acquainted her Majesty with the contents of your letters, who doth very well like of the answer that you have made unto Nau in the matter of the conveyance of his mistress' letters, for that she meaneth that the course that is now set down for that purpose shall henceforth stand and be continued still.

A daughter of one Mowbray, a lord of Scotland, is a suitor here for a passport to repair to that Queen's service, whereunto her Majesty is content to yield, seeing her here, although she had no foreknowledge of her coming. But

[1] Vol. xvi., n. 54.

for the better prevention of any practice or conveyance of letters, her Majesty's pleasure is you should so handle the matter that any such of the said Queen's women as shall have leave to depart upon her coming, may be removed to some other place out of the house before she come thither, to the end that there may no answer be committed unto her of any letters or messages that this new gent[lewoman] perhaps may bring, of the time of whose repair thither you shall receive knowledge afore-hand for that purpose.

I am glad that you find Mr. Gifford's house so fit for the well-lodging of that Queen, the rather for that my Lord of Essex seemeth still to be most unwilling to let her have the use of his. Her Majesty would have you also to certify the strength of it, and what gent[lemen] well affected do dwell near hand whose service may be used upon any sudden occasion that may happen.

Touching the smallness of the brewhouse, I have con-ferred with my Lord Treasurer therein, but we can devise no means how the same may be helped than by causing as much beer to be brewed there aforehand as the shortness of the time will permit, which may be reserved, and that little quantity also that shall hereafter be further brewed there from time to time for the said Queen's own drinking, yours and such others as you shall think convenient, and order given for other drink to be brewed for the greater number in some of the market-towns or other meet places that are nearest hand, wherein if you find so great difficulty that you cannot conveniently so do, there must then be order taken for the building up of another brewhouse in some void place about the house. An estimate of the charges whereof you shall do well to send hither with some speed in case you find there is no other remedy but to erect a new brewhouse.

And touching the straitness of lodging for the train, you must help that as well as the commodity of the place will permit by making some partitions in the barns and other outhouses that may serve for chambers for the mean sort. Upon the receipt of your answer to all with particularities, if it be found meet to have your charge bestowed in the said house, there shall be order given presently unto Mr. Gifford to remove his corn out of his barns.

Mauvissière at his departure left with me an hundred four score and ten pounds for that Queen, which, if the Receiver of the Duchy in those parts will deliver unto you there, I will presently take order it shall be paid to his use here.

Here inclosed I send you the copy that I promised you of that Queen's letter to the Ambassador, containing many passionate complaints specially touching the badness as she pretendeth of her lodging at Tutbury, which after you have perused I pray you to return unto me again, together with your opinion what is fit to be answered to every point of her said complaints, &c.

Poulet to Walsingham.[1]

Sir,—By your former letters you required me to view Chartley and Tixall, the houses of the Earl of Essex and Sir Walter Aston, which I did accordingly. By a later letter you wrote that I should cause a view to be taken of Mr. Gifford's house, wherein I supposed you had given me the larger commission because you held the matter as desperate, or at the least unlikely that a gentleman's house might be sufficient to receive this great household. Hereupon I sent Mr. Darrell thither, whose report touching the house and state of all things appertaining, as far as he could see or gather by the informations of Mr. Gifford's servants, hath been certified unto you, and I believe assuredly that you shall find it true in all points.

Touching the state of the country and the neighbours adjoining, I have taken care to inform myself by the

[1] Vol. xvi., n. 56.

mean of some men of credit in these parts, and do find
that the gentlemen of calling and countenance and best
affected in religion, as Sir Walter Aston, Mr. Bagot,
Mr. Gresley, and a few such like, have their dwellings
distant from Mr. Gifford's house, some ten miles, some
twelve, and the nearest nine. Only Mr. Littleton, a very
honest religious gentleman, as I hear, dwelling within three
or four miles or thereabouts. Mr. Gifford having two
brethren, near neighbours to his house, the one of them
rich and of good credit in the shire, and both of them
backward in religion, so as the said house seemeth to
be barren of good neighbours.

The strength of the house deserveth little better
commendation, the windows of the one side lying open
upon the fields, and the windows of the other side, where
this Queen should be lodged, lying open upon the garden,
which is environed with a wall of no great height than
as a man may reach to the top. Only the third court,
which serveth for wood and fuel, is walled about, so as
if it be meant that this Queen should make any long
abode there, I must needs say for my discharge that the
said house is not of sufficient strength for so weighty a
charge. But if it had been intended that she should
have remained there only during this winter season, and
then to have returned hither, which is the only fit house
for all purposes to receive this Queen in this shire, the
weakness of the said Mr. Gifford's house would have been
supplied with diligence and careful attendance.

But if this house were as well neighboured and of
as competent strength as might be wished, yet surely in
my simple opinion, there are other imperfections more
than sufficient to stay our remove thither, and especially
in the matter of the brewhouse there, which might serve
the turn to be used in such form as you set down in
your letters, if it were possible to get drink for the household, which is not to be had in those parts for any money

And whereas in default therof, you require an estimate
of the charges of the erecting of another brewhouse, it
seemeth worthy of consideration that so long time will
be spent in making of the said estimate, in sending of
the same to the Court, and in returning of answer, and
then being agreed upon, in providing as well of timber,
stone, and other necessaries for the buildings, as also
of brewing vessels (being not easy to find timber fit for
that purpose, as I have found by experience for the
service of this house, having been forced to provide a.
vessel whereof I stood in need, out of Worcestershire),
and lastly, in finishing the said buildings, besides that
the beer brewed will ask to be somewhat stale before
it be drunk, that when all diligence possible shall be
used, it will be impossible to remove yet these two or
rather three months, at which time the days will be at
the shortest for carriages, which will be in number very
many, the ways extremely foul, Mr. Gifford's house distant
from hence twenty miles, and the winter so far spent as
the cause of this remove proceeding of the coldness of
this castle, will seem then to be taken away.

But if all these defects were tolerable, and might be
supplied in some reasonable sort, yet if this one thing be
true which Mr. Darrell now telleth me, it sufficeth to
overthrow this intended remove, which is that there is
not water enough there to furnish so large a brewhouse,
affirming that the brewhouse of the house hath been always
provided of water by means of a well adjoining, which
hath been made dry at every brewing of one tun of beer,
and there is no other water belonging to the house, saving
in a conduit in the first court, the water whereof cometh
out of a marsh ground, and is at no time in any abundance,
but is sometimes dry when the marsh is dry. And thus I
do not see that either there is any mean to remove in
convenient time, or if we do remove, how we may be
sufficiently provided of drink.

The straitness of the house might be supplied by such means as you write, and yet it were convenient that the greater number of my servants were lodged within the gates.

I have therefore thought good to declare to this Queen the great care which is had above to give her full satisfaction touching her desired remove, that Chartley is found to stand so low, and environed with such abundance of water, as considering the state of her body, is not likely to content her when she shall see it, and then there will be as great trouble to remove her from thence as there was to bring her thither, and that therefore other houses have been sought, and at the last one house found which might seem sufficient to serve the turn for three or four months, and yet not without many imperfections, but it is of necessity that a new brewhouse must be erected, which will not be finished and the beer brewed to serve for the household in less time than three months or near thereabouts, at which time the ways will be ill for carriages, and the hardness of the winter well near spent.

Hereupon I prayed her to consider if it were not best for her to content herself to spend this winter in this castle, where she was provided with all things needful, which haply would not be found in another place, all her train well lodged, only herself had cause to complain of her lodgings, which might be amended in many things if she would resolve upon her tarrying, and that for her better satisfaction I would be content to resign unto her the great chamber wherein I do now dine and sup, and would nail up the door which leadeth out of my bed-chamber into the said dining-chamber, so as the same should remain wholly to herself, and then she might remove her bed into her now dining-chamber, which she herself reporteth to be the warmest room she hath. I told her I would make a door where is now a window in my utter chamber, and from thence by the help of a new stair to be made, would make a way by a low entry to the stair foot which leadeth to the hall, and would make the star-chamber, which is directly over against the hall door, my dining-chamber.

She answered me plainly that she would not accept of this offer, that she will seek no new helps in this house, that sithence she cannot be removed after so long a suit, she will die in her bad lodging, and then her death shall be imputed to the authors thereof, with many other bitter words (whereof she is no niggard when she is moved with passion), which proceedeth not so much of this mislike of the let of her remove, as of the packet sent now with your letters, by the which she receiveth no answer from the new French Ambassador of the contents of her late letters, complaining or rather exclaiming that she may not send her letters into France by the mean of the French Ambassador as in time past, and therewith her old griefs touching the Countess of Athol and Fontenay were renewed with great vehemency, and her son was not forgotten, which was perchance remembered the rather by reason of a letter received with this packet, by the which a gentleman of Scotland writeth to this Queen that her son had received of late from her Majesty six couple of bloodhounds,[1] wherein he took singular pleasure, and that he preferred the amity of her Highness before all other Princes of the world.

I did all that I could to appease her, and the rather because I found her lying in her bed, and grieved with three defluxions at that instant, in her shoulder, her arm, and above her heel, as indeed she is very seldom free from one grief or other, so as it seemeth that the diet which she took in the beginning of this summer hath done her little good, and more than five weeks or thereabouts she hath not come out of her chamber, her grief removing from one place to another.

---

[1] From this passage the mention was taken of the six couple of "blood-hounds" on page 26. No doubt Poulet should have said "buckhounds."

She imputeth her lameness, and all her disease, to this house, although indeed she brought the same hither with her. But I told her that her passionate and discontented mind did more increase her sickness than the coldness of this house, or any other thing whatsoever.

I would wish she were removed, although, all circumstances considered, it seemeth to be a matter of very great difficulty, and, indeed, will prove very chargeable to her Majesty, and very offensive to the country, for the great number of carriages which must be employed to carry from hence, and to bring wood, coal, hay, &c., to the new house, and whithersoever this remove shall be made, it will be five or six weeks before it can be performed.

I find nothing in this Queen's packet worthy the advertisement, saving that which is before remembered touching the bloodhounds, &c. Only this one thing may not be hidden from you, that Curle, having been assured of long time to Mowbray, a gentlewoman attending on this Queen, by the assent of her mistress, her father and mother have now given their good wills by their letters, so as it is likely that this marriage will proceed to his full effect shortly.

Your letters do not import that I should say anything to this Queen touching Mowbray, mentioned in your said letters, neither hath she as yet said anything to me therein, as likewise I do not hear that any of this Queen's women here shall depart upon her coming hither. Upon direction received from you, I will not fail to do as you shall appoint.

I will talk with the Receiver of the Duchy touching the money resting in your hands for this Queen, and have signified unto her the care which you take to see her satisfied of such money as cometh to your hands in her behalf.

You write that you have sent unto me inclosed in your letters the copy of this Queen's passionate letter to the French Ambassador ; but I have not received it.

I thank you most heartily for your French advertise-ments, which I return unto you herewith.

Whereas you write that you know that this Queen hath not as yet gotten any secret means for the convey-ance of her bye packets, I can assure you that all open means are clearly taken away, and all her people within the gates so narrowly looked unto, as they can do no hurt if they would; but if this Queen hath as good friends in this country, as it is reported, she may by her laundresses convey what she will. It may be that being removed from her old acquaintance, she will hardly find new friends that will be content to hazard themselves upon hope of uncertainty.

I trusted to have received Mr. Bagot's letter of assist-ance from you before this time, which I desire greatly, because when this Queen shall crave to ride abroad, which she will do in her coach as soon as she is able, I may perchance be unable to ride, and then she will think herself ill handled, if she may not take the air when her health will permit it.

And thus I commit you to the mercy of the Highest. From Tutbury, the 16th of October, 1585.

　　　　　Your most assured poor friend,

　　　　　　　　　A. POULET.

This last evening I conferred with Nau, who thought it very reasonable that his mistress should yield to the offers which I had made, promising to deal with her effectually therein, and having attended his answer four or five hours, he telleth me that this Queen will not hearken to this motion, alleging that she holdeth this house as unfortunate, that she began her imprisonment here, that she shall end her days here, and that she may thank Nau of her coming hither. Nau telleth me that her physician is against this remove, and thinketh that it will rather impair his mistress' health than otherwise.

Poulet to Walsingham, October 18, 1585.[1]

I trust you will consider that Spain borroweth little of an open enemy, France is not much better, and this lady so discontented, as I may not hope that she will forbear any practice to procure her farther liberty, and therefore you will either keep her where she is, or remove her to a house of no less strength.

I have, according to your direction, sent to Mr. William Agar, Receiver of the Duchy, for the payment of one hundred four score and ten pounds to this Queen, which he undertaketh to see performed the 4th of the next month, whereof I have advertised Nau, who was well satisfied therein.

The next letter[2] is interesting because it relates to Mary's chaplain, and gives us a curious description of his disguise. "Sir John," Poulet had called him in July, and as we have seen he had conjectured he was a Priest as far back as May, within a month of his appointment to succeed Sir Ralph Sadler, but now he says that no doubt remained as to Du Préau's profession.

Poulet to Walsingham.

Sir,—I remember that in perusing the letters and memorials touching this Queen which you delivered unto me by order from her Majesty at my last being at the Court, I found that this lady had made sundry motions for liberty to exercise the Romish religion for herself and her family. I am also deceived if her Majesty did not tell me that she would have no more marrying thereafter in the Scottish family, thereby to avoid the inconveniences which had ensued in times past by reason of midwives, gossips, nurses, &c., besides the increase of the household in children.

I have therefore thought agreeable with my duty to advertise you that a Frenchman, one of this Queen's

[1] Vol. xvi., n. 57.   [2] Vol. xvi., n. 59.

retinue, and called by the name of her reader, apparelled in court-like suit, a brooch in his hat, silver buttons, his garments of all colours, is suspected to be a Priest, whereof I have had this appearance, that at the time of their assembly, which is twice every day in this Queen's dining-chamber, some of my company have heard this man read in the Latin language.

This is the man that hath been accustomed to distribute the alms, and upon these occasions I have termed him in my letters unto you before this time by the name of Sir John, but he hath now discovered himself so plainly as it may not be doubted hereafter of what profession he is, being evident by many manifest presumptions that Curle was married to Mowbray, this Queen's principal gentlewoman, the 24th of this present, praying you for my better discharge to impart the same to her Majesty.

It is not my place to prescribe orders, but to execute faithfully such as shall be prescribed unto me, and yet I trust I shall not offend greatly to deliver unto you my simple opinion herein, which is that no known Popish Priest ought to dwell within these gates.

If they be disposed of malice or blindness to transgress the laws of God and man, and can carry their doings so cleanly as no just suspicion may be conceived thereof, their sin is upon their own heads, and others that have had no part therein are sufficiently discharged. But these open doings reach not only to the actors, but to all such others as shall wink at them.

And thus referring the same to your better consideration, I take my leave of you, beseeching God to increase you in health and honour.

From Tutbury, the 26th of October, 1585.

Your most assured poor friend,

A. POULET.

I trust I shall be so happy not to hear from you touching our remove until about Shrovetide, and then if we shall remove, to remove to some house where we may continue.

Poulet to Walsingham, October 27, 1585.[1]

I had forgotten, in my letters of yesterday, to signify unto you that Chérelles writeth to Nau that it pleased you to do him the honour (as he calleth it), in the delivery of this Queen's packet to the French Ambassador, to leave his letter unopened, or at the least, those which were inclosed in his letters, seeming to stand in some doubt if his own letters were opened or no, which I take to be advertised to no other purpose than to give boldness to Nau to send unto him hereafter letters of moment, inclosed in his letters under base titles, upon trust to have the freer passage. I am not ignorant that your greater business will not permit you to attend to these trifles, and yet, to deliver my opinion plainly unto you, I think it very needful, as a very good mean to keep this people in good order, that all their letters be always perused, and so delivered open, as they may know that they have been perused. . . .

It is now most manifest that Curle was married upon Sunday last, and yet this Queen saith nothing thereof to me.

On the 11th of November,[2] Poulet's preparations for removing the Queen of Scots to Chartley, which were then far advanced, were stopped by him on receipt of counter-orders from Walsingham. He then proposed Dudley Castle as a fit place for her, and on the 18th,[3] he forwarded a letter from Edward Lord Dudley, placing himself and his castle at her Majesty's commandment. Chartley was, however, ultimately decided on, and the final orders to remove were given by Walsingham on the 23rd of November, as we shall see when we come to Poulet's letter of

---

[1] Vol. xvi., n. 61.   [2] *Ibid.*, n. 63.   [3] *Ibid.*, n. 68.

the 30th of that month, contained in the next letter-book. The actual remove was effected on the vigil of Christmas, the 24th of December. But other subjects first claim our attention.

It was in October that Gilbert Gifford visited Morgan in the Bastile, and obtained from him the following letter[1] as his credentials to the Queen of Scots. Morgan's suggestion that Gifford should take a place under Poulet in the household would have facilitated the arrangements for the deception of Mary Stuart.

Morgan to the Queen of Scots.

It may please your Majesty, many of sundry nations and honourable members have found the means to visit me in this undeserved captivity of mine, and among others there was with me of late one named Gilbert Gifford, a Catholic gentleman to me well known for that he was brought up in learning of this side the seas this many years past, where I have been always his friend to my power, as I would be profitable to all that deserve well.

The said gentleman returneth to his country, and offered to do me all the friendly offices that he may do. His father is named John Gifford, a Staffordshire man, a gentleman of a good house and well friended in that country, but he is at this present a prisoner for our religion at London, and so he hath been of a long time.

The said John Gifford hath a brother named Robert Gifford, who is also a Catholic gentleman, and dwelleth within ten miles or thereabouts of the place of your continuance. These Giffords be kinsmen and friends to Baynard (Fr. Throckmorton), and to Barasino (Tho. Throckmorton), and otherwise well disposed towards your Majesty.

Knowing the honesty and faith of these gentlemen and considering their habitation and credit in their country, and as far as I can perceive your intelligence discontinued (though in that point both before and sith my captivity I

[1] Vol. xvi., n. 50.

remembered to discharge my duty as shall appear unto your Majesty, if they on that side perform their part according to my careful and ample instructions given in that behalf), I thought it my part for the more surety and increase of the number of your servants and advancement of your service, to deal with the said Gilbert to pratique with his parents and friends for the furtherance of the same.

This he promised to put in execution with care, and I hope he will show his good will and diligence in the cause. He required my letters to your Majesty, thereby to give him credit and a mean to enter into intelligence with your Majesty. For this purpose I gave him these few lines, assuring myself of his faith and honesty, and for such I recommend unto your Majesty the persons above named.

I have been in hand with the bearer to place some honest gentleman and woman to serve your host and hostess for your sake, whereby your service may be the better advanced. He is also instructed how to pratick with your host, his people and such as depend of him or his wife. He is also instructed how to haunt the market-towns adjoining the place of your continuance, to see whether he may thereby find any of your Majesty's people. In all these points he hath promised to travail effectually.

I have dealt with him to see if he can place himself to serve your host. This he will attempt. Yet his coming from these parts will be suspicious in the sight of the curious and watchful sort that have a special regard to all such as be placed about your host, whereof I gave the bearer warning, leaving him nevertheless to use his own discretion when he came to the country and saw the condition and state of things.

His uncle Robert above named was acquainted with your host in this country. I have instructed the bearer to cause his uncle to visit your host and to renew with him their former acquaintance, whereby some familiarity may

I

be drawn between them, under the colour whereof some-what may fall out to your Majesty's advantage.   This I desire as God knoweth, who knoweth my heart, and that I have no other desire in this life but to serve God, your Majesty, and my country.   Thus with my prayers in this captivity for your preservation and consolation, I most humbly take my leave and commit your Majesty to God, who ever preserve your Majesty.

Written this 15th of October.

> Your Majesty's most humble
> and obedient faithful servant
> during life to command,
>
> X

This letter is in Phelippes' hand, and in the postscript there is the following passage relating to himself, in the margin of which he has written, "Philips to be dealt withal."

It is very like that one Phelippes hath great access to your host in this time and peradventure hath some charge under him.   It is the same Phelippes of whom I made mention heretofore. . If you do use him according to my former instructions, it may be that he may be recovered to your service, but try him long and in small matters before you use him, being a severe Huguenot, and all for that state, yet glorious and greedy of honour and profit.   By this means he may perhaps be won to your service, but I dare not assure you of him as I would I could ; but present commodity and promise of preferment hereafter will weigh much with him, and I told him heretofore upon such conference as passed between him and me, and upon the hope that he gave me to serve and honour your Majesty, whereof he seemed well pleased, and told me that he would do good offices.   If he be there you may cause some of your principal people to take him in hand, and to let him know that you have been well informed of him, and of his good disposition towards your Majesty, and assure him and his friends that you will acknowledge their good wills, and so see how far he can be wrought to your service.

The said Gilbert is instructed how to send your letters to my hand to these parts.

And now the State Papers become crowded with letters addressed to, or written by, the Queen of Scots, "in the hand-writing of Mr. Phelippes," the very Phelippes of Morgan's letter. Walsingham's resolve to destroy her was taken, and his servant, so well known as Thomas Phelippes the decipherer, was employed to weave the fatal web. On the honesty and veracity of this man Mary's life depended. It is significant that while he was busily engaged in this work, May 3, 1586, Sir Francis Walsing-ham writes[1] to tell him that "the Queen has signed his bill for a pension of one hundred marks,[2] and takes his services in good part." Hardly less significant is Poulet's promise to him a month later, that he "will let him know if he hears of anything of Lord Paget's meet for him."[3]

In a letter previously given, Elizabeth had promised to be "otherwise good to him." We see what the expression meant, when we examine this man's subsequent career during her reign. He was appointed "Customer," that is, Collector of Petty Customs of the Port of London, in which office he had for a colleague Mr. Justice Richard Young, with whose name the Catholics of that time were so well acquainted. Now it will hardly be credited by those who know how extremely penurious Elizabeth was, that Phelippes contracted in two years to the Crown a debt of 11,683*l.* 6*s.* 6¾*d.* He lost his office, but he was treated with great lenity. He was liberated from prison, his annuity continued, and his land restored to him, on a promise to pay his debt within eighteen months. He did not pay it, at least in full, and he seems to have dictated his own terms, for the draft of the Warrant of the Exchequer was drawn up by him.[4]

---

[1] Vol. xvii., n. 60.
[2] *Mark*, a coin worth 13*s.* 4*d.*   *Halliwell.*
[3] Vol. xviii., n. 1.
[4] *Dom. Eliz.*, vol. cclxxv., n. 78; Docquet-book, October 8 and 10, 1598.

On the accession of James I., Phelippes had other terms to look for from the son of the Queen, whose death was brought about by his means. His "apology" (in May, 1603), for meddling in the affairs of the Queen of Scots, falsely declares that the only part he took was deciphering for Government the letters relating to Babington's conspiracy.[1]   Then in January, 1604, there is a packet of pretended intercepted letters, endorsed in Cecil's hand, "Letters written by Phelippes, and suggested by him to be counterfeited."[2]   The fact was that he spent his life in counterfeiting, and after Walsingham's death he seems to have carried on the old trade that he might get possession of Catholic secrets to sell.   As Mrs. Green points out in her preface to one of the volumes of the Calendar of State Papers, his position in the Custom House was favourable to the receipt and despatch of letters.   There is a very curious collection of drafts of letters "suggested by Phelippes," to be written by his instruments, Thomas Barnes and others, to Charles Paget and other Catholics, who little dreamt who their correspondent really was.[3]

At last he corresponded directly with Hugh Owen, who was implicated by Fawkes' confession in the Gunpowder Plot.   When arrested on suspicion, he at once offered to carry on the correspondence for the purpose of betraying the secrets confided to him, as the price of his own liberty.   Neither this offer, nor protestations of innocence, with assurances that his sole faults in intriguing with Owen were "seeking some recompense," and "delay in making disclosures till he had things fully ripe," saved him from the Tower.   Curiously enough, his old spy and instrument, Thomas Barnes,[4] reported the substance of his correspondence with Owen, and the Lieutenant of the Tower during his imprisonment was Sir William Waad, the same who had been sent to rifle the Queen of Scots' cabinets, when the Babington conspiracy exploded.   Mr. Tytler gives at length, in

---

[1] *Dom. James I.,* vol. i., n. 119.

[2] *Ibid.,* vol. vi., n. 37.

[3] "Mr. Barnes is an honest man here, and his dealing with Phelippes, that enemy to the cause, is allowed; he but dissembles to the heretic." Robert Robinson [William Sterrell] to Mr. Morice [Phelippes]. *Dom. Eliz.,* vol. ccxlii., n. 37.

[4] *Dom. James I.,* vol. xvii., n. 61.

proof of the writer's utter baseness and unscrupulousness, the memorial[1] that Philippes addressed to Waad,[2] in which he acknowledges under his own hand the forging of a whole series of letters addressed to an agent of the Spanish Government.

Is this the man, having it in his power, unchecked by fear of discovery, to tamper with the letters he had to decipher, well rewarded for exceptional services, and knowing perfectly what would be acceptable to his employers—is this the man to be quoted as an irreproachable witness, whose evidence is conclusive against Mary? Mr. Froude has not a word of blame for the part taken by Phelippes in the scheme for Mary's destruction, a part revolting to the moral sense even under the light in which he sets it; nor has he a word of warning to the reader, as to the character of the person on whose evidence everything depended.

For on the veracity of Phelippes, as Mary's life depended then, so do her character and her history depend now. In the Calendar of the "Mary Queen of Scots" State Papers, no less than one hundred and eight are expressly stated to be in this man's handwriting, either that we are dependent on him for the decipher, or that the copy surviving is in his hand. When Mary's papers were seized, it is extremely improbable that the letters in cipher only should have been preserved, and the deciphers made for her use by her secretaries should have all

---

[1] *History*, vol. viii., Appendix.

[2] "At my return to the Tower I went presently to Mr. Phelippes' chamber, and took him with me to another chamber, where I presently searched all his pockets and found nothing of importance but some notes of a matter of steel. I charged him he had not dealt friendly with me, having used him with all courtesy, to fall to relapse in his practices. He protested he never wrote letter sithence he was in the Tower, that might not be showed to any of your lordships. After a deep protestation he said he knew whence this suspicion had its fountain, in that his wife had entertained a matter with his privity with one whom I had heard of, who had the secret to make steel. The party's name was Ball, to whom there should money be given for that secret. This man James is with his wife.

"I send your lordship one of the papers that was in his pocket. Whether this steel device be a jargon, or whether there may be any such new invention, I know not, but I know in former intelligences he conveyed great matters under such like invented names of 'stuff' and 'toys,' and I must needs think that Ball was a man very ill picked out for him to deal withal." Sir W. Waad to the Earl of Salisbury, Dec. 26, 1607. *Addl. MSS.*, 6178, p. 819.

been destroyed. Yet the Calendar attributes but fifteen to Curle, and none to Nau; and of those by Curle most, if not all, were deciphered when he was a prisoner. This Curle himself has been careful to record, though the Calendar neglects to notice it. Over and over again[1] we come upon "Deciphered by me, Gilbert Curle, 5th October, 1586." Then we have to another letter[2] his endorsement, "Upon notes of the Queen's Majesty my mistress, written by me, Gilbert Curle, 5th October, 1586." And again,[3] "From me to Barnaby [Gilbert Gifford] at the Queen's Majesty, my mistress' commandment, Gilbert Curle, 5th October, 1586." Curle and Nau were arrested in August, and their lives were in grave danger. A note[4] of "matters wherewith Curle is to be charged respecting Babington's letter to the Queen of Scots," is dated September 21, and in September Sir Francis Walsingham wrote[5] to Curle "that the favour already granted to him is extraordinary, considering the foulness of his offence," and that he should "have better ground to intercede for him when he shall lay himself open, and show a disposition to deserve the Queen's favour." Under this pressure Curle made[6] the deciphers that have been mentioned.

It comes then to this: the deciphers made for Mary have been destroyed, and those made by Phelippes alone survive. When the secret letters are quoted, this should always be borne in mind.

As an example, take the postscript to Curle, "which," says Mr. Froude, "it was certain the Queen of Scots would see: 'There be many means in hand to remove the beast that troubles all the world.'"[7] This exists only in Phelippes' hand.[8] Which

---

[1] Vol. xvi., n. 21; vol. xvii., nn. 7, 56; vol. xviii., n. 6 (two letters), and 10.

[2] Vol. xvii., n. 80.

[3] Vol. xviii., n. 10.

[4] Vol. xix., n. 107.

[5] Vol. xix., n. 119.

[6] If these deciphers were not made at this time, but only attested by Curle, the case is all the stronger, for if these were forthcoming, who suppressed the rest? Prince Labanoff (tom. vi., p. 322) gives an attestation by Curle, dated September 2, 1586, of a letter intended for use in Mary's trial, in which a paragraph mentioning Poley and Blount was omitted.

[7] *History*, vol. xii., p. 131.

[8] Vol. xviii., nn. 13, 14.

is the more probable, that Morgan had the "inconceivable imprudence," as Mr. Froude well calls it, to put such words on paper, or that Phelippes should have added it to his decipher of this letter? If Elizabeth learnt that "the beast was to be removed," as Mr. Froude tells us,[1] was there not motive enough for the forgery in the wish to excite her fear and hatred of Mary?

With regard to this man's visit to Chartley, Mr. Froude has the following passage.[2] "Mary Stuart knew Phillipps by sight; a spare, pock-marked, impassive, red-haired man, something over thirty. She had been already struck by his appearance. Morgan had suggested that he might not be proof against a bribe. She had tried him gently and without success, but she had no particular suspicion of him."

Mary had written to Morgan,[3] July 27, 1586, "I remember of one named Phillippes, a gentleman who you had dealt withal long ago to have served me, about Secretary Walsingham. There is one of that name who had been here five or six days with my keeper about Christmas, and whom at that time I made be sought about, to try if he had been your man or not. But neither on his side or mine could know the same, no more than I have yet done in the space of a fortnight that he hath of late been here and departed but this day: albeit both myself and some of mine have given him occasion to have declared himself at hunting and otherwise, if he had been the man you wrote of.

"This Phillippes is of low stature, slender every way, dark yellow haired on the head and clear yellow bearded, eated in the face with small pocks, of short sight, thirty years of age by appearance, and, as is said, Secretary Walsingham's man: which I have thought good hereby to utter, to the end against his next return, in case it happen, I may before by you, if it be possible, be informed by these signs whether it be your man or not, and accordingly to use him."

Mr. Froude, having Mary's letter before him, repeats her own personal description of Phelippes, a photograph of a mean-

---

[1] *History*, xii., p. 135.

[2] *History*, vol. xii., p. 138.

[3] Vol. xviii., nn. 74, 75, one copy in Curle's hand and one in Phelippes' own; Labanoff, tom. vi., p. 423.

looking scoundrel, charitably mending his appearance by sub-stituting "impassive" for the "short sight" and "low stature." Morgan, he goes on to say, had given Mary a hint to bribe Phelippes, and accordingly she makes tentative efforts, which are foiled by his impassiveness. The document itself simply states that such a person had been at Chartley, and that Mary and her attendants have tried unsuccessfully to make out whether he were the identical Phelippes whom Morgan had tried long ago to bribe. Mr. Froude adds that Mary "had no particular suspicion of him." But Mary wrote to M. de Châteauneuf, March 24, 1586, and Phelippes copied the letter himself[1]—"Si c'est, comme je doute, un nommé Philippes, serviteur de Walsingham, qui, vers Noel, a séjourné en ceste maison plus de troys semaines, donné vous garde d'y vous commettre d'avantage, car, ores qu'il ayt promis de me faire service, je sçay qu'il joue double jeu."

The transfer to Chartley, as we have said, took place on the 24th of December. The second letter-book, which was written there, opens with some letters which relate rather to Jersey than to Mary Queen of Scots. It has seemed better, however, not to omit them, as they are not among the State Papers.

To Sir Francis Walsingham, 27° Decembr., 1585.

Sir,—It may please you to peruse this letter inclosed, which I received this present day from Sir Thomas Leighton, who had written to the same effect to my son, Anthony Poulet, as may also appear by this copy inclosed. My said son giving me farther to understand that the Count Brisac[2] prepareth certain ships at Newhaven, but to what end he cannot yet learn.

I would not doubt of the Spaniard's good will if he were a near neighbour, but I have no great opinion that the French would be hasty to stir up new enemies, and to have so many irons in the fire at once; and yet living here a prisoner, I dare not judge of the actions abroad, and therefore do refer myself herein to your better

---

[1] Vol. xvii., n. 36 ; Labanoff, tom. vi., p. 262.

[2] Charles de Cossé, afterwards marshal of France. Birch's _Elizabeth_, vol. i., p. 163.

knowledge of the state of foreign parts. But if you shall find that this attempt carrieth any apparent colour of truth, I shall most heartily pray your friendly mediation towards her Majesty for supply of men and munitions for the Isle of Jersey. Besides that it shall be very needful that the inhabitants of Jersey be encouraged in all times of danger by the assistance of some English supply, it is also certain that the ordinary garrison maintained by the captain is less than sufficient to defend the castle of Jersey against the enemy.

It may be that the castle is sufficiently furnished of munitions to pass over some little time of peace and quietness, but in case of danger, it is of necessity that the same be furnished with a new store of powder, calivers, &c. Forbearing to set down the particularities of this supply until I shall hear from you how the same shall be needful, I have been always of opinion that in these like suspected times one or two of her Majesty's smaller vessels might be commanded to attend these isles, as well for their service upon all occasions occurring, as also to bring advertisement of their necessity, if any should happen.

And thus I leave, &c.

Two other letters of the same date, one to Walsingham,[1] and the other to Burghley, relate to the provisioning of Chartley. The words inclosed in brackets in the following letter are supplied from the original.

To Sir Francis Walsingham, 27° Decembr., 1585.

Sir,—This Queen's packet sent with your letters of the 19th of this present contained no matter worthy of advertisement. Returning unto you herewith your Scottish occurrents with my most hearty thanks, I am very glad to hear (and I take it as an especial favour done to myself) that you have procured a new Privy Seal for a new supply

---

[1] Vol. xvi., n. 76.

of money, whereof our need here is so great as it is acco[mpani]ed both with shame and loss, and therefore I shall most heartily pray you to hasten the execution of the said Privy Seal as much as you may. It is true that I received 1,000*l.* at my coming from London for the service of this household, but this money was spent before my coming hither, so as I found this house indebted, the charges here being greatly increased sithence the end of the last harvest by reason of the great dearth of corn. Our bread and our beer being dearer by the third penny, our beef and mutton little bet[ter], provender for horses no less, all sorts of poultry little under that rate, [wine] in like manner, and the more by reason of the far carriage ; and now lately, this Queen, troubled with a weak stomach, drinketh much sack,[1] so as I am driven to make an ordinary provision thereof. I speak nothing of our dear carriages of wood and coal, the charges whereof are also greatly increased.

And now it may not be thought that the Lord Paget's revenues, although they came wholly to my hands, can be sufficient to entertain this great household without some help of her Majesty's coffers. God is my witness that I have great and singular care of her Majesty's profit in this service, and have already cut off all fees of Court and a great number of other superfluous charges, reducing all things to such order as if I lived in my own house in Somersetshire ; and even now, making my profit of the straitness of this house, have reformed many disorders to her Majesty's benefit and to the surety of my charge, which could not have been done so cleanly before this time.

This Queen's servants are always craving, and have no pity at all of English purses, so as if I kept not a strait hand on them, forcing them to address all their complaints

---

[1] *Sack,* sherry. The term was also given to any Spanish white wine. *Halliwell.*

to myself and to no other, her Majesty's expenses here [would be far greater than they are], and yet they will not cease to cavil; but I dare affirm that they are intreated with all reasonable courtesy, and to her Majesty's honour.

I make this despatch to no other end than to pray your speedy relief of money; my little store, as also my credit in this strange country, being utterly spent.

And thus, &c.

To my Lord Treasurer, 27° Decembr., 1585.

My very good Lord,—Mr. Secretary, by his last letters of the 20th of this present, writeth in these words, that because the monies rising of the revenues of the Lord Paget seemeth to be already spent, he had procured that a Privy Seal should be directed for a new supply to the end there should be no want. And therefore, presuming that Mr. Secretary's knowledge of the necessity of this household proceeded from your lordship, as likewise the procuring of this Privy Seal, and desiring greatly the expedition thereof, I have thought good to write unto him more particularly herein, which I have done in the same words in effect as were contained in my last letters to your lordship, as may appear by this copy hereunder written.

And thus resting always at your lordship's commandment, I leave, &c.

The next letter,[1] however, shows that Poulet had misunderstood Walsingham, and that the new Privy Seal was not yet issued.

The bearer, old acquaintance with whom Poulet claims, was probably Phelippes, who was at Chartley about Christmas, "plus de troys semaines," as Mary said in the extract already given from her letter to M. de Châteauneuf. The friendly terms that existed between Poulet and Phelippes will plainly appear in some letters that will be given in their chronological place. No one but Phelippes could have had the "sufficiency" to relate what Poulet's "short lines" left unsaid.

[1] Vol. xvii., n. 3.

To Sir Francis Walsingham, 10° Januarii, 1585.[1]

Sir,—I have received your letters of the 1st and 2nd of this present, and whether the mistaking [was] in your writer or in me touching the Privy Seal mentioned in my letters to have been procured by you, the fault is not great. Thanking you for your promise to hasten the grant of the same, having done somewhat already for my relief herein, as it seemeth by that my Lord Treasurer hath written his letters to some of the Collectors of these parts to pay their debts to my hands.

If the King of Scots hath begun already (as you write) to work a conceit in his nobility that until they have estranged themselves from England, they can never stand assured of his good opinion and favour, it seemeth that he cannot dissemble so cunningly as his mother and Nau report of him, and, indeed, it is very gross that he should discover himself so soon after this great accident.

The embroiderer[2] having sent hither to this Queen's physician at two sundry times for physic for his wife, finding that no relief in money came from hence upon the first sending, at the second took occasion to write to the physician that without my succour he had been greatly distressed; upon sight whereof this Queen sent him four angels.[3] The sick woman continuing in extremity of madness, so as being watched nightly by two hired men, her keepers were forced to bind her hand and foot six or seven days after the receipt of the said four angels. The

---

[1] The reader must be pleased to remember that the year began on Lady Day, March 25, in England up to the year 1752.

[2] Audrey's wife Poulet had been afraid to discharge, as he says in his letter of August 18, 1585, because she was "a woman of judgment and understanding." Mary's desire to dismiss the embroiderer and his family was repeated November 30 (Vol. xvi., n. 69). They were left at Tutbury. The Queen's opinion of the embroiderer is given in her letter to M. de Châteauneuf, March 24, 1586. "Sitost que mon brodeur sera par delà, faites-le passer en France, estant un fort mauvais et corrompu poltron" (Vol. xvii., n. 36; Labanoff, tom. vi., p. 266).

[3] *Angel*, a gold coin, varying in value from about 6*s.* 8*d.* to 10*s. Halliwell.*

embroiderer writeth to this Queen's physician in such terms as may appear unto you by this copy inclosed. It is manifest by the physician's answer in writing, that this Queen was troubled with this letter, and much the more because she knew the same had passed through my hands.

Whereas you write you have been advertised that some letters have passed between the Queen and her son by the mean of some gentlewoman dwelling not far from Tutbury, who hath been used as an instrument therein, and hereupon require me to inform myself what gentlewomen likely to be so employed are dwelling within ten or twelve miles of that place. The truth is, that I have not seen any other gentlewomen in this country than the Lady Aston, Mrs. Gresly, lately deceased, and Mrs. Bagot, whom I have seen in their houses, and do think and believe them to be of good credit, and faithful subjects to her Majesty.

There are many recusants and other suspected Papists within twelve miles of Tutbury whose wives are not unlikely to do bad offices. The Lady Grace, wife to Mr. Henry Candishe, is an old acquaintance with this Queen, and with all the retinue, as you know. The other gentlewomen of these parts are utterly unknown to me, and therefore I am bound to judge the best of them, and may not be too hasty to accuse in a matter of this weight without good ground, praying you to believe that no gentlewoman or other woman of this country hath had access to this Queen sithence my coming to this charge. And I may say as much for all the gentlewomen in this country of all degrees, yea, even in the day of her remove hither.

I have advertised heretofore that this Queen's laundresses had great liberty to do what mischief they would at Tutbury, being lodged out of the castle and out of the danger of the watch and ward, so as they might carry and receive all things at their own pleasure. This is all I can say herein. Neither do I know how to inform myself better. It seemeth that the advertiser might be entreated or compelled to express his knowledge in plain terms, and it is likely that he that can say that a gentlewoman hath done it, doth also know or may learn of his author who she is.

I can say no more touching Tutbury, but of this house I may affirm, and therein I take God to witness, that the laundresses being lodged within the house as now they are, and the residue of this Queen's train watched and attended in such precise manner as they be, I cannot imagine how it may be possible for them to convey a piece of paper as big as my finger, and I think if you were here with me you would say as I say. And yet I dare assure nothing in so nice a point, but I speak plainly and truly as I think.

Mr. Phelippes hath assisted me in perusing of this Queen's packet, wherein I refer you to this abstract here inclosed, by the which you may perceive that new servants are expected, wherein I trust you will not be hasty. The two gentlewomen lately admitted have filled this house full of news, and you must look for larger measure if any servants come out of France.

I find, by a memorial sent by the carrier from Nau to Chérelles, that he is desired to be a suitor unto you for a woman-servant for Carell's [Curle's] new wife, so as now it cannot be avoided but you must be acquainted with the marriage,[1] and therefore it may please you to prepare your answer.

You may believe that this bearer, for the old acquaintance between him and me, was very welcome unto me, thinking myself beholden unto you for this friendly choice, and now his sufficiency shall excuse my

---

[1] Poulet means that the presence of the Priest is thus acknowledged. See the letter of October 26, 1585.

short lines. I shall think myself happy to have heard of your dangerous sickness and of your recovery by one self-[same] messenger.

Beseeching God, &c.

It is necessary to repeat that the original of this letter is amongst the State Papers, which, when they suit him, are freely quoted by Mr. Froude. Let us now compare one of Mr. Froude's assertions with the source from which he drew. When Walsingham had written that he knew that "this Queen hath not as yet gotten any secret means for the conveyance of her bye packets," Poulet wrote in reply from Tutbury, October 16, 1585, to assure him that all open means are clearly taken away, but that "she may by her laundresses convey what she will." So again, Poulet now says that at Tutbury "the laundresses had great liberty to do what mischief they would, being lodged out of the castle, and out of the danger of the watch and ward, so as they might carry and receive all things at their own pleasure." Of Tutbury he can say no more, but at Chartley Poulet takes God to witness that he "cannot imagine how it may be possible for them to convey a piece of paper as big as his finger."

With this before him, Mr. Froude wrote in his *History*, respecting the secret correspondence between Mary and her friends which Walsingham intended should be carried on through Gilbert Gifford, "Nothing could be done while the Queen of Scots was at Tutbury. The approaches to the castle were too difficult, the guard too effective to be evaded. The Queen of Scots was clamorous to be removed, in the hope, poor creature, that she might find communication elsewhere less impossible. Walsingham, for the same reason, was equally anxious to humour her. . . . Paulet had affected to persuade her to remain at Tutbury, though Elizabeth had consented to her removal. He had made her only, as he probably intended, the more eager to go. . . . She went Walsingham's way, believing it to be her own."[1]

A romance writer relies for the interest he excites on the multiplicity of details that he weaves into his plot. Historically,

[1] Froude's *History*, vol. xii., pp. 111, 115.

as to this detail of this particular plot, it is plain that it was a matter of perfect indifference to Walsingham and of no consequence to the success of his plans against Mary, whether she remained at Tutbury or was removed to any of the houses he suggested. It is true that Mary did not use the laundresses as a means of communication at Tutbury, so that Poulet's suspicion of them was as it happened misplaced, and she remained without private letters from her friends until she was moved to Chartley. This was not because Chartley was more accessible than Tutbury, for with Poulet's connivance letters could have been introduced into the one house as easily as into the other; and indeed the Burton brewer, who was the instrument of communication at Chartley, served Tutbury Castle with beer. Mr. Gifford's house was too far from Burton to be supplied with beer by him; and it does not seem to have been true that Walsingham would have greatly preferred it to Chartley, as Mr. Froude supposes, and that he was baffled by Poulet in his simplicity, while yet in ignorance of the Secretary's plot.

Again Mr. Froude is inaccurate. "The coachman who exercised her horses, the laundress who carried out the clothes, the almoner who distributed her charities in the adjoining village, all were employed on her correspondence. . . . Letters stole in despite of Poulet's care. . . . La Rue's communication must have been almost the last which she received for many months, and Poulet's skill at last stopped the channels by which her own private letters were carried out."[1]

Here Mr. Froude sketches how peculiarly tantalizing it must have been for Mary to find her intelligence cut off, just after the receipt of Père La Rue's letter, "on the eve of the expected triumph of the Catholic cause." But Mary did not receive Père La Rue's letter till it was more than a year old, and then it came through Walsingham's contrivance. Mr. Froude might have seen her own statement in the Public Record Office,[2] or in Labanoff, dated Chartley, June 30, 1586. "Mon père, je croy que vous aurez esté assez adverty de l'interruption de toutes mes intelligences depuis mon changement de garde, ce qui a esté

---

[1] *History*, vol. xi., p. 579.

[2] Vol. xviii., n. 24; Labanoff, tom. vi., p. 349.

cause de me faire recevoir si tardivement les deux dernières lettres[1] que vous m'avez escriptes."

Mr. Froude must have forgotten how dramatically he had shut up Mary Stuart with Père La Rue's letter in her hand, when later on[2] he says that his letters in cipher were with the others, "which had been lying at the French Embassy, unforwarded for want of opportunity."[3] Yet he adds, "Some of them, those especially from La Rue, have been already, quoted," as having been in Mary's hands a twelvemonth before she received them.

We may be sure that Poulet's persuasions to Mary to remain at Tutbury were not "affected," nor intended to make Mary more anxious to go. Her gouty keeper did not like changing houses in the winter, and if he could have put the plasterers in to ceil Mary's room without removing her, he would have done it. In the very October, when Mr. Froude imagines he was by a feigned opposition inducing Mary to wish to leave Tutbury, he was himself writing[4] to Walsingham that he hoped to hear no more of the remove "until about Shrovetide," that is, not before spring.

To my Lord Treasurer, the 10th of January, 1585.

My very good Lord,—I think myself bound to your lordship for your letters directed to the Collectors of these parts as for a singular turn, and do take it as a sure testimony of your friendly care of my poor service, and yielding unto your lordship most humble thanks for the same. I wish that the Privy Seal intended to be procured may extend to one thousand pounds, and that Mr. Baynham may be required to make payment unto me of the last half year's receipt of the Lord Paget's lands,

---

[1] May 8, 1585, vol. xv., n. 86; November 14, 1585, vol. xvi., n. 64.

[2] *History*, vol. xii., p. 120.

[3] "Lorsqu'elle fut ès mains dudit Sadler et Paulet, elle perdit tout moyen d'avoir lettres secrétes de quelque part que ce fut, et durant lesdites années 1584 et 1585; de sorte que le sieur de Mauvissière, partant de sa charge d'Ambassadeur en Septembre 1585, laissa ès mains du sieur de Châteauneuf, son successeur, grande quantité de paquets secrets pour ladite dame, lesquels il n'avait pu lui envoyer durant les dites années (*Châteauneuf's Memoir*; Labanoff, tom. vi., p. 278).

[4] Vol. xvi., n. 59; *Supra*, p. 111.

J

as likewise of that which shall be due hereafter, and then I trust I shall not need to be hasty to pray any new supply. It is very true that this household is greatly indebted at this present.

It pleased your lordship to signify unto me by your letters in the end of this last summer, that the patent of the stewardship of the Lord Paget's lands should be sent unto me as soon as the seal could be procured. If it be forgotten, it may please your lordship to call it to your remembrance. If upon any occasion your lordship shall think to stay it, or to revoke it, I refer myself most willingly to your lordship's good pleasure.

And thus, &c.

To the Justices of Stafford, touching the contribution of money for wood and coke [coal], &c., 11° Januarii, 1585.

After my very hearty commendations, whereas upon conference between you and the Justices of the county of Derby, at the instance of Sir Ralph Sadler, then having the charge of the safe keeping of the Queen of Scots, it was agreed, the 20th of February last past, that certain sums of money should be levied for the necessary carriages of wood and coal for one whole year unto the Castle of Tutbury, for the governor and household attending there upon the said Queen, *vizt.*, in the county of Stafford four score and ten pounds, in the county of Derby four score and ten pounds, and in Leicestershire four score pounds; which, upon due consideration of the proportion of wood and coal requisite for the said service, and of the short carriage of the same by reason of the nearness of the Queen's woods, seemed to be reasonably rated.

Having considered that the time agreed for will be expired very shortly, and understanding of your assembly at Stafford this day, and being unwilling to be more troublesome unto the country than necessity enforceth,

I have thought good to pray you to take order for a competent sum of money to be levied within your county for the purpose before rehearsed, for the year to come, wherein it shall be meet to have regard as well of the far and dear carriage of wood and coal to this house of Chartley (the certainty and truth whereof cannot be unknown to some of you), as also that it is unlikely that the county of Derby will yield to any great contribution to this service, by reason that this household is removed so far from them. And thus, not doubting but that you will not only tender the quietness of your neighbours, but also have due regard to her Majesty's service, expecting your answer by this bearer, I leave you to your own discreet considerations.

And whereas order hath been given heretofore for a watch by night of two persons, and of a ward by day of one person, to be kept in the townships and parishes within ten miles of the castle of Tutbury, and also of a weekly search to be duly made within the said precinct, as by this note inclosed of the order then prescribed, may more plainly appear unto you; these shall be to pray you to have no less care of her Majesty's service in this place, and to that purpose to revive the said order, with strait charge for the due execution of the same.

And thus, &c.

This copy, altered in one or two points, was sent also to the Justices of Derby.

The next letter is out of its proper place. It must have been written at Tutbury, and the only sentence that it contains relating to the Queen of Scots is the first, which gives us the date of the final order for the transfer to Chartley. The rest of the letter is about an appeal case from Jersey, which George Poulet had come over to defend; and as he had applied to his brother, Sir Amias, for letters of recommendation to the Court, so this letter has naturally been placed with that which follows it.

J 2

To Sir Francis Walsingham, ult° Novembr., 1585.

Sir,—Having received your letter of the 23rd of this present for the removal of this Queen [to] Chartley, wherein all diligence shall be used, I have not now wherewith to trouble you in anything concerning her Majesty's service, but am bold to trouble the post for my private business in a matter concerning my government in Jersey, wherein I am most heartily to pray your good favour, and yet no otherwise than as the same may stand with justice and equity.

It was ordered in anno 1572, by the Lords of her Majesty's Council (the order being extant in the chest of the Council Chamber), that no appeal in any case or matter, great or small, should be permitted or allowed by the Justices of the said isle before the same matter were fully examined and ended by definitive sentence, or other judgment having the force and effect of a sentence definitive, thereby to avoid many great inconveniences tending to the hindrance of justice in general, and to the great loss and trouble of the parties, as well plaintiff as defendant, in particular.

This order hath been duly obeyed until now very lately that one Andrew Harrys, of the Isle of Guernsey, hath appealed before the sentence definitive, and would not be persuaded by any prayers, entreaty, or other advice of the Justices, to desist from the same; but hath found sureties to maintain his doings herein, when he shall be called to answer the same before the Lords of her Majesty's Privy Council.

Hereupon my brother, George Poulet, now Bailiff of that isle, at the instant request of the Justices, fearing lest this breach might breed a great ruin, is repaired into England to prosecute this cause, staying himself in the west parts with his sick wife, to avoid the expenses of his vain attendance at the Court without the presence of his party. And like as I doubt not but that the Lords of her

Majesty's Council will maintain their own doings, wherein I am most humbly to pray their lawful favour; so I shall most heartily desire you to send a pursuivant for the said Harrys at the peril of the party that shall be found to have transgressed. And upon the arrival at the Court of the said Harrys, and the same signified unto me by your letter, my brother shall not fail to wait on you with all speed, or sooner if you shall think so meet, wherein it may please you to give me your direction.

I am not ignorant that the calling of the said Harrys by a pursuivant will breed charges and expenses to him that shall be found faulty, and I could be content that the matter were carried with less damage to the offender; but I consider that the calling of him in this sort will serve to great purpose to terrify all such wilful and malicious fellows, and to keep them hereafter within the bounds of obedience. Neither do I see how he may be called by any other assured mean.

There is also another cause of my brother's repair into England, which is that one Hellyer Paine, inhabitant of the Isle of Jersey, hath also appealed of a late sentence given by my said brother. And forasmuch as it hath fallen out these few years last past that the party appealing hath been accustomed to leave the prosecuting of his appeal, and to procure a Commission from the Lords of the Council, referring the deciding and hearing of the cause and controversy unto Commissioners, to the great hindrance of the due execution of justice, to the utter abolishing of the laws and privileges of the said isle, and to the great slander of the Bailiff and Justices there; the Justices, fearing lest this appeal of Hellyer Paine might have like success, have prayed my said brother to answer the said cause in person, in which behalf I am to trouble you with two suits. The first, when Hellyer Paine shall make his repair to the Lords of the Council, which, by order established by their lordships, he must do within three months, that he may be commanded to justify his appeal, as by law he is bound to do, and that he may not hide his wilfulness under the cloak of a Commission. My second suit is, that when the said Hellyer shall arrive at the Court, that it may please you to give me knowledge thereof, whereupon my brother shall not fail to make his immediate repair thither.

I confess that it were my brother's duty to attend, but being willing to avoid idle expenses, and also to accompany his sick wife, if it shall please you to be content to forbear him until one of his parties shall be in place, I shall thank you heartily for it, and shall take it for a favour done to myself.

I am so well persuaded of the integrity of my said brother, as I do not doubt but he will answer all his doings to the good satisfaction of my Lords of the Council; and, indeed, I placed him in the office of Bailiff in that isle for no other cause than that by his upright and sincere dealing justice might be duly administered to the inhabitants there in this time of my absence. I am very sorry that among your weighty and manifold business, the isle of Jersey should minister any occasion of trouble unto you.

And thus, &c.

To my Lord Treasurer, 15° *Januarii,* 1585.

My very good Lord,—Whereas at my last being in Jersey I placed this bearer, my brother, George Poulet, in the office of Bailiff in that isle, for no other cause than that, by his upright and sincere dealing, justice might be duly administered to the inhabitants there in this time of my absence, and do not doubt but that his proceedings are, and will be, such as will be answerable to my expectation. My said brother being repaired to the Court at the instant request of the Justices of the said isle, to defend his and their doings in a matter of appeal

before the Lords of her Majesty's most honourable Privy
Council ; these are most humbly to pray your lordship to
afford him your favour, the rather at my desire, and yet
no otherwise than as the same may stand with justice.
and equity.

And thus, &c.

The next letter[1] makes open mention of Mary's chaplain.

To Sir Francis Walsingham, 15° *Januarii,* 1585.

Sir,—Whereas Bastian's wife looketh to be delivered
of child shortly, I am to pray your direction for my
behaviour at the time, which I shall not fail to follow
in all preciseness. In former times, besides that the
midwife and nurse were provided out of the country, the
child was also baptized by the next minister, and English
godfathers and godmothers admitted. This Queen is now
so well provided, and useth her chaplain so boldly, as
there will be no question of the baptism, as I take it.
But what shall be done touching the midwife and nurse,
I refer to your better consideration. The access of midwives and nurses cannot be admitted without peril, but
how they may be avoided in cases of extremity, I refer to
your better judgment.

I remember that it pleased her Majesty to say unto
me, that she had considered of the inconveniences which
had ensued by these occasions, and would provide the
remedy. It is likely that Curle's wife will be sick of the
same disease very shortly, and some say she complaineth
already. As likewise it is to be expected that there will
be no end of marrying in this great household, when they
may marry without controlment, according to their own
religion.

This Christmas time, joined with this frosty weather,
hath deprived us of all kinds of sea fish, which is so ill
taken, as they threaten to complain by their letters. And

[1] Vol. xvii., n. 4.

yet I assure you, as great care hath been used to provide it as was possible. Indeed, this house is ill seated for that kind of provision. There is no end of their cavilling, and therefore I would be glad they did complain, that I might convince them of their unreasonableness, wherein there is no measure.

And thus, &c.

Passing over the letter to Walsingham of January 25,[1] which is about linen and laundresses, the next, to Lord Burghley, is about Queen Mary's money matters.

To my Lord Treasurer, 27 Januarii, 1585.

My very good Lord,—Whereas Mr. Wm. Agar hath made payment to this Queen only of 100*l.*, and hath given his band[2] for the other 500*l.*, to be paid the 26th of this next month, wherewith this Queen is as well satisfied as if she had received all the money in hand, having prayed me to make him a discharge of the whole sum, which I have done under my sign. It is so that this Queen is advertised, by letters received very lately, of other 600*l.* arrived at London, wherein she hath prayed me by Nau to request your lordship's favour for speedy payment to be made unto her of those other 600*l.*, which if your lordship cannot do by the mean of her Majesty's receivers, or other like officers, then she desireth you to require Mr. Agar to bring the said money with him from London at her adventure, which, indeed, he hath proffered to do; and to this purpose he shall receive the said sum of the French Ambassador in gold. This Queen pretendeth to have great need of this money, and that the same is already due to her servants here for their wages.

And thus, &c.

The Queen of Scots at this time had a serious illness. On the 30th of January, Poulet wrote to Walsingham.

---

[1] Vol. xvii., n. 12.   [2] *Band,* a bond, a covenant. *Halliwell.*

To Sir Francis Walsingham,[1] *30 Januarii, 1585.*

Sir,—I thank you most heartily for your last despatch, wherein you did my brother great pleasure, who had forgotten that all his papers remained with me, without the which he can do no good in his business.

I have thought good to trouble you with this abstract here inclosed of the French Ambassador's letters to this Queen, finding nothing else in the packet worth the advertisement.

This Queen is much grieved at this present, sleeping little, and eating less. The humour removeth from one place to another, and doth now possess many places at once.

I am very glad to hear that you are returned to the Court in good health, where God maintain you in the same.

Chartley.

To Sir Francis Walsingham,[2] *2 Februarii, 1585.*

Sir,—This Queen hath kept her bed this six or seven days, being very much grieved with ache in her limbs, so as she is not able to move in her bed without great help, and when she is moved, endureth great pain. She hath caused me to be informed, that when she came to Tutbury this last year, the bed appointed for her own use was stained and ill-favoured, whereof she complained to Mr. Somer, who, being willing to redress it the best he could, delivered unto her his own bed, which is no better, indeed, than a plain ordinary feather bed, and is so much as the feathers come through the tick. She saith that hitherto she hath contented herself with this bed, but being not able to ease herself in her bed, as when she enjoyed her health, she findeth herself annoyed (the rather by reason of her long lying) with the hardness of the feathers, and therefore prayeth to be provided of a bed of down, which

[1] Vol. xvii., n. 14.　　[2] *Ibid.,* n. 17.

seemeth so reasonable as I could not in honesty and charity, refuse to move it. There is honour and conscience in this trifle, and therefore it may please you to have consideration of it.

And this, &c.

This copy was also sent to my Lord Treasurer.

In the next letter Sir Amias returns to the linen.

To Sir Francis Walsingham, 17 *Februarii,* 1585.

Sir,—It seemeth that Mr. Yonge hath been abused in the provision of the linen sent lately hither, which hath been greatly misliked by this Queen and all her officers ; and after some ill favoured speeches, so much thereof as was to serve this Queen's table was utterly rejected upon the first view, and rendered again immediately to Mr. Darrell, and the residue accepted rather of necessity, because they could not spare it, as they said, than for any liking they had thereof. The next day the whole proportion was returned to Mr. Darrell by order from this Queen, upon information given by Nau and some others of his fellows, that the linen provided for their use was not meet to be received. They complain of the coarseness of all this linen, and of lack of breadth and length in the napkins and cupboard cloths, and therefore have delivered unto me a pattern of every sort of those which they had in Sir Ralph Sadler's time, desiring to be furnished, if not of better, yet of as good at the least.

I have thought good to send back this linen unto you, to the end you may cause it to be seen by such as have knowledge therein. Indeed the whole portion was very ill chosen, and was so thin as it carried the show of cloth that had been already worn, the Scottish people affirming plainly that the towels had been made of sheets, which also did appear by the threads which had been ripped and sewed again. I am so of opinion that in such provisions the best and the strongest is best cheap, and especially for this people which make no spare of it in washing and wearing. It shall make for her Majesty's profit that this linen be sent without delay, because this linen of the finer and better sort, which might have lasted until Christmas next as they say, is now worn daily for lack of change.

I would have been bold to have stayed this linen for the provision of her Majesty's household here, whereof there is great need, and might have served the turn very well for so long as it would last, but I durst not presume so far, and did forbear the rather because I doubted it might be thought that I had assented to the refusal made by the Scottish people to the end I might retain it to my own use. Their demand now is somewhat increased, as may appear by this note inclosed, which Mr. Darrell received of this Queen's master of household, who hath been intreated with some difficulty to accept of the dresser cloths and wipers.

And thus, &c.

I think myself greatly beholden unto you for your favour extended towards my brother, which I do acknowledge with all thankfulness.

To Sir F. Walsingham,[1] *eodem die.*

Sir,—I have thought good to accompany my other letters sent herewith by reason of this Queen's linen with a word or two concerning her disposition of body, which is that she remaineth fast lodged in her bed, where she hath continued now this month and more, subject to many painful defluxions, and within these two days was taken in one of her sides in very extreme manner, so as all her trustiest servants were sent for with speed, who have not seen her so dangerously grieved at any time heretofore, as

[1] Vol. xvii., n. 23.

'Nau and others have reported. After seven or eight hours this violent pain was assuaged, and the night following she took indifferent good rest.

And thus, &c.

The letters to Walsingham of the 26th of February relate to a visit of M. Arnault,[1] and they are followed by a civil little note in French from Poulet to M. Arnault himself.

A Monsieur Arnault, 26 *Februarii,* 1585.

Monsieur,—Allant coucher le soir apres votre partement je donnay charge a mon secretaire de vous aller voir le matin et vous a porter mes lettres a Monsieur Walsingham. Estant couche et endormy Monsieur Nau m'envoye l'extraent inclose, lequel ie n'avois enchores veu quand mon secretaire s'en allast vers vous, qui est la cause que ic ne le vous ai envoye pour lors, vous priant de m'excuser. Je vous supplie de croyre que vous avez acquis une grande obligacion sur moy, de la quelle ie m'acquitteray a la premiere occasion qui se presentera, en appes [*sic*] de quoi ie vous baise bien humblement les mains, priant Dieu, Monsieur, vous tenir en sa digne et saincte garde.

To Sir Francis Walsingham, ult. Februarii, 1585.

Sir,—Mr. Darrell having received advertisement from the Court of the late decease of Mr. Rutland, one of her Majesty's household officers there, by occasion whereof it falleth out that every other officer according to his place is to attain to some higher degree of preferment, forasmuch as by the alteration Mr. Avenor[2] (as it seemeth), is to be preferred to the Greencloth, and so consequently Mr. Darrell, being one of the Clerks of the Avery, to arise in his degree.

---

[1] Vol. xvii., nn. 25, 26.

[2] The Greencloth was the counting house as well as the court of justice of the royal palace. The Avenor was the chief clerk of the Avery, and was an officer under the Master of the Horse, having the charge of the provender for the royal stables.

I can do no less than to recommend his cause to your favour, and most earnestly to pray you to have such friendly consideration of him that he may in his course attain to such preferment as by order is due unto him. It is often seen that men out of sight are out of mind, but his service here being in care, travail, continual writing, and daily attendance far beyond the service of any of his companions about the Court, it were unreasonable that his absence should be hurtful unto him, deserving to be better regarded and rather to be recompensed extraordinarily than to have anything taken from him.

I may affirm unto you that besides that the gentleman serveth here so painfully and carefully, as I will not hope that he will be succeeded with his like; so he is also religious, honest, and endued with many good virtues. I pray you once again, as heartily as I can, to assist him with your good favour.

And so, &c.

On the 2nd of March,[1] Poulet communicated to Walsingham the desire of Sharp, the coachman, and of [Burgoigne], the physician, to be discharged from the service of the Queen of Scots. The first request "seemed so strange, as I said I could hardly believe that he was of that mind." Sharp, however, persisted, "praying the like for his sister and sister-in-law, who serve here as laundresses." This "I would suspect to be grounded upon great cunning, if I did not know that they were already provided of sufficient means to perform all the treacheries that they can devise." This clearly is an allusion on Poulet's part to the plan of communicating with the outer world through Gilbert Gifford and the Burton brewer, which Walsingham had devised, and which was now beginning to work.

As these treacherous individuals play so considerable a part in this tragedy, we avail ourselves of the present opportunity to lay before the reader some observations on Mr. Froude's statements respecting Gilbert Gifford and his employer, Sir

[1] Vol. xvii., n. 27.

Francis Walsingham.   After an elaborate argument to show
that Walsingham was acting with perfect uprightness in setting
a trap for Mary Stuart and her Catholic correspondents, he
pronounces Elizabeth's Minister innocent of bringing about
her death by tempting her to join in the Babington conspiracy.
"It has been represented as set on foot by Walsingham
to tempt the Queen of Scots to ruin herself. It was utterly
unconnected in its origin either with him or with his instruments. The channel of communication which Gilbert Gifford
had opened was made use of by the conspirators, but the
purpose had no existence in Walsingham's original design, nor
does it appear that Gifford himself was even trusted with the
secret, or was more than partially, accidentally, and externally
connected with either Babington or his accomplices."[1]

Froude then introduces Ballard as "the original instigator" of
the plot, acting under the patronage of Mendoza, whose personal
hatred for Elizabeth was sharpened by eager desire to avenge
himself for his summary expulsion from England. Ballard saw
Morgan in the Bastile, who introduced him to Gifford. "Gifford,"
he goes on to say, "though he accompanied Ballard from Paris to
England, was personally ignorant of what was going forward. ·It
was not till afterwards that he learnt it, in conversation, from
Ballard himself. Though he probably saw Walsingham in London,
therefore he had nothing of moment to make known to him."[2]

Then again.[3]   "The Queen of Scots was the victim of
treachery, so it has been often said, and so it will be said again,
and if by treachery it is meant that she was deceived, the charge
is just. But it is false, absolutely and utterly, that the plot was
set on foot by agents of Walsingham to tempt her to join it in her
desperation, and then to destroy her."

In Gifford, says Mr. Froude, "the Jesuit training produced a character of a different type" to that of his brothers.
"He was taken from England when he was eleven years
old, and the Order therefore had him entirely to themselves,

---

[1] *History*, vol. xii., p. 124.

[2] *Ibid.*, p. 132. Perhaps not personally; for as Châteauneuf says, Gifford
all along "communiquait le tout avec Walsingham par le moyen de Phelippes"
(Labanoff, tom. vi., p. 288).

[3] *History*, vol. xii., p. 147.

to shape for good or evil."[1] Gilbert Gifford had no "Jesuit training," and "the Order" never had anything to do with him. Mr. Froude may be excused the mistake in this instance, for M. de Châteauneuf has committed the same error; but it is necessary to note that all through Mr. Froude's *History* he habitually styles "Jesuits" those who never had anything in the world to do with the Society of which St. Ignatius Loyola was the founder. Thus Anthony Tyrrell and Foscue, or Fortescue, better known as Ballard, are "two young English Jesuits."[2] So also "neophytes, when their conversion was completed, were drafted off to Douay or Rheims, were admitted, most of them, while their imaginations were still fevered, into the Order of Jesus."[3] When this curious system of misnaming men is understood, it is of course possible to make allowances when reading the book, so as not to be perpetually misled; but as some were really Jesuits and some were not, among the multitude whom Mr. Froude so calls, it is, to say the least, confusing: and as the appearance of the word in Mr. Froude's pages is the signal for an offensive attack, perhaps those who really are Jesuits may not like it. For instance, the Order that helped to keep the English Catholics patient through their persecutions may think it hard that it should be said, "So for ever sang the Jesuits," that "one brave shot or dagger-stroke" would send "the carcase of Jezabel to the dogs," and would write the name of the assassin "among the chivalry of Heaven."[4]

The College that was founded at Douay, and which was removed there again after fifteen years spent at Rheims, was, it is hardly necessary to say, in the hands of the English Secular Clergy. In that Seminary it was that Gilbert Gifford "had been ordained deacon, and had been reader of philosophy;" so that there is no need to contradict the statement that "being a good linguist, he had travelled on the business of the Order." Travelling on this errand, according to Mr. Froude, he incidentally makes acquaintance with Morgan, Paget, and Throgmorton, and was in no way connected with Walsingham until the late spring or early summer of 1585.

[1] *History*, vol. xii., p. 110.   [2] *Ibid.*, vol. xi., p. 43.   [3] *Ibid.*, vol. x., p. 513.
[4] *Ibid.*, vol. xi., p. 395.

Again, we have seen that, in reference to Babington's conspiracy, Mr. Froude directly says that it does not "appear that Gifford himself was even intrusted with the secret, or was more than partially, accidentally, and externally connected with either Babington or his accomplices." And his narrative of events is skilfully contrived to justify this statement. But Blackwood states[1] that two years earlier Gifford was acting as Walsingham's spy at Rheims, and had come twice to London to incite Savage to regicide.[2] And both Morgan's correspondence and Châteauneuf's Memoir mark out Gifford as the prime mover in the plot. For eight months before it was fully organized he had been living in close intimacy with Morgan and the other refugees in Paris. Gifford, Poley, and Phelippes were all in Paris during the summer of 1585, insinuating themselves into the confidence of Mary Stuart through Morgan. Walsingham's agents were already associated with Babington,[3] for letters from Morgan and Paget of that date recommend the trio, Babington, Poley, and Gifford, as persons able and willing to serve the Queen of Scots. In December, 1585, Gifford returned to England, furnished with ample recommendations to Mary from Morgan and from the Archbishop of Glasgow.[4] After presenting himself at the French Embassy in London, he went straight to Phelippes' house, where he lived during the month of January, "practising secretly among the Catholics," that is, insinuating himself into the confidence of Babington and his friends, and opening Walsingham's route of communication with Chartley. The secret packets for Mary which, acting under Walsingham's directions, he obtained

[1] Jebb, *De vita et rebus gestis Mariæ*, 1725, vol. ii., p. 281. "Ledit Gifford (comme il se verra ci-après) était un homme suscité par les seigneurs du Conseil d'Angleterre pour perdre la Reine d'Escosse, comme par toutes les cours de l'Europe ils ont des hommes, lesquels, sous ombre d'être Catholiques, leur servent d'espions, et n'y a Collége de Jésuites, ni à Rome ni en France, où ils n'en trouvent qui disent tous les jours la messe pour se couvrir et mieux servir à cette Princesse [Elizabeth]; même il y a beaucoup de prêtres en Angleterre tolérés par elle pour pouvoir, par le moyen des confessions auriculaires, découvrir les menées des Catholiques." *Châteauneuf's Memoir*, Labanoff, tom. vi., p. 279.

[2] Gifford's name appears in the indictment of Savage as having urged him to assassinate Elizabeth. Howell's *State Trials*, vol. i., p. 1120.

[3] Labanoff, tom. vi., p. 213, 328.

[4] *Châteauneuf's Memoir*, Labanoff, tom. vi., p. 281.

by fraud and falsehood from the French Ambassador, contained nothing which could justify putting her to death; the sufficient "occasion" or "opportunity," as Poulet frankly calls it, had still to be sought. Accordingly, during the spring and summer, Gifford, in concert with Babington and Ballard, was actively developing the conspiracy, crossing frequently to Paris, where he associated himself with Morgan and Paget, and laid their projects of revolt and regicide before Bernardino de Mendoza, the Spanish Ambassador, who, smarting under his own expulsion from England, and resenting on his master's behalf the action of the English Government in the Low Countries, lent a ready ear. "A cette occasion," says Châteauneuf,[1] "le dit de Mendoza n'oublia rien de belles promesses, tant au dit Gifford et à ceux qui étaient à Paris, qu' aux autres qui étaient en Angleterre pour les y inciter, avec promesses d'une armée de mer et de tous les moyens de son maître." Of these facts Mr. Froude, though he draws a good deal of material from Châteauneuf's Memoir, takes no notice whatever.

Nor is this all. Châteauneuf's statements are confirmed in full by a letter,[2] of which Mr. Froude has made ample use, from Mendoza to Philip, August 13, 1586. In Mr. Froude's resumé of this despatch,[3] Ballard is represented as laying before Mendoza the full details of a formidable conspiracy. He describes the state of religion in England, and gives the particulars of the strength of the Catholic party in the different counties, with a roll-call of noblemen and gentry prepared to rise in revolt.[4] In short, the envoy furnishes full information respecting a triple conspiracy, including a plan for a general Catholic rising, a scheme for Elizabeth's assassination, and proposals for a Spanish invasion. So "Ballard told his story" to the Spaniard, who heartily approves everything, particularly the plan of assassination. "Ballard's story" is pretty accurately repeated by Mr. Froude from his authority, with one startling variation. He has from first

---

[1] Labanoff, tom. vi., p. 287.

[2] Simancas Archives, B 57, printed by Teulet, *Histoire de l'Ecosse au XVI. siècle*, vol. iii., p. 423, Bannatyne Club edition.

[3] *Hist.*, vol. xii., p. 128.

[4] Among them appears "milord Gifford, persona de hedad, es padre del gentilhombre que me ha venido a hablar."

K

to last substituted Ballard's name for that of Gifford in the original. Mendoza opens his report by informing Philip that, some months previously, "*un clerigo*"[1] had come over to acquaint him with the Catholic movement in England,[2] but that, the information supplied being incomplete, he had answered only in general terms, at the same time requiring further particulars. In consequence, he reports, the Catholics had sent a second envoy,[3] a gentleman named Gifford, of good family, well accredited, and furnished with ample instructions. Mendoza writes in full confidence towards Gifford, or, as he more often styles him, "*el gentilhombre*," as will appear from the passage which Mr. Froude has had the courage to reproduce and apply to Ballard.[4] So the letter proceeds. Throughout it is Gifford, not Ballard, to whom the mission of the Catholic party is confided, who unfolds the secrets of the confederacy and lays opens the plan for regicide. It is Walsingham's agent whom Mendoza unsuspectingly welcomes as the negotiator of proposals "so profitable in the interests both of religion and of the King of Spain."

The manner in which the plot was carried out by Gifford and Phelippes is related by Mr. Froude with an inaccuracy that is truly remarkable. "Phillipps came to reside at Chartley under the pretence of assisting Paulet in the management of the household." This continued residence of Phelippes is entirely inconsistent with fact, and indeed the correspondence seems to show that he only paid Chartley two short visits, the former at Christmas, and therefore about the time of Mary's arrival, ending in all probability, as we have seen, on the 10th of January, the other, in which the fatal work was done, beginning on the 14th and ending on the 27th of July.

"Every letter conveyed to the Queen of Scots and every letter which she sent in return was examined and copied by him

---

[1] Ballard is always so designated in Mendoza's letters.

[2] Mendoza to Idiaquez, May 12, 1586. Simancas, B 57, n. 310; Teulet.

[3] "Han me embiado los Catholicos un gentilhombre llamado Maistre Gifford, de buena casa, con señas en su creencia."

[4] *Hist.*, vol. xii., p. 130. The whole document, in which the Queen of Scots is only slightly mentioned, will repay examination. Gifford had evidently imposed grossly exaggerated statements upon Mendoza respecting the Catholic party.

before it was forwarded to its destination, and Morgan's introduction of Gifford, which betrayed her into Walsingham's hands,
was the first on which he had to exercise his skill. Gifford
himself, too young and innocent looking, as he appeared to
Paulet, for so involved a transaction, had organized his own
share of it with a skill which Sir Amyas' blunter mind failed
at first to comprehend. Sir Amyas thought that his remuneration
from Walsingham ought to have contented him. Gifford, wiser
than he, knew that gratuitous services were suspicious. He
wrote to the Queen of Scots, saying that he was honoured in
being of use to her, but reminding her that he was risking his
life, and capitulating for a pension." The mind of Sir Amias
was not so blunt, and he too was conscious that gratuitous
services were suspicious, as he wrote to Walsingham, "I could
think that your friend's substitute at London should procure his
reward from this Queen, and if it be not sought at her hands she
shall have just cause to think ill of it."[1]

Mr. Froude gives the manner in which communications were
opened with Mary, from M. de Châteauneuf's Memoir.[2]

It is thus told by him: "Gifford s'adressa à celui qui four-
nissait la bière pour la provision de la Reine; laquelle, à la mode
d'Angleterre, se porte toutes les semaines, et ayant fait faire
un petit étui de bois creux, il mettait ses paquets dans le dit étui
bien fermé et les jetait dans un vaisseau de bière; lequel le
sommelier retirait et le baillait à Nau, qui, au prochain voyage du
charretier, rendait le vaisseau avec la réponse. Le dit fournisseur
de bière se tenait en une lieue de là, où l'on allait quérir les dites
lettres."

"At points between Burton and London," continues
Mr. Froude,[3] "he had found Catholic gentlemen with whose
assistance the packets were transmitted. They were told no
more than that they contained letters of supreme importance to
the cause. One of them, who resided nearest to Burton, received
a bag weekly from the brewer, and carried it on to the next, by
whom it was again forwarded. So it was passed from hand to
hand to the Jesuit agency in London. The treachery was at

---

[1] Vol. xviii., n. 22; *infra.*   [2] Labanoff, tom. vi., p. 284.
[3] *Hist.*, vol. xii., p. 117.

K 2

Chartley only. From the time that the letters left the brewer's house they were tampered with no more. The London Jesuits receiving them by their confidential channel, and little dreaming that they were transcribed already, distributed them to their ciphered addresses, and returned answers in the same way, which again, after inspection by Phillipps, were deposited in the cask."

The ensuing correspondence will show that there is not a word of truth in this paragraph. The series of Catholic gentlemen handing on a weekly post-bag from one country house to another, had no existence; and there was no Jesuit agency in London to act as a general post office.

It is true enough that Gifford told a falsehood to M. de Châteauneuf, which has deceived not only him, but Mr. Froude. "Qu'entre Londres et Chartley, qui sont distants l'un de l'autre environ de quarante lieues, il y avait deux maisons de gentils-hommes Catholiques, ses amis; que le plus proche de Chartley enverrait toutes les semaines quérir les lettres chez le faiseur de bière, puis les enverrait chez l'autre gentilhomme plus proche de Londres, lequel les enverrait à Londres, au logis du dit Sieur Ambassadeur, par un des siens tantôt vêtu en serrurier, tantôt en crocheteur, tantôt en menuisier, tantôt en charretier, et ainsi en diverses sortes."

This was Gifford's contrivance to prevent the French Ambassador from making any inquiries into the character of the messengers whom Gifford deputed in his absence to carry the correspondence to and fro. Characteristically greedy scoundrels as they all were, Gifford wound up, " partant, qu'il ne lui fallait jamais faire paraître que cela vînt de la Reine d'Escosse, suffirait à chaque voyage lui donner un angelot pour l'encourager à bien faire." So they were to be paid by Walsingham, by Mary, and by de Châteauneuf.

Gifford, in his letter to Walsingham of the 11th of July, shows us how completely the letters remained in their hands throughout. "Barnes" (who is called by Poulet "the second messenger") "hath not yet appeared in any of his frequented places, so that I think he came not yet to town. I know not whether he hath been with the Ambassador, for I dare not go thither till such time as I bring the packet with me. I trust Mr. Phelippes will meet the said packet by the way and peruse it, that it need no delay in delivery." The packet in question was intercepted by Phelippes on July 7 at Stilton, was carried by him back to Chartley, and sent by Poulet to Walsingham with his letter of July 14, having been first opened by him, and a letter withdrawn. Is this a packet that from the time it left the brewer's house, was "tampered with no more?"

There were no Catholic gentlemen employed here. Why should there have been? Provided only that the persons at the two ends of the journey were unsuspected, what did it matter who carried the letters? Even Phelippes himself was the bearer of a letter from Babington to Mary, the answer to which is promised "at the return of the honest man." The letter from Mary to Babington was delivered by one of Phelippes' agents, probably by Barnes, as in writing to Walsingham on the 19th of July, Phelippes says, "If he be in the country, the original will be conveyed into his hands, and like enough an answer returned."

The treachery was not "at Chartley only." It was wherever it was convenient for Phelippes to be. Nor is it true, as Mr. Froude proceeds to say, that "six persons only were in possession of the full secret: Elizabeth and Walsingham, by whom the plot had been contrived, Gifford and the brewer who were its instruments, Phillipps by whom the ciphers were transcribed and read, and Paulet whom it had been found necessary to trust. All the rest," he adds, "were puppets who played their part at the young Jesuit's will." By "the young Jesuit" Mr. Froude means Gifford, and it is in keeping that he should have the management of the unconscious puppets who made up "all the rest." But it was Sir Amias who engaged "the substitute," who was one of the Earl of Leicester's men found for Poulet by Mr. Bagot. Gifford called him his cousin, but as we know no more of him, we are not bound to take the relationship on Gifford's word. As to this cousin, Mr. Froude makes him "an unconscious instrument in the ruin of the lady whom he worshipped as his Queen."[1] It would have been more

[1] *Hist.*, vol. xii., p. 118.

dramatic no doubt had it been so, but it is not true. He was a venal knave like the rest. Poulet was required by Walsingham to reward him, and proposed[1] to give him five pounds, in addition to whatever he could get from the Queen of Scots.

Gifford's falsehood to the French Ambassador gave Mr. Froude two Catholic gentlemen, and he has swelled the little invention into a series, who passed the packets from hand to hand; but the Jesuit agency in London to which they were consigned is Mr. Froude's own fabrication. There were at this time but three Jesuit Fathers in England, and of these two did not arrive till Mary's correspondence was drawing to its close. Edmund Campion and Thomas Cotham had been martyred; Robert Persons, Jasper Haywood, and William Holt were on the Continent; William Weston, *alias* Edmonds, who had been for some time the only Jesuit Priest in England, was apprehended before Ballard,[2] and most undoubtedly, if he could in any way have been shown to have been implicated in Babington's plot —and that any confidential messenger between Mary and Babington would have been held to be—he, being in custody, would have been put on his trial with the conspirators. Two other Jesuit Fathers reached England in 1586, as Mr. Froude will have learned from a letter of Morgan to Gifford, under the names of Thomas Germyn to Nicholas Cornellys, July 3, 1586.[3] "There are two Jesuits sent into England, both very young men, Father Southwell and Father Garnet; God prosper them and their labours." Besides these there was a Lay-brother, Ralph Emerson, shut up in the Counter in the Poultry. What pretext can Mr. Froude possibly have for saying that any of these men received the letters that Gifford and the other messengers from Chartley brought to London? If he has none, who were there to constitute the "Jesuit agency in London?" Who were the "London Jesuits" who "distributed the letters to their ciphered addresses and returned answers in the same way?"

However, the reader will be able to gather the true details for himself of the manner in which Mary's secret communications were carried on, as far as they are recorded in the correspondence we proceed to give. Phelippes had taken his departure in the

---

[1] Vol. xix., n. 7; *infra.*   [2] Vol. xix., n. 4.   [3] Vol. xviii., n. 31.

early part of January, 1586. On the 16th of that month, Mary received the letter of introduction dated October $\frac{6}{15}$, brought to her from Morgan by Gifford. She answered it on the 17th January, "conform to the ancient computation," that is, old style, inclosing letters for the Duke of Guise and the Bishop of Glasgow. Of Gifford she says, "I thank you heartily for this bringer, whom I perceive very willing to acquit himself honestly of his promise made to you, but, for such causes as presently I will not write, I fear his danger of sudden discovery, my keeper having settled such an exact and rigorous order in all places where any of my people can go, as it is very strange if they receive or deliver anything which he is not able to know very soon after."[1]

Gifford's return after taking this answer to London was expected by Poulet when he wrote the following letter to Phelippes. It is unnecessary to say that neither this nor any of the subsequent letters relating to the secret communications makes its appearance in Poulet's letter-book. We print them from the holograph originals in the Public Record Office. The reference in the first to Francis Bacon is noteworthy. Phelippes was for years on familiar terms with Bacon.[2]

Poulet to Phelippes.[3]

Sir,—Your letters have been very welcome unto me, and I take them as an earnest penny for more to come hereafter, which shall receive like welcome. I find it very strange to understand by your letters that Reynolds should make suit to depart from me, having used him in all this time of his service with many extraordinary favours, such as I never showed the like to any man that served me. And besides that I have trusted him with all that hath passed from me, I have also loved him very heartily. I will say no more but that in honesty and good manner he ought to have acquainted

---

[1] Vol. xvii., n. 5 ; Labanoff, tom. vi., p. 254.

[2] "The Marquis of Worcester is desirous to be acquainted with Francis Bacon by Phelippes' means." *Dom. Eliz.*, vol. ccxliv., n. 103.

[3] Vol. xvii., n. 13.

me with his meaning, and I know him and his disposition so well as I dare affirm that when he shall leave my service he shall go out of God's blessing into a warm sun, not doubting but that it will be easy for me to provide myself of some man as honest as he and as well qualified. If you had asked me, I would have said that he had loved me heartily and faithfully.

I look daily to hear from your friend.[1] Let this suffice, I pray you, until some new occasion shall minister better matter. And thus I commit you to the mercy of the Highest, with my most hearty commendations, and the like from my wife to yourself and our good friend, Mr. Francis Bacon.

Chartley, the 25th of January, 1585.

Your assured friend,

A. POULET.

To my very good friend, Mr. Thomas Phelippes, attending on Mr. Secretary, at the Court.

Poulet to Walsingham.[2]

Sir,—I received a letter from your friend the 3rd of this present, by the which he prayed me to send a trusty messenger unto him at a place appointed, which I did with two or three words in writing, signifying by the same that I had learned not to trust two where it sufficed to trust one; and therefore, although I had a very good opinion of the messenger, yet I advised him to return his mind in writing. Hereupon he thought good to repair unto me in person, which he did late in the night, the 5th of this present, and then delivered unto me the two packets and two letters sent herewith, showing me also a cypher which he had received from Curle, but prayed that it might remain with him because he was to advertise

---

[1] "Your friend" is Poulet's name for Gifford; the "secret party" is Phelippes'.
[2] Vol. xvii., n. 20.

Curle of the receipt of the said packets, which he could not do without the cypher.

He desired that these packets might be sent unto you with speed, and that his father might be advised by Mr. Phelippes to call him to London as soon as were possible, to the end he might deliver these letters to the French Ambassador in convenient time for the better conservation of his credit that way.

He promiseth to do great service, affirming that he hath good means to do it, and pretendeth to depend wholly of your favour. He resolveth to 'leave a counter-paper with the honest man at their next meeting for the credit of any such as he shall hereafter send unto him, with the like paper.

Being uncertain if you will command him anything else touching this service before his return to London, he hath instructed me where to find him.

I will hope the best of your friend, but I may not hide from you that he doubled in his speech with me once or twice, and [it] cannot be denied but that he received these or other packets sooner than he confessed.

The honest man hath made many leaps abroad sithence this matter was first made, and God knoweth if under the cloak of this trifle greater treacheries may be contrived.

In my simple opinion you shall do well to assure yourself of the honest man, which I may easily do, and then besides that your friends doings will be the more manifest, you shall also have the better mean to entertain this intelligence.

It escaped your friend to tell me that the packet to the French Ambassador had a cypher in it, but because I had tripped him once or twice before, I thought good to forbear to ask how he knew it, doubting he might conceive that I suspected him. He pretended to have showed me all that he had received from this people, which being true I cannot imagine how he should be informed of this.

cypher. It may please you to put him to the question, letting him to know that I informed you of it.

And thus, leaving these things to your better consideration, I commit you to the mercy and favour of the Highest.

Chartley, the 6th of February, 1585.

Your most assured poor friend,

A. POULET.

It may please you to give me leave to recommend my brother to your good favour.

Addressed by Poulet's secretary in the usual form to Sir Francis Walsingham, and endorsed as usual.

Poulet to Walsingham.[1]

Sir,—Your letters of the 4th of this present came to my hands the 8th of the same in the morning, being glad to hear that your friend returneth hither, and indeed I do not see how by any other mean your purpose could be continued with surety.

· Choice is made of a substitute of honest credit, good wealth, good understanding, and servant to the Earl of Leicester, from whom I look to hear hourly of the delivery of the first packet according to the direction received from you, and of a day to be appointed for their meeting again, at which time the second packet shall also be delivered, and then the third as time will permit, wherein I follow your instructions.

The letters contained in this Queen's packet came from Mauvissière and his servant Mareshall to this Queen and to Nau, with another letter from one Foster, a Scot, to one of the gentlewomen here. There is no matter in these letters worthy of advertisement, saving that Mauvissière writeth to this Queen that Claude Hamilton is returned

[1] *Harl. MSS.*, 285, f. 282.

into Scotland by the commandment of the King her son, and that he is well affected to her service.

I thank you most heartily for your friendly advertisements of the state of foreign parts, being sorry to hear that our actions in the Low Countries are no better backed at home, which will give no small comfort to the enemy, and may prove dangerous to the general cause.

Your letters touching the recusants in this county were delivered here the 8th of this present.

I think it meet that you hear from me sometimes, and therefore have made this despatch to the end you may know how far I am gone in the execution of your last letters.

I have been advertised from my brother of your friendly favour and effectual dealing in his behalf at the Council table, wherein I think myself greatly bound unto you, and do thank you for it most heartily.

God increase your honour and health.

Chartley, the 10th of March, 1585.

> Your most assured poor friend,
>
> A. POULET.

Sithence the writing of the premises, I am advertised that the honest man hath received the packet, and doth like very well of the substitute, but in respect of his private business, would not be persuaded to appoint the day of their next meeting until the 20th of this month.

Addressed by Poulet's clerk—To the right honourable Sir Francis Walsingham, knight, her Majesty's principal Secretary.

Endorsed by Phelippes — 9 March, 1585. From Sir Amias Poulet.

Phelippes to Walsingham.[1]

It may please your Honour,—The secret party was with me this morning, and tells me that Chérelles prays him in any case to stay until to-morrow at night, for that

---

[1] Vol. xvii., n. 28 ; *Cotton. MSS.*, Calig., C. ix., f. 219.

before that he hath talked with one Mr. Pierrepont again, he cannot despatch him. But the Ambassador himself hath been inquisitive of him for some apt mean to send a packet into Scotland, which is some secret matter. I thought good to send your honour word hereof, to the end that if Poley be not in the way, whom it is likely they will use, you may think of some other that may deliver it, and the secret party shall demand the same.

If Poley receive it, I do not think but he will bring it unto you. But you may try his good dealing at this time if he be in these parts. For as appeared by Morgan's last,[1] he is recommended as a fit man for that convoy of Scotland. Howbeit, it may be they would not be at so full a charge as the express sending of a messenger. Poley I think may be sent to the Ambassador by a sleight with some whispering intelligence what he will offer touching the convoy of these letters, which if he commit it to Poley, you shall either have it, and carried at their costs, or else know Poley thoroughly, for my secret friend shall know what becomes of it. If they do not commit it to Poley, it may please you [to] consider how it may [be] conveyed otherwise and give me direction, and my secret friend shall accept it and call for the packet at your pleasure.

The mention hereof puts me in mind that Mr. Justice Young said yesternight that he had a special spy about the Ambassador, by whose direction he dealt with Aldred, and I consider he may do the like with my secret friend, which would be very prejudicial to the service. I told him if he had commission from you to take that course it was another matter, but if he had not, I said, without your privity he might as soon do harm as good with his spials. And further, that as I took it, you were not curious to watch the Ambassador. "But they have been careful," said he, "heretofore." I answered, the times

---

[1] January $\frac{18}{28}$, 1586, vol. xvii., n. 6; Murdin, p. 440. Cf. Labanoff, tom. vi., p. 320.

were altered, and perhaps his spy was known, wherefore he were best to follow such order as you would prescribe. For anything I find by your honour or him, he hath no commission. If not, it may please you to limit him by some peremptory speech, or he will mar all to have work.

And so I humbly take my leave of your honour.

London, this 19th of March, 1585.

Your honour's most humble at commandment,

THO. PHELIPPES.

From these exciting topics we turn back to Poulet and his money matters, as recorded in the letter-book.

To my Lord Treasurer, 7 Martii, 1585.

My very good Lord,—Mr. William Agar hath made payment to this Queen of 500*l.* in full satisfaction of 600*l.*, appointed to be paid by letters from Mr. Chancellor, written to that purpose by direction from your lordship at Christmas last or thereabouts. Also he hath [made] payment to this Queen of six hundred and four score pounds, which he received now lately of the French Ambassador, and hath brought the same hither at your lordship's commandment, as he hath affirmed to Nau, who telleth me that this Queen thinketh herself greatly beholden unto you therein.

Farther, the said Mr. Agar hath undertaken to furnish this Queen yearly of 2,000*l.*, to be received again by him at London of the French Ambassador at two certain days in the year to be agreed upon between them, so as your lordship shall be no more troubled with any suit from hence in that behalf.

I have received your lordship's letters touching the tenement of Shulborowe, supposed to be in her Majesty's hands, and desired by one of your lordship's servants, the grant whereof shall be stayed until your lordship shall advertise your pleasure. And thus, &c.

To my Lord Treasurer, eodem die.

My very good Lord,—It may please your lordship to
give me leave to pray your direction in a matter or two
which import her Majesty's profit and service very much.
Upon conference between Sir Ralph Sadler, then serving
in this place, and the Justices of Stafford and Derby, it
was agreed, the 20th of February, 1584, that certain sums
of money should be levied for the necessary charges of
wood and coal for one whole year for the governor and
household attending upon the Scottish Queen, *vizt.,* in
the county of Stafford, four score and ten pounds, and in
the county of Derby, four score and ten pounds, which
upon due consideration of the proportion of wood and
coal requisite for the said service and of the short carriage
of the same by reason of nearness of the Queen's woods,
seemed to be reasonably rated. So as her Majesty was
charged only with 2*d.* for the carriage of every load of
wood, and with 6*d.* for the carriage of every load of coal.

It is so that the county of Stafford hath made full
payment of this contribution, as likewise the county of
Derby, saving in Skarsdale, where Mr. Leake refuseth
utterly to pay the portion assessed upon his limit, amounting to 22*l.* 10*s.,* although Mr. John Manners, being likewise
rated, hath already made payment of 15*l.,* and is ready
and willing to pay the residue, if Mr. Leake and his
neighbours will be content to do the like.

Mr. George Agar took upon this service at the
request of Sir Ralph Sadler, so as if he be not satisfied
of this money at Mr. Leake's hands, it is of necessity
that he must be recompensed by her Majesty's officers
here, which were an unnecessary charge to her Highness,
and unreasonable in my simple opinion. I have not
spared to ask this money by my sundry letters, and
now lately at the sessions holden sithence Christmas, I
wrote therein to the whole Bench, but have received no
answer from them, although I doubt not but that they

have dealt earnestly with Mr. Leake herein. The whole sum due by Mr. Leake and Mr. Manners amounts to 30*l.*, of the payment whereof there is no stay but in Mr. Leake. And now it may please your lordship to consider if this money shall be paid by her Majesty or by them.

The other matter wherein I desire your lordship's direction is, that whereas during and being at Tutbury, her Majesty was no farther charged with wood and coal than as is before mentioned, sithence the coming of this Queen hither, by reason of the far distance, the carriage of every load of sea coal doth cost 10*s.*, every load of charcoal 5*s.*, and every load of wood 3*s.* 4*d.*, besides the making of the said sea coal, charcoal, and wood, which falleth out weekly to so deep a sum by reason of the great expence in this great household, which is also increased by the occasion of this Queen's sickness, who now keepeth four continual fires in her own lodging.

As I fear it will be nothing pleasing to her Majesty, which I have thought to ease by some contribution for the year to come, the last contribution being expired the 20th of February last past, and to that purpose wrote to the Justices of the county of Stafford and Derby the last sessions to such effect as may appear by this copy inclosed.

The assembly of the Justices at Derby was very slender at that time by reason of the great frost and snow, promising by message to confer with their fellow Justices, and return answer, whereof I have as yet received none, and therefore do presume that they will do nothing.

From the Justices of Stafford I have received answer that they are willing to contribute as they did last year, praying earnestly to be pressed no further, in respect that the country is charged this year many ways very deeply, as they affirm. This contribution of four score and ten pounds by the year is far behind the yearly charge of the carriage of the year to come, which by the estimation made this last year by Sir Ralph Sadler will amount, as the carriages are now rated, to the sum of 333*l.* 18*s.* 3*d.* at the least.

This house is not so near bordering upon Derbyshire as was the Castle of Tutbury, and therefore I doubt how that she will be persuaded to yield to any contribution. If her Majesty will not be content to bear this heavy charge of wood and coal, how her Highness may be relieved therein, I refer it to your lordship's better consideration.

The necessity of this household is so great, as I have chosen rather to send for the money remaining yet at London of the 1,000*l.* granted by Privy Seal and to abide the adventure of the carriage than to forbear it with discredit to myself and hindrance to her Majesty's service, and therefore have despatched this bearer, my servant John Cade, expressly for that purpose, praying your lordship to take order that the said money may be delivered unto him, whose acquittance for the receipt thereof shall be a charge unto me as far forth as if I had received it myself. The man is of honest credit and sufficient substance to answer a greater sum of money than this cometh unto.

Having compared the state of this household with our present store of money and with that which is likely to accrue unto us by the demesnes of Burton, the tithing corn belonging to the same, and the herbage of the Lord Paget's three parks, with the profits of the iron mills, which, as is affirmed by the ministers, will not exceed the sum of 500*l.* this year, I have thought good most humbly to pray your lordship that Mr. Darrell may be commanded to make his repair to the Court, there to yield his account for this year past, which is wholly within his charge, although two months thereof were spent before my coming, trusting that upon the yielding of his accounts and due consideration had thereof, order will be taken, the rather by your lordship's good mean, that her Majesty's master of household here may have some money always in store, and not be indebted as he hath been continually sithence my coming hither, with slander to this household and loss to her Majesty. There is owing to me at this present 500*l.*, Mr. Darrell being not able to make payment of any part thereof.

And thus, &c.

Poulet speaks out plainly his indignation at the shabby way in which he, in common with all Elizabeth's servants, was treated. Her closeness was such that the most necessary sums had to be wrung from her.

The three following letters are not to be found in the State Papers.

To Sir Francis Walsingham, 12 *Martii,* 1585.

Sir,—Curle repaired unto me the 11th of this present, to pray me to provide a more sufficient merchant to furnish this Queen and her family with woollen cloth, linen cloth, and such other mercers' wares as they have occasion to use, alleging that the merchant of Stafford appointed to that purpose was not able to serve their turn for want of stuff fit for them, and that the Queen his mistress was now to make provision, after her accustomed manner, of [blank] woollen cloth and linen cloth to be given to the poor on Maundy Thursday, which this merchant of Stafford could not furnish. I told him that I was very glad that he had acquainted me thus far with his mistress' intent, because this matter was strange to me, but did remember that the French Ambassador wrote not long sithence to this Queen, that he would not fail, according to her instructions, to move her Majesty touching her alms, so as it was likely she should hear from him shortly therein. He answered that she might perchance have written to the French Ambassador touching her alms in general, but knows that she made no doubt of her

L

liberty on this point, as a matter which hath not been
denied unto [her] sithence her coming into England. I told
him that the question of her alms in general was decided
by her Majesty the last summer to his mistress' good
satisfaction, and therefore I had cause to think that her
late advertisement to the French Ambassador concerned
her Maundy, which he insisted to deny, concluding that
the Queen his mistress would think herself very hardly
used if she should be restrained herein. I prayed him to
tell me of the manner of the last year's Maundy. He
said that forty-two young maidens had every of them
a yard and a half of woollen cloth, two yards of linen
cloth, and 13*d.* in money, and eighteen little boys, wherein
she had respect to her son, had also every of them a yard
and a half of woollen cloth, two yards of linen cloth, and
13*d.* in money, and that on Good Friday she bestowed
6*l.* among the elder sort of the poor of Tutbury town. I
find that the Priest was the chief minister in this distri-
bution, and that he went from house to house and made
choice of all this poor company at his discretion. It is my
manner to walk in the broad highway, and therefore it
may please you to give me your direction herein. If you
shall think good to continue this custom, it seemeth meet
that the choice [of] poor folks be made by the constable
and other officers of the next parishes adjoining, and that
the money be distributed by them. Phillipps, the carrier,
of [blank], bringeth these letters unto you, who will return
in time convenient for your answer herein, if it shall
so please you.

And thus, &c.

Although you have, perchance, no opinion that among
the great matters here in question between us and our
neighbours, they will vouchsafe so much as to think upon
the little Isle of Jersey, yet it may please you to be a
mean that the poor isles may be remembered as time and

occasion shall require. My son writeth unto me that the drum is stricken up in all the towns of Normandy, and that Monsieur Brisac prepareth to go to the sea. The carrier hath broken his day, wherewith the Scottish people are not pleased, who look for many things from thence; but no doubt he will be there very shortly. This letter cometh now unto you by one of my brother's servants.

In the next he shows that the royal "parsimony" is still on his mind. In this case it is "in matters of State" and not of household expense. Under the terms cóncluded between Elizabeth and James, he was to have had five thousand pounds a year, and Elizabeth would not give him more than four thousand, which made him very angry. Poulet was of course anxious that James should be secured to Elizabeth's interest.

To Sir F. Walsingham, 22 Martii, 1585.

Sir,—I have been much troubled of late with a cold, which I had taken in such extremity as I have been sick with it divers days, and after cast into an ague, but am now in some towardness of recovery. I thank God for it.

I thank you most heartily for the copy of Mr. Randolph's letter,[1] beseeching God to give success to his travail there, whereof there will be no doubt, if we could be removed from our old error of parsimony, a dangerous fault in matters of State, the nature whereof, not unlike to a canker, is plausible enough in his beginning, but payeth surely at the last.

It seemeth that Claude Hamilton is very liberal of his friendship (such as it is), which you can remember he hath offered with many words to this Queen by his sundry letters.[2]

[1] Randolph was Elizabeth's Ambassador to Scotland.

[2] Mary wrote to Lord Claude Hamilton, apparently in July (Vol. xviii., n. 27 ; Labanoff, tom. vi., p. 371) ; but she does not acknowledge the receipt of any letters from him. Amongst the State Papers there are two of much earlier date, from Paris, July 16 and October 8, 1585 (Vol. xvi., nn. 13, 52), and one written long after this time, August 10, 1586 (Vol. xix., n. 31).

This Queen having kept her chamber nine or ten weeks is now delivered of her pain and grief, but not yet able to go or stand, wherewith she is greatly perplexed. Our Scottish churches do now grow to some perfection, first by marrying, and now by christening of Bastian's young child, whose wife was delivered very lately.

As knoweth, &c.

To Sir Francis Walsingham, 28 Martii, 1586.

Sir,—You may see by the great packet sent herewith, that this Queen and her people are at good leisure. Having no other cause of this despatch at this time, it may please you to do me the favour to command one of your servants to deliver these letters inclosed to my Lord Norreys, or to my lady his wife. I trust you have received my letters of the 22nd of this present.

And thus, &c.

Your letters of the 24th of this present came to my hand this last evening, the contents whereof shall be performed in the best sort I may. I thank you heartily for your French and Scottish advertisements.

We here intercalate a holograph letter[1] from the Record Office from Poulet to Phelippes. "Your friend" is Gilbert Gifford, and Poulet has by this time got over his suspicions of his fidelity.

Châteauneuf says that Gifford came to England in December, 1585, and spent all the month of January practising secretly with the Catholics who were favourable to the Queen of Scots, coming from time to time to the Ambassador's house to speak with his secretary, Cordaillot;[2] and that

---

[1] Vol. xvii. n. 45.

[2] "L'ambassadeur de France avait entre les secrétaires un nommé Cordaillot, auquel il avait donné la charge des affaires de la Reine d'Escosse, et celles de ces pauvres Catholiques Anglais réfugiés, pour recevoir leurs lettres, les faire tenir et leur en envoyer la réponse, avec l'argent que leurs parens et amis leur fournissaient" (*Châteauneuf's Memoirs*, Labanoff, tom. vi., p. 281).

when at last he was on his way to Chartley the Ambassador gave him a letter to the Queen written in the cipher with which she used to communicate with his predecessor, De Mauvissière. Châteauneuf is wrong in saying that Gifford spent all January in London, for it was on the 16th that Mary received Morgan's first letter, and she answered it on the following day. Her first letter to Châteauneuf was sent by some other channel, "par aultre voye," as she calls it. Her object was to send him a new cipher. On the 31st of January she re-wrote her former letter, and inclosed it in another which she intrusted to Gifford. It contained this request, "envoyez-moi par ce porteur, tous les paquetz que vous et Chérelles avez entre les mains pour moi, les enferment en une petite boite ou sac de cuir fort." This letter was not delivered at the French Embassy till the 1st of March, N.S. On the 5th of February Gifford placed the packet in Poulet's hands, desiring that it might be sent to Walsingham "with speed," that it might be delivered to the French Ambassador "in convenient time;" and yet for a fortnight it was retained in Walsingham's office for Phelippes' manipulation of the ciphers. There were, Châteauneuf tells us, letters inclosed to be forwarded to the Archbishop of Glasgow, Mary's Ambassador in France.

In consequence of the request of the Queen of Scots, Châteauneuf handed over to Gifford the packets which had been accumulating for two years; and as Gifford said they were too bulky, the packets were opened by him and Cordaillot and made up into smaller bundles,[1] "pour les faire tenir plus aisément et à diverses fois, ainsi que disait le dit Gifford;" the fact being that it was impossible for Phelippes to decipher so many at a time. Gifford told Châteauneuf that as soon as he had sent these letters to Mary, it was his intention to return to France to inform her friends there of what had been done. It is not easy to say whether he really went. On the 23rd of March, Mary received Châteauneuf's letter of the 6th, with five other

---

[1] Mary complained, at the result of the covers being taken off her packets. "Je ne pourroy bien souvent sçavoir les voyes et addresses par qui ilz me seront envoyez et à qui j'en devroys envoyer la response." Labanoff, tom. vi., p. 342.

letters, "tant en chiffre que paquetz." Various packets were
carried by the substitute, who reached Chartley with them on
the 10th. The first was delivered at once. What it contained
we do not know. The second was Châteauneuf's. The consequence of its receipt was "the great packet" sent by Poulet
to Walsingham on the 28th of March. All that we know
of its contents is that there was a letter[1] from Mary to
Châteauneuf, and a letter[2] also from Nau to Chérelles, inclosing letters and a cipher. The third packet Poulet promised
should be delivered "as time will permit, wherein I follow your
instructions." So that Walsingham regulated even the order
in which the letters were to reach Mary's hands.

Phelippes, as we learn from the following letter, forwarded the
next batch within a week, within which time Gifford, who had
been detained in London by Chérelles till the 20th, but was now
at Chartley, had promised Mary a further delivery. The rest
came dropping in all through the month of April. On the 20th
she received a letter from the Bishop of Ross, two from Liggons,
and two from the Spanish Ambassador in Paris, Mendoza. On
the 23rd one from D'Esneval; on the 25th two from Father
Persons, and two from Father Holt; and in the course of
the month five from the Archbishop of Glasgow, two from Sir
Francis Englefield, two from Fuljambe, five from Charles Paget,
"with an infinite number of other letters in cipher," as she
says; and "at divers times, but almost all at once," eight
from Morgan. The deciphering of this mass of letters took
so long a time, that when she came to answer Morgan on the
20th of May, she had only yet been able to have three out of
Morgan's eight deciphered for her. As Mary's letters of the 20th
of May were ready for despatch, she received one more from
Paget and four others from Morgan. Gifford did not remain
all this time at Chartley. Towards the end of March, says
Châteauneuf—it must really have been the middle of April—
he went over into France, and made two or three voyages to
and fro without remaining long at a time either in Paris or
London, up to the end of July. Here we may leave him for
the present.

---

[1] Vol. xvii., n. 36 ; Labanoff, tom. vi., p. 261.　　[2] Vol. xvii., n. 39.

But the evidence afforded by these dates is the confutation of an important theory of Mr. Froude's. He very elaborately maintains[1] that access to Mary's secret correspondence was the only means by which Walsingham could acquire really trustworthy information. "There was one way, and only one, by which all these questions could be answered. The Queen of Scots must be again enabled to open a correspondence which she and her friends could believe to be perfectly safe, and her letters and theirs must be passed through the hands of Walsingham.". . . "One letter or one packet would not be enough. What Walsingham wanted was a, sustained, varied correspondence with many persons, protracted for an indefinite time—with the Pope, with Philip, with her son, with the Archbishop of Glasgow, with Guise, Mendoza, and the English refugees.". . . "The first prize was an accumulation of ciphers from Morgan, Paget, Père la Rue, and the Archbishop of Glasgow, which had been lying at the French Embassy unforwarded for want of opportunity." Such is Mr. Froude's theory, and it is intended for a defence of Walsingham's plot on the plea of political necessity. But it will not bear comparison with the facts. Elizabeth's Minister had brought his spy system to such high perfection, and letters were so frequently intercepted, or drawn by treachery from their unconscious writers, that Walsingham was in possession of the fullest information. The secret correspondence of the King of Spain and of Mendoza found its way into the Secretary's office;[2] the French Ambassador's letters were intercepted:[3] and if such sources of information were not sufficiently regular, in addition to the reports of numberless spies, Phelippes carried on for years a systematic correspondence himself, in the name of an imaginary person, with Hugh Owen, the agent of Philip's Government,[4] and by Barnes and others with Charles Paget at Paris, while offers from treacherous or pretended Catholics are not wanting to maintain similar intercourse with leading Catholics on the

[1] *History*, vol. xii., pp. 106, 108, 120.
[2] *Cotton MSS.*, Calig., C. ix., f. 568.
[3] Vol. xix., n. 80 ; *Dom. Eliz.*, vol. cxcvii., n. 11.
[4] *Dom. James I.*, vol. xx., n. 57.

Continent for Walsingham's information.[1] As for Mary herself, not only had her secret correspondence through the French Ambassador been regularly sold to Walsingham by Chérelles, but her action in Scottish affairs and the whole State policy of her son were systematically betrayed through the Master of Gray, the notorious Archibald Douglas, and the less conspicuous traitor, Fowler. Walsingham had at will, therefore, precisely what Mr. Froude maintains he contrived the plot solely to obtain, "a sustained, varied correspondence with many persons, protracted for an indefinite time."

Now, with such facts before us, we find with no surprise that Walsingham, holding in his hands an order from Mary, the delivery of which would have made him the possessor of "the first prize," by which "the very inmost secrets of the Catholic confederacy were to be open for his inspection," allowed a fortnight pass without making any use of the talisman he held. Let it be understood that he knew quite well that her letters would not furnish evidence on which she could be condemned, that the Babington conspiracy was not yet matured, and that his main object was to implicate Mary in some way that might serve as a pretext for her death, and there is no difficulty in the fact that the perusal of her correspondence was a matter of secondary importance to Walsingham.

---

[1] Thomas Rogers (*alias* Nicholas Berden) to Walsingham, March, 1586. States the names of parties abroad by whom he was procured to come home, viz., Charles Paget, Charles Arundell, Stephen Brynkley, Godfrey Foulgiam, and Thomas Fitzharberd, to receive and deliver their letters, and to transmit intelligence to them from England. States the purport of the letters in his portmanteau. The designs of Spain. Proposes a system of secret correspondence with the above parties. From Paget he should receive letters from the lord his brother, Throgmorton, and others; from Arundell letters of Sir Francis Englefyld; from Brynkley the whole affairs of Allen and Parsons; from Foulgiam the affairs of the Queen of Scots, and from Fitzharberd the devices of the Queen Mother. Proposes to keep up an entire correspondence with all the parties, for the avowed purpose of communicating it to Walsingham. *Endorsed by Phelippes*—"From Berden to Mr. Secretary Walsingham, the accompt of his employment putt uppon him by them beyond the sea." [There can be little doubt this important communication was the basis of the secret intelligence which enabled Walsingham to counteract the designs of Spain, resulting in the destruction of the Spanish Armada. *Mr. Lemon's note in the Calendar.*] (*Dom. Eliz.*, vol. clxxxvii., n. 81.)

Poulet to Phelippes.

Sir,—Your letters arrived here jump with the time appointed between your friend and me, whereof he was not a little glad for his credit sake with his friends of this country. I am very well persuaded of the fidelity of the man. The fruit proveth the goodness of the tree. You shall hear of some further matter by Mr. Secretary. Your friend hath prayed me to convey this letter inclosed unto you. Your friendly letters increase my debt more and more, which shall be acquitted as soon as I may. In this meantime accept my goodwill, I pray you. God bless your labours.

From Chartley, the 1st of April, 1586.

Your assured friend,

A. POULET.

The next letter relates to "our intended Maundy." Its angry conclusion is ominous. Later on, Poulet gives still more vehement expression to his wish to live so long as to see Mary's "damnable Popish wickedness" plucked up by the roots. The letter is in the Record Office,[1] but in the Calendar it is misdated April 1.

To Sir Francis Walsingham, 10 Aprilis, 1586.

Sir,—It fell out very happily that the merchant was not yet come with the cloth and linen for our intended Maundy, when your letters to that purpose of the 24th of the last were delivered the 27th of the same. Where-upon I sent for Curle, who is the only merchant and dealer in such things, and declared unto him that according to the former speech between him and me, I had advertised his mistress' determination touching her Maundy, but had received no answer for my warrant therein, which perchance I might do before the day of that ceremony, whereof I thought good to give him to understand, to the end he might forbear to provide the cloth and linen for

[1] Vol. xvii., n. 46.

that purpose, or at the least, to indent with the merchant to take his ware again, in case I received no direction from you in convenient time.

Curle said he knew his mistress would not fail to provide the cloth and linen, and if she did not bestow it this way, she would employ it to some other use. I told him that for my discharge in honesty towards his mistress, I thought good to give him this advertisement, referring her for the rest to her own consideration. The 30th of the last, Curle cometh unto me to know if I had received any direction touching the Maundy. I told him that I had heard from you the day next before, as indeed I had by Mr. Phelippes, but without any mention of the matter in question. It is no innovation, saith he, that is desired, but only their continuance of the former course, which I might allow without any further warrant. I prayed him to consider that the matter was new to me, and that I might not permit it without special direction, and the less because I had prayed satisfaction therein. He answered that his mistress would think herself very hardly used, and that the denial hereof tended to no other end than to deprive her of all regal dignity, as he called it. I wished him to give it a more reasonable interpretation, and to impute it to your vast charge in this busy time, wherein matters of greater weight are forgotten sometimes. He insisted to persuade me with many words, and with proffer of new conditions, to satisfy his mistress' request, which I refused, and so we departed in more quiet than I expected. Immediately after the departure of Curle from me, the broadcloths provided for this Maundy were carried through the hall to this Queen's chamber, and the same brought back again in remnants, as it should have served if the Maundy had holden.[1] Chérelles hath sent to this

---

[1] In the "inventory of the jewels, &c., found in the custody of the several servants of the late Queen of Scots," there appears "Certain cloth bought at Chartley for her intended Maundy," in the custody of Robert Mooreton, one of the tailors of her wardrobe (Vol. xxi., n. 20, I. ; Labanoff, tom. vii., p. 272).

Queen by the carrier, by your permission, as he writeth, a box full of abominable trash, as beads of all sort, pictures in silk of all sorts, with some *Agnus Dei*, &c. I was far more willing to have burnt it than to permit it to be delivered. I am a near neighbour to much damnable wickedness, trusting to live so long to see it plucked up by the roots.

And thus, &c.

On the following day Poulet wrote the same letter both to Burghley and Walsingham,[1] respecting his expénses.

To my Lord Treasurer, 11th of April, 1586.

My very good Lord,—Mr. Darrell cometh herewith unto your lordship to account with your lordship for the household defrayments here from the time of my first entrance into this service. And although the expenses shall appear to be great, yet when the occasions moving the same shall be duly considered, I trust both he and I shall be excused, wherein I make mention of myself, not that I think that I am any way answerable for the same, but that I can be content to join with Mr. Darrell herein, because he hath acquainted me with all his doings from time to time, and hath used my poor advice upon all occasions occurring. For myself, I may affirm that I have always wanted of the number of the men and horses allowed unto me. I have taken away all kind of fees from all the officers of this household, which amounted to a round sum by the year. I have cut off some unnecessary officers, and thereby saved both their diet and their wages. The diet for her Majesty's family here hath been very temperate. This Queen before my coming and some time after, had upon the fish days twenty-four dishes at every meal for her whole family, which I reduced to twenty. Finally, I may say truly, and I say it before God, that I have had as great care to moderate her Majesty's charge as if the money had issued out of my own purse, and have made it a matter of consideration to myself to avoid all spoils and wilful wastes.

Touching Mr. Darrell, I must confess that I have been an eye-witness of his painful and diligent service, and do verily believe that his dealing hath been just and faithful. The occasion moving the large expense may partly appear by this bill inclosed,[1] but your lordship shall be best

[1] *A conference between the prices paid for victuals at the beginning of this year at Tutbury, and the prices now paid at Chartley in this month of April.*

	Tutbury.	Chartley.
Wheat of great measure	2*s.* 6*d.* bush.	6*s.* bush.
Beer	33*s.* 4*d.* tun.	40*s.* tun.
Ale	7*d.* gall.	10*d.* gall.
Gascon wine	14*l.* tun.	18*l.* 10*s.* tun.
Sack	11*l.* butt.	13*l.* 6*s.* 8*d.* butt.
Beef	3*l.* 12*d.* carc.	5*l.* 12*d.* carc.,
Mutton	4*s.* 6*d.* c.	7*s.* carc.
Veal	6*s.* 5*d.* c.	9*s.* c.
Lamb	2*s.* 6*d.* c.	3*s.* 9*d.* c.
Pork	8*s.* pec.	9*s.* pec.
Lard	6*d.* lb.	8*d.* lb.
Pigs	8*d.* pec.	14*d.* pec.
Capons	14*d.* pec.	18*d.* pec.
Chickens	2*d.* pec.	3*d. ob.* pec.
Pigeons	16*d.* doz.	22*d.* doz.
Hay	6*s.* 8*d.* carr.	10*s.* carr.
Oats	6*s.* qrtr.	9*s.* 4*d.* carr.

Poultry
Freshwater fish
Sea fish   } increased exceedingly.
Spices

(Vol. xvii., n. 48, I.).

Certain abridgments used in household causes at Tutbury Castle and Chartley, for bringing down of the household charges there, since the government of Sir Amias Poulet.

First there was abridged from the Governor's servants sitting in the hall two livery messes of meat before served.

The diet of this Queen's laundresses is now furnished out of their general proportion, and so the charges of it clearly saved to her Majesty.

All fees that may be used in any service are generally taken away. And the ordinary messes, as well of the Governor's own table as the rest, are now furnished with them instead of other dishes of charge.

The two messes of meat served to the steward and porters are now less than before by eight dishes every day.

informed therein by the report of the said bearer. The continual want of money hath been prejudicial to this service, and it may be affirmed that a store of money beforehand would be profitable to her Majesty. I received at London 1,000*l.* for this service, which were spent before my coming hither, so as I found this household in debt to the sum of 24*l.*, and it is very true that Mr. Darrell hath been indebted to the purveyors continually from week to week sithence my coming hither, which is neither ho[nourable] nor profitable to her Majesty. It may please your lordship to be a mean to her Majesty that this household may be better provided of money hereafter, and that we may be always assured of a new supply before the old store be spent.

Poulet then says that Mary's servants are unreasonable in their complaints, and begs that Mr. Darrell may be sent back again, as "it is no small advantage to the Governor here to have a master of household that is sound in religion and upright in duty towards our Queen his mistress, and will not be carried away with the flattery of this people." He asks Lord Burghley's help "for the trial of her Majesty's title to certain lands granted unto me by her Highness among other things for

The dishes of most kinds of meat are much less now than before.

There is saved in wages by the discharging of divers household ministers, by estimation about 30*l. per ann.*

Certain causes of surcharge, more now than in times past.

The general increase of prices in all kinds of provisions, as may appear by the particularities written on the other side.

The loss, as well of hay as of grass, by reason of the great floods which were this summer, both in the grounds reserved at Burton, as in certain other grounds hired about Tutbury.

The charges of fuel much increased to her Majesty by reason of the great prices paid for carriage thereof at Chartley, which could not be avoided, because the contribution made by Sir Ralph Sadler was not expired before the 20th of February.

The charge of the remove, as well in carriages as in preparations at Chartley, and other losses growing by that occasion.

The continual want of money, so as nothing could be provided beforehand, whereby much money might have been saved in this time of dearth (Vol. xvii., n. 49).

the term of forty years." And in a postscript to Walsingham he
returns to the linen, "because this Queen occupieth her best
linen of damask work every day," and winds up with the contents
of Mary's packet of letters.

In the next letter some of Lord Paget's Catholic servants get
into trouble.

To Sir F. Walsingham, 17 Aprilis, 1586.

Sir,—Yesterday Mr. Richard Bagot cometh hither to
me, requested thereunto by the Dean [of] Lichfield and
others the Justices and officers of that city, to acquaint
me with the examination taken by them of a convicted
prisoner remaining in the gaol there, who accuseth Ensor
and Bold, late servants to the Lord Paget, of some things
to have been done by them against her Majesty's Crown
and State. This examination was not signed by the
Justices and officers when it came to my hands, as also the
same had been taken nine days before, and therefore I
returned it unto them, advising them by Mr. Bagot to
discharge their duties in giving you advertisement thereof,
and notwithstanding, for my better discharge, have thought
good to give you to understand of my knowledge herein,
which I do the rather because these men are accused to
have been employed in bad offices for this Queen under
my charge. I leave the accuser and the parties accused to
their trial. But it is too true that divers of the better
calling of the late servants of the Lord Paget's are ill
affected in religion, come seldom to the church, and that
for fashion's sake only, and come not to the communion
at all.

And thus, &c.

To my Lord Admiral, 7° Aprilis, 1586.

My very good Lord,—This tickle and dangerous time
will give me occasion to send often to Jersey with speed
and upon short warning; to which purpose it shall be
meet for me to be always assured of ready passage. I

shall therefore most humbly pray your lordship to give me your warrant for a barque called "the Edward," of the burthen of twenty tons, belonging to the port of Lyme, where Edward Lymberye, owner of the said barque, dwelleth, and that by virtue of your lordship's said warrant, the said barque, being discharged of all arrests and other services, may be always in readiness to be employed by my direction for her Majesty's service for Jersey upon all occasions occurring.

This small barque is fitter for this purpose than a ship of greater burthen, the owner and master of the said ship having haunted those isles many years, and therefore well acquainted with those coasts. I presume of the continuance of your lordship's good favour towards me, which I will be always ready and willing to deserve in that I may ; and therefore do trust that your lordship will not refuse me in this small suit, tending to the furtherance of her Majesty's service, without any private benefit to myself.

And thus, &c.

Two letters addressed to Walsingham on the 25th April and the 5th of May are among the State Papers.[1] Of these the first begins thus, "Having not seen this Queen sithence the departure of Chérelles, which I impute either to her great writing business, or that she would not discover her lameness, she prayed me the 21st of this present, after noon, to repair unto her, whom I found sitting upon the side of her bed, and not yet able to use her feet."

Mary complained of Elizabeth's delay in not receiving the French Ambassador, M. de Châteauneuf, the successor of M. de Mauvissière, "which she thought to be delayed of purpose to hinder her causes. I told her that the French Ambassador, by his last letters unto her, was better satisfied herein, acknowledging that the deferring of his audience had no other ground than her Majesty's indisposition by reason of a rheum. 'Yea,' saith she, 'this was an excuse to delay the audience.' 'What can her

---

[1] Vol. xvii., nn. 57, 62.

Majesty,' quoth I, 'win or lose thereby, when of ordinary course
the audience cannot be denied any long time?' She answered
that perchance her Majesty would not be willing to hear of the
French causes at this time, finding the King to be resolute in
this action. I said that I thought her Highness would be the
more willing to hear the French Ambassador, as her best mean
to be truly informed of his master's disposition towards her son.
Other speeches passed between her and me touching the French
troubles, wherein we differ in opinion very much, and I have
many times heretofore delivered my mind so plainly unto her
in the like causes as she taketh no great pleasure to confer
with me therein. She insisted so slenderly upon all these
things as I might well perceive the cause of her sending for
me was yet behind, as indeed it was."

The subject Mary had in her mind was Bessie Pierrepont,
the niece of Henry Cavendish, now seventeen years old, who
had "been with her from her infancy, and in all this time used
no other bed or board than her own," but who she thought ought
now to leave her. The name of this young lady occurs frequently
in the subsequent corespondence. On the 13th of June[1] her
father sent some of his servants to conduct his daughter to him
at Holbeck Woodhouse, but the Queen was then unwilling to
let her go. Elizabeth expressed her surprise at this change in
a letter to Sir Amias,[2] which however is endorsed "Not sent."
At the end of July,[3] Mary renews her request through the French
Ambassador. Poulet was puzzled at the wish,[4] and advised that
she should be removed suddenly. The fact is that Nau, the
Queen's Secretary, was in love with the young lady,[5] and was
prosecuting his suit with her father through Chérelles. Mary
did not approve, and thought that she would be safest under
her father's roof,[6] "pour plusieurs respects, mesmement pour

---

[1] Vol. xviii., n. 7.
[2] *Ibid*, n. 26.
[3] Vol. xix., n. 15.
[4] Vol. xviii., n. 3.
[5] Vol. xvii., nn. 27, 34, 35; vol. xxi., n. 17.
[6] "Se traitait le dit mariage secrètement entre le dit Nau et la dite fille,
contre la volonté de la Reine d'Escosse leur maîtresse" (*Châteauneuf's Memoir*
Labanoff, tom. vi., p. 283).

rayson de sa grande mère," [1] the Countess of Shrewsbury;
though when the time came for her removal the Queen found
it difficult to part with her, for "she could not deny that she
loved the young gentlewoman very well, and if it might stand
with her benefit would be glad of her continuance with her all
the days of her life." Poulet suspected that Nau desired to
marry the young lady, and says of it, "The invention is so gross
in my simple opinion as they are likely to be taken in their own
snare." Mary speaks openly about her in her last letter to
Morgan.[2] "Show me what you do mean in your last by
advising me to ask Sir Gervase Clifton's consent in bestowing
of Bess Pierrepont, whom I have never sought to bestow in
marriage on any, neither before nor since I caused the same to
be propounded, at the Countess of Shrewsbury's solicitation, and
by her means to the Lord Percy, now Earl of Northumberland,
whereof I think you have heard, nor have had any intention for
any other, but rather contrariwise have suited by the Queen of
England's licence this half year and more to be rid of her, by
reason she is now at her best, brought up my bedfellow and
at board, ever sithence she had four years of age, so carefully
and virtuously, I trust, as if she had been my own daughter,
and, failing of my own means, accordingly to have her preferred
that her own parents, for discharge of my conscience and my
honourable using of her, might relieve me of her loss of time
and other inconveniences, after that I had offered her as a
piece of my nourriture (to do her honour) to serve about the
Queen of England; which is not granted, but yet on a sudden
they would have had her from me, which I could not yield unto,
for that such honest furniture as then I had in hand for her
departure was not yet ready, as she and it both are now for
an hour's warning. But to be plain, I would be the rather quit
of her, for that I see too much of her grandmother's nature in
her behaviour every way, notwithstanding all my pains for the
contrary, and therefore now would be sorry to have her bestowed
upon any man that I wish good unto."

[1] Vol. xvii., n. 76; Labanoff, tom. vi., p. 344.
[2] Vol. xviii., n. 74; Labanoff, tom. vi., p. 424.

M

The great "linen" question came to an end at last, for the closing sentence of this letter of April 25th is, "The bed and linen provided for this Queen was brought hither by the carrier the 22nd of this present, and was well accepted."

On the 5th of May, Poulet wrote two letters to Walsingham. From the first[1] we learn that Elizabeth at length allowed them a more liberal supply of money. This is Poulet's "domestical success."

To Mr. Secretary, 5° Maii, 1586.

Sir,—Like as your foreign advertisements mentioned in your last letters were very welcome because they contained matter full of honour and profit, so you may believe that I was not a little comforted to hear of the good success of our domestical causes, and that her Majesty had yielded to yield a warrant dormant, which I impute to your friendly furtherance, and although the profit thereof shall redound to her Majesty, yet having tasted to my great grief of the slander and discredit which have grown to this house through want of money, I think myself beholden unto you for it, as for an especial good turn, and as much as I can I thank you for it.

It is very true that I was informed by a gentleman belonging to a nobleman and a councillor that himself and many others above have been credibly informed that I enjoyed the Lord Paget's demesne, grounds, and parks here to my own use, and for his part did confess that he had so reported of me, as many others had done the like to his knowledge, praying me to excuse his fault as done of ignorance.

I say unto you before God that I never received benefit of anything belonging to the Lord Paget to the value of one penny. Whereof I prayed Mr. Darrell to inform you, as one willing to remove from you this opinion, if haply you had received it upon sinister information.

[1] Vol. xvii., n. 62.

I was advised by a friend better acquainted with the state of this country than myself to desire the stewardship of the Lord Paget's lands in this shire, thereby to have the tenants the more at commandment upon all occasions of service occurring, and to keep them in the better obedience to her Majesty's laws and proceedings in matter of religion, wherein they had been greatly seduced by the Lord Paget and his ministers. This stewardship I have from my Lord Treasurer with a fee of 40*s*. by the year, whereof as yet I have received nothing, and this all the profit which I have made of the Lord Paget's lands, although I may say truly that the late Lord Paget's tenants are somewhat reformed sithence my coming to this stewardship.

Poulet then says that five or six of the Scottish Queen's retinue were sick of a tertian ague, "of which number Curle's servant is one." Curle, therefore, begging that another might be provided, "I asked where he would find this maiden-servant, wherein he referred himself to my choice, or would be content with a young woman in Tutbury, god-daughter to this Queen, if I could like of it. I have no great opinion that (as things go in France at this present) the supply of servants desired by this Queen will be yielded unto, and therefore it were not amiss, in my simple opinion, that this one servant were admitted, which would greatly satisfy their discon[ten]ted minds. A woman of her quality cannot be dangerous if the matter be so carried as she be brought hither before she know the cause of her coming; and here I would wish it might be lawful for me to indent with her that she should resort twice or thrice at the least in every week at our sermons and prayers, which may perchance restrain them from alluring her to their idolatrous service. . . .

"I have kept this Queen fasting from all sort of news, good or bad, ever sithence I was so loudly belied upon the advertisement which I gave of the last alteration in Scotland, which they spared not to write to have been delivered by direction from above, and I know by good mean that this Queen pretendeth to be grieved that she cannot hear how the world goeth, and I would

M 2

believe she were so if I did not think that she had secret means to be advertised thereof."

This letter keeps alive our compassion for Lord Paget's poor Catholic tenants, who must have groaned under their new steward, as the next letter pretty plainly shows us. That the "advertisement of the last alteration in Scotland" was made to the Queen of Scots by order "from above" is more than likely, for on the 7th December, Sir Francis Walsingham instructed Poulet "to show a certain letter to the Queen of Scots in regard to the present alteration in Scotland, *and to note carefully the speeches she shall use on perusing the same.*"[1] If this is the "advertisement" Poulet alludes to in May, he kept his captive "fasting from all sort of news, good or bad," for a long time. His allusion to her "secret means" of receiving news is curious, and it is as plainly expressed as it could be without betraying what was going on to his Secretary.

The following, which is entered in the letter-book as a separate letter, was despatched as part of the foregoing.

To Mr. Secretary, eodem die [5°] *Maii,* 1586.

Sir,—Following the direction of the Lords of her Majesty's Council signified by your letters of the 26th of the last, touching the confessions sent unto you from Lichfield, I failed not, immediately upon the receipt of your said letters, to cause the houses of the parties suspected to be searched by some of my servants of honest credit, and with Mr. Richard Bagot's assistance took the examinations of John Godwyn, Robert Taylor, and Bryan Bold, Richard Ensor being departed towards London before my letters came to my hands, forbearing to send the said examinations unto you until Richard Ensor hath also been examined. By these searches and examinations it falleth out that the marriage of Robert Taylor, servant to Richard Ensor, at a Mass six years past, or thereabouts, is confessed by himself, and that sithence that time he hath not presented himself to the

[1] Vol. xvi., n. 72.

communion, as also that Richard Ensor's study was found furnished with Popish books of all kinds, whereof my servants the searchers brought hither with them thirteen, besides a good number which they left remaining there, praying to be advertised from you what you will have done with these books. No other thing contained in the accusation yet is proved. The Priest which married the said Taylor is called by the name of Barloe, and hath been heretofore in the Marshalsea, and now lately hath been committed to the gaol in this shire by the Justices here where he now remaineth.

And thus, &c.

In the next letter,[1] the Priest reappears in a very curious way, showing an inattention that we should hardly have expected in Walsingham. Perhaps he did not know that " Camille " was the same person as " Du Préau," whom Poulet has frequently mentioned as Mary's chaplain. Or perhaps he knew it was the Priest of whom he was writing, and not being willing to recognize his existence, even in writing to Poulet, calls him, out of contempt, the *valet de chambre.*

To Sir Francis Walsingham, 12 Maii, 1586.

Sir,—Whereas by your direction John Magale, Frenchman, hath been permitted to have speech with one Camillo, whom in your letters you term *valet de chambre,* the truth is that the said Camillo, surnamed Du Préau, is the Massing Priest of whom I have heretofore advertised you. This Magale had conference with him in my presence and hearing, not above half an hour, the chief cause of his coming being a matter of debt, wherein Préau hath dealt very liberally, and, as I may say, brotherly with him, and I am greatly deceived if he be not indeed his brother, resembling him in countenance very much, which is also to be gathered by other circumstances.

Although for his [sake] I would not have troubled the

---

[1] Vol. xvii., n. 66.

post at this time with so slender matter, but that my Lord Treasurer requireth my opinion with speed by what mean her Majesty's charges of household here may be diminished, and what superfluous persons in this family may conveniently be spared, whereof he would be advertised before the return hither of Mr. Darrell. It is not my place to give orders, but to obey such as shall be prescribed unto me, and therefore my opinion herein is soon given.

And thus, &c.

It is ingenious in Poulet to discover in Elizabeth's desire for the reduction of their expenditure, a reason for getting rid of the Priest, in order to put a stop to the christenings and marryings.

To my Lord Treasurer, eodem die, [12] *May,* 1586.

My very good Lord,—Your lordship's of the 2nd of this present came to my hands the 9th of the same. And as I think myself much beholden to your lordship for your favourable endeavour to satisfy her Majesty touching Mr. Darrell's accounts for the expenses of the family, so for my part I can say no more therein than hath been already delivered by your lordship, and it is so far off that I can promise the lessening of the said charges, as I may assure your lordship that it will be increased if the general dearth do continue.

The diet of this household and the other defrayments incident to the same, are so certain and ordinary as there can be no great abuse therein, and order was taken before my coming to reduce the same to a certainty, which was then rated at 3,000*l.*[1] by the year, and I know that Sir Ralph Sadler's[2] expenditure during his being in this

---

[1] It is not clear in the manuscript whether it is iijM*li.* or iiijM*li.*, that is 3,000*l.* or 4,000*l.* The warrant for the Queen of Scots' diets, granted April 23, is for a sum not exceeding 3,600*l.* a year (*Cotton. MSS.*, Calig., C. ix., f. 23).

[2] Sadler tells Walsingham, January 13, 1585, that 70*l.* a week is set down for the Queen's diet (Vol. xv., n. 19).

charge did far exceed that rate.[1] I think the Earl of

[1] *A brief of the account of Marmaduke Darrell, gent., for all such sums of money as he hath received towards the household defrayments of the Scottish Queen and her family at Tutbury Castle and Chartley, between the last day of April, 1585, and the 3rd day of April, 1586, following, viz.:*

Received by virtue of a Privy Seal, out of the receipt of the Exchequer and by the hands of certain collectors of the subsidy, within the time of this account ... ... 1,000*l.*

Received of Richard Bagot, esquire, out of the profit growing to her Majesty of certain iron works, late the Lord Paget's, within the time of this account ... ... 1,610*l.*

Received of Sir Amias Poulet, for the rent of certain grounds, tithes, and parks, late also the Lord Paget's, due for one whole year ended at our Lady Day next ... 358*l.* 12*s.* 8*d.*

Received more of his honour, which he hath lent towards these household defrayments at sundry times ... ... 350*l.*

And received for the hides and tallow of beeves, muttons, &c., and for certain household provisions sold upon especial causes within the time of this account, as may appear ... ... 121*l.* 19*s.*

Sum. 3,440*l.* 11*s.* 8*d.*

Against the which there hath been discharged which was owing upon the last former account, ended the said last day of April, 1585 ... ... 20*l.* 17*d.*

And there hath grown due within the time of this account for victuals, necessaries, wage, and other household charges, as may particularly appear ... ... 3,618*l.* 6*s.* 9*d.*

Sum. 3,638*l.* 8*s.* 2*d.*

Remaineth owing to the country upon this account, ending the 2nd of April ... ... 197*l.* 16*s.* 6*d.*

A brief of the expenses within the time aforesaid.

There did remain in victuals and other provisions at the beginning of this account, the 1st day of May ... ... 258*l.* 11*s.* 2*d.*

And there hath been disbursed within the time of this account in household defrayments, as before appeareth 3,618*l.* 6*s.* 9*d.*

Sum. 3,876*l.* 17*s.* 11*d.*

Towards the which

There hath been returned to her Majesty for hides, tallow, and certain household provisions sold within this time ... 121*l.* 19*s.*

And there doth remain in divers kinds of victual at the end of this account, the 2nd of April ... ... 103*l.* 2*s.* 3*d.*

Sum. 225*l.* 15*d.*

And so

Appeareth to have been clearly expended within the time of this account ... ... 3,651*l.* 16*s.* 8*d.*

In diet	2,599*l.* 3*s.* 2*d.*
In necessaries, &c.	290*l.* 13*s.* 7*d.*
In hire of labourers	51*l.* 13*s.* 7*d.*
In household wage	85*l.* 4*s.* 2*d.*
In soldiers' and posts' wage ...	393*l.* 10*s.*
And in foreign payments ...	230*l.* 12*s.* 2*d.* (Vol. xvii., n. 50).

Shrewsbury will not confess that his bargain was profitable unto him when he had 1,500*l.* for this Queen's diet, yet it may be affirmed that his lordship might better do it with 1,500*l.* than her Majesty with a double sum, which may be proved by many reasons not unknown to your lordship, and therefore I forbear to make mention of them.

And whereas it is thought that the number of persons, as well in this Queen's family as of those of my company is over great and superfluous, and that the discharge of some of them might shorten the charges, wherein it pleaseth your lordship to require my opinion with speed, Mr. Darrell can inform your lordship of all the particular names of this Queen's family,[1] with the qualities and conditions of their service, referring the allowing or disallowing of them to her Majesty's good pleasure, only I will say that as long as her Highness shall allow a Sir John

[1] *The names and offices of such persons as do attend upon the Scottish Queen.*

Mr. Nawe, Seretary.	
Mr. Melvin, Mr. of the Household.	
Mr. Curle, Mr. of the Horse.	
Mr. Burbon, physician.	
Mr. Prewe, reader.	
Every of them a servant.	
The apothecary.	
The surgeon.	
The embroiderer.	
Four grooms of her chamber.	} 35
Two yeomen of her pantry.	
Two yeomen of her warder.	
Two cooks.	
A pastelar.	
Four turn-broches.	
Four grooms of her stable.	
Bastian's son.	
Two others.	

Mrs. Pearpointe.	
Mrs. Bewregarde.	
Mr. Curle's wife.	
Mr. Curle's sister.	
Mrs. Mowbraye.	
Mrs. Camdaye.	} 16
Mrs. Bastian.	
Her two daughters.	
Two English Sisters.	
Mrs. Curle's woman.	
Mrs. Perpoint's woman.	
Her three laundresses.	

The whole number of the Queen's people } 51

The Governor's forty servants.
The Mr. of the Household and two servants.
Thirty soldiers in garrison.
Three posts. } 76

The number of both families. } 127   (Vol. xvii., n. 53).

in this house, and that there is christening and marrying among them, there will be no want of unprofitable servants.

There are two or three old men which are entertained especially in respect of their service past. The younger sort, by reason of this Queen's infirmity, have no doubt their hands full, which I may not deny unless I will be careless of her Majesty's honour, and also deal uncharitably with those who are afflicted with sickness. I do not account Mrs. Pierrepont or her maid of this number, who are not used or intreated as servants.

Touching my company, I may affirm that I have been very careful to keep myself within the compass of the number prescribed unto me, which was rated at forty servants and thirty horses, wherein I have been the more curious to make satisfaction, in part for her Majesty's gracious favour in permitting my wife to be here with me, although I may say truly that her oversight in the kitchen and other offices of this household is not unprofitable.

Divers of my said forty servants are placed in offices, as kitchen, cellar, buttery, pantry, &c., having nevertheless their wages and liveries of me, and if I looked no farther than to myself and to the service of my own person, I might spare some others and might save the wages and liveries, but the strength of this house consisting only in the serving[-men], the soldiers taking their diet and lodging always out of the house, I think no man of any discretion will take upon him to answer for this great Scottish family with a less guard than of forty serving-men, and indeed might be in danger to have his throat cut and to lose his charge, if his own company were not stronger than the Scottish retinue. Thus having delivered unto your lordship all that I know or think in this matter, I will conclude with this assertion, that if I have honesty, truth, or conscience in me, I have been more niggardly in this charge than ever I was in my own house.

As knoweth, &c.

Fearing the malice of evil tongues, I thought good to acquaint your lordship that I have had here with me, the better part of this last year, one of my sons and his servant, for whom I have spared so many of the number of my ordinary servants prescribed unto me, and as they have not been more chargeable to her Majesty than two common servants should have been, so I may say truly, that my son hath done me very good service in this place.

Also, I have here with me a young gentlewoman, a ward, of my own name, whom I bought of my Lord Audley for my said son, and having procured her coming hither, to try how my son and she could like one of the other, it is now resolved that at the next Whitsuntide they shall be married, by the grace of God, and within four days after, I intend to send them into the west parts, where they shall remain, meaning nothing less than to keep any married folks in her Majesty's family here.

Moreover, by reason of your lordship's little god-daughter, and my little jewel, her nurse hath been here sithence my coming, but the child being weaned, the nurse departeth this Whitsuntide. Thus, for fear of some whispering and undermining harm, although I trust your lordship will not be hasty to condemn me upon report, I have thought good to lay open these trifles unto your lordship, which I call trifles, because, all the foresaid persons being put in reckoning, it shall be found that I have wanted of my prescribed number, so as her Majesty hath not been charged by this occasion.

The letter to Walsingham of May 22,[1] begins with an interview between Nau and his brother's servant, Boulenger, at which the only matter of any consequence was Nau's assertion, " which he uttered with passion, redoubling his speeches, that the Queen his mistress was neither *hydroppique,* nor *cancresse* in her legs, *ny malade a la mort* (I use his own words), as had been given forth

[1] Vol. xvii., n. 81.

by some who perhaps wish the same, but that she increased in health and strength daily, hoping to see her perfectly recovered in time, to the comfort of all her good friends."

Apparently, Poulet was afraid that some letters were received by Mary that did not pass through his hands, for in the following passage he can hardly refer to those that came by Gifford and the Burton brewer, all of which he said: "Nau, in his speech with me after the departure of his brother's servant, asked if I had received the French Ambassador's letter of the 7th of this present. I answered, No. Then he prayed me to put you in remembrance of them. I told him that the French Ambassador's letters made mention of another packet of the 14th of the last, which he said he did not remember. It is to be feared lest this packet hath been delivered by some secret mean, because Nau taketh no pleasure to hear of it, and if it be so, then the French Ambassador hath forgotten himself, to make mention of this packet in his open letters."

Mary's singular request, that Elizabeth would take Bessie Pierrepont into her own service was not forgotten. "The Ambassador's wife writeth also to this Queen, that she will not fail to solicit her Majesty touching Pierrepont, and will follow the matter with all diligence."

Lastly, Poulet forwards, together with Nau's letters, "another packet of letters from the Priest here to the Frenchman lately sent hither unto him to be delivered unto the French Ambassador."

In an autograph postcript Poulet adds, referring evidently to Mary's secret letters dated May 18 and 20, which were very numerous,[1] "I have been prayed by a friend of mine to convey unto you this packet inclosed which I received yesterday, and have nothing else to write unto you touching the same, whereof I am nothing sorry, because I assure you my hand is lame at this present, so as I write my name with some difficulty."

The letter-book ends with the following fragment of a letter, showing that the scornful tone of Poulet's last letter about money matters had not induced Elizabeth to pass his accounts.

---

[1] May 18, to the Archbishop of Glasgow, Liggons, the Bishop of Ross; May 20, to Mendoza, Charles Paget, Sir Francis Englefield, and Morgan. Labanoff, tom. vi., p. 294—330.

To my Lord Treasurer, 25th of May, 1586.

My very good Lord,—Understanding by your letters that her Majesty was not pleased with the expenses of this family, and required to be advertised from me how the same might be diminished, I thought good to forbear to make answer to your lordship's letters until the return of Mr. Darrell, because the charge belonging in part unto him. . . .

Between the end of this and the beginning of the last letter-book, there is again a very long interval. Poulet's letters in the Public Record Office are of two sorts. There are his public letters, which series would be more interesting if it contained his report to Elizabeth of the conduct of his charge when forcibly separated from her servants, and his letters to the Lord Treasurer "from day to day" during the transfer to Fotheringay. But besides these, there is another set of letters, also addressed to Walsingham, but unsigned, and altogether in Poulet's own handwriting. These are the letters in which Poulet communicates with Walsingham on the various stages of their plan for entrapping Mary. And it was during this interval that the plot was completed, the evidence prepared, and the Queen of Scots tried and condemned.

The following short letter is interesting, not only on account of the reward bestowed upon Phelippes, the significance of which has already been noticed, but also on account of the reference to Lord Burghley, who is here, and in a subsequent letter from Phelippes to Walsingham, called "the great person." It is plain that Mary thought that Burghley was inclined to be friendly to her, for she wrote to Châteauneuf:[1] "Il n'y auroyt point de mal que en touchassiez un mot à mylord Burghley, mais . . . comme de vous mesmes, . . . sans luy laisser aulcun lieu ou subject de soupçonner que le vent vient d'icy." And to the Archbishop of Glasgow:[2] "Donnez advis de cecy au grand trésorier par l'Ambassadeur Staffort." However, both these were written

---

[1] Vol. xviii., n. 44 ; Labanoff, tom. vi., p. 370.
[2] *Cotton. MSS.*, Nero, B. vi., f. 400 ; Labanoff, tom. vi., p. 382.

later, and are not the letters alluded to by Walsingham. "That packet" we shall probably never see, for Walsingham "saved" it, lest Elizabeth's Minister or "the cause" should suffer. Mary's death was "the cause," and for it Walsingham was ready to do more than suppress Mary's letters.

Walsingham to Phelippes.[1]

Her Majesty hath signed your bill for a pension of an hundred marks, and you will not believe in how good part she accepteth of your service.

I have saved that packet that toucheth the great person, as neither he nor the cause shall take lack. Some warning is to be given to G., and Foxley[2] looketh for an answer. I would be glad to-morrow, in the morning, to see you here. God keep you.

At the Court, the 3rd of May, 1586.

Your loving friend,

FRA. WALSINGHAM.

Addressed—To his (*sic*) servant, Tho. Phelippes.

Endorsed by Phelippes—From Mr. Secretary Walsingham, 3rd May, 1586.

The five following letters are placed together, as they relate to the same subject, and not being dated, it is not easy to decide upon their proper chronological place. For the first the Calendar suggests May. If so it must be very early in the month. Mary wrote a very large number of letters in May, but in April hardly one. The brewer's wife, though "acquainted with the practice," was not apparently acquainted with her husband's double dealing.

Poulet to Walsingham.[3]

The substitute was · at the place appointed the 22nd of the present, when he remained from morning to night,

---

[1] Holograph. Vol. xvii., n. 60.

[2] Foxley is Gratley, the Priest (*Dom. Eliz.*, vol. cxcix., n. 95), who, in concert with Gilbert Gifford, wrote a book against Father Persons and the Jesuits, which book was submitted to Walsingham and Phelippes.

[3] Holograph. Vol. xvii., n. 82.

but the honest man did not appear.   Hereupon, the
substitute sought the honest man the next morning early
at his house at Burton, from whence he was departed
before the coming of the said substitute, to make provision of malt, as his wife affirmed.

The honest man had heretofore declared to the
substitute that if at any time he failed of his promise,
the substitute should repair to his house, where in his
absence his wife should satisfy him in all things, who
was acquainted with the practice.   This woman telleth
the substitute that her husband was advertised from this
Queen his mistress (so she termed her), that her letters
could not be ready until the end of this week now in
hand, and that returning thither after four days, he should
find her husband at home, who would agree with him
upon the time and place of their next meeting.

She told him that her husband had great credit
with this Queen, and that he carried himself so well
as he had no less credit with me, and that I had given
him letters into other shires for provision of malt, as
indeed I had.

She said that this Queen had dealt liberally with
her husband, and that she was bountiful without measure
to all such as deserved well of her.   In all her speech
she called this Queen her husband's mistress.

Endorsed by Phelippes—A note from Sir Amias Poulet.

To Mary the brewer's services were, as she believed, simply
invaluable.   She had no means of knowing when he received
her letters, or how long he kept them.   He could do as he
pleased, excuse himself as he liked, and make his own terms
with her.   This letter does not speak of his extorting money
from her, but it does of his consciousness of his power over
Poulet.   Mr. Froude puts it well when he says,[1] "The brewer was
first paid by Walsingham ; next he was assured of lavish rewards

---

[1] *History*, vol. xii., p. 116.

from the Queen of Scots, which to secure her confidence it was necessary to permit him to receive. Lastly, like a true English scoundrel, he used the possession of a State secret to exact a higher price for his beer." Gifford says that he had " 20*l.* besides many good angels."[1] The 20*l.* probably, and the "many good angels" certainly, came from Mary. How many, no one knew, and Poulet doubted "lest the honest man kept the better part for himself" of the rewards Mary sent to the others through him. Another letter speaks of 10*l.* in money, besides the former rewards. "There was never so fortunate a knave," said Gifford, who was himself a greater knave than he. Gifford extorted money from Morgan,[2] by pretending that the brewer was bribed by him. "He gave him that made the intelligence to your Majesty eight angels, and promised to make it some twenty nobles,[3] which is twenty crowns, which he will never account to your Majesty."

Poulet to Walsingham.[4]

. I have written unto you before this time that the honest man playeth the harlot with this people egregiously, preferring his particular profit and commodity before their service, because he knoweth he can satisfy them with words at his pleasure, and that they cannot control anything that he saith.

The house where he dwelleth is distant from hence only ten miles, and yet I do not remember that he hath delivered at any time any packet unto this Queen until six or seven days after the receipt thereof. He appointeth all places of meeting at his pleasure, wherein he must be obeyed, and hath no other respect than that he may not ride out of his way, or at the least that his travel for this cause may not hinder his own particular business. And therefore having appointed his last meeting within one mile of his own house, with resolution to lodge

---

[1] The angel was about 10*s.*
[2] Vol. xvii., n. 32 ; Murdin, p. 498.
[3] *Noble,* a gold coin worth 6*s.* 8*d.* *Halliwell.*
[4] Holograph. Vol. xvii., n. 83.

there that night, he sendeth thither late in the evening a boy to signify unto the substitute that his business would not permit him to be there that night, praying him to have patience until the next day at ten of the clock, at which time he came indeed and brought with him the last packet which you received from hence.

At his coming he beareth the substitute in hand that he could not have the packet until that morning, whereas in truth he was despatched from hence the day before in the morning. The displeasure which was likely to grow hereof was this, that the said boy whom he used for his messenger, was son to one who is the ordinary carrier to the honest man for his malt, and this carrier is a near neighbour to the substitute, so as the boy knew him as soon as he saw him. The substitute very discreetly dealt so roughly with the honest man for sending unto him a foolish messenger in this manner that he rested satisfied and looked no further into the matter, and indeed if he have wit to consider it, in bewraying the substitute, he shall bewray himself.

It seemeth that the honest man is persuaded that I cannot spare his service, having of late required an increase of price for his beer in unreasonable sort, and yet so peremptorily as I must yield to his asking or lose his service. I think his new mistress and her liberal rewards make him weary of all other service.

That the next letter belongs to May is clear from the mention in it of Whitsuntide. The letter from Curle to Gifford, alluded to by Poulet, has not been preserved. The application for "pensions and I cannot tell what," that frightened Poulet, was probably a petition to Mary, made perhaps to keep up appearances, perhaps because he thought it possible that he might hold it, that he might have the prebend in St. Quintin's, that Morgan had promised[1] him in Mary's name. To Morgan

[1] Vol. xvii., n. 32 ; vol. xviii., n. 13.

Mary answered,[1] "By my next open depesche there shall be sent to you two brevets for prebends, and your man shall be set upon my estate amongst my pensioners." And July 4, Morgan wrote to Gifford under the names of Thomas Germyn to Nicholas Cornelly's,[2] that A. [the Queen of Scots] thanked him for his services, and granted him a prebend.

The "last week's meeting" being "disappointed," means of course that Mary's letters were not ready. Poulet trusted "that yet now at the last some good success would have followed." Upon these words only one construction can be put. Poulet was waiting and hoping from week to week that every packet from Mary would contain "sufficient to hang her," as he puts it elsewhere. He fears this may be frustrated through some warning conveyed by Gifford, who he thinks is bidding too high with the Queen of Scots to be faithful to Walsingham.

Poulet to Walsingham.[3]

Sir,—The last week's meeting was disappointed, and a new day and place set down by the honest man, which was performed yesterday, at which time I trusted that yet now at the last some good success would have followed, although, to say plainly as I think, I have been in great doubt of it ever sithence I received from your friend a letter in cipher from Curle to him, by the which it seemed that his mistress, finding herself pressed to make speedy answer, did forbear when she was before resolved to have written.

Surely I do not mistrust the fidelity of your friend, but I fear lest his young years and want of experience have not been answerable to his goodwill, and that for want of judgment he hath played the wanton in writing to this Queen, which I suspect the rather, because he hath capitulated with her for pensions and I cannot tell what, and perchance to show his forwardness hath bewrayed his indiscretion.

---

[1] Vol. xvii., n. 80; Labanoff, tom. vi., p. 327.
[2] Vol. xviii., n. 31.   [3] Holograph. Vol. xvii., n. 67.

N

I may easily judge of his own several letters unto
me that he wanteth that sufficiency of discretion, which
were requisite in him that hath to deal with so many
fine and subtle heads. His service, no doubt, was very
acceptable to this people in the beginning, and with
temperance his credit towards them would have increased
daily. It may be that all things will come to good pass,
and that I have no cause to write thus largely unto you,
but the suspicion of the contrary is so apparent, as in
my simple opinion I should do wrong to my place if
I did not inform you of it, leaving the same to your
better consideration, and yet resting in some little hope
of better success.

At the yesterday's meeting the honest man told the
substitute that as yet he could get no despatch from this
Queen his mistress, which she hath deferred until Whitsuntide, and hereupon a new meeting is appointed upon
Tuesday in the Whitsun week [May 24, O.S.]. The substitute found himself grieved that he had lingered here in vain
these three weeks for answer, and that his cousin looked
to have seen him at London before this time. The honest
man prayed him with a merry countenance to have
patience, saying that this Queen had sent him word
that she could not send him so good news now as she
hoped to do within these three weeks. (This clause
seemeth to carry some other meaning.) The substitute
concluded that he or his cousin would not fail to keep
the appointed time of meeting.

The packet for this Queen received yesterday from
Mr. Phelippes shall be carried by the substitute to the
honest man's house, having no other means to deliver
the same with such speed as is required. It may be
that this new packet will give new credit to the substitute.

[Not addressed.]

Endorsed—A secret note, *and by Phelippes*—A secret
note from Sir Amias Poulet.

The next letter, it is clear, was written between the 7th and the 17th of May. Gifford was not sent to "assure the honest man," that is, to make trial of him, before the beginning of July. On May $\frac{18}{28}$,[1] Mary acknowledges the receipt of a letter from the Archbishop of Glasgow of the last of March,[2] together with Père de la Rue's[3] of [Nov.] $\frac{14}{24}$.

Poulet to Walsingham.[4]

The packet sent for this Queen was delivered to the honest man at his house the 7th of this present by the substitute, who could not by any mean intreat him to deliver the same here before the 14th ensuing, excusing himself especially for this reason, lest his often going and coming might minister just cause of suspicion. And whereas in my last I signified unto you that the honest man had appointed the Tuesday in the Whitsun week for his next meeting with the substitute, he hath now shortened the time and hath agreed to meet with him the 17th of this instant, so as there is good hope of better success than my last letters did import, the substitute finding the honest man very well satisfied and altogether void of suspicion.

If the substitute shall receive nothing from hence about this Whitsuntide, I am of opinion that it shall be well done to assure the honest man, thereby to know if he have any other vent for his letters.

[Not addressed.]

Endorsed—Advertisement from Sir Amias Poulet.

The brewer was led to believe that he was the only traitor. The consequence was that round-about courses were necessary to preserve the "credit" of the others who were employed. The date of this letter must be the first week in June, and this suits the "short light nights." It is hard to see how, with these

---

[1] Vol. xvii., n. 84 ; Labanoff, tom. vi., p. 295.
[2] Vol. xvii., n. 31. [3] Vol. xvi., n. 64. [4] Holograph. Vol. xvii., n. 68.

words in the letter, Mr. Thorpe can have calendared it in February. Poulet exults over the possession of this packet, because the letters of the end of May were very numerous, and Mary had hardly written any since the "great packet" at the end of March. He feared lest the brewer was forwarding her letters honestly, and this is why he so devoutly thanks God that "all is now well," and that "the honest man is engaged for ever." Poulet is glad that Bessie Pierrepoint had not left, because he thought that if she had gone, she would have been the bearer of these letters, which thus would never have reached Walsingham's hands. He says so, plainly, in his letter of June 15th. This letter is probably of later date than that.

Poulet to Walsingham.[1]

Sir,—I think myself very happy that among so many changes and chances that have fallen out of late, this expected packet is come safely to my hands, which was delivered unto me by the honest man the 3rd of this present in the morning, at which time your friend was not far from me ; but for the better consideration of his credit in this action it was agreed between him and me that I should stay the said packet in my hands until the 4th in the evening, and then to send it to the honest man's house at Burton, where your friend would be ready to seize on it.

Your friend arrived here the 1st of this present, and taking his old lodging with Mr. Newport, steward to the Earl of Essex, I have had more safe conference with him by a continual intercourse of letters than if he had come unto me in person in these short light nights, especially considering that many of this Queen's family are stirring all night by reason of her infirmity at this present.

You see all is now well, thanks be to God, and the honest man is engaged for ever. It seemeth that this people make good account of this packet, in that the honest man telleth me that with the packet he had 10*l.* in money, besides all former rewards from this Queen not unknown unto you.

Your friend can tell you that he hath been troublesome to Mr. Newport many times, and must be hereafter, as often as he cometh into these parts. It seemeth meet that some consideration were had of it.

I account it a great happiness that this packet cometh to your hands before the departure of Mrs. Pierrepont.

Your friend is very careful in this service and professeth to have vowed himself wholly to your devotion, as one bound thereunto by your singular benefits.

It is not for nothing that Nau hath not gone out of this house above once this month without riding or walking abroad after his accustomed manner. He hath been worse occupied at home.

This Queen hath not gone out of her chamber this month and is yet troubled with defluxions in divers parts.

Great cost is bestowed on Mrs. Pierrepont in garments of all sorts, wherein cloth of silver and gold and silver lace are not spared.

Your friend could [not receive the packet at the honest man's hands so soon as he expected, which is the cause that it cometh so slowly unto you.

This Queen in her speech with me yesterday, complained that she was not better answered touching her servants[1] and change of lodging. But she complained very coldly of the latter, which I impute to nothing else than that she feareth lest her remove from hence would overthrow her intelligence.

It is true that this Queen hath in every of her legs an issue, which, as they say, is her last remedy. I found her lying on her bed.

Endorsed—1586. From Sir Amyas Poulett.

[1] Mary wrote to Walsingham on the 3rd of May, asking for passports for some new servants (Vol. xvii., n. 61 ; Labanoff, tom. vi., p. 272).

We now come to letters to which Poulet is neither ashamed nor afraid to sign his name.

Poulet to Phelippes.[1]

Sir,—I pray you impute my long silence to my diligent servant the gout, which had possessed my hand so as I could hardly write my own name, which is the true cause that I have not written unto you of late. You may find by my former letters to Mr. Secretary, that I have been jealous of her Majesty's service, a fault not worthy of great blame, wherein also I had some particular interest because I was a party in the action.

Your friend had committed two great and gross faults in this country, which moved me the rather to suspect the worst. I trust the last despatch from hence was so effectual as will suffice to salve all sores.

You write of your coming into these parts, which as I desire greatly, so I will not fail to further if I shall hear of anything belonging to the Lord Paget meet for you.

And thus not doubting but that you have your hands full of business, I leave to trouble you with idle words, and so do commit you to the mercy of the Almighty.

From Chartley, the 3rd of June, 1586.

Your assured friend,

A. POULET.

I pray you do me the pleasure to convey this letter, sent herewith, to my servant Hackshaw.

Addressed by Poulet — To my very good friend, Mr. Thomas Phelippes, esquire, at the Court.

Endorsed by Phelippes—3rd June, 1586. Sir Amias Poulet.

The letter that follows is quoted by Mr. Froude,[2] but in such a manner as to call for remark. Mary, he says, "happy

---

[1] Holograph. Vol. xviii., n. 1.   [2] *History*, vol. xii., p. 132.

in the removal to Chartley and the secret access which she possessed once more to the outer world, had recovered her health and spirits. She had been treated with unusual indul‑gence. Her legs had swollen in the winter, and on her first arrival she had been unable to walk; but as the spring came on she was driven out in a carriage, or was wheeled in her chair through the garden. We catch a glimpse of her enjoying 'a duck-hunt' in one of the ponds; and when summer came, her spirits lifting her body, she was able to mount her horse again and gallop with the hounds, or strike a deer with a crossbow." The latter Mary said of herself to Morgan[1] July $\frac{17}{27}$, doubtless with intent to show that if an attempt were made to rescue her, she was able to ride, not only "as this afternoon I intend to do, within the limits of the park," but also "other where, if it were permitted."

But the letters we have already given show how far from the truth Mr. Froude is in his account of Mary's health. On the 25th April, Poulet found her "sitting upon the side of her bed, and not yet able to use her feet." In June her lameness was "desperate." When the nights were short and light, she was still so ill that "many of her family were stirring all night;" she had "not gone out of her chamber for a month," and had "in every of her legs an issue, which, as they say, is her last remedy." True, as Mr. Froude says, we do "catch a glimpse of her enjoying a duck-hunt;" but we catch no glimpse in Mr. Froude's pages of her being carried to the pond, as "yet able to go very little, and not without help of either side." In fact, Mary was so helpless and infirm, that even a professional advocate of Queen Elizabeth's hardest proceedings against her wrote the following passage, and then erased it as too true and telling too severely against the cause for which he was pleading. He wrote that Queen Elizabeth "had been many times heard to say that she had resolved with herself rather to hazard her person and estate to all uttermost danger that perverse fortune or the malice of the said lady could work for the residue of her time, *than to take away that poor life of hers, as a prisoner of such years, so sickly and impotent, and so strongly guarded, her*

---

[1] Vol. xviii., n. 74; Labanoff, tom. vi., p. 426.

Majesty thought it impossible should be able any ways to annoy her, or to do her any great harm."[1]

As to the unusual indulgence with which she had been treated, Mary herself did not so describe it. "Mon gardien," she wrote to Châteauneuf in July,[2] "continue tousjours ses rigueurs et innovations;" and again, "depuis quelques jours, se démonstre beaucoup plus rigoureux et insolent que de coustume;" and Phelippes' commentary on it is,[3] "You may see how she is weary of her keeper, who in truth hath made no such change of his behaviour, but thought it policy to colour matters with his ordinary proceeding used before, thinking remissness would have discovered the practice;" that is, indulgence would arouse Mary's suspicions.

Poulet to Walsingham.[4]

Sir,—Your letters of the 29th of the last, with a packet for this Queen, came to my hands the 1st of this present in the morning. Finding nothing in the said packet worthy the advertisement, saving that Chérelles writeth to Nau that the French King will write to her Majesty for a new supply of servants for this Queen, and for the change of her lodging, concluding in his letter with these words: "On tient que la paix se fera, pour ce qu'on ne peult plus fournir a la guerre." These news are as welcome to this Queen as if he had cast salt in her eyes.

The French Ambassador writeth to this Queen that her new servants will not be granted until their names be advertised, and touching the conflict between the Prince of Condé and the regiment belonging to the Duke of Maine, he writeth that Monsieur de Laval and his two brethren were slain in that fight.

---

[1] This passage occurs in a document which has become, with the letter-books, the property of the Bodleian Library. It is evidently the work of one of the Crown lawyers, and the words printed above in italics have had others substituted for them by the author.

[2] Vol. xviii., n. 44; vol. xix., n. 15; Labanoff, tom. vi., pp. 369, 428.

[3] Vol. xviii., n. 61.

[4] Vol. xviii., n. 2.

The French Ambassador's wife in her letters to this Queen writeth very honourably of her Majesty, which I impute rather to that she knoweth that her letters must pass through my hands, than to any great devotion she beareth to her Highness.

This Queen hath now gotten a little strength, so as she goeth sometimes abroad in the coach, and at other times is carried in her chair to one of the ponds adjoining to this house to see duck-hunting, but is yet able to go very little, and not without help of either side.

It may please you to do me the favour to convey this letter inclosed to my Lord of Leicester, by the next convenient messenger. And thus, with my most hearty thanks unto you for your liberal advertisements of the occurrents of foreign parts, and giving God like thanks for His merciful providence towards her Majesty, His afflicted Church, and this our country, I commit you to His mighty protection.

From Chartley, the 3rd of June, 1586.

Your most assured poor friend,

A. POULET.

It may please you to command one of your servants to deliver this letter to Mr. Phelippes.

The request to be removed from Chartley does not appear in Mary's private letters. It was probably made in a letter openly addressed to Châteauneuf, but no such letter is in existence. Mary can only have asked to be removed in order to avert suspicion from her correspondence which she supposed to be secret. Poulet must have been in the right when he said that she would be sorry to be taken at her word.

Poulet to Walsingham.[1]

Sir,—I am not ignorant that this Queen hath desired to be removed from hence, wherein for my part I rest

---

[1] Vol. xviii., n. 4.

in my old opinion to be no suitor for any remove, or to nominate any house for that purpose, but to follow therein such direction as I shall receive from above. Only I have thought good to put you in remembrance that it shall stand much with her Majesty's profit that the certainty should be known as soon as may be, for provision to be made of hay, wood, coal, and many other things for the service of this house the next winter. I have written thus much to my Lord Treasurer by this bearer. And thus, wishing unto you all happiness, I , commit you to the merciful protection of our good God. From Chartley, the 9th of June, 1586.

Your most assured poor friend,

A. POULET.

On the 6th June Poulet wrote,[1] under the false impression that Mary wished Bessie Pierrepont to marry Nau. "Now being commanded to signify unto you how it cometh to pass that this Queen desireth to be rid of Mrs. Pierrepont, I can say nothing therein but by way of surmise ; but I believe verily that this Queen did never expect that this young gentlewoman should be taken from her upon this motion, for doubt of the intelligence which this gentlewoman so assured unto her might carry abroad, wherein this Queen being refused she might have the better colour to perform the intended marriage with Nau. This is all I can say or think herein, and so I pray you to deliver it to her Majesty. . . . I think convenient in my simple opinion that she should be taken from this Queen in such sudden manner as she may have no time to confer with her after her warning to depart. . . . My meaning herein tending to no other end than that if young Pierrepont depart from this Queen, she may not carry with her any treacherous or lewd instructions."

Poulet carried out his own suggestion, and overdid it. The suddenness offended the Queen of Scots, who refused to part with her *protégée* till her wardrobe was prepared. Mary said so in a letter to Châteauneuf of June 25, which letter no longer

[1] Vol. xviii., n. 3.

exists. She afterwards repeated,[1] "Tout le retardement survenu en cela n'est procédé que du peu temps que mon gardien me donne, m'estant venu advertir sur l'apres-diner, pour la faire partir dans le mesme jour." Mary was really anxious that she should go.

Poulet to Walsingham.[2]

Sir,—Mr. Pierrepont upon the receipt of your letters the 10th of this present in the morning, declared to the messenger, my servant, that his daughter lost her time with this Queen, and therefore being willing to bestow her in marriage, as also for his own comfort, his house being not very well furnished with children, he had been a suitor unto you of late that his daughter might be restored to him; but coming out of London in haste, so as he did not see you at his departure, did understand by your letters that his suit was granted, and did trust that this Queen would not refuse to deliver her, praying the messenger to signify unto me that his servants should be here to that purpose the 14th of this present; who arriving here at the prescribed day in the evening, and bringing with them this letter inclosed, I prayed to have access to this Queen. Wherein being refused upon pretence that she had a pain in her side (as indeed she hath been diseased these nine or ten days), and therefore desiring to be forborne until the next day at nine or ten of the clock in the morning; having access unto her at the time appointed, I declared unto her that according to the motion made unto her Majesty by the French Ambassador in her behalf,[3] for licence to be given to young Mrs. Pierrepont to return to her father, her Highness had caused her pleasure therein to be signified as well to Mr. Pierrepont as to myself, and Mr. Pierrepont having sent men and horses for his daughter, I prayed that she might be delivered unto them.

[1] Vol. xix., n. 15; Labanoff, tom. vi., p. 428. [2] Vol. xviii., n. 7.
[3] Vol. xvii., nn. 76, 89.

This Queen answered that she is entreated therein as
in her other suits for her servants, and touching her poor
folks at Easter, having received no answer in either of
both, and now she trusted to have heard from her Majesty
of her assent to this motion by her own letters.

• I told her it was sufficient, unless the matter were more
weighty, to understand her Highness' pleasure by me,
and she had reason to be satisfied in that her request
was granted.

"Yet," saith she, "it had been reasonable I should
have been advertised in time convenient to have prepared
all things necessary for the young gentlewoman," wherein
she had to consider of her own honour, and that her tailor
was now hurt (as indeed he was, in a drunken fray between
two of her servants), so as nothing could be prepared
for her.

I answered that it was well known that she was not
unprovided of sufficient clothes, and that she went from
hence to her father's house whence she was no stranger.

"I must tell you," saith this Queen, "that she is
unprovided of smocks, which are now in making, and she
may not want them."

"Madam," quoth I, "one smock is sufficient to bring
her home."

"I have brought her up," saith she, "now many years,
and I would be loth to leave her, but with the satisfaction
of her friends, and I know not if they have been truly
informed of my meaning herein."

I said I could assure her that her father had been truly
informed of the substance of the speech delivered by the
French Ambassador, which he had signified unto me by
his letters.

"Will you be content," quoth she, "to show me those
letters?"

"Yea, truly, madam," quoth I, "for your satisfaction;"
and so sending for them, showed them unto her, which

also I have sent unto you[1] to the end you may know that nothing was contained in them meet to be kept from her.

After many other words I prayed her to consider that the motion came from herself, her Majesty had yielded unto it, and the gentlewoman's father, dwelling fifty miles from hence, had sent nine or ten horses for her, and therefore wished her to take order that she might be delivered. Hereupon she prayed me to give her respite for one hour, at what time she sent Curle to signify unto me her resolution, which was that having made this motion unto the French Ambassador, she would not suffer the gentlewoman to depart until she had answer from the said Ambassador how her Majesty was satisfied therein, as a thing which touched her in honour.

I answered Curle that the message was of such weight as I would not receive it at a second hand, and therefore prayed to have access again to his mistress ; which being granted, this Queen telleth me the same in substance (although with greater plenty of words) that had been before delivered by Curle, adding that she could not tell if Sir Francis Walsingham had truly delivered her Majesty's mind, because she had been ill-handled that way divers times heretofore.

I prayed her to think that you would not misreport her Majesty, and that it would be thought above that her Highness' pleasure signified by your letters and reported by me, ought to carry as good credit with her as anything that should come from the French Ambassador.

" Yea," quoth she, " but I prayed the Ambassador to move many other circumstances, wherein I am not yet answered."

" Madam," quoth I, " you have the substance of your request, which is that the young gentlewoman should be delivered to her father."

[1] Sir Henry Pierrepont to Sir Amias Poulet, vol. xviii., n. 7, I.

"If I should deliver her," saith she, "after this sort, it would be the slander of the gentlewoman, as though she departed from me for some fault."

I answered that her departure was not sudden, and that the matter had been long in question, and that her father had been informed of the true cause thereof to this Queen's honour, and to the full discharge of the gentlewoman, as might appear by her father's letters unto me, which she had seen. Then she came again to her clothes, which I said would be no answer above.

When I saw that she would come to no reason, I told her that I was commanded to deliver her to her father's servants when they came for her, and therefore as far as I could, I required that she might be delivered unto me; which being denied, I prayed her to give leave to signify my commission to the young gentlewoman in her presence, which I did, in the hearing of all those in the chamber, which were many, and there declaring to the young gentlewoman the motion made by the Queen her mistress, the causes moving the same, her Majesty's yielding thereunto, your advertisement thereof, as well unto her father as to me, that her father had sent his servants to fetch her, and finally the refusal of this Queen to deliver her, upon weak grounds, which I then also confuted as well as I could; I required her to be content to depart with her father's servants, wherein she should show herself dutiful and obedient to the Queen my mistress, and should also do good service to this Queen, although she did not so take it.

After many words and many reiterations of my former motion to the young gentlewoman, this Queen concluded that she would not depart until she had heard farther, and the young gentlewoman said she would do nothing without her direction. Then I told her that I could not draw her out of her mistress' chamber by force, but required her as far as I could, to depart with her father's servants; wherein

I could get no other answer, and so I left them, and surely I left this Queen as much perplexed as I have seen her sithence my first coming to this charge, and no doubt, howsoever it cometh to pass, she hath been overreached in this matter, and now she cannot tell how to help it.

Hereupon I sent word to Mr. Pierrepont's servants that this Queen would not assent to the delivery of the young gentlewoman at this time, and that their master should not send again for [her] until he had received new direction from above.

I think my simple guess was not much out of the way, which was that this Queen looked for nothing less than that the young gentlewoman should be taken from her. But if she should depart hereafter, I do not doubt but that you will consider that her mistress will not fail to make her profit largely of it, and although she may have a good opinion of her other secret means, yet you may believe that she will prefer this mean before all other.

Being willing to follow her Majesty's direction, signified by Mr. Nicasius'[1] letters, as near as I might, I caused one of my servants to lie in wait for Mr. Pierrepont's men and to stay them from coming near to the house, to the end this Queen might receive the first advertisement of this message from myself, and therefore my audience being denied in the evening, I did also refrain to advertise the cause, until my coming to this Queen's presence.

And thus leaving these women's causes to your better consideration, I commit you to the mercy and favour of the Highest.

From Chartley, the 15th of June, 1586.

Your most assured poor friend,

A. POULET.

Autograph postscript—I thank you most heartily for this letter inclosed and for your other foreign advertisements.

[1] Nicasius Yetsweirt, two letters from whom will be given later.

The "packet inclosed" in the following letter is not forth-coming now. Pasquier was one of Mary's servants; "half a secretary," Poulet afterwards called him.

Poulet to Walsingham.[1]

Sir,—I received this last evening the packet inclosed, after I had already despatched the post with my other letters unto you, signifying unto Nau this morning the cause of the stay thereof. Hereupon he sendeth Pasquier unto me yesterday at noon, to tell me that it hath not been the custom that his mistress' letters have attended any opportunity, but have been sent away with speed.

I prayed him to tell Nau that his mistress did me wrong to charge me with any such custom, and as I had observed no such custom heretofore, so I would not bind myself to any such custom hereafter, and that if this Queen's letters had been delivered unto me before the departure of the post, I would have sent them with mine, and that now I would send them as I might.

Although I know no cause why this Queen's letters should be sent away in post, or that her business should in reason require it, and therefore will not bind myself unto it; yet because these letters are likely to concern Mrs. Pierrepont's cause, and were written, no doubt, in heat and choler, I have thought good to send them unto you, wherein I have omitted of purpose one day, to the end that Nau should know I did not like with his arrogant message.

I did forget to signify unto you in my other letters that among this Queen's other shifts for the detaining of Mrs. Pierrepont, she alleged that the Countess of Shrewsbury did not love her, and would be glad to take any advantage against her, and that therefore it behoved her to send Mrs. Pierrepont from her in good order.

[1] Vol. xviii., n. 9.

Also I remember that this Queen told me that she had prayed the Ambassador to deal with Mr. Pierrepont touching his daughter, wherein she was not yet answered, but she would not dwell upon it, so as it seemed that she repented to have said it.

Because it is likely that I may hear further in these matters, I think it shall not be amiss to advertise me of your pleasure touching Mrs. Pierrepont, before you shall require the execution thereof, to the end I may forbear the same until you shall hear again from me, if I shall find good and reasonable cause. And thus wishing you all happiness, I commit you to the safe keeping of our good God.

From Chartley, the 17th of June, 1586.

Your most assured poor friend,

A. POULET.

This Queen, willing to recover her desperate lameness, hath taken much physic of late, wherewith she is now faint and weak, and yet intendeth, as I am secretly informed, to practise some other experiments which she received of Mr. Doctor Baylye at his being with her, so as it is not likely that she will come out of her chamber these many days.

It may please you to cause one of your servants to deliver this packet to Mr. Nicasius.

We have in the next letter a good specimen of the way in which Mary's letters were treated. The "second messenger" was Thomas Barnes. When Babington wrote in July, he begged that Mary's answer might be sent to Lichfield. Perhaps because he was there, this new agent of Walsingham's was told to make Lichfield his head-quarters. In order that he and the brewer might not know each other's treachery, Mary's letter is brought to Poulet by the brewer, sent to Walsingham in London, for Phelippes' perusal, returned by Walsingham to Chartley, and then sent by Poulet to Burton that Barnes might receive it from the brewer's hands.

O

Poulet to Walsingham.[1]

Sir,—The honest man having received this present morning this packet inclosed for the second messenger, who (as it seemeth) stayeth at Lichfield of purpose for the same, I have willed him to tell the said messenger that this Queen is sick and troubled other ways, so as he can receive no answer at this time, but is promised that he shall not fail to have it on Saturday shall be sevennight, being the 2nd of July, so as it is of necessity that I must receive this packet again from you the last of this present month at the farthest, because the next day I must send it to the honest man's house. If you think the time which I now give you to be too short for the perusing of the packet, it may please you to signify unto me what time I shall appoint hereafter.

I send unto you herewith all your copies and letters, for the which I thank you as much as I can. And thus I leave you to the mercy of the Highest.

From Chartley, the 21st of June, 1586.

Your most assured poor friend,

A. POULET.

I cannot yet have opportunity to have sufficient talk with the honest man, but I have given him four angels, because he shall know that I have forgiven all that is past.

In this case the delay for deciphering and perusal is in another stage of the proceedings. The brewer received the letter back from Poulet, that the substitute might have it, by whom it was brought back again to Poulet. It is by no means clear that Walsingham would take Poulet's view of the unimportance of the packet because it was "so little." It was Mary's first letter to Babington, which being dated the 25th was delivered to Poulet by the brewer on the very day on which it was written. Walsingham was "expecting" Mary to write to

[1] Vol. xviii., n. 12. Holograph.

Babington, for Morgan's letter of April 29 [May 9th] had passed through his hands, in which not only was the Queen of Scots urged to write to him, but a draft of the letter she was recommended to write was sent her. Answering Morgan,[1] on July $\frac{17}{27}$, she says that at Gifford's "last return from these parts, she had at once three of his letters; one dated the 13th of June,[2] the most part in Pietro his commendation; another the 9th of May [N.S., April 29, O.S.] concerning Babington;[3] and the third[4] of the 20th of July, '85."

But Mary had received one letter[5] from Morgan before this, "touching Babington," and Walsingham's treatment of it deserves attention. It was dated July 26, 1585; Poley brought it to England at the end of July. Walsingham kept it in his hands till late in May in the following year, for Curle acknowledges its receipt "as the bearer was ready to have been despatched" with Mary's letter[6] of May 20, 1586. The reason is obvious when we remember that signs of the Babington conspiracy did not show themselves till about the middle of May, 1586. Nothing could be more significant.

Poulet to Walsingham.[7]

Sir,—The honest man on Saturday last, the 25th of this present, brought unto me this little packet inclosed, which being so little as could be nothing answerable to that which you expect, and was not likely to contain any great matter, and the day of meeting between the substitute and the honest man approaching so near, I thought good to stay the said packet in my hands for these few days, to the end the honest man should not think that I had intelligence with the substitute, and therefore sent the said packet again to the honest man the 28th of this

---

[1] Vol. xviii., n. 74; Labanoff, tom. vi., p. 421.

[2] Vol. xviii., n. 13.

[3] Vol. xvii., n. 58; Murdin, p. 513.

[4] Vol. xvi., n. 7; Murdin, p. 446.

[5] There is no copy of it in the Record Office, but it is given by Murdin, p. 453.

[6] Vol. xvii., n. 80; Labanoff, tom. vi., p. 328.

[7] Vol. xviii., n. 22. Holograph.

present to be delivered to the substitute the 29th, and so being returned unto me by the substitute I send it unto you.

It may please you to signify unto me what course I shall take with the substitute hereafter, which resteth to be considered only by you, who are acquainted with the secrets of the cause. And whereas you require me to reward him, I purpose to give him five pounds, if I hear not from you to the contrary by your next letters; but I would think that your friend's substitute at London should procure his reward from this Queen, and if it be not sought at her hands, she shall have just cause to think ill of it. The truth is that he hath had many journeys by this occasion, and therefore doth deserve to be well recompensed.

The 27th of this present, at ten of the clock at night, I received letters from Mr. Phelippes of the 25th, together with two several packets, the lesser being the same which I sent unto you the 21st of this instant, and which was delivered to the honest man for the second messenger, who attended his answer at Lichfield, and it is very likely that this packet was delivered for him, because the day appointed for meeting between the honest man and the substitute was not yet come. Howsoever, this matter was mistaken by this people or by the honest man, I see no danger or inconvenience if we can be content to have patience until the arrival of your friend, who as it seemeth will be here shortly.

Mr. Phelippes hath set down a course for many things to be done, which surely I dare not put in execution for fear of the worst, wherein I am also the more fearful because it seemeth there is hope that the 3rd of this present, great matter will come from this people, which might be in danger to be stayed if, [by] any mean, cause of suspicion were ministered by any of the agents in this intercourse.

Mr. Phelippes would have the substitute to seize upon this little packet now returned from you unto me, whereunto the honest man will never assent without my especial direction, because he is now to receive the said packet at my hands. This adventure might breed many dangers, and seemeth to serve to no other purpose than thereby to deliver a letter from the substitute to Curle, the said letter containing no matter that requireth especial haste, and which may not be done more safely by your friend at his coming.

All is now well, thanks be to God, and I should think myself very unhappy if upon any instructions to proceed from me, this intercourse, so well advanced, should be overthrown. I have therefore resolved to open the returned packet, and to deliver only to the honest man the letter for the second messenger therein contained, reserving the rest according to Mr. Phelippes' direction, so as if any question grow thereof hereafter (which is not likely) it shall be said that the substitute finding the said packet in the honest man's hands, seized upon it and took out thereof what pleased him. Thus you see that I am curious to conserve as well myself as the cause out of peril or hazard thereof, wherein I am the more bold because I see nothing in the other course that presseth, and yet being miscarried between the substitute and the honest man, might bring imminent danger.

The honest man believeth verily that this second messenger came by direction from your friend, because he bringeth a true token, which was that in such a place your friend gave him two angels, and telleth me further that the second messenger seemed to mislike greatly that this Queen delayed to answer him, and said that his business would not permit him to tarry so long in these parts, but concluded that he would fetch fresh letters and would return the 4th or 5th of this next month of July. He calleth himself Barnes, and saith (untruly I doubt not), that he is nearly allied to Sir Walter Aston and Mr. Richard Bagot.

And thus I commit you to the mercy of the Almighty, who give you strength of body and mind to overcome the troubles of this troubled time.

From Chartley, the 29th of June, 1586.

Your most assured poor friend,

A. POULET.

The honest man bringeth to the substitute at this time two angels from this Queen, which surely I think should have been delivered long before, and I marvel that the reward is so slender, doubting lest the honest man hath kept the better part for himself. I find that the honest man hath played his part at this time very well with the substitute according to my instructions.

Addressed by Poulet to Walsingham and endorsed by Phelippes.

Poulet to Phelippes.[1]

Sir,—You have set down a very reasonable and probable course in your letters as things appear unto you there, but I find here by reason of the circumstances so many difficulties as I dare not proceed to the execution of your direction in all things, which I forbear the rather because I find nothing in your letters that presseth, and do return your packet unto you inclosed herein.

I have written more at length to Mr. Secretary, and thus willing to send a new packet unto you with speed, I pray you excuse these short lines, which shall be longer another time.

From Chartley, the 29th of June, 1586.

Your assured friend of old acquaintance,

A. POULET.

To my very good friend, Mr. Thomas Phelippes, esquire.

[1] Vol. xviii., n. 23. Holograph.

Poulet to Walsingham.[1]

Sir,—Your three packets of the last of June came to my hands the 3rd of this present, at four in the morning, and having perused all the letters addressed to this Queen, I find nothing much worthy of advertisement, and yet I thought good to trouble you with this note inclosed.

I have refused to perform the content of this letter inclosed from the Ambassador,[2] as well because I would not wade in matters of this quality without warrant, as also that I would give no such precedent which might make them bold hereafter upon like occasions.

Mr. Darrell, having taken order of late by my discretion, and upon very good ground, for the restraining of some things concerning the diet of this Queen's family, the Master of her Household was sent unto me to know if I were acquainted with it; which, being avowed by me and reported unto her, she commanded her Master of Household to signify unto me that in other things I was accustomed to say unto her that I had no commission to do this or that, and therefore if I had no especial direction from her Majesty or from the Lords of her Highness' Council, she would not yield unto it. I answered that I would not fail to cause the order to be put in execution the next morning, and if his mistress complained she should know my commission.

Yesterday, having first sent unto me her Master of Household with a new complaint about the matter, and receiving from me a resolute answer, she sent Curle to pray me to come unto her to her chamber, where I yielded such reasonable matter for the justification of my doings as, after some words, she was satisfied.

---

[1] Vol. xviii., n. 36.

[2] In behalf of a young Scotchman who had served in France, who is desirous to return to Scotland, and wishes to see his mother, an attendant on the Queen of Scots (Vol. xviii. n. 36, I.).

Then she prayed me to advertise Mr. Pierrepont that when he should send for his daughter, she should be delivered. I said that without new direction from her Majesty I could do nothing therein, whereupon she prayed me to signify her proffer.

Cordaillot, among other things sent to Nau by the carrier in his last journey, sendeth this paper inclosed, by the which he bewrayeth his lewd opinion of our nation, and therefore I thought good to retain the said paper before it came to Nau's hands, and now I would wish that it were rendered to Cordaillot, whereby he may perceive that his slanderous conceits are bewrayed. Having compared the said note with his other writing, I find it to be written with his own hand. And thus I commit you to the mercy of the Almighty.

From Chartley, the 7th of July, 1586.

Your most assured poor friend,

A. POULET.

It may please you to do me the favour to cause this letter inclosed to be delivered to my Lord Norreys.

In sending Gifford to be a spy upon the brewer and Barnes, Phelippes was acting on the adage, "Set a thief to catch a thief."

Gilbert Gifford to Phelippes.[1]

Sir,—Two principal points (whereof many secondary were derived, as we discoursed at our last being together) were the cause of my coming hither for the trial of the honest man, and the discovery of the second. In the first we have so proceeded that the honest man is *totaliter* ours, who is too glad to have thus escaped with his 20*l.*, besides many good angels, than to incur the same danger. He seeketh nothing more than to win credit with the governor in this service. There

---

[1] Vol. xviii., n. 37.

was never so fortunate a knave, so that there cannot possibly be anything added to this point, and I think he is sufficiently charmed for admitting any other but the first man.

For the second, at my speaking with the honest man, he told me that the second messenger was gone to London a sennight and more before, and that his appointment with him was uncertain.

Whereof this morning I have amply written to Sir Amias, declaring the necessity of my return. The conclusion of my letter is—either this party is at London or no: if not, he will not be long in these parts, as well for that I have his letter, as also to finger more packets. Besides that, I will leave with the honest man an earnest letter for his coming up.

If he be already at London, as is probable, not repairing to the honest man in so long a space, then it is likely that I shall find him there coming up speedily, whence we will dispose of him. His name is Barnes. I know him well, but I think he hath no chamber in London, neither were it expedient you lean harder of him for the case I told, for that would spoil all; but assure yourself, and I promise and undertake of my credit, to cut him clear off from this course, and to that end I have written to Z, the copy whereof you shall see at our meeting.

I have no leisure but to commit you to God, this 7th of July.

Yours to command,

G. G.

I trust you have displayed [? delayed] the journey of P. Let them be dainty at the first, let scarce one of them be seen. I would gladly deliver this packet to you myself.

Addressed—To my very loving friend, Mr. Thomas Phelippes.

The packet that was intercepted by Phelippes was a large one
if it contained all Mary's letters of the end of June and the
beginning of July. We have letters of hers[1] dated June 30 to
Cardinal Laurea and Père la Rue, and July 2 to Mendoza,
Morgan, and Charles Paget. We have not got the letter to the
Ambassador which Phelippes made "fit for his handling." The
request to Walsingham to "resolve thoroughly and speedily" of
Babington's matters, is noteworthy. Gifford told Curle that *he*
had met with the packet on the way, and meant to deliver it
himself.[2]

Phelippes to Walsingham.[3]

It may please your Honour,—According to your direction, meeting with the packet of Sir Amias between
Stilton and Stamford, I have opened the same, and I
have found a packet for the French Ambassador, from
the which I thought best to take with me to despatch
here and send you up fit for his handling with all
speed, because I know he expecteth the same earnestly.
By Sir Amias' letter to your honour, and our friend's
to me, I find all things to stand in so good terms as
my abode there will be the less but for Babington's
matters, which I beseech you resolve thoroughly and
speedily of. And so I humbly take my leave.

Stilton, this 8th of July, 1586.

Your honour's most humble at commandment,

THO. PHELIPPES.

I departed London yesternight at nine, and had been
at Chartley at this time but for the extreme carelessness
of constables, and contempt of some of them, wherein
your honour must needs take order upon special services,
as this is. I forgot to know your honour's pleasure touching

---

[1] Vol. xviii., nn. 41, 24, 28, 29 ; Labanoff, tom. vi., pp. 347—360.

[2] Vol. xviii., n. 74 ; Labanoff, tom. vi., p. 423.

[3] Vol. xviii., n. 38.

the mad book that G. G. brought you of Foxley,[1] &c. The greatest necessity of it is only the saving of G. G.'s credit, who pretends no other errand. In which respect, if you think good, it might be on the press in the meanwhile.

Gifford missed Barnes on the road between Chartley and London. This letter, written immediately on his reaching London, makes one wish that a few more of the letters between the same parties had escaped destruction.

Mr. Froude[2] is thinking of this letter when he says that "Gifford, though he accompanied Ballard to England, was personally ignorant of what was going forward; it was not till afterwards that he learnt it in conversation from Ballard himself." We have already seen[3] that in truth, though not in Mr. Froude's pages, it was Gifford who brought Mendoza to accept the plan of regicide, when Ballard had failed with him.

So far from learning anything from Ballard in this conversation, which Mr. Froude supposes to have been Gifford's initiation into the plot, Gifford himself remarks that Ballard so spoke as "thinking him privy to the course," and he was apparently about to say, what Walsingham did not need to be told, that Ballard was not far wrong in saying so.

Gifford said to Walsingham what he thought it prudent to say and he is careful to disclaim much previous acquaintance with a man who he knew would soon be tried for high treason. But it is not easy to believe that he "was never well acquainted with" Ballard.[4] According to Châteauneuf, whom Mr. Froude generally

---

[1] This is the book against Father Persons and the Jesuits, the joint work of Gifford and Gratley, mentioned in a previous note (*supra*, p. 189). Gifford, when a prisoner in Paris, said that he would have been released if Gratley had not been taken, who was in the Inquisition at Padua for the book against Persons (*Dom. Eliz.*, vol. ccxiv., n. 35). The book was evidently printed by Walsingham, to whom Henry Cæsar wrote, "the which book Phelippes your man did send unto Lily" (*Domestic, Addenda, Elizabeth*, vol. xxx., n. 120).

[2] *History*, vol. xii., p. 132.

[3] *Supra*, p. 146.

[4] Gifford said to Phelippes more than he had said to Walsingham, denying with an oath that "ever I had any other acquaintance with him or knew him otherwise than man I never saw" (Vol. xx., n. 45). But this was written after he had fled to Paris, for fear lest he should be tried with Babington's accomplices.

follows, it was Gifford who "fit passer en Angleterre" this miserable conspirator.

Mr. Froude gives this account of the interview related in this letter. "Ballard, who, without mentioning names, had now communicated the secret to Gilbert Gifford, told him that before any active step could be taken, 'he must obtain the Queen's hand and seal to allow of all that must be practised for her.' Without this his labour was vain, and nothing could be done. He had himself promised that he would not write to her; but Babington was about to make use of Morgan's introduction to send her a few words, and Gifford must convey his letter by the secret channel." Babington "about to make use of Morgan's introduction" in the middle of July, when, in consequence of Morgan's letter of April 29, Mary had written to Babington on the 25th of June! When had Ballard "promised he would not write to her?" As a matter of fact, he did not write to her, for Mary says to Morgan,[1] "I have heard of that Ballard of whom you write, but nothing from himself, and therefore have no intelligence with him."

Gilbert Gifford to Walsingham.[2]

Right Honourable,—Barnes hath not yet appeared in any of his frequented places, so that I think he came not as yet to town. I know not whether he hath been with the Ambassador, for I dare not go thither till such time as I bring the packet with me. I am assured he shall no sooner come to the town but I shall hear of him, and needs he must come for I have his letter with me from Q[ueen of Scots].[3]

I trust Mr. Phelippes will meet the said packet by the way and peruse it, that it need no delay in delivery.

Touching the practice in hand, before my last coming over in discourse with Morg[an] I smelled something afar

---

[1] Vol. xviii., n. 74; Labanoff, tom. vi., p. 425.

[2] Vol. xviii., n. 40.

[3] Probably Mary's letter to Barnes of June 19 (Vol. xviii., n. 10), in answer to his of the 10th (*Ibid.*, n. 6).

off, and he told me that he had sent one to solicit interest
here; promising me that in time I should know all, as
occasion should serve; for it is their custom to discover
things by little and little, albeit they trust one never
so much.

Now yesterday, by great inquiry, one Ballard found
me out. I never was well acquainted with him, but he
told me that he had sought me greatly, and that he
knew my endeavour thoroughly in the behalf of the
cause, and that he purposed verily to have come to
me in the country, "for," said he, "I thought you were
there." After great entertainments, at the length he
brake with me into great complaint of Morg. and Charl.
P[aget], saying that they promised him intelligence very
oft, and that he never heard from them since his coming
over. Hereof I gave him some reasons of their delay.
Then he told me that at his coming over he was directed
to me, and that finding me not, he was in great perplexity,
thanking God that we were met together to be an help
one to another. He told me that he was on Saturday
night with the Ambassador,[1] and he expecteth letters
daily.

"But," said he, "if they will not perform that they
promised, we will do at the least our parts," by which
words I perceived that I [he] thought me privy to the
course [which indeed *erased*].

I asked him what was to be done on our parts. He
replied that I must needs obtain of Q[ueen] her hand

---

[1] Gifford "fit passer en Angleterre un prêtre Anglais, nommé Ballard, qui
avait autrefois servi d'espion à Walsingham contre les Catholiques, et qui
depuis, reconnaissant sa faute, s'était du tout départi de son accointance,
ainsi que l'on disait. Le dict Ballard était pour sa doctrine fort estimé des
Catholiques, la plupart desquels ignoraient ce dont il s'était autrefois mêlé;
il vint à Londres, et quelques jours après, il vint au logis de l'Ambassadeur de
France, avec un autre, savoir s'il n'y avait point de lettres de France pour lui
qui lui étaient adressées sous un nom supposé, et là salua l'Ambassadeur dans
sa galerie, sans entrer en propos aucuns, ni se découvoir à lui, ni a son
secrétaire, sinon pour Catholique" (*Châteauneuf's Memoir*, Labanoff, tom.
vi., p. 288).

and seal to allow of all that should be practised for her behalf, "without the which," said he, "we labour in vain, and these men will not hear us."

I answered that it was a matter of great importance, and that we should expect Morg. and P. to do it. He said the matter would go long and that he was in great danger.

"Well," said I, "in my opinion this was never obtained hitherto by any man, and the granting thereof will be hard. But what persuasion, what probability of success, can you leave before Q. whereby he [*sic*] can be moved to grant it?" Said he, "I will undertake within forty days to procure his [*altered from* her] liberty."

"Well," said I, "let us think of it, and to-morrow I will answer you;" so he parted out of town, and left his man with me for answer, which he is ceaseless earnest in.

This Ballard is the only man used in this practice whatever it be, which I cannot thoroughly discover the first day, but in time it will be easy, for he desireth my company and help therein.

What your honour thinketh good I shall answer him I desire to be informed, and how far I shall join with him and keep him company, which doing it is unpossible but I shall discover all.

He complained much of Sir T. Tresham and my cousin Talbot, for not only they would not hear him, but threatened to discover him, "and," saith he, "unless we obtain that from Q. all is but wind."

I beseech your honour, as soon as the packet shall arrive that it be conveyed to me by this bearer, before which time I cannot go to the Ambassador.

Ballard told me that your honour had an inkling of some things, especially of the Ambassador's intelligence with Q. Your honour hath some very corrupted men about him whereto great regard is to be taken.

He told me that Phelippes was gone to Chartley for the removing of Nau and Pro [de Préau].

I trust your honour considereth how necessary it is to entertain D[octor] G[ifford] and Gratley, for hereby they be persuaded that there is no other dealings of mine but that only, otherwise it were unpossible but I should be suspected.

D. G. coming over would colour me much, as also I can know his whole thoughts, and no doubt he would be greatly employed so that by him I should understand all their courses, for he can hide nothing from me.

Thus protesting before God that nothing shall pass my hands and hearing, but your honour shall soon understand it, beseech the Almighty long to protect your honour.

This 11th of July.

Your honour's faithful servant,

G. G.

Mr. Froude quotes[1] the next letter and adds, "Some remorse he could not choose but feel. She was in his toils, and he was too certain that she would be meshed in them. Another letter from her and the work would be done." The only sign of remorse Phelippes showed was to put a gallows on the outside of the letter which he sent to Walsingham. He quotes the warning verse as applicable to himself.

Phelippes to Walsingham.[2]

It may please your Honour,—The packet is presently returned which I stayed in hope to send both it and the answer to B[abington]'s letter at once. In the meanwhile beginning to decipher that which we had copied out before. And so I send your honour her letter to the French Ambassador,[3] which was in cipher, and her letters to the Lord

---

[1] *History*, vol. xii., p. 138.

[2] Vol. xviii., n. 48.

[3] The letter to Courcelles (now lost) was inclosed in her letter of July $\frac{3}{13}$, to Châteauneuf (Vol. xviii., n. 44 ; Labanoff, tom. vi., p. 368). The letter to Lord Claude Hamilton is only dated July (Vol. xviii., n. 27; Labanoff, tom. vi., p. 371). "The short note sent to Bab." was Nau's letter to Babington dated July 13, N.S. (Vol. xviii., n. 43), in answer to Babington's inquiries about Robert Poley (Vol. xix., n. 9).

Claude and Courcelles out of cipher. Likewise the short
note was sent to Bab., wherein is somewhat only in answer
of that concerned Poley in his. We attend her very heart
at the next. She begins to recover health and strength
and did ride abroad in her coach yesterday. I had a
smiling countenance but I thought of the verse,

Cum tibi dicit Ave, sicut ab hoste cave.

I hope by the next to send your honour better matter.
In the meanwhile humbly take my leave.

Chartley, the 14th July, 1586.

Your honour's most humble at commandment,

THO. PHELIPPES.

It may please your honour to command the delivery
of the letter to my servant wherein is some matter for
your secret friend.

If the posts make any reasonable speed, these will be
with you by to-morrow noon, and G. G. may have delivered
his packet and received the answer by Sunday, which then
despatched hither would give great credit to the action, for
otherwise we look not to depart this sevennight, and therefore as good all that belongs thereto were done here as at
London.

"The packet sent by Mr. Phelippes" was Babington's letter,
placing the plot before Mary, which thus came to her straight
from Walsingham. Its possession, no doubt, brought Phelippes
down to Chartley. "Such answer given in writing as the
shortness of the time would permit," must be Nau's letter
to Babington about Poley,[1] which Phelippes mentioned with
greater exactness in his letter to Walsingham, for Mary wrote
but two letters to Babington.

Poulet to Walsingham.[2]

Sir,—Your letters of the 11th of this present coming to
my hands yesterday at eleven before noon, I have no other

---

[1] Vol. xviii., n. 43.   [2] Vol. xviii., n. 49.

thing wherewith now to trouble you than to send unto you the packet intercepted upon the way by Mr. Phelippes, and also to advertise you that the packet sent by Mr. Phelippes hath been delivered and thankfully received, with such answer given by writing as the shortness of the time would permit, and with promise to answer more at length at the return of the honest man, which will be within three days.

I cannot thank you enough, first for your messenger, my old good friend Mr. Phelippes, and then for your messages, as well by mouth as by writing; for your favour wherein I shall rest your debtor as long as I live. As knoweth the Almighty, to whose safe keeping I commit you.

From Chartley, the 14th of July, 1586.

Your most assured poor friend,

A. POULET.

I am prayed to convey unto you this packet inclosed from this Queen to the French Ambassador.

The proposal that some one should "disguise himself like a gentleman of ability" and personate Emilio Russo to the French Ambassador is worthy of Walsingham's spy system. The gentleman in disguise was to "give credit to Berden,"[1] who was now "discovered to be a lewd fellow," as Morgan wrote[2] to Gifford at this time.

Phelippes to Walsingham.[3]

It may please your Honour, — I send you herein Mr. Harborne's letter in answer of yours sent by Captain Ellis, and therefore sealed up and deciphered by myself.

I had letters from G. Gifford by Mr. Hugh Offley. He hath great credit for his service and puts me in hope to discover somewhat of importance, smelling as he saith

---

[1] See foot note, p. 168.
[2] Thomas Sansellen to Nicholas Cornellys, July 9 (Vol. xviii., n. 39).
[3] Vol. xviii., n. 56.

P

such matters as I would wonder at, protesting that which
I doubt not of his care to discover it speedily.   He
saith he findeth that Morgan hath sent over two, as he
terms them, of great government and discretion, to set
upon some other.   Albeit I doubt not but our intercourse
continuing, they will be discovered.   Yet I wish, for more
assurance, somebody were advised of to appear in his
likeness before the French Ambassador, which is yet the
only want here.   If you think Berden a meet man, as I
see no cause truly of the contrary, for my part it should
need but to get somebody to disguise himself like a
gentleman of abil[ity] for once to come and talk with the
Ambassador as Emilio Russo, and he to give that credit
to Berden which should serve the turn hereafter, and this
might any man do.   But without question the Ambassador
will look for the party after one despatch at the farthest.
It may please you therefore to think of it one way or other.
And so I humbly take my leave, this 17th of July, 1586.

   Your honour's always most bound at commandment,

                              THO. PHELIPPES.

   At last Poulet was "wonderfully comforted," though Elizabeth
"pinched" him to the last.   Mary's third letter to Babington was
in Phelippes' hands, and a copy, with a gallows on the cover,
on its way to Walsingham and Elizabeth.   Was that copy a true
one, free from interpolations?   Or was it not until afterwards
that the interpolations were made?   That there were interpolations made no one can doubt who reads the letter as printed
by Prince Labanoff; but whether Phelippes inserted them before
Walsingham saw the letter or afterwards no one can now tell.
The probability is that the decipher sent to Walsingham was a
genuine copy of Mary's letter to Babington.   Phelippes no doubt
thought it abundantly sufficient evidence to bring her to the
scaffold.   It was an elaborate instruction how an insurrection
might be organized and war made upon the Queen of England.
Such a letter would have been high treason in a subject, beyond
all doubt; but Mary was an independent sovereign, though a

captive, and Walsingham may well have felt that something
more was required to induce Elizabeth to proceed to extremities
against her. She must be shown to be a party to the plot for
Elizabeth's assassination, and for this purpose the interpolations
were made. The reader must judge for himself whether the
passages marked by Prince Labanoff formed a part of Mary's
letter. The whole letter is too long for transcription. The
material passages are the following :

"Les choses estant ainsy préparées et les forces, tant dedans
que dehors le royaulme, toutes prestes, il fauldra [*alors mettre les
six gentilshommes en besoigne et*] donner ordre que [*leur desseing
estant effectué*] je puisse, quant et quant, estre tirée hors d'icy, et
que toutes voz forces soynt en ung mesmes temps en campaigne
pour me recevoir pendant qu'on attendra le secours estranger,
qu'il fauldra alors haster en toute dilligence. [*Or, d'aultant qu'on
ne peult constituer ung jour préfix pour l'accomplissement de ce que
lesdicts gentilshommes ont entreprins, je vouldrois qu'ilz eussent
tousjours auprès d'eulx ou pour le moings en cour, quatre vaillans
hommes bien montés pour donner advis en toute dilligence du succez
dudict desseing, aussytost qu'il sera effectué, à ceulx qui auront charge
de me tirer hors d'icy, afin de s'y pouvoir transporter avant que mon
gardien soyt adverti de ladicte execution, ou, à tout le moings, avant
qu'il ayt le loisir de se fortifier dedans la maison, ou de me
mener ailleurs. Il seroyt necessaire qu'on envoyast deux ou trois de
dicts advertisseurs par divers chemins, afin que l'ung venant à
faillir, l'autre puisse passer oultre, et fauldroyt en ung mesme instant
essayer d'empescher les passages ordinaires aux postes et courriers.*]

"C'est le project que je trouve le plus à propos pour ceste
entreprinse, afin de la conduire avecq esgard de nostre propre
seureté. De s'esmouvoir de ce costé devant que vous soyez
asseurés d'ung bon secours estrangier, ne seroyt que vous mettre,
sans aucun propos, en dangier de participer à la miserable fortune
d'aultres qui ont par cydevant entreprins sur ce sujet ; et de me
tirer hors d'icy sans estre premièrement bien asseurez de me
pouvoir mettre au milieu d'une bonne armée ou en quelque lieu
de seureté, jusques à ce que noz forces fussent assemblées et les
estrangiers arrivés, ne seroyt que donner asses d'occasion à ceste
Royne là, si elle me prenoyt de rechef, de m'enclorre en quelque

fosse d'où je ne pourrois jamais sortir, si pour le moings, j'en pouvois eschaper à ce prix là, et de persécuter avecq toute extrémité ceux qui m'auroynt assisté, dont j'auroys plus de regret que d'adversité quelconque qui me pourroyt eschoir à moy mesmes."

Supposing the italicized passages to have been in the original, the letter will have run thus : "When your preparations both in England and abroad are complete, let the six gentlemen who have undertaken to assassinate Elizabeth proceed to their work, and when she is dead—*leur desseing estant effectué*—then come and set me free; and be sure you have at least four men ready to bring me the earliest information of the Queen's death—*du succez dudict desseing.*

"But do not take any steps towards my liberation until you are in such force that you may be able to put me in some place of perfect security, lest Queen Elizabeth should take me again, and shut me up in some inaccessible dungeon, or lest if she should fail in recapturing me, she should persecute to extremity those who have helped me, which I should feel more than any adversity of my own."

Could Prince Labanoff help saying that there is here an evident contradiction? *Could* Mary have said, "Do not move till Elizabeth is dead, and after that so manage my escape that she may not be able to hurt me or my friends?"

Now will the reader believe that Mr. Froude has entirely suppressed all mention of the paragraph in Mary's letter, in which she begs that care may be taken that the attempt to rescue her may not move Elizabeth to inflict fresh and more severe persecutions upon herself and her partisans? He has done so, and we must suppose that he accounts it fair and just so to do. But besides the suppression of this passage, the meaning of the sentences of the letter is twisted throughout Mr. Froude's "condensed" version,[1] as he calls it, so as to make them refer to the scheme for Elizabeth's murder instead of that for Mary's escape and the invasion of England.

The intrinsic evidence of forgery is so strong as to be conclusive by itself, but it is supported by extrinsic evidence not less conclusive. First, there is Nau's confession[2] of September 5,

---

[1] *History*, vol. xii., p. 144.   [2] Vol. xix., n. 90.

countersigned by the Lords of the Privy Council, which ends
thus : " Quant a la lettre escripte a Babington, sa Majesté me la
bailla pour la pluspart escripte de sa main, et i'ay rien faict ny
escript comme j'ay protesté sans son expres commandement et
specialement touchant le point de son eschapper et mettant la
feu aux granges près de la mayson." It is clear what Nau
thought were the most grievous points in the letter, and he
tries to exculpate himself and to throw all the responsibility on
Mary for the project of her escape, and for the proposal to set
the outhouses on fire. Would he have been content to bear
the blame for the clauses respecting Elizabeth's assassination ?
Plainly he had never heard of them.

Secondly, in the heads of accusation that were first drawn
up against Nau and Curle, there is no allusion made to any
clause concerning "the six gentlemen." In a paper in Phelippes'
hand,[1] endorsed by Lord Burghley, " 4 September, 1586, from
Philipps," there occurs no accusation more specific than the
following—" The heads of that bloody letter sent to Babington,
touching the desseingment of the Queen's person, is of Nau his
hand likewise."

The *Hardwicke State Papers*[2] say of the trial at Westminster,
" There was also showed forth a paper written by Nau containing
the short minutes and notes of the principal points of Babington's
letter, and of the Scots' Queen's letter to Babington, which was
found among her papers at Chartley, which on being showed
to Nau by some of the Lords of the Council, he upon sight
thereof confessed it to be his own hand, saying that upon
reading Babington's letter to the Scots' Queen and her direction
given for the answering of the same, he did set down the same
notes to serve as a memorial for him for the writing of other
letters. In this paper, amongst other points is contained the
coup, which can hardly be construed to be meant otherwise
than the blow or stroke for killing her Majesty." Now one
of two things is true, and either exculpates Mary. Either
the heads produced were really those of Mary's letter to
Babington, and then those notes are identical with those
of her letters to Glasgow, Mendoza, and Paget, in none

---

[1] Vol. xix., n. 85.   [2] *Hardwicke State Papers*, vol. i., p. 235.

of which is the *coup* Elizabeth's assassination, but the enterprize upon Chartley for Mary's rescue. In this case the same heads for the letter to Babington will mean that the same things were to be written to Babington. The *coup* is not, then, the assassination, but the assault upon Chartley. Or else, which is far more likely, the heads produced at the trial were really those of the letters to Glasgow, Mendoza, and Paget, wilfully separated from Nau's statement to that effect;[1] separated, because if they had been known to be the heads of letters that were then produced, the real meaning of the word *coup* would have been unmistakeable.

Thirdly, Mary herself especially denied the authenticity of the interpolated passages. The letter[2] Mr. Froude has seen, for he quotes from it Lord Burghley's phrase, " this Queen of the Castle," but he does not quote Mary's denial. Perhaps it may be said that Mary denied everything, and that therefore her denial of these passages is of no value. But this is not true. She denied that she had received *such* a letter from Babington and had returned *such* an answer, and this the Hardwicke State Papers[3] show conclusively against the narrative published in the State Trials. She could hardly deny the assassination passages without acknowledging the rest of the letter. But when the letter was proved against her, she left the evidence to speak for itself, and

[1] Secours de dehors.
Forces dans le pais.
Armée d'Espagne au retour des Indes.
Armée of Trance au mesme temps, si la paix se faict.
Guise, s'il ne passe, tiendra la France occupée.
De Flandres, de mesme.
Ecosse, au mesme temps.
Irlande, aussy.
Coup. Sortie.
Ceulx cy sont les poinctz qu'en presence de la Roine ma maistresse et par son commandement je tiray pour faire la depesche en France, a scavoir, a l'Archevesque de Glasco, a l'Ambr. d'Espaigne, et a Charles Paget. Quant a la lettre escripte a Babington, sa Majesté me la baille pour la plus part escripte de sa main, et j'ay rien faict ny escript, comme j'ay protesté, sans son expres commandement et specialement touchant le point de son eschapper, et mettant la feu aux granges près de la mayson.   5 Sept., 1586.
                                        Ainsi signé NAU.

W. Burghley.	G. Shrewsbury.	H. Hunsdon.
H. Derby.	C. Howard.	W. Cobham.
J. Croft.	F. Walsingham.	(Vol. xix., n. 89, 90.)

[2] *Cotton. MSS.*, Caligula, C. ix., f. 533.
[3] *Hardwicke State Papers*, vol. i., pp. 233, 237.

then she made special exception against these sentences in the letter that relates to the Queen's murder. Speaking of "this day's work," October 15, the last day of the trial, Lord Burghley said to Secretary Davison, "This Queen of the Castle was content to appear afore us in public to be heard, but in truth not to be heard for her defence, for she could say nothing but negatively, that the points of the letters that concerned the practice against the Queen's Majesty's person were never by her written, nor of her knowledge; the rest, for invasion, for scaping by force, she said she would neither deny nor affirm."

But, says Mr. Froude, whether or no the passages italicized formed a part of Mary's letter, "if any part of it was hers," she was an accomplice in Babington's guilt, for it contains "a full general approbation of his intended proceedings and no prohibition of, and therefore a tacit consent to, the murder." It is not true that Mary's letter contains a single expression that can be interpreted as a "full general approbation" of all that was contained in Babington's letter. Mary tacitly rejected the plan of assassination. She writes taking Elizabeth's life for granted. But she never explicitly mentions the plot. Her letter is written exactly as though Babington had simply asked her advice how they should manage an insurrection and her rescue. Mr. Froude says that Mary told Charles Paget "that she had answered him [Babington] point by point." She does not say so. The word "answered" is Mr. Froude's, and not hers. She said,[1] "I have made them a very ample despatch, containing, point by point, *my advice* on all things requisite, as well for this side as for without the realm, to bring their designments to good effect." She did not answer Babington's letter point by point, though in her trial, as well as by Mr. Froude, it was alleged that she had so answered it. Her advice is given point by point on all the details of a simultaneous invasion and insurrection.

Mr. Froude says that the letter "was sworn to by the two secretaries in the deciphered form in which it was produced by Walsingham." The following are the hesitating attestations of Nau and Curle. "Je pense de vray que c'est la lettre escripte par

[1] *Cotton. MSS.*, Caligula, C. ix., f. 278; Labanoff, tom. vi., p. 401.

sa Majesté a Babington, comme il me souvient. 6 Septembre, 1586.
—NAU." "Telle ou semblable me semble avoir esté la response
escripte en françoys par Monsieur Nau, &c.—GILBERT CURLE."
We have no reason to believe that their depositions upon oath were
in other terms. These attestations were brought forward at the trial.
If anything more positive existed it would not have been kept back.
Mr. Froude further asserts that "Phillipps' copy of the cipher
was examined by the Privy Council and the decipher verified."[1]
But on what authority are these statements grounded? If the
cipher was endorsed by the Council, this in no way proves that
it had been tested by the key or alphabet. And as to Phelippes'
original decipher, far from this having been verified, it was not so
much as produced. Nothing but copies of Babington's letter
and Mary's alleged reply were put in evidence, nor was Phelippes
himself even brought forward to attest on oath the agreement
of those copies with his own decipher. Again, obviously with
a view to secure the reader's acceptance of the French copy
produced, as in truth Phelippes' decipher, Mr. Froude represents
Mary's own letter to Babington as written in French. But taking
it for granted, improbable as it seems, that the original was
French, then the endorsement upon this particular copy, "Tournée
d'Angloys en Francoys," will stamp it as a translation twice
removed from the original document.[2]

[1] *History*, vol. xii., p. 142.

[2] Nau stated that he drew Mary's answer in French and read it to her,
which being done, Curle put it into English by her commandment, and after
read it unto Nau, and then by her commandment, Curle put it into cipher.
Curle states explicitly that Mary ordered him to burn the English copy of the
letter sent to Babington (*Hardwicke State Papers*, p. 237). Nau affirmed
(September 21), that he took the points in the Scots' Queen's letter to
Babington of her own mouth from point to point in the same as he put in
writing, whereupon he did draw the letter in French, and after brought it
unto her, and she corrected it in such sort as it was sent to Babington (*Ibid.*,
p. 236). All letters, it was also deposed, were first drawn by Nau in French,
and after Mary had examined his draft, "*if they were to be written in English*,
then did Curle translate them out of French into English," he read them in
English to Mary, and then "he did put the same into cipher, and so they
were sent away." This was sworn to have been "the course holden" with
her letter to Babington (*Ibid.*, p. 235). The language, though not conclusive,
seems on the whole to describe the July letter to have been, like the letter
in June and Babington's answer, in English. However, be that as it may,
this "deciphered form produced by Walsingham," is nothing but a French
translation, for its endorsement is unmistakeable.

"The original cipher, having been passed on to Babington, was never recovered," says Mr. Froude. Perhaps so; yet either the original or Phelippes' copy of it was in the possession of Elizabeth's Ministers, for Lord Burghley wrote on the margin, of "A brief plot for the course of proceedings against the Scottish Queen,"[1] where he mentions her letter to Babington, "Note that the cipher be carried with us." Yet it was henceforward no more produced than the decipher that Phelippes marked with the gallows.

Mr. Froude says that Phelippes sent the original ciphered letters to Babington, and that the reason that it was not received by him for eleven days was that Barnes could not find him. This is, he says, in answer to the argument of Prince Labanoff, that the original cipher was detained by Phelippes for eleven days, in order that it might be tampered with. But even though the dates when the letter reached and left Phelippes had been those that Prince Labanoff supposes, the present question would not have been affected, for that original cipher is not forthcoming, and we are concerned only with the translation into French, and that Phelippes had undoubtedly the leisure to manipulate at will.

Mr. Froude contends that Mary's letter to Babington of July $\frac{17}{7}$ was forwarded to its destination on the very day after it reached Phelippes' hands, "like the rest of her letters." The facts show that from first to last all Mary's letters remained for some time in the decipherer's hands. Take for instance her packet to the French Ambassador intercepted by Phelippes at Stilton, on his way down to Chartley, July 8, of which he writes to Walsingham that after having manipulated it "he will send it with all speed." Poulet does not forward the packet to Walsingham until July 14. Phelippes' letter to Walsingham, July 19, by no means proves that the original cipher to Babington had already passed out of his hands. His chief evidently knew that he still held it, for writing to recall him in answer to Phelippes' letter, he simply requests the decipherer to bring with him the original. Phelippes took it up with him July 26, O.S. Babington did not receive it till the 29th, O.S. Of course Babington was easily persuaded that the delay was solely due to his absence from Lichfield.

[1] *Cotton. MSS.*, Caligula, C. ix., f. 507.

It is worthy of notice that, as the Hardwicke Papers[1] and Camden[2] show, Babington received his first letter "by a boy unknown to him,"—Barnes' boy, in fact. His answer he sent "by the same unknown boy." Upon which "she answered twenty or thirty days after in the same cipher by which he wrote unto her, but by another messenger." The first letter to Babington was, we see, really sent through Barnes and delivered by his footboy. The second letter, that which Phelippes calls the "bloody" one, which did not reach Babington till twenty or thirty days after his letter to her, came "by another messenger." Naturally this letter had been from the 17th to the 29th in the hands of Phelippes and Walsingham, and was delivered to Babington in London, not by Barnes' messenger, but by theirs, "a homely serving-man in a blue coat."

Phelippes to Walsingham.[3]

It may please your Honour,—You have now this Queen's answer to Babington, which I received yester-night. If he be in the country, the original will be conveyed unto his hands, and like enough an answer returned. I look for your honour's speedy resolution touching his apprehension or otherwise, that I may dispose of myself accordingly. I think under correc-tion you have enough of him, unless you would discover more particularities of the confederates, which may be [done] even in his imprisonment. If your honour mean to take him, ample commission and charge would be given to choice persons for search of his house. It is like enough for all her commandment, her letter will not be so soon defaced.[4] I wish it for an evidence against her, if it please God to inspire her Majesty with that heroical courage that were meet for avenge of God's cause and the security

---

[1] *Hardwicke State Papers*, vol. i., p. 227.

[2] *Annales Rerum Anglicarum*, 1625, p. 434.

[3] Vol. xviii., n. 61.

[4] "Ne faillez brusler la présente quant et quant" (Vol. xviii., n. 51; Labanoff, tom. vi., p. 394).

of herself and this State. At least I hope she will hang
Nau and Curle, who justly make Sir Amias Poulet take
upon him the name she imputes to him of a gaoler of
criminals. He trusteth that her Majesty will have better
consideration of all things necessary for his charge than it
appeared to him by my Lord Treasurer lately she had,
saying he had so many soldiers, and pinching at the
charges, which is no small offence to him, I assure you.
But being wonderfully comforted with these discoveries.

I have sent your honour herewith of this Queen's
letters in the packet was last sent those to the Bishop of
Glasgow, Dr. Lewis, and Morgan.[1] You may see how she
is weary of her keeper, who in truth hath made no such
change of his behaviour, but thought it policy to colour
matters with his ordinary proceeding used before, thinking
remissness would have discovered the practice. She is
very bold to make way to the great personage, and I fear
he will be forward in satisfying her for her change till he
see Babington's treasons, which I doubt not but your
honour hath care enough of not to discover which way
the wind comes in.

I am sorry to hear from London that Ballard is not yet
taken, and that some searches by forewarning have been
frustrate. There was great mean made unto me at my
coming away for one Thorowgood by your honour's favour
to pass the sea. It was pretended that he sought to avoid
Mr. Vice-Chamberlain's wrath, being one touched with the
death of Best. But it was a notorious enemy who was the
setter on of the suit and Mr. Vice-Chamberlain's man, and
it was whispered unto me that it should be Ballard to pass
under that feigned name. I was not assured, and therefore
rejected the motion, although a good gratification were
spoken of, which made it the more suspicious. Howbeit,
I have had, even in this country, inkling it should be he or

---

[1] *Cotton. MSS.*, Nero, B.vi., f. 400; vol. xviii., nn. 78 and 74; Labanoff,
tom. vi., pp. 381, 412, 420. The letter to Dr. Lewis no longer exists.

as bad a man. If it please your honour by Berden and my man to try it by a warrant, which you may stop by a counter-warrant to be. sent to the port of Rye, where he may be apprehended. If good come of it, I would be glad ; if not, he shall have no great injury if it be Thorowgood, and Mr. Vice-Chamberlain may bear the name.

And so attending your honour's speedy resolution whether we shall attend any longer here, I humbly take my leave.

Chartley, this 19th of July, 1586.

> Your honour's most humble at commandment,
>
> THO. PHELIPPES.

It may please your honour by Berden or my man to inform yourself whether Babington be at London or no, which known we will resolve presently upon return.

We come now to the forged postscript, the authenticity of which Mr. Froude boldly maintains against every respectable authority on the subject, from Camden downwards. The generally received view of this forgery—that after its fabrication by Phelippes, that particular scheme for connecting the Queen of Scots with the six conspirators being abandoned, the sentences fixing guilt upon her were interpolated into the body of her letter— this very probable hypothesis is presented by Mr. Froude, with a half-sneer at the "chivalry" which suggested it, as a theory set up by Prince Labanoff. Mr. Froude apparently forgets that the Prince simply reproduces Mr. Tytler's line of argument, and that the judgment pronounced on the postscript is not merely that of a chivalrous partisan, but the judicial verdict of a high historical authority.[1]

Prince Labanoff has pointed out that eight contemporary copies of Mary's letter to Babington are in existence, some

[1] The whole history of the Babington conspiracy and Walsingham's plot has been impartially investigated by Mr. Tytler, and the reader is especially referred to his "Historical remarks on the Queen of Scots' supposed accession to Babington's conspiracy" (*History*, vol. viii., App., n. 14).

in English and some in French, and that in none of them
is this postscript found.   Nothing is produced for it whatever from among the papers of the Queen of Scots that were
seized at Chartley, nor is any mention made of it in any of
their letters by Phelippes or Poulet.   Nothing was said about
it at Mary's trial, nor at any of the previous examinations of
her secretaries.   Nau's letter to Babington about Poley was
produced, but of this important postscript not a word was heard.
The copies of the Babington correspondence sent over to Paris
by the English Government before the trial at Fotheringay did
not include it.[1]   Surely in such a case the negative argument is
conclusive proof, and to it may be added the fact that the cipher
endorsed by Phelippes, looks to the eye extremely unlike those
which are Curle's undoubted work.   In fact what Mr. Tytler
found in the Record Office,[2] endorsed by Phelippes as " The
postscript of the Scottish Queen's letter to Babington," is his first
draft of an addition made by him to the letter to Babington, in
which, as it was only a draft, it was not worth his while to imitate
Curle's ciphers.   The sentence erased in the middle of the postscript bears out this view.

Camden informs us[3] that the postscript was " craftily added
in the same cipher" to the letter sent to Babington.   "Subdole
additum eodem charactere postscriptum, ut nomina sex nobilium
ederet, si non et alia."   Now why should such a postscript have
been added if the inculpating passages were in the original letter?

---

[1] The summary of Mary's letter to Babington made by Mendoza for
Philip is conclusive on this point.   Mr. Froude asserts that Mendoza believed
that Mary was a party to the assassination plot, and "told the King that she
had implicitly acknowledged it in a letter to himself."   This letter Mendoza
expressly says is not in cipher.   Would Mary have been so imprudent as to
write of Elizabeth's murder without that safeguard?   Besides, all her correspondence having passed through Walsingham's hands, can it be supposed that
such a letter as Mr. Froude suggests was actually written and no copy of it
produced at the trial?   The letter really referred to the Spanish invasion.
So far was Mendoza from belief in Mary's guilt that he replied to Elizabeth'
Government in respect of Mary's letter to Babington, that this was not the
first occasion upon which Walsingham and Cecil had forged letters, and that
having the ciphers of the Queen of Scots in their hands, they could insert
at will passages inculpating her (Mendoza to Philip, 8th November, 1586
Teulet).

[2] Vol. xviii., n. 55.

[3] *Annales,* p. 438.

Babington was intended to gather from it that Mary approved of the assassination, which in the body of the letter she had tacitly condemned, assuming, as we have seen, the life of Elizabeth and not her death. The postscript had its purpose to serve with Babington, but it would not have been evidence against Mary, and therefore the postscript was abandoned and the insertion made in the text of the letter.

Mr. Froude says[1] that Prince Labanoff "conceives that Phelippes intended first to make a mere addition, that he changed his mind, and recomposed afterwards the entire letter, that it was detained for that purpose, and that although one of the most dexterous manipulators of cipher in Europe, he did his work so clumsily that it can be seen through with ease by a critic of the nineteenth century."

Granted that Phelippes was a most skilful decipherer, he was here employed in copying or translating, and not in deciphering. Though "one of the most dexterous manipulators of cipher in Europe," the insertions are clumsily done, so that "they can be seen through with ease by a critic of the nineteenth century." If Phelippes had brought his skill in ciphering to bear, he might have baffled us no doubt, but he had no unusual skill that would enable him to insert phrases into a letter that were inconsistent with its tenour.

Mr. Froude finds it hard to say what other name should be given to Prince Labanoff's argument from the postscript than the epithet "preposterous," for it implies that "Phelippes preserved, endorsed, and placed among the papers to be examined by the Privy Council, his own first draft of a forgery which he rejected as unsuited to his purpose." That Phelippes preserved and endorsed the paper is true, but how does Mr. Froude know that it was placed before the Privy Council? If it had been, it would have been signed by the Lords of the Council. It was given to Walsingham no doubt, and thus it has come down to us amongst the State Papers. If Walsingham was in possession of a note so compromising to Mary in the original cipher, why did he not produce it against her? We are told that the original cipher of the letter to Babington was sent to him and could not be

[1] *History*, vol. xii., p. 143.

recovered. According to Mr. Froude, Barnes or Emilio took charge of this postscript together with the letter. How came the cipher of one to be recoverable and not of the other ? Having it, we should suppose that they would have supplied for the absence of the original of the long letter, by at least producing that which they had, the cipher of the postscript, which itself contained matter that would bring Mary's head to the block. What explanation is there but that of Prince Labanoff, preposterous as it seems to Mr. Froude, that Phelippes and his-master were content with one forgery without producing a second ? If this postscript had been produced, some recognition of it would have had to be extorted from Nau and Curle. It was easier far to get from them who knew that a long letter had been written, an attestation of a copy into which passages had been inserted without their knowledge, than it would have been to induce them to authenticate a fabricated postscript. And how does it happen that Nau and Curle were not taxed with having written it ?[1]

But Mr. Froude has discovered a proof of the authenticity of this conclusive yet unused postscript, in the letter which is next submitted to the reader. "A note from Curle to Emilio," he says " explains the mystery. Some 'addition' to the letter had been sent by mistake. It had perplexed Emilio, who had written to know what it was and what he was to do with it. Curle answered, 'I doubt by your former, which I found some difficulty in deciphering, that myself have erred in setting down the addition which I sent you, through some haste I had then in despatching thereof. I pray you forbear using the said addition, until that, against the next, I put the whole at more leisure in better order for your greater ease and mine.' Curle was by that time aware that Babington had not been at Lichfield, and, therefore, supposed rightly that the letter was still in Emilio's keeping. His description applies exactly to the 'postscript' which forms Prince Labanoff's text."

Let the reader test this theory of Mr. Froude's by substituting the word *postscript* for *addition* in the fragment of the letter quoted

---

[1] Dr. Lingard has very fully shown what was confessed by Mary's secretaries and the bearing of their evidence upon this point (*History*, Ed. 1844, vol. viii., p. 434, note M.).

by Mr. Froude, and he will see at once that the letter is turned into nonsense. This is an evident proof that Curle's description does not "apply exactly to the postscript." How could Emilio, whoever it was who passed under that name, or Barnes, "forbear *using* the said" *postscript?* Or how could Curle "put the whole *postscript* at more leisure in better order for Barnes' greater ease, and his own?" Indeed, how was Barnes to know which was letter and which was *addition?* Did he carry open letters to Babington, and was he possessed of the key to decipher Babington's letters?

The fact is that the *addition* was not a postscript to a letter, but a supplement to the cipher by which Barnes communicated with Curle. Every one of these practisers or intelligencers had their separate alphabet or cipher. Mary's letters tell us so plainly. For instance, she says to Morgan, "Mercier, for whom you have sent me an alphabet, hath yet written nothing unto me. Herewith be three other alphabets to be distributed as you find cause, until I send you more."[1] Indeed, in her letter of the 2nd of July, she speaks of a man who, "coming near to this house sent me your foresaid last which he delivered by Pietro [Gifford] his means, and the same man having written unto me a very honest letter in Pietro his alphabet, hath omitted the uttering of his name therein, neither given me any sign whereby I may know how to discern him assuredly by [from] another. For I have not nor cannot yet employ him, albeit I have sent my answer with a particular alphabet for himself whosoever he be."[2] He was Barnes, as his own declaration at the end of his letter[3] of June 10 shows most decisively, though why he should have communicated anonymously with Mary, making an offer of his service, when he was already in correspondence with Curle, it is not easy to see. Mary's answer to him,[4] dated June 19, says, "In the meanwhile I do herewith send you a new alphabet, conform to your desire."

As Mr. Froude must have seen from the letter on which he builds his theory, Barnes brought Mary "such occurrents" that

---

[1] Vol. xviii., n. 74; Labanoff, tom. vi., p. 425.
[2] Labanoff, tom. vi., p. 355, from the Cecil Papers, at Hatfield.
[3] Vol. xviii., n. 6.
[4] Vol. xviii., n. 10.

she gave him "continual thanks for his care and travail." To communicate this news, he needed an alphabet or cipher. Curle sent him some addition to it, and as it was written down in haste, he concluded that there must in consequence have been some error in it. He therefore prayed him to "forbear the using of the said addition until that against the next, he should put the whole at more leisure, in better order as he hoped to do both for Barnes' greater ease and his own," for Curle had "found Barnes' letters difficile in deciphering, and therefore some points less intelligible then he wished." This could surely have been gathered from the letter Curle wrote to "Emilio," and even from that part of it that Mr. Froude quotes.

But we are not left to deductions. Curle says to Barnes, July 17, "Herewith is *the addition to the alphabet;*" and Barnes answers, July 20, "I received your alteration of the alphabet. . . . I wish for great expedition also in writing, that you would assign special characters for a number of the most common words."[1] Curle answered, July 22,[2] "With my next, I shall do my best to satisfy you touching the other characters."

The two letters from Mary to Babington, of which Curle wrote in the letter of July 28, were those dated the 13th and the 17th of July. The first was Nau's letter to Babington about Poley; the second was the fatal letter. Mr. Froude,[3] neglecting the information contained in Phelippes' note to Walsingham of July 14th, says that the letter "was apparently in two parts." The letters were sent by Curle to Emilio, but it is not to be forgotten that neither Gifford nor any of his substitutes were ever seen by Mary or her secretaries. The letters in all cases fell into Phelippes' hands, and it was by him[4] that the answers were drawn up that they sent.

Of the "boy" whom Barnes is to send to the French Ambassador he said to Curle,[5] in order to make the treachery more natural and plausible, "I was bold to pray the Ambassador

---

[1] Vol. xviii., n. 57, 63.
[2] Vol. xviii., n. 42, wrongly dated in the Calendar July 12.
[3] *History*, vol. xii., p. 146.
[4] See, for instance, vol. xviii., n. 63.
[5] Vol. xviii., n. 6, in the Calendar erroneously entered as "with n. 26."

Q

to bestow an angel upon him, which would be a great encouragement to him, being a footboy, to run it, being also the manner
of our nation, and a trifle in the whole year to her Majesty." He
is no doubt the "laquay" whom Mary recommended[1] to Châteauneuf. "Continuez, je vous prie, toujours à gratifier ce laquay de
ce que trouverez bon, toutes et quantes foys qu'il vous portera
aulcunes lettres de ma part, et l'employez sur mes parties.'
We have here the "unknown boy" who delivered Mary's first
letter to Babington.

It is plain from the allusion to Emilio's "brother" in Curle's
letter, that Mary had been told that "the substitute," whoever he
was, and Barnes, "the second messenger," were brothers, cousins
to Gifford. So she says[2] to Morgan, that it was not for her to
retain Pietro, that is Gifford, in imminent danger in the country,
"when he had established as he hath done the honest brethren,
kinsmen of his, to serve the turn in his absence."

Apparently Mary was led to believe that more persons were
employed in her affairs than there really were. Curle wrote[3] to
Barnes, "I trust you have caused [to] deliver her Majesty's
answer to the second messenger, although (to say truly) her
Majesty agreeth with your cousin Gilbert his advice not much
to employ the man, neither hath her Majesty been willing at any
time to [take] this course for her part with any other than
yourself, your brother, and your cousin Gilbert." Gifford's
motive in casting doubts upon Barnes under the title of the
"second messenger," must have been to colour the deception,
unless indeed by thus multiplying themselves the knaves could
obtain more money from the Queen of Scots.

Singular care was taken that Emilio might not be known.
Gifford, even in his ciphered letters to Phelippes, takes care not
to mention his name. "When Morgan examined me secretly,
touching the parties that conveyed letters, I was forced to name
two, whereof Barnes was one, and for that purpose I dealt with
Barnes, never thinking," he says with an oath, "but to make him
a colour for Emilio; and his writing once or twice would cause all
blame to be removed from myself when things should be opened,

---

[1] Vol. xviii., n. 44; Labanoff, tom. vi., p. 370.
[2] Labanoff, tom. vi., p. 355.   [3] Vol. xviii., n. 87.

which I knew must be shortly, . . . but I thought to have withdrawn him after that Morgan had fully perceived that the convoy
.was sure; and one thing I will tell you, if you handle the matter
cunningly, Barnes may be the man to set up the convoy again for.
Paget, and Morgan be never in rest inquiring for him. I have
feigned as though the matter is irrecuperable, and therefore I have
speculated on the point." Phelippes followed the crafty advice
and for years kept up a correspondence with Charles Paget
through Barnes. "If you have Barnes," Gifford continues, "keep
him close; if you have him not . . . feign his hand to me. His
name is Pietro Mariani, and I pray you, use Emilio no more. Let
him be one of them that were hanged, for before God they will
suspect."[1] Phelippes did as he was told, and wrote to Gifford
that Emilio was one of those that were hanged.[2]

The endorsement of this letter, "Curle to Emilio" is in
Phelippes' hand. The other letters of Curle to Barnes are
addressed to him under the name of Barnaby.

Curle to Emilio.

Sir,—Her Majesty giveth you continual thanks for your
care and travail taken to let her understand of such occurrents as you do, whereof frequently her Majesty cannot be
advertised by others, as by the rare coming of secret
letters unto her hands which pass through yours you may
well judge. Your desire to have warning beforehand shall
be satisfied so well as may be, which hither-till hath not
been much forgotten, and specially for the sending of this
inclosed packet, whereof I wrote to you ten days before the
day appointed for despatching thereof, and should have
been sent unto you on Monday last were it not that those
which came with yours the same day caused it thus so
long to be stayed. Her Majesty prayeth you now to send
it away by your boy to the French Ambassador, so soon as
you may goodly. And if you think that you can find
Babington at London by the same means to make her
Majesty's two letters, which you have already, be surely

---

[1] Vol. xx., n. 45.   [2] *Domestic, Elizabeth,* vol. ccii., n. 38.

delivered unto him. Doubting by your former (which to tell you truly I found difficile in deciphering, and therefore some points less intelligible then I wished) that myself have erred in setting down the addition which I sent you,[1] through some haste I had then at despatching thereof, I pray you to forbear the using of the said addition until that, against the next, I put the whole at more leisure in better order, as I hope to do both for your greater ease and mine. If I have not mistaken your meaning, touching the mark that is for you, it is your desire that in your absence her Majesty's letters or mine requiring speedy deciphering, that on the back thereof for your brother his better direction as you name it, your said mark may be written twice or thrice, which until you let me know the contrary shall be so. God Almighty preserve you.

Friday, the 7th of August [July 28, O.S.].

CURLE.

The "papers sent herewith" were Mary's letters[2] to Charles Paget, Sir Francis Englefield, Châteauneuf, and Mendoza, which, as far as we know, complete the packet. Poulet's pious rejoicings as Mary's danger increases, correspond very little with Froude's belief[3] that "he probably liked ill the work that he was about, when he found the turn which it had taken."

Poulet to Walsingham.[4]

Sir,—I should do you wrong to trouble you with many words, the papers sent herewith containing matter enough of trouble for some time. God hath blessed your faithful and careful labours, and this is the reward due for true and faithful service.

And thus trusting that her Majesty and her grave Councillors will make their profit of the merciful providence

---

[1] *In the marg.* Against Curle.
[2] *Cotton. MSS.*, Caligula, C. ix., f. 354; vol. xviii., n. 76; vol. xix., n. 15, 2 ; Labanoff, tom. vi., pp. 399, 404, 427, 431.
[3] *History*, vol. xii., p. 139.
[4] Vol. xviii., n. 62.

of God towards her Highness and this State, I commit you to the mercy and favour of the Highest.

From Chartley, the 20th of July, 1586.

Your most assured poor friend,

A. POULET.

We have in the next letter an admission that throws all necessary light on Walsingham's subsequent conduct. Mary was heir apparent to the throne of England, and if Elizabeth were to die, she would be Queen. "Little comfort for their travail" was in store under such circumstances for the "instruments in the discovery." Up to this time, all that had been done might possibly have been concealed from her. Henceforward this is impossible, and Mary must die, if these "instruments" are to live. It will not be Walsingham's fault if "a good course" is not "held in this cause."

Walsingham to Phelippes.[1]

Sir,—At your return you shall from her Majesty's self understand how well she accepteth of your service. I hope there will be a good course held in this cause. Otherwise, we that have been instruments in the discovery shall receive little comfort for our travail. At your return come as quietly as you may, for that the practisers are jealous of your going down, and the gallows upon the packet sent hath greatly increased their suspicion. Some of them are very inward with our post of London.

Hope Bal. will be taken before your return. My friend remaineth still here. And so in haste I commit you to God.

At the Court, the 22nd of July, 1586.

Your loving friend,

FRA. WALSINGHAM.

Bab. shall not be dealt withal until your return. He remaineth here. The original letter unto him you must bring with you.

---

[1] Vol. xviii., n. 68.

Poulet to Walsingham.[1]

Sir,—I should do you great wrong to trouble you with long letters at this time, when Mr. Phelippes cometh unto you, who can inform you of the true state of all things here.

Mr. Waad shall be very welcome, and I trust his message will bring me great satisfaction many ways.

This Queen writeth very truly that I am no fit keeper for her, and she may say as truly that this house is no fit lodging for her.

I leave all these things to the better consideration of her Majesty, and so do take my leave of you, committing you and your labours to the direction of the Highest.

From Chartley, the 26th of July, 1586.

Your most assured poor friend,

A. POULET.

Poulet to Phelippes.[2]

Sir,—Besides the familiar use of letters between you and me, I did not know if anything were contained in this letter inclosed, which might require present execution, and therefore was bold to open it. I trust you are safely arrived at the Court, and it seemeth by Mr. Secretary's letters that upon your coming thither some resolution will be taken. God grant it be good, to whose blessed tuition I commit you.

From Chartley, the 29th of July, 1586.

Your assured friend,

A. POULET.

To my very good friend, Mr. Thomas Phelippes, esquire.

Poulet to Walsingham.[3]

Sir,—Your letters of the 24th of this instant arriving here on the 27th of the same at six in the evening, Mr. Phelippes was then twelve or fourteen miles on his

---

[1] Vol. xviii., n. 73.   [2] Vol. xviii., n. 88. Holograph.
[3] Vol. xviii., n. 89. Holograph.

way towards you, not doubting but that he is safely
arrived with you.

I thank God with you for the happy news you have
received from Sir Francis Drake, and do thank you most
heartily for your advertisement thereof.

You make mention in these letters of a counter-cipher
in these words, viz., "I pray you, sir, send me word
whether the counter-cipher I delivered unto you, for that
there will be use thereof in respect of the causes we are
to deal in hereafter." It seemeth that there is defect of a
word or two which maketh the sense unperfect, so as I
can give you no other answer than that to my remembrance I had no cipher of you sithence my entrance into
this service, whereof I thought good to advertise you,
because I do not know what hasty use there may be
thereof.

And so I commit you to the mercy and favour of
the Highest.

From Chartley, the 29th of July, 1586.

Your most assured poor friend,

A. POULET.

None of the letters next mentioned as having been written
"with greediness" are in the Record Office. Those that are in
the Calendar under the date July 27, are of July 17, O.S., and
were taken by Phelippes. Mr. Thorpe has changed some of the
new style dates into old style, but not all, which is very confusing.

Poulet to Walsingham.[1]

Sir,—I have no other cause of writing at this time than
to convey unto you this packet inclosed, which bewrayeth
that this people is sharp set, and writeth with greediness,
as knoweth the Almighty, who keep you now and ever.

From Chartley, the 30th July, 1586.

Your most assured poor friend,

A. POULET.

[1] Vol. xviii., n. 91.

The plan proposed by Poulet in the following letter was new perhaps in some of its details, but in the main similar orders had been given by Elizabeth several years before, though they were then recalled. Elizabeth gave instructions,[1] January 16, 1580, to Lord Shrewsbury, Sir Ralph Sadler, and Sir Henry Pelham, to remove Mary from Sheffield to Ashby, and then, she continues, "immediately upon your imparting to her this our commandment, you shall seize upon all her writings and letters, both in the custody of herself and also of her secretaries, and of any others that deal with her secret affairs; which if she, or her secretaries, or any other, shall refuse to deliver, or suffer you to take in quiet manner, in that case our pleasure is that you shall use all means to have the same, by taking their keys or otherwise by breaking their coffers, desks, cabinets, and other things where the same writings may be found; and then, without further perusing of the same, or any of them, to put all such writings and letters into convenient or sure coffers or trunks, and sealing up the same with the seals of you all three, or of two of you, you our said cousin [Lord Shrewsbury] shall bring the said coffers and writings safely unto us." These instructions were not the consequence of a Babington conspiracy.

Poulet to Walsingham.[2]

Sir,—I heard from Mr. Waad yesterday, at six after noon, and this morning I met with him in the open fields, where I conferred with him at good length, as may appear by these notes inclosed.

Mr. Bagot deserveth to be thanked by letters for his faithful service. He procured the substitute, and was the only messenger between him and me. He hath been charged and troubled many ways, as knoweth the Almighty, who always preserve you.

From Chartley, the 3rd of August, 1586.

Your most assured poor friend,

A. POULET.

---

[1] *State Papers* of Sir Ralph Sadler, vol. ii., p. 355.
[2] Vol. xix., n. 7. Holograph.

Inclosure in Poulet's handwriting—

A memorial for Mr. William Waad.

1. That her Majesty doth think meet Sir Amias Poulet should consider in what sort the Queen his charge's writing might be best seized, whether remaining there or removing her to some other place under the colour of hunting or taking the air.

> This Queen will be easily entreated to kill a stag in Sir Walter Aston's park,[1] where order being taken with her, some gentlemen of credit may be sent forthwith to possess her chamber and cabinets in this house, and to remove out of them the gentlewomen which they shall find there.

2. That he also consider how Curle and Nau may be best apprehended, and in what sort.

> It seemeth meet that Nau and Curle be apprehended at the very instant of the challenge made to this Queen.

3. That there shall be some especial gentleman sent from hence to conduct them up, if he find none other or shall so think meet.

> I would not advise that this shire should be unfurnished of any gentlemen of trust and credit, but that two gentlemen be sent from above to take the charge of the conducting of Nau and Curle, thereby to keep them from conference. Pasquier is half a secretary and much employed in writing, and perchance not unacquainted with great causes.

4. That he consider whether it be not fit to remove her, and to what place he shall think meet she should be removed; what necessary persons are to be retained about her, and in what sort she shall be kept.

---

[1] " The park was a very noble one, five or six miles about, with five or six hundred head of deer, with about thirty or forty red deer" (Sir Edward Southcote's *Narrative; Troubles of our Catholic Forefathers*, first series, p. 403).

The cabinets and other places cannot be duly searched unless she be removed, because the doing thereof will require some leisure, and she cannot be lodged in any other place in this house than where the cabinets are. Three gentlewomen, her master cook, her panterer, and two grooms of her chamber may seem to suffice in the beginning of this remove, which may be increased when things shall be settled.

5. To advertise in what sort he thinketh meet she should be removed, and under what guard.

Sir Walter Aston's house seemeth for many causes the fittest for this remove, who may convey her directly from his park to his house with the assistance of my horsemen and others. I think he will require to be assisted with my guards of soldiers, who may take their table and lodging in the village adjoining, and because the house is of no strength, if I were in Sir Walter Aston's place I would require some stronger guard.

6. Whether he have not already sufficient commission for the calling of the assistance of the well-affected gentlemen unto him, and if he have not, then to advertise what further commission he will require.

I have already her Majesty's commission for the levying of forces in very ample manner.

7. Whether he do not think it meet to have some especial gentleman sent from hence to acquaint that Queen with the cause of her Majesty's attempts towards her.

I do not see how any man here can take knowledge of these secrets, and therefore meet to commit the same to some gentleman to come from you.

8. That some servant of his own be sent up with all speed with his resolution touching these points, as also such other matters as he shall find requisite to receive

informatiom from hence. That the party that shall be sent be in no sort made acquainted with the matter.

> One of my servants cometh herewith, utterly ignorant of all these things.

9. That her Majesty hath thought meet you should stay there to assist him wherein he may have use of you.

> Mr. Waad stayeth here, but Mr. Bagot's house being much resorted unto, he retired to the house of a gentleman of meaner calling of his acquaintance.

10. That he carry a watchful eye over his charge, and that in such sort as may engender no suspicion.

> This shall be performed as near as I may.

11. That the extraordinary posts be commanded to use more diligence, and to that purpose to keep two horses at the least in the house for the packets.

> It seemeth meet that this order come from you, and I will also require it.

12. To signify his opinion touching the gentlemen in that county, and in other counties next adjoining, who are well affected and fit to be used for this service.

> I have lived as a prisoner in this country and therefore not well acquainted with the state thereof, but I have conceived upon good experience a very good opinion of Sir Walter Aston, Mr. Bagot, and Mr. Gresley, all three neighbours to this house. Mr. Trentham is one of the lieutenants of this shire and of very good report, but I have had little to do with him.

13. To consider what order shall be taken with the unnecessary number of her servants, especially with young Pierrepont.

> Although I take Mr. Melvyn to be free from all practices, and indeed liveth as a stranger to his own company, and hateth Nau deadly, yet I think meet that he be removed from his mistress to some gentleman's house, as likewise Mrs. Pierrepont; who

may be sent, the one to Mr. Trentham, and the other to Mr. Bagot, directly from Sir Walter Aston's park. The residue of the servants may remain in this house until further order shall be taken.

Endorsed—Sir A. Paulett's postills[1] to Mr. Waad's Memorial.

Poulet's plan was adopted, but definite orders to carry it into execution cannot have reached him before the 10th. But if the orders were received late in the afternoon of the 8th, it can hardly have been " le même jour," as Prince Labanoff says,[2] that they were carried into execution. John Allen wrote a report,[3] February 11, of the communications that passed between himself and Nau.

Poulet to Walsingham.[4]

Sir,—This bearer, your servant Mr. John Allyn, arrived here with your letters unto me this present day at six after noon, who hath delivered unto me your full mind in the matter touched in your said letters, which shall be duly performed, by the grace of God, to whose blessed tuition I commit you and your heavy and troublesome charge.

From Chartley, the 8th of August, 1586.

Your most assured poor friend,

A. POULET.

The following instructions, the draft of which is in Walsingham's hand, were brought to him by Mr. Gorge. Poulet was not able to follow these instructions literally, for, as he says in a subsequent letter, he had his " hands full" at Tixall. The gentlemen who were employed on this service, were, we learn from Camden,[5] John Manners, Edward Aston,[6] Richard Bagot,

---

[1] *Postil*, Fr. postille, a gloss, a marginal note. *Johnson.*

[2] Tom. vi., p. 437.

[3] Vol. xxi., n. 17.

[4] Vol. xix., n. 22. Holograph.

[5] *Annales*, p. 441.

[6] Sir Walter Aston died in 1589. Sir Edward his son was made a knight banneret by Queen Elizabeth on his coming of age. He was the father of Walter, first Lord Aston, so that the statement (*supra*, p. 99) that Lord Aston was the son of Sir Walter needs correction.

and William Waad. The draft of the letter of Elizabeth to Poulet was also written by Walsingham.

Instructions for A. P.[1]

You shall, with all convenient speed as you may, under the colour of going a hunting and taking the air, remove the Queen your charge to some such house near to the place where she now remaineth as you shall think meet for her to stay in for a time, until you shall understand our further pleasure for the placing of her. And to the end she may be kept from all means of intelligence, we think it convenient you give order that such as are owners of the house where you shall place her for a time shall be removed, saving such persons as are to furnish all necessaries of household, of which number there would be no more left remaining in the house than necessity shall require.

You shall return [to] Chartley from the place where you meanwhile remove her, cause her servants Curle and Nau to be apprehended and to be delivered to the hands of some trusty gent. of that county, or the counties next adjoining, such as you shall know to be discreet, faithful, and religious, to conduct them to London with some convenient guard, where there shall be order given for the bestowing of them.

You shall also take order with the said conductors to see them brought up in two several troops, and to have an especial care that they may be kept from conference with any person in their way towards London, and to appoint, in places where they shall lodge, good standing watches to be kept in the night season.

You shall, immediately after she shall be departed from Chartley, search all such papers as shall be found either in her own lodging, or in the lodging of any that appertain to her (taking care that all secret corners in the said lodging

---

[1] Vol. xix., n. 31.

be very diligently sought), to be seized and to be put up in some bags or trunks, as by you shall be thought meet. In execution of which service we think it very convenient for many respects that you should use, besides our servant Waad, two principal gentlemen of credit either of that county, or of some shire of the counties next adjoining; for which purpose we think John Manners the elder and Sir Walter Aston very meet to be used, if they shall [be] found in the country, or some of like quality, whom we would have in no sort made acquainted with the said service until the said Queen shall be removed, and they brought to the place when and where it shall by you [be] thought meet to be performed.

You shall cause the said gentlemen, together with Mr. Waad, to seal [with] their seal of arms the said bags or trunks where the said letters and papers shall be placed, and to send up two of their trusty servants, together with Waad, with the said writings.

You shall do well, during the time of her abode in the the place and house to the which you shall remove her, to cause some substantial watches to be kept both about the house, as also in the town next adjoining, wherein we doubt not but that you will have an especial regard to use the services of such the justices and gentlemen in that county as you shall know to be well affected, giving them especial charges to make choice of well affected men to be employed in the said watches, and not such as are known to be recusants, or otherwise ill affected.

And in case you shall see cause, for the better strengthening of yourself, to use some other well-affected gentlemen in the counties next adjoining, you may therein use your own discretion, for which purpose we have sent unto you certain letters signed by us, referring the direction of them to yourself.

And whereas our meaning is not that hereafter she shall have such number of attendants upon her person as she hath heretofore had, we think meet, therefore, that you make choice of so many of her train, both men and women, as you shall see only necessary to attend on her person. And for the rest of her train, we think it convenient that they should be kept together at Chartley, in such sort as there may be no access had unto them until you shall understand our further pleasure how we shall afterwards think meet they shall be bestowed.

For your better assistance in this service, we have thought good to send unto you this bearer our servant, Thomas Gorge, one whom we know to be most faithfully devoted unto us, to be by you used in such sort as shall appertain to one of his place and calling. We have in no sort made him acquainted with the cause of his employment, but have referred him to receive directions from you, who we think meet should deliver as much in speech with the said Queen as is expressed in our letters to you.

Endorsed—August 9, 1586. Instructions for Sir A. Poulet.

Queen Elizabeth to Poulet.[1]

Right trusty, &c.,—We having of late discovered some dangerous practices, tending not only to the troubling of our estate, but to the peril of our own person, whereunto we have just cause to judge both the Queen your charge and her two secretaries, Nau and Curle, to have been both parties, and assisting in a most unprincely and unnatural sort, and quite contrary to our expectation, considering the great and earnest protestations she hath heretofore made of the sincerity of her love and goodwill towards us. Our pleasure therefore is, that first you cause the two secretaries to be apprehended, and to be sent up unto us under good and sure guard, and that you do presently remove the said Queen unto some such place as by you shall be thought meet, and there to see her securely kept, with so many

[1] Vol. xix., n. 30.

only of her train to tend on her person as by you shall be thought necessary, until you shall understand our further pleasure therein.

Endorsed—A minute of a letter to Sir A. P.

Châteauneuf's letter to Mary—the last he wrote to her—is dated August 5.[1] Of this journey of Du Jardin, and of another journey that followed it, Châteauneuf says in his Memoir,[2] that on July $\frac{20}{30}$ Gifford came to Cordaillot and said that it was of importance that he should send a messenger into France in all haste, for letters to and fro were too slow for their purpose. Gifford was accompanied by Savage, one of Babington's accomplices, and a third person, who was to be the messenger. "Pour lors l'ambassadeur dépêchait un des siens vers le roi, nommé Du Jardin, qui revenait d'Escosse, où ledit sieur ambassadeur l'avait envoyé pour le service du Roi; et, se présentant cette occasion, le secrétaire lui dit que leur homme pourrait passer comme serviteur dudit Du Jardin, portant sa malle, et cela fut ainsi arrêté entr'eux; et furent avertis du jour du partement, qui était le lendemain au soir à la marée, par la voie de Calais." The next evening, just as Du Jardin was starting Gifford came, equipped for the voyage, and saying that he had changed his mind about sending a messenger, and would go himself. On this the Ambassador took him aside, and in the presence of Du Jardin and Cordaillot spoke to him seriously of the danger he was bringing on the Queen of Scots. His frequent journeys, he told him, betrayed the existence of some plot, and he begged him not to be urged by those who were out of the reach of danger, and especially by Mendoza, to undertake anything that might cause risk to Mary, "à ne perdre pas cette princesse, laquelle avait des ennemis près la Reine." The Memoir here unfortunately breaks off, the latter portion being lost. Du Jardin crossed that evening, July 21,[3] and Gifford went with him, never to return. He left behind

[1] Vol. xix., nn. 15, 16.
[2] Labanoff, tom. vi., p. 292.
The despatch he carried is in the Bibliothèque Nationale at Paris, and shows the correctness of this date. Labanoff, tom. vi., p. 292.

him, Camden says,[1] the half of a torn paper with the French Ambassador, with instructions that letters from the Queen of Scots or any of the Catholic exiles were to be given only to the person that should produce the other half of the paper; and that other half he left with Walsingham. On the 15th August he wrote from Paris both to Phelippes and Walsingham, hoping that his sudden departure was not judged "sinistrously." Phelippes and Walsingham answered him through Cordaillot—which seems strange—but he said he had left his cipher behind him and could not read their letters.[2] As the Catholics had discovered all, he was in great disgrace with them, but Walsingham and Phelippes would find him the same man as long as they would deal secretly. On the 3rd September he wrote again to Walsingham, entreating to know how he could serve him, and assuring him that he never meant to deal otherwise than plainly. Gifford went to Rheims and Rouen, where he passed under the name of Jacques Colerdin.[3] It was on the occasion of this visit to Rheims that Gifford was ordained Priest.[4] He was, it will be remembered, a deacon when he began his communications with the Queen of Scots.

In April, 1587, he returned to Paris,[5] and towards the end of the year he was arrested and confined in the prison of the Bishop of Paris. "Gifford, being a Priest, lived in Paris, and was apparelled as our disguised Priests are in England, whereat divers men were offended." "The occasion of his first taking was for that he was taken of a sudden in a suspected house." So a Priest, who signed his letter Henry Cæsar, wrote to Walsingham.[6] Sir Edward Stafford, the English Ambassador at Paris, thought[7] "that they will put him to a hard plunge, for they mean to take him upon this point, which indeed letters (as I hear that they have of his

---

[1] *Annales*, p. 441.

[2] Vol. xix., nn. 45, 46, 70, 71, 82.

[3] *Domestic, Elizabeth*, vol. cxcix., nn. 20, 95.

[4] In the Douay Diary, amongst those promoted to the priesthood in 1587, occurs the name, "Gilbertus Giffordus, Lichfildien."

[5] *Domestic, Elizabeth*, vol. cc., nn. 48, 65.

[6] *Domestic, Addenda, Elizabeth*, vol. xxx., n. 120.

[7] *Ibid.*, n. 69.

R

with his own hand written to Phelippes) will make hard against him, that he became a Priest by cunning to deceive the world, and that he had, being become a Priest with that intent, said Mass after." Sir Edward did his best to obtain his liberty, saying,[1] "If I can and he will, I will find means to send him into England, for if he were away, what letters soever be taken there [could] be said to be counterfeit; but if he be here to avow them by constraint, they will make their profit of them greatly. They say they find that by Phelippes' mean he kept intelligence with her Majesty."

Though Gifford turned against the Ambassador, who called him "the most notable double treble villain that ever lived, for he hath played upon all hands in the world," yet under the name of Jacques Colerdin, or Francis Hartley, he found means in prison to carry on his correspondence with Phelippes and Walsingham. Thus from his French prison he reported[2] the arrival on the English mission of Father John Gerard, and of other Priests with him in 1588. He remained in prison till he died, which, as we learn from one of the letters[3] of Father Henry Walpole among the Stonyhurst Manuscripts, was in 1590.

Poulet to Walsingham.[4]

Sir,—I find nothing in this Queen's packet, received here the 5th [? 8th] of this present month to be imparted unto you saving this copy inclosed of a letter sent to this Queen from the French Ambassador in Scotland, by Du Jardin, belonging to the French Ambassador gone and lately returned out of Scotland as it seemeth.

---

[1] *Domestic, Addenda, Elizabeth,* vol. xxx., n. 53.

[2] *Domestic, Elizabeth,* vol. ccxvii., n. 3.

[3] Recently edited with great care for private circulation by the Rev. Augustus Jessopp, D.D. The letter is dated Brussels, November 29, 1590, and the passage speaks of Morgan as well as Gifford. "Morgan's matter is here now to be ended one way or other, such order being come out of Spain. I hear that they that handle it say that there is very much information against him, but he avoideth without full proof in great matters. 'Tis doubtful whether they will put the poor man to the torture or no. Gilbert Gifford is dead in prison in Paris."

[4] Vol. xix., n. 23.

The French Ambassador writeth to this Queen that there is no hope of her remove from hence, or of any passport to be granted for a new supply of servants, and touching Pierrepont he writeth that he findeth her Majesty indifferent for her stay here, or for her return to her friends, as this Queen shall think good. And thus I leave to trouble you, beseeching God to strengthen you with His mighty Spirit to endure the trouble of this busy time.

From Chartley, the   August, 1586.

Your most assured poor friend,

A. POULET.

The two following letters come straight from Elizabeth, who certainly gave her direction in very minute detail. It is important to notice that Nau and Curle were imprisoned in Sir Francis Walsingham's own house. Francis Mills, Walsingham's secretary, said in October,[1] that he was "tied to the custody of Nau." We shall see subsequently that Walsingham was determined to have both Nau and Curle in his power, by drawing from them admissions which would put their lives at Elizabeth's mercy.

Nicasius Yetsweirt to Walsingham.[2]

Right Honourable,—My duty humbly remembered. About ten of the clock I received a packet from your honour wrapped in the letter to me, which packet I delivered forthwith unto her Majesty. When she had read both Sir Amias' and yours, she marvelled that the clause her Highness wrote in the foot of my letter should so trouble you, and you construe the same so, as if her Highness had put you in the number of those she meant, considering that you could not but be assured of the assured good opinion she had of you all manner of ways, and of your great care and diligence you ceased not to use in her affairs, with many other good and gracious words which I cannot here express.

---

[1] *Domestic, Elizabeth*, vol. cxciv., n. 18.   [2] Vol. xix., n. 47.

R 2

Her Majesty hath written to Sir Amias and to your honour, whereby I doubt not but that both he and your honour shall know amply of her pleasure. The letters be both unsealed and wrapped up in a paper sealed with my seal.

Her Majesty willed me to let you know how thankfully she taketh the trouble and charges from time to time you bear with those that are committed unto you, and now for the lodging and guarding of Nau and Curle, you have already prepared for them as you have written to her Majesty. In the keeping and guarding of whom, as her Majesty doubteth not but shall be with all safety, so she would not have you to bestow too large a diet upon them, but as becometh prisoners. And her Majesty thinketh that they shall not need to have anybody to attend upon them in their chambers, but have their meats and necessaries brought unto them by such as by you shall be appointed, and so left in their chambers under lock and key, for her Majesty thinketh that they be not so desperate as either to hang or kill themselves.

Further, her Majesty would have you in your letters to require Sir Amias Poulet to write unto her the whole story of those things done in this matter to the Queen of Scots and to hers, not for any other cause but that her Majesty might take pleasure in the reading thereof. And whereas her Highness doth understand that the charge of the Queen of Scots' household folk are [is] committed to Mr. Darrell, who attendeth there, she thinketh him not sufficient for such a charge, and therefore would have Sir Amias to consider thereof as is needful. And touching the Queen's chaplain, how he shall be used, her Highness doth refer the same to his wisdom and discretion.

As touching the three prisoners, Babington, Barnewall, and Savage, remaining at Mr. Vice-Chamberlain's,[1] her

---

[1] Sir Christopher Hatton, who was made Lord High Chancellor, April 29, 1587.

Majesty doth not mean that they shall be sent to the Tower before they be thoroughly examined.

Whereas in my last letter I wrote unto your honour that none should have sight of the letters she delivered unto you at your being here with her Majesty, her Highness has willed me to signify unto you that she is well pleased that Mr. Vice-Chamberlain have a sight of them, knowing his loyalty and faithfulness to be such towards her as she dareth trust him with her life.

Her Majesty hath signed the letter to my Lord Mayor of London of her gracious acceptation of the joys and affections the people there declared for the apprehension of these traitors, which I send unto your honour in this packet.

And thus I humbly take my leave of your honour.

From Windsor, this 19th of August, 1586.

Your honour's humble at commandment,

NICASIUS YETSWEIRT.

Addressed—To the Right Honourable Sir [Amias Pou. *erased*] Francis Walsingham, knight, principal Secretary to the Queen's Majesty, and one of her Highness' most honourable Privy Council.

Endorsed—August 19, 1586, from Mr. Nicasius.

Nicasius Yetsweirt to Walsingham.[1]

Right Honourable,—I have declared unto her Majesty the contents of your honour's letter I received this evening, and her Highness liketh very well the order taken for the safe bringing of Nau and Curle, and the things that Mr. Gorge and Mr. Waad hath charge of also besides, which I perceive be caskets with writings. And her Majesty being very careful to have those caskets safely brought, though I told her that according to her pleasure, signified unto your honour in my letter this day, you had

---

[1] Vol. xix., n. 50.

despatched a discreet person to assist Mr. Gorge and Mr. Waad in his charge, yet her Highness is scant satisfied with that, and would have you to provide yet better herein, and specially that the said caskets might be brought under sure conduct and by sure persons before, for her Highness esteemed more of the caskets and of the things contained in them than of Nau and Curle, for in comparison, little she esteemeth them in respect of the caskets.

This afternoon the French Ambassador resident here, and M. d'Esneval, who is come out of Scotland, had audience, and her Majesty told me that she never saw a man more perplexed than the legier[1] Ambassador here, for when he was about to speak, every joint in his body did shake, and his countenance changed, and specially when this intended enterprise was somewhat mentioned by her Majesty. Whereupon, seeming to take some more heart unto him, said unto her Majesty, "I would have moved some suits unto you, but that I see that your Majesty is somewhat troubled with these *jeunes follastres* that are apprehended." "Yes," said her Majesty, "they be such *jeunes follastres* as some of them may spend ten and twenty thousand francs of rent, and it may be that there are some may spend more."

Her Majesty seemeth to me afraid that this Ambassador might work some mischievous means to disturb the quiet and sure bringing up of these men and things before named; wherefore she willed me in any wise to put your honour in remembrance that special care be had thereof.

Her Majesty is marvellously glad of the apprehension of Roger Yardley, and prayeth you that he may be well looked unto. It seemeth unto me that her Majesty hath heard before of his quality. I had no time to tell

---

[1] *Leger* (from Dutch *legger*, to lie), anything that lies in a place, as a leger Ambassador, a resident; a leger-book, a book that lies in a counting-house. *Johnson.*

her of M. de Civille, which I will perform, God willing, to-morrow in the morning.

And thus, humbly taking my leave of your honour, I pray God have the same always in His blessed keeping.

From Windsor, this 21st of Angust, 1586, at nine of the clock at night.

Your honour's humble at commandment,

NICASIUS YETSWEIRT.

Châteauneuf's report of this audience to Henry III.[1] is widely at variance with Elizabeth's statements to Yetsweirt, and the Ambassador's account is corroborated by d'Esneval's letter to Courcelles,[2] September 2, intercepted by Walsingham. The latter runs thus : "Depuis M. de Chasteauneuf ayant faict demander audience à la Royne d'Angleterre, nous l'allasmes trouver Dimanche dernier a Vindsor où elle est, et receut M. de Chasteauneuf et moy aveques toute favorable demonstration. Et apres beaucoup d'honnestes langages passez entre nous," &c. But he goes on to say that Elizabeth, when she heard that Courcelles was left in Scotland in the place of d'Esneval, "aussy tost faict une grande exclamation ;" that in reply d'Esneval said that he was a faithful servant of his King, "ce qui la mit fort en cholere," &c.

Another letter[3] from d'Esneval to Courcelles, dated October 7, contains passages respecting the Queen of Scots' apprehension, well deserving of insertion here.

"Monsieur,—Ayant faict mes affayres a Londres, je suis venu en ce lieu de Rye pour me trajetter a Dieppe, dont je ne veulx partir sans vous advertir de ma bonne santé.

"Touteffoys pour faire scavoir comme se passe le faict de la Royne d'Escosse que j'ay appris plus particulierement depuis vous avoir escript a quelques jours, que Sir Amias Poulet mena la dite Dame Royne pour aller a la chasse, ou s'estant acheminée

---

[1] Von Rammer, *History of the Sixteenth and Seventeenth Centuries*, p. 123. Teulet.

[2] *Scotland, Elizabeth*, vol. xli., n. 12.

Scotland, Elizabeth, vol. xli., n. 30.

avec tous les siens, mesmes Nau et Courles ses secretaires, Gorges l'aysne la vint trouver et luy feit entendre qu'il avoit charge de la Royne sa maistresse la mener a une maison a troys lieues de Charteley, nommé Tixsal, qui est a Sieur Edouard Haston, et aussy de se saysir des personnes de Nau et Curle, ce qui la mit en telle colere qu'elle l'outragea fort de parolles et sa maistresse : mesmes voulust que les siens se missent en defence.　Touteffoys Gorges estant le plus fort, Sir Amias Poulet la mena ou il avoit charge, et Gorges emmena ses secretaires. Pendant les quelles entrefaites il y avoit un secretaire du Conseil, nommé Wade, a Chartley, qui fouilla tous les papiers de la dite Dame Royne, des quelz il se saisit et les fist mener avec les prisonniers, et vantent que ce sont les plus secretz et importans. Je ne sçay s'il est veritable, ou si c'est pour s'en prevaloir de cela en quelque artifice, des quelz ils sont tant inventeurs comme de leur part Maistre [blank] m'a voulu dire ce jours icy, qu'ilz avoyent trouvé le testament de la dite Dame, par le quel elle donnoyt l'Angleterre et l'Escosse au Roy d'Espaigne, qui n'est comme vous jugerez bien, que pour aigrer contre elle le Roy d'Escosse son filz, vers le quel vous luy sçaurez je m'asseure bien faire les bons offices desquelz elle a besoing. . . .

"Cependant Monsieur de Chasteauneuf a envoyé ces jours icy vers Monsieur le Grand Tresorier son secretaire, par le quel il luy escripvoyt que ayant entender que Nau et Curle estoyent prisonniers, il avoyt desiré scavoir la verité, et si ainsy estoyt les advertir qu'ilz estoyent serviteurs du Roy de France mis par sa Majesté pres la dite Dame pour les affaires de son Douaire. Que estantz telz il le promit d'advertir la Royne souveraine et Messieurs du Conseil qu'ilz y eussent esgard.　Le dit Grand Tresorier sans faire aultre response addressa le dit Sieur a Walsingham qui estoyt la present, et luy bailla la lettre du dit Sieur de Chasteauneuf, laquelle il leut, et apres luy dit que la Royne d'Escosse estoyt une tres mauvaise femme, et ses secretaires tres meschantz, et que la Royne sa souveraine en feroyt justice, et qu'ilz n'advanceroyent rien en cela qu'ilz ne le communicassent a Monsieur l'Ambassadeur, et qu'il trouveroyt de telles meschancetez qu'il s'asseuroyt qu'il ne vouldroyt ny Madame de Chasteauneuf (qu'il sçavoyt aymer la Royne d'Escosse) parler pour elle a la Royne sa souveraine, la quelle envoyeroyt encores un gentilhomme[1] vers le Roy de France pour luy faire entendre le faict. Il semble que Walsingham veuilla desja divertir ceulx qu'il scayt se devoir employer pour la dite Dame. Mais cela ne retiendra pas le dit Sieur Ambassadeur qu'il n'a obmis ny obmettra, non plus que je feray estant en Cour, aucune chose qui puisse apporter ayde et secours aux affayres de la dite Dame Royne, de laquelle je n'ay par ceste aultres nouvelles, si non que je suis parti de Londres on y devoyt amener une de ses damoyselles prisonnière, nommée Pierrepont. Il y a beaucoup de personnes en peine pour ce fait, une bonne nombre est prise (*sic*) et les aultres poursuiviz. Je vous envoye les noms. C'est tout que vous aurez de moy a present."

As a supplement to d'Esneval's account of the seizure of the Queen of Scots, we may add a record that shows that something more than papers were "taken away" from Chartley.

"A note of such things as were taken away which were the Queen of Scots."[2]

"First, a glass furnished with two crystals and two tables or covers on each side. Within the one is the picture of the Queen of England, within the other the picture of the Queen of Scots, and the said tables are enamelled and garnished with diamonds, rubies, and emeralds.

"*Item*, a little chest garnished with diamonds, rubies, and pearls.

"*Item*, a set garnished with diamonds, rubies, and pearls, and emeralds in the midst.

"*Item*, a pair of bracelets of agate, garnished with little rubies.

"*Item*, a jewel pendant, garnished with diamonds, rubies, and emeralds.

"*Item*, one other jewel to hang, wherein is a sapphire garnished with small rubies.

"*Item*, one other little jewel, enamelled with white and carnation.

"*Item*, one other little jewel of the fashion of an agate.

---

[1] Sir Edward Wotton was sent on this mission to France. Camden, *Annales*, p. 443.

[2] Vol. xx., n. 44.

"*Item*, a little pincase of gold, a chain to wear for a girdle for a woman, enamelled with white and red.

"*Item*, a chain for a man, all plain without enamel, weighing six marks, five ounces, and five pennyweights.

"*Item*, in white money about a seven score pounds.

"*Item*, one piece of twenty ducats.

"Two doublets, the one of russet satin, the other of canvas.

"*Item*, one black velvet cap, with a green and black feather in the same; three mufflers of embroidery, whereof two be of black velvet.

"*Item*, two carcanets[1] or bad [? badge] chains, embroidered with gold and silver.

"*Item*, other black set with pearls.

"*Item*, four vessels of sweet powder.

"*Item*, one pair of silk stocks."

Endorsed—Goods stolen from the Queen of Scots.

The well known letter that follows has no date, but its place in this series is indicated by the mention of it in Poulet's letter from Tixall of the 22nd of August. It has been often printed. Strype[2] gives it "as transcribed from a copy thereof taken by Michael Hacket, the Lord Treasurer's Secretary." There it is headed, "To my faithful Amias."

Mr. Froude prints[3] this letter with the remark that in it Elizabeth's "better nature struggles with her affectation with rather more success than usual." When Elizabeth wrote it, probably in her own mind she had fixed upon Poulet as the man who, as she hinted to her Parliament in November, was to be "found willing," by the murder of his prisoner, "to put his own life in risk for his sovereign."[4] Be that as it may,

---

[1] *Carcanet* (Fr. carcan), a chain or collar of jewels. *Johnson.*

[2] *Annals of the Reformation*, vol. iii., p. 361.

[3] *History*, vol. xii., p. 163.

[4] In her second speech to her Parliament, November 24, O.S., Elizabeth, after extolling her own magnanimity, and dwelling upon the obloquy which must accrue to her were she to give public consent to the execution, states her conviction that Mary's death was essential to her own safety, winding up with these significant words : "But this she considers, that many a man would put his life in danger for the safeguard of a King ; she does not say that so she will, but prays them to believe that she hath thought upon it" (Holinshed. Nicolas' *Life of Davison*, p. 57).

this outburst of gratitude and affection towards Mary's keeper, prompted, we are told, by the Queen's "better nature," reads curiously like the opening of King John's famous speech to Hubert :

> O my gentle Hubert,
> We owe thee much; within this wall of flesh
> There is a soul, counts thee her creditor,
> And with advantage means to pay thy love :
> And my good friend, thy voluntary oath
> Lives in this bosom, dearly cherished.
> Give me thy hand. I had a thing to say,—
> But I will fit it with some better time.
> By Heaven, Hubert, I am almost ashamed
> To say what good respect I have of thee.

Elizabeth to Poulet.[1]

Amias, my most faithful and careful servant, God reward thee treble-fold in three double for thy most troublesome charge so well discharged. If you knew, my Amias, how kindly, besides dutifully, my grateful heart accepteth and praiseth your spotless actions, your wise orders, and safe regards, performed in so dangerous and crafty a charge, it would ease your travails and rejoice your heart. In which I charge you carry this most just thought, that I cannot balance in any weight of my judgment the value that I prize you at, and suppose no treasure to countervail such a faith ; and shall condemn myself in that fault, which yet I never committed, if I reward not such deserts. Yea, let me lack when I most need, if I acknowledge not such a merit with a reward, *non omnibus datum.*[2] Let your wicked murderess know how with hearty sorrow her vile deserts compelleth these orders ; and bid her from me ask God forgiveness for her treacherous dealings towards the saver of her life many a year, to the intolerable peril of her own ; and yet, not contented with so many forgivenesses, must fall

---

[1] Vol. xix., n. 55 ; *Cotton. MSS.*, Caligula, C. ix., f. 606.
[2] It is so printed by Strype. The usual form is to put as a separate sentence, *Non omnibus est datum.*

again so horribly, far passing a woman's thought, much less a prince's; and, instead of excusing[s] (whereof not one can serve, it being so plainly confessed by the authors of my guiltless death), let repentance take place, and let [not] the fiend possess her, so as her better part be lost; which I pray, with hands lifted up to Him that may both save and spill.

With my most loving adieu and prayers for thy long life, your most assured and loving sovereign, as thereto by good deserts induced,

E. R.

Poulet to Walsingham.[1]

Sir,—Among many other great favours received from you of late, I account this the greatest that your friendly or rather partial report hath wrought in her Majesty to good acceptation of my poor service, as hath appeared by her most gracious letters: and as the comfort is singular which I have received by the same, so it may please you to think that I account my obligation herein towards you so much the greater, and so I must remain your debtor.

Whereas you refer to my consideration, my continuance here, or my remove to Chartley, only requiring that the house there be first duly searched, which hath been done effectually by Mr. Waad and the other commissioners; I see now no cause at all of our longer abode here, but rather just reason of our return to Chartley, as well in respect of the lessening of her Majesty's charge, and in avoiding the trouble of this country in extraordinary watching and warding about this house, besides the watches and wards in all the towns adjoining; as especially for the better surety of this charge, the house of Chartley being of far better strength by reason of the water than this house is. I am therefore resolved to return to Chartley as soon as I may, and to that purpose to crave the assistance of the well-affected gentlemen of

[1] Vol. xix., n. 51.

these parts, for the furnishing of one hundred horsemen at the time of the remove.

I must confess unto you that I am very willing to remove the Priest, and yet I will not take upon me to discharge him and to set him at liberty without especial direction from you, and indeed I do not think it meet that he should be set at liberty to return into France until the matters in hand were somewhat overblown. I will therefore remove him to Mr. Gresley's house, where he shall remain until it may please you to resolve what shall be done with him. If I should leave him at Chartley until this lady's arrival there, he would not be removed without great difficulty.

It may please you to remember to send your direction touching Mrs. Pierrepont, Melvin, and Pasquier, who are bestowed with Mr. Trentham, Mr. Bagot, and Mr. Littleton. I will not fail according to your direction to advertise her Majesty as soon as I may, of all the circumstances of the proceeding sithence the pretended hunting, although I doubt not but that her Highness hath been duly informed before this time by Mr. Gorge and Mr. Waad of all things done before their departure, and sithence this lady's coming hither, I have not spoken with her, or seen her.

It may please her Majesty to believe that I have had so good experience of Mr. Darrell's faithful devotion to her Highness' service, and of his cold affection towards this lady, as I would sooner commit the charge of the company at Chartley unto him than to any other in these parts, and I know he hath discharged it faithfully. I can assure you that this people hath had no intelligence at all sithence their coming hither, to which purpose I kept them from pen, ink, and paper, and the next day after my arrival here did remove Sir Walter Aston's servants who served to deliver necessary things. This lady hath not gone out of her chamber and gallery, and none of her people have gone beyond the hall door sithence their coming hither.

I do not intend to have any speech with this lady during my being here, but after my next speech with her, it is likely I shall have some greater matter for you.

It may please you to write two or three words of thanks in her Majesty's behalf to Sir Walter Aston, which surely he hath well deserved, as knoweth the Almighty, to whose blessed tuition I commit you.

From Tixall, the 22nd of August, 1586.

Your most assured poor friend,

A. POULET.

Nicasius Yetsweirt's letter of the 19th ordered Walsingham, in Elizabeth's name, "to require Sir Amias Poulet to write unto her the whole story of those things done in this matter to the Queen of Scots and to hers, not for any cause but that her Majesty might take pleasure in the reading thereof." We now learn that Poulet did what he was commanded, but as his letter to Elizabeth was not left in Walsingham's custody, it is not among the State Papers, and we cannot share with Elizabeth the "pleasure in the reading thereof."

Poulet to Walsingham.[1]

Sir,—Forasmuch as you required me by order from her Majesty to advertise her of that which hath passed between this lady and me in the execution of this late charge, and also how she hath behaved herself sithence the apprehension of her secretaries, I have considered that the sooner I performed this duty the better it would be, although indeed there hath fallen out nothing worthy of her Majesty, and therefore I send unto you inclosed herein my letter to her Highness. It may please you to consider what shall be done with Nau's servant, who is of this country, and came to his service from Mr. Pierrepont, and with Curle's servant, who is a Scot, they both being now unprofitable here. And touching the residue of the

----

[1] Vol. xix., n. 52.

Scottish family, I think good at my next convenient leisure
to send you a note of their names, surnames, and charges,
whereupon you may consider to reserve and to remove as
you shall think meet.

It is intended that this lady shall remove to Chartley
this next morrow, as here this household can have no
long continuance without imminent danger, and extreme
charges to her Majesty in many things this winter, by
reason that provisions have not been made beforehand.
I hear of traitors that are carried towards you every
day. God be thanked for it, to whose merciful tuition
I commit you.

From Tixall, the 24th of August, 1586.

Your most assured poor friend,

A. POULET.

Poulet did with the Priest as he had proposed, and sent
him from Chartley to Mr. Gresley's, before he returned with the
Queen of Scots.

Walsingham to Poulet.[1]

Sir,—Mr. Gorge and Mr. Waad came safely to London
on Sunday at night, with their several charges, and her
Majesty resteth marvellously well satisfied with the care
and endeavour that hath been used by you in the search of
the house, expressing as well generally to all my lords of
the Council, and particularly to every one that she spake
withal in such gracious terms her good liking of your wise
and discreet manner of proceeding in the whole course of
that your charge, and now in the execution of this late
service, as it is not possible for any Prince to give
greater commendation to the good desert of a servant,
nor to rest better contented withal. Her Majesty doth
well allow of your purpose to remove your charge to
Chartley again for the reasons that you set down in
your letters, of the strength of the house, and easing

[1] Vol. xix., n. 56.

the country of their continual watches.   But upon
report made by Mr. Waad of the unsoundness of the
country, her Majesty meaneth that your said charge shall
be shortly conveyed to some other place, and not there
remain with that liberty that she enjoyeth now, but in the
state of a prisoner, attended only with few persons such as
she must have of necessity, and therefore her Majesty
would have you to consider to what number the said
persons may be restrained.   I mean to know her Majesty's
pleasure touching the Priest, whom in the meanwhile you
have done well to sequester into my cousin Gresley's
house.   And you shall also know what is to be done with
young Pierrepont and Melvyn.   For young Pasquier, her
Majesty would have you to send him hither under sure
guard, such as to yourself shall seem convenient for the
purpose, because it is supposed he was privy to the writing
of these letters that were in cipher.

There are letters of thanks written to Mr. Manners,
Sir Walter Aston, and Mr. Bagot. Anthoine Tuchiner hath
been lately taken, so as we want now but only Edward
Abington of the whole number of the six conspirators.

From the Court at Windsor, the 25th of August, 1586.

Endorsed—To Sir Amias Poulet.

Before the return of Mary to 'Chartley, the transfer to
Fotheringay Castle was almost determined.   The Privy Council
repeats "that it is not meant she shall henceforth have that
scope and liberty that heretofore she hath enjoyed."   "Scope
and liberty" are singular terms to apply to Mary's captivity
since Poulet was appointed her keeper.

Burghley and Walsingham to Poulet.[1]

After, &c.,—The Queen's Majesty, upon information
given unto her by Mr. Waad, according to such direction as

[1] Vol. xix., n. 59.

he received from you for that purpose, of the unsoundness of that country, doth think meet to have the Queen, your charge, removed from thence to some other place of more safety, and for such purpose hath thought upon Fotheringay Castle, in Northamptonshire, and wills us particularly to consider of such things as are necessary for the said remove. Whereupon we have directed our letters unto Sir Walter Mildmay to view the said castle and to certify us of the state thereof, and how the household may there be furnished, both of necessary provision of wood and meat, and of a convenient quantity of beer by some brewer in the town of Fotheringay, or otherwise ; and do also pray you that you will likewise send either Darrell or some other apt person thither, accompanied with one of the wardrobe, to consider in what sort the stuffs and hangings that are now with you may furnish some convenient lodging for the said Queen, for that it is not meant she shall henceforth have that scope and liberty that heretofore she hath enjoyed, but remain in the state of a prisoner, with some regard nevertheless of her degree and quality. Other particularities wherein we desire to be resolved by you, we have set down in the inclosed articles, wherein we pray you that you will yield us answer with as much speed as conveniently you may.

August 26th, 1586.

Endorsed—The Lord Treasurer and Mr. Secretary to Sir Amias Poulet.

Mr. Froude has a curious reason to assign why Mary should have been sent back to Chartley. "The house," that is, Sir Walter Aston's house, Tixall, he says,[1] "was small and inconvenient ;" a singular description of a house where there were "on the point of a hundred persons uprising and downlying," as its master described his "great family." Mr. Froude then draws for his narrative on the following letter, and therein furnishes

---

[1] *History*, vol. xii., p. 161.

another specimen of inaccuracy.   Mary "went to her own apart-
ments, to find drawers and boxes open and empty, and her most
secret papers gone.   'Some of you will be sorry for this,' she said
sternly to Paulet, who was attending on her."[1]   "I was not present
when the words were spoken," Poulet wrote ; and the expression
follows so closely upon the words uttered by Mary that it seems
wonderful that Mr. Froude should have succeeded in copying the
one sentence without catching sight of the other.   "She said
sternly to Paulet," says Mr. Froude, who is indebted to his
imagination for the fact ; and every one who reads the passage
understands by it a threat on Mary's part to punish the perpe-
trators of the outrage, if ever it was in her power.   Poulet
understood it to mean that her papers would compromise others,
who would have cause to be sorry that they were taken.   In what
sense that could apply to him he did not know.   This he knew,
that he could be sorry for others, but "there was nothing in her
papers that could give him cause to be sorry for himself."

But the threat suited Mr. Froude best.   He wanted it to
introduce this paragraph—"Elizabeth had no braver subject
than Paulet, not one who would have broken lance with
lighter heart in her behalf against the stoutest knight in
Christendom, but there was something in this fiery woman that
awed and frightened him.   He dreaded a rising in the country.
He urged her removal to some stronger place, as a matter of
pressing necessity, wishing evidently that she was in the Tower,
and that he was rid of his responsibilities with her."   Mr. Froude's
reference for this is the letter now before the reader.   Who would
have thought that all this could have been drawn out of Poulet's
postscript ?   "Our remove," concerns "her Majesty's service very
greatly."   Her Majesty was grumbling at the number of his
soldiers, and begrudging him his expenses.   The removal from
Chartley had been, in his mind, a question of "provision to be

---

[1] Dr. Lingard has a similar mistake.   "When she entered her former
apartment, and saw her cabinets opened, and her seals and papers gone, she
paused for a moment, and then turning to Poulet, said with an air of dignity,
'There still remain two things, sir, which you cannot take from me, the royal
blood which gives me a right to the succession, and the attachment which
binds me to the faith of my fathers'" (*History of England,* 1844, vol. viii.,
p. 214).

made of hay, wood, coal, and many other things for the service
of this house the next winter," as he wrote in June : that was
the benefit to her Majesty ; and Poulet himself would get
away from a place where his health suffered severely. Certainly
he knew that Staffordshire was a county of recusants, the
"unsoundness" of which he requested Waad to represent to
the Privy Council, but there is nothing of "pressing necessity"
about it. So also in October Poulet represented "the weakness
of one part of the Castle of Fotheringay," so that it would not be
safe in case a "desperate attempt" were made "in this doubtful
time in favour of the Queen his charge." That he would have
been glad to be "rid of his responsibilities" is true, but it is
utterly untrue that he was "awed and frightened" by Mary. He
would have been as surprised to hear it as to have received a
summons to set his gouty foot into the stirrup, and break a lance
with the hand that sometimes could not hold a pen. He did not
fear Mary personally ; he hated her, and he feared above all
things the result of her surviving Elizabeth and becoming Queen
of England. He hated her with a steadily increasing hatred, and
perhaps the personal inconvenience he had to share with his
prisoner tended to embitter his mind against her. But there is
no sign anywhere that he was awed or frightened by her. His
complaint is rather of her "tediousness." Perhaps Mary was not
quite "the fiery woman" Mr. Froude imagines her to have been.

Poulet to Walsingham.[1]

Sir,—This lady was removed hither the 25th of this
present, conducted by Sir Walter Aston, Mr. Bagot,
Mr. Gresly, Mr. Littleton, Mr. Chetwynd, and others to
the number of one hundred and forty horses at the least.
At her coming out of Sir Walter Aston's gate she said
with a loud voice weeping, to some poor folks which were
there assembled, "I have nothing for you, I am a beggar
as well as you, all is taken from me ; " and when she came
to the gentlemen she said, weeping, "Good gentlemen, I
am not witting or privy to anything intended against the

[1] Vol. xix., n. 62.

Queen." She visited Curle's wife (who was delivered of child in her absence), before she went to her own chamber, willing her to be of good comfort, and that she would answer for her husband in all things that might be objected against him. Curle's child remaining unchristened, and the Priest removed before the arrival of this lady, she desired that my minister might baptize the child, with such god-fathers and godmothers as I would procure, so as the child would bear her name ; which being refused, she came shortly after into Curle's wife's chamber, where laying the child on her knees, she took water out of a basin, and casting it upon the face of the child she said, "I baptize thee in the name of the Father, the Son, and the Holy Ghost," calling the child by her own name, Mary. This may not be found strange in her who maketh no conscience to break all laws of God and man..

At her coming hither, Mr. Darrell delivered the keys, as well of her chambers as of her coffers, to Bastian, which he refused by direction from his mistress, who required Mr. Darrell to open her chamber door, which he did, and then this lady finding that her papers were taken away, said, in great choler, that two things could not be taken from her, her English blood and her Catholic religion, which both she would keep until her death, adding further these words—"Some of you will be sorry for it," meaning the taking away of her papers. I was not present when these words were spoken, but no doubt they reached unto me, in what sense she only knoweth. I may be sorry for others, but I know there is nothing in her papers that can give me cause to be sorry for myself.

I considered that Mrs. Pierrepont's maid would be unnecessary here, and that remaining in this house until the coming hither of this lady she might not be sent away afterwards without peril. I therefore removed her to Mr. Chetwynd's house, where she remaineth until you have resolved what to do with Mrs. Pierrepont.

I consider that you are overwhelmed with business, and therefore I am loth to trouble you with any unnecessary matter from hence, of which kind I must confess all the premisses to be, and yet I think agreeable with my duty to advertise you of this lady's remove hither, which I would have done sooner, but that I thought she would have desired to have spoken with me after her coming hither, wherein I perceive I am much deceived, and that she is not hasty to see me or speak with me, only she sent to know if I would convey her letters to her Majesty, which I refused, saying that no letters should pass out of this house without order from above, and I do not doubt but that upon the examination of her servants some good occasion will be ministered to deliver some message unto her which may give her just cause to write. She made the like proffer at Sir Walter Aston's house, which I then also refused, and prayed your direction therein.

I trust you do remember to consider, as time will give you leave, what shall be done with Pierrepont, Melvin, and Pasquier, thinking assuredly that you shall find good cause to command Pasquier to be brought unto you.

And thus I leave you to the mercy and favour of the Highest.

From Chartley, the 27th of August, 1586.

Your most assured poor friend,

A. POULET.

After the signing of these letters I received yours of the 25th, this present day at eight in the evening, by the which you continue to increase my joy by your report of her Majesty's gracious acceptance of my unworthy service, although trusty and faithful. I will not fail to send Pasquier unto you with convenient speed, and at that time will give you my simple opinion touching this lady's family. God be thanked that so many of the principal conspirators are apprehended, and God make us thankful for these singular mercies.

Autograph postscript—I beseech you most heartily to further our remove from hence as much as you may, as a matter importing her Majesty's service very greatly.

The first sentence in the following letter applies to Dr. Gifford. Gilbert Gifford wrote from France to Phelippes,[1] 'What as [if] Morgan should say that D. Gifford meant not to deal sincerely with Mr. Secretary. I never doubted it but that he would not, and so always I told you." The consideration had for Gilbert Gifford's travail was not less than a promise of 100*l.* a year.[2] No doubt he was well content, at such a price, that Walsingham and Phelippes should " both write and speak bitterly against him."

Walsingham to Phelippes.[3]

I return you Morgan's letter, by the which it appeareth what trust is to be given to Papists. It shall now suffice to assure G. G. that both he and I have been greatly abused ; and that there shall be that consideration had of his travail as shall be to his contentment.

It were convenient that Paynter did convey over unto him some of that stuff that Mr. Douglas gave unto you for the secret manner of writing, and to instruct him how to use it. Then may he direct his letters to his uncle Offley, containing outwardly but matters ordinary. He must be content that we both write and speak bitterly against him. And as for D[octor] G[ifford][4] and Gratley, they deserve it. I have sent Arthur to attend you this day in copying out the letters I sent you.

---

[1] Vol. xx., n. 45.
[2] *Domestic, Elizabeth*, vol. cxcix., n. 96.
[3] Vol. xix., n. 63.
[4] Dr. Gifford was afterwards Archbishop of Rheims.

And so I commit you to God. In haste, the 28th August, 1586.

Your loving friend,

FRA. WALSINGHAM.

Addressed—To my servant Thomas Phillippes.

Endorsed by Phelippes—August 28, 1586, from Sir Francis Walsingham.

Poulet to Walsingham.[1]

Sir,—Pasquier cometh unto you herewith, conducted by three of my servants, not doubting but they will discharge this service to your satisfaction, and indeed I could not think of any other good means to send him unto you.

Having now resolved and prepared for the sending of Pasquier unto you, I received this last evening at ten of the clock at night letters from my Lord Treasurer and you, with articles inclosed, which shall be answered with as convenient speed as I may. I have no other thing wherewith to trouble you at this time, beseeching God to bless you and all your actions.

From Chartley, the 29th of August, 1586.

Your most assured poor friend,

A. POULET.

Poulet to Burghley and Walsingham.[2]

It may please your Honours to be advertised that, receiving your letters of the 26th of this present the 28th of the same, late in the evening, I have according to your direction despatched Mr. Darrell this present morning towards Fotheringay for the view of the lodgings there, which no doubt will be furnished with the hangings belonging to this house, whereof there is good store of all sorts of height and breadth.

---

[1] Vol. xix., n. 64.   [2] Vol. xix., n. 66.

I send unto you herewith my simple opinion touching your articles addressed unto me, and have sent the copy as well of the articles as of my postills to Sir Walter Mildmay, to the end he may in his letters to your honours supply all defect by his better judgment and knowledge of these countries.

I think myself very happy for many causes to be removed out of this country, and now I should think myself twice happy if this Queen with the change of the lodging might also change her keeper, and, indeed, a gentleman of that country might supply this place with less expense to her Majesty, and better surety of his charge, having his servants, tenants, and good neighbours at hand.

Although I am bold to write as I wish, yet I will never desire it but as it may stand with her Majesty's good pleasure, as one that embraceth all her Highness' commandments with all willing obedience.

And thus humbly taking my leave, I commit your honours to the mercy and favour of the Almighty.

From Chartley, the 30th of August, 1586.

Your honour's to command,

A. POULET.

Addressed—To the right honourable my very good lord, the Lord Burghley, Lord Treasurer of England, and to Sir Francis Walsingham, knight, her Majesty's principal Secretary.

The postscript of the first of the two following letters is important as showing that the minutes of Mary's letter to Babington were not found among her papers at Chartley, neither the French minute by Nau nor the English by Curle,[1] nor her

---

[1] Curle is represented as stating in the examination of September 21, that he burnt the English translation by Mary's order (*Hardwicke State Papers,* p. 237).

own autograph draft, if, as Nau says, she made one. In the letter to Phelippes of the 4th September, Walsingham says again, "The minute of her answer is not extant."

Dr. Lingard[1] gives an extract from a confession by Nau,[2] of the same date as this letter of Walsingham's, which mentions "une minute de lettre escripte de sa main, qu'il lui plust me baillier pour la polir et mectre au net, ainsi qu'il apparoit a vos hon. *ayant l'une et l'autres entres vos mains.*" Relying on this, Dr. Lingard says, "At her trial, the minute by herself and French letter by Nau, which were in the hands of the prosecutors, were suppressed." Prince Labanoff[3] gives up Mary's autograph minute, but takes for granted that Nau's French minute was found. "La correspondence de Walsingham et de Phelippes prouve qu'il fut impossible de découvrir la minute autographe dont Nau avait parlé, et que la seule chose que l'on trouva, lors de la saisie. . . . ce fut la minute française écrite par Nau." It is very surprising that Nau should have taken for granted that Mary's minute and his draft were in Walsingham's hands, and that they should not have been found. It is very suspicious, for if Mary's letter was to be altered, the original drafts would have been an embarrassment to the forger; but forger as Walsingham undoubtedly was in the matter of this letter, it seems impossible that he could have written as he has written to Phelippes, if either of these minutes had been taken at Chartley.

But though the minutes were not found, there was the cipher which Burghley noted was to be taken to Fotheringay, and there was the decipher made by Phelippes for Walsingham as soon as the letter reached his hands, and neither of these were produced at Mary's trial, or are now forthcoming. The argument does not need to be strengthened.

The copy of d'Esneval's letter sent by Walsingham to Phelippes with his letter of September 3rd had come to Chartley in a packet from Châteauneuf to Mary, August 5th [? 8th], as we have seen from Poulet's letter of that date.

---

[1] *History of England*, 1844, vol. viii., p. 214.
[2] *Harl. MSS.*, n. 4649.
[3] Tom. vi., p. 397.

Courcelles had sent to Mary through Châteauneuf this copy of d'Esneval's letter to him.

Davison wrote a letter to Phelippes[1] a few months later, which speaks of other intercepted letters and the way they were treated. "The French Ambassador hath written to my Lord Treasurer complaining of the apprehension of his servants and detention of his packets. Her Majesty therefore would that they should be made up ready to be delivered unto him, but that you do first let my Lord Treasurer and me [be] advised in what state the packets are before they be delivered." It is curious to see how perfectly the Ambassador's packets could be made up again,[2] so that they should give no sign of having been opened or tampered with. Elizabeth simply takes this for granted, though it does not seem that when the packets were taken, there was any thought that they would have to be returned to the Ambassador. It is not likely that Phelippes was often idle, as Elizabeth was pleased to suppose in December, when Davison thus wrote[3] to him. "Her Majesty delivered me the ticket here inclosed to be sent unto you for your exercise, because she thinketh you now be idle. When you have made English thereof, I doubt not but you will return it back to her Highness."

The number of letters to or from the French Embassies in England and Scotland intercepted about this time was very considerable. In two volumes of the State Papers[4] there are thirty letters to or from d'Esneval, Courcelles, and Châteauneuf, between August, 1586, and September, 1587. Even bills are there for silks, &c., supplied to Courcelles by Henry Nisbet, merchant, of Edinburgh, and the Ambassador's note of hand for eight hundred crowns borrowed from the same man.

The bearing of Walsingham's treatment of Nau and Curle on the value of their evidence is obvious. To Curle he wrote,[5] "I can be but a mediator, and therein I shall have the better

---

[1] *Domestic, Elizabeth,* vol. cxcvii., n. 11. Holograph.

[2] The man who tampered with the seals was Arthur Gregory (Camden, p. 438).

[3] *Cotton. MSS.,* Caligula, C. ix., f. 569.

[4] *Scotland, Elizabeth,* vols. xli., xlii.

[5] Vol. xix., n. 119.

ground to deal for you when you shall lay yourself so open, as
her Majesty may see in you remorse for that which is past, and
a disposition to deserve her favour by acquainting of her with
your knowledge of such things as may any way concern her
estate." Curle's "confession," dated however the day after this
letter, is given among the State Papers[1] in English. This was
written at the foot of a copy of Babington's letter. "There
must, and I do confess to have deciphered the like of the
whole above written, coming written in one sheet of paper, as
from Mr. Babington. And the answer thereunto, being written
in French by Mr. Nau, to have been translated in English
and ciphered by me.—GILBERT CURLE, 5 September, 1586."
On the copy of Mary's letter he simply wrote, "The foresaid
I acknowledge to have put in cipher. 5 September, 1586.—
GILBERT CURLE." The other attestation by Curle, already
quoted, being dated the 5th, it would almost seem as though
those just given must have been dated the 3rd. He refers to
them thus :[2] "Telle ou semblable me semble avoiresté la
response escripte en françoys par Monsieur Nau, laquelle j'ay
traduict et mis en chiffre, comme j'en fais mention au pied d'une
copie de la lettre de Mr. Babington, laquelle Monsieur Nau a
signé le premier.—GILBERT CURLE, 5 September, 1586."

Walsingham to Phelippes.[3]

Sir,—I send you these inclosed copies, the one of
d'Esneval's, and the other of Chasteauneuf's letters unto
Courcelles,[3] which were intercepted, whereof I would be
glad to know the substance, and therefore I pray you take
some pain in perusing them that I may be acquainted
therewith as soon as conveniently you may. And so I
bid you heartily farewell.

From Barnelms, the 3rd of September, 1586.

Your loving friend,

FRA. WALSINGHAM.

---

[1] Vol. xix., n. 88.   [2] Labanoff, tom. vi., p. 395.
[3] Vol. xix., n. 80.

Autograph postcript—I pray you take care to find out such minutes as have been drawn by Nau, who is not so deeply charged as Curle is, who wrote the letters sent to [Sir *erased*] Englefield and to Charles Paget, which by subscription he hath acknowledged to be his ; but that the minutes were first drawn by the Queen,[1] their mistress. Both he and Nau are determined to lay the burden upon their mistress. By no means ; they will be yet brought to confess that they were acquainted with the letters that passed between Babington and her. I would to God those minutes were found. I pray you send me word what course you have taken for young Pasquier's despatch. It toucheth my poor credit (how hardly soever I am dealt withal) to see our friend beyond the seas[2] comforted.

Addressed—To my servant Thomas Phelippes at Court.

Walsingham to Phelippes.[3]

This morning I received the inclosed from Fra. Mills, and this afternoon he made report unto me of his proceeding with Curle, accordingly as is set down in the inclosed, by the which you may perceive that Curle doth both testify the receipt of Babington's letter, as also the Queen his mistress' answer to the same, wherein he chargeth Nau to have been a principal instrument.

I took upon me to put him in comfort of favour in case he would deal plainly, being moved thereto for that the minute of her answer is not extant, and that I saw Nau resolved to confess no more than we were able of ourselves to charge him withal.

---

[1] It is noteworthy that while in the earlier interrogations Nau swore that he wrote Mary's letter to Babington from a minute in her own hand, in the examination of September 21, of which we have only an imperfect account drawn up by Phelippes, Nau is made to say that Mary dictated the letter to him by word of mouth, and Curle, for the first time, states that he burnt the English copy by Mary's order.

[2] Gifford at Paris.

[3] Vol. xix., n. 83 ; in Mills' hand.

If it might please her Majesty upon Curle's plain dealing, and in respect of the comfort I have put him in to receive grace for the same, to extend some extraordinary favour towards him, considering that he is a stranger, and that which he did was by his mistress' commandment, I conceive great hope there might be things drawn from him worthy of her Majesty's knowledge, for which purpose I can . be content to retain him still with me, if her Majesty shall allow of it. I pray you therefore procure some access unto her Majesty that you may know her pleasure therein with as convenient speed as you may. And so God keep you.

From Barnelms the 4th of September, 1586.

Your master and friend,

FRA. WALSINGHAM.

Addressed—To my servant Thomas Phelippes at Court.

Two letters follow of direction " from above," as Poulet likes to call Elizabeth and Walsingham. These are printed from the drafts. They are remarkable as showing Walsingham's fear lest the treatment Mary was now to receive should "cast her into some sickness, whereby the purpose of the said remove should be hindered." He thinks it "likely" that the course on which Elizabeth had now resolved, of seizing Mary's money, separating her from her servants, and of showing her no "great favour" in other respects, would so aggravate her chronic ill-health as to frustrate, by her death, his plans for her degradation by trial and execution. As Elizabeth insists on these harsh measures, "if afterwards the inconveniences happen thereof that are doubted, her Majesty can blame none but herself for it." Elizabeth is then personally responsible for these proceedings.

Walsingham to Poulet.[1]

Sir,—The inclosed I received yesterday from Mr. Waad, containing her Majesty's pleasure how she would have you

[1] Vol. xix., n. 86.

to deal with that lady, whereupon I took occasion to write back again that if that course were held with her before the intended remove, it were likely to cast her into some sickness, whereby the purpose of the said remove would be hindered ; but because I hear nothing yet in answer of my said letter, I have in the meanwhile thought good to acquaint you with her Majesty's purpose and meaning towards the said Queen, to whom you may easily perceive she hath no disposition that there should be any great favour showed, and we are now here in consultation to have her brought directly to the Tower, as a thing which is thought most necessary, and afterwards proceeded against according to the statute made in the last Parliament. If this course hold, then the intended repairing and furnishing of the Castle of Fotheringay may stay. In the meanwhile you shall, in my opinion, do well to forbear the touching of the money or removing of her servants, &c.

September 4, 1586.

Endorsed—M[inute of letter] to Sir Amias Poulet.

Walsingham to Poulet.[1]

Sir,—How her Majesty doth continue her former resolution to have that lady's money seized and her servants divided from her, you may perceive by the inclosed extract of a letter that I received this morning from Mr. Waad, and therefore her pleasure being such, I do not see why you should now any longer forbear the putting of the same in execution. If afterwards the inconveniences happen thereof that are doubted, her Majesty can blame none but herself for it. I am now absent from the Court by reason of an inflammation that I have in my right leg, grown of the pain of a boil that is risen in it, and therefore I cannot debate the matter with her Majesty as I would. This afternoon my Lord Chancellor, my Lord Treasurer, and

---

[1] Vol. xix., n. 87.

Mr. Vice-Chamberlain meet together at London, whereupon I think you shall be presently advertised of the resolution that will be taken, either for the removing of that lady to Fotheringay, or bringing of her directly hither to the Tower.

September 5th, 1586.

Endorsed—M. to Sir Am. Poulet.

We have already seen that in Nau's confession[1] of September 3, he took for granted that Mary's autograph minute of the answer to Babington, and his own French minute drawn up from hers, were found at Chartley. The following letter from Waad affords evidence that at all events they had not reached the hands of. Queen Elizabeth. "What does he mean by "I suspect one packet you deciphered ?"

In Nau's later confession[2] of September 10, the following passage occurs—"La lettre de Morgan et sa minutte pour Bab. doibvent estre parmy les papiers dudict Curle." This minute of Morgan's, Prince Labanoff says was found, and is now among the Cecil Papers at Hatfield House.

Waad to Phelippes.[3]

Sir,—Her Majesty's pleasure is you should presently repair hither, for that upon Nau's confession it should appear we have not performed the search sufficiently, for he doth assure we shall find amongst the minutes which were in Pasquier's chests, the copies of the letters wanting both in French and English. I suspect one packet you deciphered. You must bring with you likewise the minutes of letters you had here. So I commit you to God.

From Windsor, the 7th of September, 1586.

Your most assured loving friend,

W. WAAD.

I pray you send us some messengers hither.

Addressed—To the worshipful, my very loving friend, Mr. Thomas Phillips.

---

[1] *Harl. MSS.*, n. 4649.   [2] Vol. xix., n. 98.   [3] Vol. xix., n. 94.

The long letter that describes the seizure of the money of the
Queen of Scots is printed by Robertson,[1] and Sir Egerton Bridges
remarks upon it as damaging to Poulet's character. It is hard,
however, to see why the blame should fall upon him. Some men
perhaps would not have accounted honourable the details of the
work entailed by the office he held. But he read Mary's letters,
and now took possession of her money because he was ordered to
do so. This letter corrects another of Mr. Froude's inaccuracies.
" Paulet, with Secretary Wade," he says,[2] " who had accompanied
Gorges down, galloped back to Chartley, where drawers, boxes,
and cabinets were broken open and searched." Poulet did not
gallop back to Chartley. " As you know, I was no commissioner
in this search, but had my hands full at Tixall."

Poulet to Walsingham.[3]

Sir,—I did forbear according to your direction, signified
by your letters of the 4th of this present, to proceed to
the execution of the contents of Mr. Waad's letters unto
you for the dispersing of this lady's unnecessary servants,
and for the seizing of her money, wherein I was bold to
write unto you my simple opinion (although in vain, as it
now falleth out) by my letters of the 7th of this instant,[4]
which I doubt not are with you before this time.

But upon the receipt of your letters of the 5th (which
came not to my hand until the 8th in the evening, by
reason as did appear by an endorsement that they had
been mistaken and were sent back to Windsor, after that
they were already entered into the way towards me), I
considered that being accompanied only with my own
servants, it might be thought that they would be entreated
to say as I would command them, and therefore I thought
good for my better discharge in these money matters to
crave the assistance of Mr. Richard Bagot, who repairing

---

[1] *History of Scotland,* App., p. 426 ; also Ellis, vol. iii., p. 6.
[2] *History,* vol. xii., p. 160.
[3] *Cotton. MSS.,* Caligula, C. ix., f. 378.
[4] This letter is not among the State Papers.

unto me the next morning, we had access to this Queen, whom we found in her bed troubled after the old manner with a defluxion which was fallen down into the side of her neck, and had bereft her of the use of one of her hands, unto whom I declared that upon occasion of her former practices, doubting lest she would persist therein by corrupting underhand some bad members of this State, I was expressly commanded to take her money into my hands, and to rest answerable for it when it shall be required, advising her to deliver the said money unto me with quietness.

After many denials, many exclamations and many bitter words against you (I say nothing of her railing against myself), with flat affirmation that her Majesty might have her body, but her heart she should never have, refusing to deliver the key of her cabinet, I called my servants, and sent for bars to break open the door, whereupon she yielded, and causing the door to be opened, I found there in the coffers mentioned in Mr. Waad's remembrance five rolls of canvas containing five thousand French crowns, and two leather bags, whereof the one had in gold one hundred and four pounds, two shillings, and the other had three pounds in silver, which bag of silver was left with her, affirming that she had no more money in this house, and that she was indebted to her servants for their wages.

Mr. Waad's note maketh mention of three rolls left in Curle's chamber, wherein no doubt he was misreckoned, which is evident as well by the testimonies and oaths of divers persons, as also by probable conjectures, so as in truth he found only two rolls, every of which containeth one thousand crowns, which was this Queen's gift to Curle's wife at her marriage. [*In marg.* Curle can tell you the truth of this matter.]

There is found in Nau's chamber in a cabinet a chain of gold worth by estimation one hundred pounds, and in

T

money in one bag nine hundred pounds, in a second bag two hundred [and] fifty-nine pounds, and in a silk purse two hundred, four score, and six pounds, eighteen shillings.

All the foresaid parcels of money are bestowed in bags and sealed by Mr. Richard Bagot, saving five hundred pounds of Nau's money which I reserve in my hands for the use of this household, and may be repaid at London where her Majesty shall appoint out of the money received lately by one of my servants out of the Exchequer.

I feared lest this people might have dispersed this money in all this time, or have hidden the same in some secret corners, for doubt whereof I had caused all this Queen's family, from the highest to the lowest, to be guarded in the several places where I found them, so as if I had not found the money with quietness, I had been forced to have searched first all their lodgings, and then their own persons. I thank God with all my heart as for a singular blessing that it falleth out so well, fearing lest a contrary success might have moved some hard conceits in her Majesty.

Touching the dispersing of this Queen's servants, I trust I have done so much as may suffice to satisfy her Majesty for the time, wherein I could not take any absolute course until I heard again from you, partly because her Majesty by Mr. Waad's letter doth refer to your consideration to return such as shall be discharged to their several dwellings and countries, wherein it is seemeth you have forgotten to deliver your opinion; partly for that I have as yet received no answer from you of your resolution upon the view of the Scottish family sent unto you, what persons you do appoint to be dismissed.

Only this I have done. I have bestowed all such as are mentioned in this bill inclosed in three or four several rooms as the same may suffice to contain them, and have ordered that they shall not come out of their chambers, and that their meat and drink shall be brought unto them by my servants.

It may please you to advertise me by your next letters, in what sort, and for what course, I shall make their passports, and also if they shall say that they are unpaid of their wages, what I shall do therein. It is said that they have been accustomed to be paid of their wages at Christmas for the whole year. [*In marg.* This lady hath good store of money at this present in the French Ambassador's hands.] Her Majesty's charges will be somewhat diminished by the departure of this people, and my charge by this occasion will be the more easy. But the persons all, saving Bastian, are such seely and simple souls, as there was no great cause to fear their practices, and upon this ground I was of opinion in my former letters that all this dismissed train should have followed their mistress until the next remove, and there to have been discharged upon the sudden, for doubt that the said remove might be delayed, if she did fear or expect any hard measure.

Others shall excuse their foolish pity as they may ; but for my part, I renounce my part of the joys of heaven, if in anything that I have said, written, or done, I have had any other respect than the furtherance of her Majesty's service, and so I shall most earnestly pray you to affirm for me; as likewise for the not seizing of the money by Mr. Manners, the other commissioners, and myself, I trust Mr. Waad hath answered in all humble duty for the whole company that no one of us did so much as think that our commission reaching only to the papers, we might be bold to touch the money, so as there was no speech of it at all to my knowledge, and as you know, I was no commissioner in this search, but had my hands full at Tixall. Discreet servants are not hasty to deal in great matters without warrant, and especially where the cause is such as the delay of it carrieth no danger.

T 2

Your advertisement of that happy remove hath been greatly comfortable unto me, I will not say in respect of myself, because my private interest hath no measure of comparison with her Majesty's safety and with the quiet of this realm. God grant a happy and speedy issue to these good and godly counsels.

And so I commit you to His merciful protection.

From Chartley, the 10th of September, 1586.

Your most assured poor friend,

A. POULET.

My servant repairing to my Lord Treasurer's according to your commandment, found his lordship ready to enter into his coach towards the Court, as so as he said he could not write, but commanded him to signify unto me that I should prepare to remove with all speed, and that I should put all things in good safety. His lordship asked him if you had written, and it seemed that he thought you had written unto me touching this remove, wherein as yet I have heard nothing.

Endorsed by Phelippes—Septemb. 10. Sir Amyas Poulet.

Poulet to Walsingham.[1]

Sir,—I find by your letter of the 12th, received this last night at midnight, that you were not acquainted with my Lord Treasurer's first and second letter unto me of the 8th, the contents whereof may appear unto you by my answer to the same, sent to his lordship. I find this lady very willing to remove upon hope to hear often from the French Ambassador, by reason that her lodging is within thirty miles of London, and now twenty carts are appointed to be laden here this next morrow, and I think we shall remove from hence about the middle of this next week, if we be not stayed by contrary news, whereof I thought

---

[1] Vol. xix., n. 102.

good to advertise you. Sithence my last letters unto you I found in a casket in Nau's chamber 5*l.* 10*s.* in gold and 27*s.* 3*d.* in white money, and among the same the silver piece inclosed, by the which you may easily judge of his malicious, cankered, and traiterous heart towards her Majesty. All this Queen's seals were in this casket, which are in great number, and to serve for privy packets and all other purposes.

And thus I leave you to the mercy and favour of the Almighty.

From Chartley, the 15th of September, 1586.

Nau had bestowed these pieces of silver among a number of Agnus Dei.

Your most assured poor friend,

A. POULET.

Poulet to Walsingham.[1]

Sir,—I have not failed according to the direction given unto me to advertise my Lord Treasurer from day to day of my proceedings in this late journey, which being now finished, thanks be to God, Mr. Thomas Gorge repaireth to the Court to make report to her Majesty of all the circumstances belonging. I shall be glad to hear that you are recovered of your late grief. And thus wishing unto you all happiness, I commit you to the merciful protection of our good God.

From Fotheringay, the 25th of September, 1586.

Your most assured poor friend,

A. POULET.

Endorsed—25th September, 1586. From Sir Amyas Paulett. Of his arrival with the Scottish Queen to Fotheringay.

---

[1] Vol. xix., n. 113.

The Commissioners, of whom Walsingham was one, were those who were sent to Fotheringay as Mary's judges. The accounts of the trial must be sought elsewhere, as it does not enter into the series of letters that are here reproduced.

Poulet to Walsingham.[1]

Sir,—I have received your letters of the 28th of this present, and am very glad to find by the same that you are so well recovered of your late grief, and that you are appointed a commissioner to come hither, trusting now to be so happy to see you once again before I die, which I should never have done if I had continued one year more in that unhealthy house at Chartley, finding myself already well amended in my health sithence my entrance into this journey. I have no other matter for you at this time.

And so do commit you to the mercy of the Almighty. From Fotheringay, the 29th of September, 1586.

Your most assured poor friend,

A. POULET.

Poulet to Walsingham.[2]

Sir,—I was very willing to have provided a chamber for you and had taken order for it, but Sir Walter Mildmay hearing thereof hath given me to understand that the chamber appointed for him near adjoining to the council chamber shall serve for you and him, and that he knoweth you would have it so. He hath also made provision for your diet in that chamber. I have taken order for room for ten or twelve of your horses in the stable appointed for my use. I take it for an especial favour and cannot thank you enough for your friendly proffer, touching the traffic desired by the merchants of the west parts to be established in Jersey and Guernsey, wherein I can say little without conference with the merchants, only I shall most heartily pray you that if this traffic be granted it

---

[1] Vol. xix., n. 115. Holograph.   [2] Vol. xx., n. 3.

may be left indifferent to both the isles, and then my neighbour Sir Thomas Leighby [Leighton] and I shall agree very well I doubt not.

You will not be here so soon as I wish for you, and indeed I think every day three until you come. And thus with my second thanks for your friendly remembrance touching this Jersey cause, I commit you to the mercy of the Almighty.

From Fotheringay, the 5th of October, 1586.

Your most assured poor friend,

A. POULET.

Queen Elizabeth to Sir Amias Poulet.[1]

Right trusty, &c.,—Forasmuch as heretofore the Queen your charge hath taken exception to such Ministers of ours as have been sent to treat with her, for that they came not accompanied with letters of credit from us directed to herself, we have therefore thought meet to the end she may take no exception unto the Commissioners we now send, being persons of that quality and honour they are, for lack of letters of credit directed from our-self to her, to send you the inclosed herewithal, which our pleasure is that you shall deliver unto her, at such time as by you and the rest of the said Commissioners shall be thought meet. And so, &c.

October 6th, 1586.

Endorsed—Minute of a letter to Sir Amys Paulet.

The Commissioners arrived at Fotheringay Castle on the 11th of October, and on the 15th the Court was adjourned to the Star Chamber at Westminster. It was by Elizabeth's express order that sentence was not passed at Fotheringay. "She caused me to write a few hasty and scribbled lines at midnight," Davison wrote[2] to Walsingham on the 14th, "for the stay of the sentence

---

[1] Vol. xx., n. 5.   [2] *Domestic, Elizabeth,* vol. cxciv., n. 43.

against the said Queen until your return to her Majesty's presence to make report what you have done, notwithstanding by your general verdict there she be found guilty of the crimes whereof she standeth charged." But the next day he wrote[1] that Elizabeth feared lest this "stay of pronouncing the sentence . . . may have wrought some hindrance to the rest of that course you are to take, as proceeding to the verdict upon the indictment and proofs against her, a [thing which] in truth would as little please her as there is little cause to doubt."

"We had proceeded presently to sentence," Walsingham wrote[2] to Leicester, "but that we had a secret countermand, and were forced under some other colour to adjourn our meeting until the 25th of this month at Westminster. I see this wicked creature ordained of God to punish us for our sins and unthankfulness, for her Majesty hath no power to proceed against her as her own safety requireth." The "colour" for the adjournment is given by Burghley in a letter[3] to Davison on the same day. It was his business to hide the fact that Elizabeth had given this "secret countermand," and he pledges the Queen to permit sentence to be passed at the next meeting. "We had great reason to prorogue our Session, which is done till the 25th, and so we of the Council will be at the Court the 22nd. And we find all persons here in commission fully satisfied as by her Majesty's order judgment will be given at our next meeting; but the record will not be perfected in five or six days, and that was one cause why if we should have proceeded to judgment we should have tarried five or six days more, and surely the country could not bear it, by the waste of bread especially. Our company there and within six miles [is] above two hundred horsemen. But by reason of her Majesty's letter, we of her Council, that is the Lord Chancellor, Mr. Vice-Chamberlain, Mr. Secretary, and myself only did procure this prorogation for the other two causes."

It happened as Elizabeth feared, and the adjournment took place without any verdict having been given. Burghley received

---

[1] *Domestic, Elizabeth,* vol. cxciv., n. 44.
[2] *Cotton. MSS.,* Caligula, C. ix., f. 502.
[3] *Ibid.* f. 533; Ellis, vol. iii. p. 12.

Davison's letter on Sunday the 16th, at his house at Burghley, which caused him to write[1] to Walsingham, "I have showed how unpossible it is to convene us together afore the 25th, both because it should be an error in law, the commission being adjourned, and almost in fact unpossible to come sooner than our day appointed. I have given hope that the matter will take a good end, and honourable for such a cause, which would not upon two only days, or rather but upon one day and a half hearing be also judged; for so we might verify the Scottish Queen's allegation, that we came thither with a prejudgment, and that as she said it was so reputed commonly."

Burghley to Walsingham.[2]

Sir,—Being come to this town of Royston this Wednesday, at night, I first received a letter from Sir Amias Poulet by a servant of his own that came hither, and by that he wrote to me that he had advertised you[3] of some speeches of late betwixt the Scottish Queen and him, but his special cause of sending to me was to have some money, which at my coming to London on Friday I will accomplish.

And after that I had supped, there came a letter directed to you from him also, which I thought might be the letter whereof he made mention to me, although if it so be, it appeareth that the post maketh less haste than the ordinary pursuivant.

If there be any matter that hath passed from that Queen worth knowledge, I pray you advertise me.

The letter that yesterday came to me from you, sent by Mr. Davison, was written on Saturday, so as hitherto I cannot understand how her Majesty accepteth of our same Saturday's work in adjourning our commission. I mind to be at Theobalds to-morrow at night, and at Westminster on Friday at night.

[1] *Domestic, Elizabeth*, vol. cxciv., n. 45.
[2] *Domestic, Elizabeth*, vol. cxciv., n. 49. Holograph.
[3] This letter to Walsingham is not among the State Papers.

My Lord of Shrewsbury, as I think, lodgeth this night at Huntingdon, and my Lord of Rutland at Stilton.

From Royston, 19th October, 1586.

Yours assuredly,

W. BURGHLEY.

Poulet to Walsingham.[1]

Sir,—I send unto you inclosed herein the copy of my articles postilled by you, together with the names of the Scottish retinue at Chartley.[2] And whereas by direction

[1] Vol. xx., n. 16. Holograph.

[2] The names of the Scottish Queen's family remaining at Chartley the 29th of August, 1586 [four days after Mary's return from Tixall], and in what rooms they serve:

MEN SERVANTS.

French	Mr. Burgoigne	... ...	Physician: Ralf, his servant, English.
,,	Gervais	... ...	Chirurgeon.
,,	Nic. de la Marre	... ...	Apothecary.
,,	Bastian Pagez	... }	Grooms of her chamber.
,,	Hanniball	... }	
,,	Symon	... ...	Page of her chamber.
,,	+ Baltazar, old and impo-tent	... }	Tailors of her wardrobe.
English	Robert Mooreton	... }	
French	+ Charles Plouvart	...	Embroiderer.
,,	+ Dedier, an old man	}	Panterers.
Scottish	John Lawder	... }	
French	Martyn	... ...	Master cook.
,,	Nicholas	... ...	Pasteler.
Scottish	Hamilton	... ...	Under cook.
English	Percye	... }	
French	Silvester	... }	Boys and turnbroches of the kitchen.
English	+ Little Hamerlyn	... }	

,, + Thomas Welshe, one of this number, hath been discharged within these two days for his misdemeanour.

,,	Roger Sharpe	... ...	Coachman.
,,	Lawrence Barloe	... }	
,,	John Jackson	... }	Grooms of her stable.
,,	Robert	... }	
,,	+ Henry	... ...	Nau's servant.
Scottish	+ Lawrence	... ...	Curle's servant.
English	+ George	... ...	Melvin's servant.

WOMEN SERVANTS.

Scottish	+ Curle's wife	... }	
French	+ Beauregard	... }	
Scottish	☧ Jane Kenethye	... }	Gentlewomen of her chamber.
,,	☧ Elizabeth Curle	... }	
	Gillis Mowbray	... }	

from my Lord Treasurer and you, I sent two of my servants to Chartley to bring hither Mr. Melvin, Bastian's daughter, and Mr. Melvin's servant, the charges in the journey for the whole company in coming and going amounting to the sum of 105*s.* or thereabouts, it seeming reasonable that the Scottish Queen should bear the charge thereof, because it was done for her service and contentment, wherein I pray your direction. I pray you let me hear from you if it will be expected that I should see my charge often, which as I do not desire to do, so I do not see that any good can come of it so long

English	Catharine Braye	...	} Maidens to serve the Queen's gentle-
Scottish	A Scottish maid	...	} women.
,,	Bastian's wife	...	...
,,	Her two daughters	...	...
,,	Her son	...	...
English	Elizabeth Butler	...	}
,,	Alice Sharpe	...	} Laundresses.
,,	+ Alice Foster	...	}

38.

Of which number these following seem to be unnecessary if this lady shall be restrained of her liberty.

Men Servants.

Baltazar	...	...	...	... Tailor of her wardrobe.
Charles Plouvart		...	...	... Embroiderer.
Didier	...	...	...	... Panterer.
Hamilton	...	...	...	... Under cook.
Roger Sharpe, Coachman		...		}
Lawrence Barloe		...	...	} May be spared if their mistress be not
John Jackson	...	...	...	} allowed to ride abroad.
Robert	...	...	...	}
Henry	...	...	...	... Nau's servant.
Lawrence	...	...	...	... Curle's servant.
George	...	...	...	... Melvin's servant.

Women Servants.

Curle's wife	...	...	...	... Gentlewoman of her chamber.
Catharine Bray	...	...	...	... Who serveth the gentlewomen.
Bastian's wife	...	...	...	}
Her two daughters		...	...	}
Her son	...	...	...	}

The three laundresses may be reduced to two.

19.

If Bastian's wife be discharged, it is like that Bastian will desire to go with his wife, wherein there were no great loss, because he is cunning in his kind, and full of slight to corrupt young men.

Endorsed—The Scottish Queen's family (Vol. xix., n. 65); Labanoff, tom. vii., p. 250.

as I stand assured that she is forthcoming. God send you a good journey to the Court, and prosper all your doings to His glory. Wishing the like to Mr. Vice-Chamberlain.

From Fotheringay, this present Saturday [? October 22], 1586.

Your most assured poor friend,

A. POULET.

Mary knew full well the peril of her life in which she stood, and Poulet's letters disclose to us her brave carriage in this trying time.

Poulet to Walsingham.[1]

Sir,—I took occasion yesterday afternoon, accompanied with Mr. Stallenge, to visit this Queen, who hath been troubled these two days last past with a defluxion in one of her shoulders, intending to take physic this next morrow. I see no change in her from her former quietness and security certified in my last letters, careful to have her chambers put in good order, desirous to have divers things provided for her own necessary use, expecting to have her money shortly rendered unto her, taking pleasure in trifling toys, and in the whole course of her speech free from grief of mind in outward appearance.

I tarried with her one hour and a half at the least, which I did of purpose to feel her disposition, and moving no new matter myself, suffered her to go from matter to matter at her pleasure. She had long speech of the Countess of Shrewsbury, of the Lord of Abergavenny, and of some other things not worthy of advertisement. This only I thought good to signify unto you, that falling in talk of the late assembly here, and having glanced at the Lord Zouch for his speech in her chamber, and also at the Lord Morley for some things delivered by him to the lords sitting next unto him, which she said she overheard and told him of it in the open assembly, she was curious

[1] Vol. xx., n. 17.

to be informed of the names of one such sitting in such a place, and of others sitting in other places, saying that one had said little, another somewhat more, and others very much. I told her that I might easily perceive by her hard conceit of the lords which she had named already she was much inclined to think ill of all those that spake, and therefore I would forbear to name any man unto her, praying her to conceive honourably of the whole assembly, and to think that those which spake, and the rest which were silent, were of one consent and mind to hear her cause with all indifferency.

She added that the histories made mention that this realm was used to blood. I answered that if she would peruse the chronicles of Scotland, France, Spain, and Italy, she should find that this realm was far behind any other Christian nation in shedding of blood, although the same was often very necessary where dangerous offences did arise. She was not willing to wade farther in this matter, and indeed it was easy to see that she had no meaning in this speech to reach to her own cause, but did utter it by way of discourse after her wonted manner. Thus you see that I am bold to trouble you with trifles, as one willing to be blamed rather for lack of good matter, than for want of diligence. And so I commit you to the mercy and favour of our good God.

From Fotheringay, the 24th of October, 1586.

This note inclosed being found among Nau's things, and your name being mentioned therein, I thought good to send it unto you.

Your most assured poor friend,

A. POULET.

Autograph postcript—It seemeth by all circumstances that this Queen hath had no intelligence of the prorogation of the late assembly, and that she is utterly void of all fear of harm.

The following letters show, in addition to those already given, that several letters from Poulet were received after the trial and before the date of our next letter-book, which are not to be found among the State Papers in the Public Record Office.

Davison to Burghley.[1]

My especial good Lord,—The letters here inclosed came to me yesterday from Mr. Secretary, which having imparted with her Majesty I thought immediately to have sent to your lordship, but that some speech her Majesty let fall of your return hither yesternight made me in expectation thereof retain them by me.

Sir Amias Poulet his complaint of the weakness both of his number and the place where he is, to resist any desperate attempt [which] might in this doubtful time be made in favour of the Queen his charge, is a thing her Majesty thinketh fit to be provided for ; which in her own opinion may best be done by a levy of some one hundred or two hundred, to be disposed in some apt places near him ready against any sudden [attempt] for his relief, which her Highness willed me to signify unto your lordship to consider of and take order for, if you find not some other way, as by arming some of the best affected gentlemen thereabouts, more expedient.

To remove her thence, especially to any place nearer, I find no disposition in her. For his other wants of powder and shot, she is so willing to have him supplied as breeds some doubt she will not hastily ease him of his present cares.

Some lack her Majesty noteth in himself that he doth not advertise her Highness what speeches and discourses do fall from her, since your lordships being with her ; and hath willed Mr. Secretary to let him know that she looketh for more particularities in these things from him.

---

[1] *Domestic, Elizabeth*, vol. cxciv., n. 66. Holograph.

Of our Ambassadors' letters I found her Majesty to take little taste, containing as she took it nothing worthy the charge they put her to. With them I send your lordship the copy of an instruction from the King of Navarre to de Reaux, touching the interview betwixt the Queen mother and him, which it seems hath some other subject and scope than an intent to meet on the one side or the other, at the least to any good purpose in her behalf. Which is all I have now to trouble your lordship with, whom I most humbly recommend to the grace and providence of the Almighty.

Richmond, this 29th of October, 1586.

Your lordship's humbly at commandment,

W. DAVISON.

John Wallis is this morning despatched from Mr. Secretary into France, and will in his way attend upon your lordship to see what it may please you to command him.

Burghley to Davison.[1]

Sir,—I have read Mr. Paulett's[2] letters which you sent me, and finding thereby his opinion of the weakness of one part of the Castle of Fotheringay, and of lack of shot and powder, of both which I perceive her Majesty would have regard had. For the first, I think best in my opinion that he had an increase of forty or fifty soldiers for watch and ward, who being well chosen by himself will serve to better purpose than two hundred without the castle, or arming of any gentlemen thereabout. For shot and powder I will take order with a servant of his that is an agent for him here in London for the provision thereof.

And considering I mind by God's grace to be there[3] to-morrow at night, I do forbear to proceed any further

---

[1] *Domestic, Elizabeth*, vol. cxciv., n. 68. Holograph.
[2] In the Calendar it is printed " Mr. Parlett." It is Sir Amias.
[3] " There," that is at Windsor.

herein until her Majesty may direct the same, and yet I will presently write to Mr. Poulet about both these matters, so as his further mind may also be known, either to-morrow at night, or on Tuesday some time.

And so until my return I forbear to write any more. To-morrow in the afternoon the Commissioners must meet at the Star Chamber, so as, the cause being of great length, to hear and conclude upon the whole process in form of a record. It will be late before I can come thither, specially seeing I shall bring the gout with me in my foot, which nobody, either here nor there, will accept from me I am sure. But I thank God my hand is free.

30th October, 1586.

Your letter is dated yesterday, and yet came not to me until past twelve this 30th.

Yours assuredly,

W. BURGHLEY.

Poulet to Walsingham.[1]

Sir,—Although I have no matter worthy of you, yet having a convenient messenger without troubling of the post, I thought good to advertise you that this Queen hath taken physic this week three times, and by occasion thereof according to her wonted manner hath been sick, so as she hath not come out of her bed these five or six days and there remaineth as yet.

Your letters of the 26th have comforted me greatly, and I thank you for them as for an especial favour, praying you to do the like as you shall proceed further. And so I commit you to the mercy of the Highest.

From Fotheringay, the 30th of October, 1586.

Your most assured poor friend,

A. POULET.

---

[1] Vol. xx., n. 19. Holograph.

Burghley to Walsingham.[1]

Sir,—I know it [is] unreasonable to send you any matter to take care thereof, considering how otherwise your mind is burthened, with a care not easily to be removed;[2] but yet having received in a packet to me addressed from Sir Amias Poulet a letter[3] to myself and another to you, not knowing what might be in yours, I venture under your patience to send them both to you, not finding in mine, to the principal point for strengthening of the place, any resolute opinion but argumentation, doubtful to both sides; and therefore I would for answer to be made to mine, that Mr. Secretary Davison might report his answer, and receive her Majesty's resolution: and if both our letters be sent to him, I think her Majesty's answer shall be best for us both. For I still find by experience that such directions must be taken as princes shall give after counsel given.

Nov. 2, 1586.

It is curious to see how completely Burghley looked on Mary's death as inflicted for religion. It is for the good of the Church that she is to die, and the sacredness of the cause removes the case from the operation of the rule of the old Canon Law that Bishops were to take no part in trials for life or capital sentences.

Burghley to Davison.[4]

Sir,—Yesterday in the Parliament chamber grew a question whether it was convenient for the two Archbishops[5] and four other Bishops to accompany the other lords temporal in their petition to her Majesty for

---

[1] *Domestic, Elizabeth,* vol. cxcv., n. 1. Holograph.

[2] Walsingham had just lost his son-in-law, Sir Philip Sydney, who died October 16, 1586, of the wound he received at the battle of Zutphen, on the 22nd of September.

[3] These letters are not among the State Papers.

[4] *Domestic, Elizabeth,* vol. cxcv., n. 11. Holograph.

[5] John Whitgift and Edwin Sandys.

U

execution of the Scottish Queen. Some scruple I had whether her Majesty would like it, because in former times the Bishops in Parliament were wont to absent themselves. But yet I do not think unlawful for them to be present and persuaders in such causes, as the execution of the sentences tend to the state of the Church as this doth.

I pray you do use some speech thereof to her Majesty, that it may be felt whether she will like or mislike, for so will my Lord of Canterbury direct the course. Return me word with that speed you can. I have spoken with Sir Drue Drury, whom Mr. Secretary will despatch this afternoon. With too much haste,

Yours assuredly,

W. Burghley.

This Friday, [? Nov. 4].

If Mary had read the letter that follows, she would not have been able to retain the opinion she had formed, that she might expect fairness from Lord Burghley. He flippantly compares the sentence to a young child that is now old enough to speak. Dr. Lingard quotes[1] Burghley's letter to Hatton that Nau and Curle "would yield somewhat to confirm their mistress' crimes if they were persuaded that themselves might escape and the blow fall upon their mistress betwixt her head and her shoulders;" and he adds, "Was then the decapitation of Mary a subject of merriment to the Lord Treasurer? The wary courtier knew to whom he was writing, and to whom his letter would be shown."

Burghley to Davison.[2]

Mr. Secretary,—I have considered how Ash Wednesday falleth this year coming, which shall be a full month after Candlemas, so as it will be unto Ash Wednesday three full months, that is a quarter of a year. Ash Wednesday shall

---

[1] *History of England,* 1844, vol. viii., p. 219.
[2] *Domestic, Elizabeth,* vol. cxcv., n. 22.

be the 1st of March, and Easter Day the 16th of April, about which time it will be meet that all persons be in the countries maritime, to provide for defence.

I pray you remember her Majesty to send in writing the manner of the speeches that my Lord Chancellor shall use to-morrow at the prorogation of the Parliament. I knew her Majesty meaneth to thank them for their pains, and specially for their care and continuance therein for her safety. But if they have not some comfort also to see the fruits of their cares by some demonstration to proceed from her Majesty, the thanks will be of small weight to carry into the countries; and then the realm may call this a vain Parliament or otherwise nickname it a Parliament of words. For there is no law made for the realm, and if also there be no publication presently of so solemn a sentence, the sentence against the Scottish Queen will be termed a dumb sentence, whereof the nobility that have given it, and all the Parliament that have affirmed it, may repent themselves of their time spent.

The sentence is already more than a full month and four days old. It was full time it should also speak.

If her Majesty will sign it this day, both the Ambassador of Scotland may be prevented this day in that point, as done to satisfy the importunity of the noblemen in commission, and of all the [E]states in Parliament; and to-morrow also my Lord Chancellor[1] may declare the same to the liking of the Parliament.

And for hope of the last part for execution, if her Majesty shall be content that it be said that therein she will prefer no other men's advices or any stranger's for her surety afore her own people, she shall leave hope of execution. And to that hope I beseech God give full perfection.

Thus you see I cannot but utter my opinion, long afore day light, for I have been up since five.

---

[1] Sir Thomas Bromley, who died April 12, 1587.

U 2

Poulet to Burghley.[1]

My very good Lord,—I can hardly express unto your lordship the great joy which I have conceived of your choice of Sir Drue Drury for my assistant in this charge, wherein, although I know that your lordship's chief and principal regard hath been to further her Majesty's service, yet because your lordship cannot be ignorant of the old acquaintance and good friendship between this gentleman and me, I take it for an especial favour that among so many others meet for this place, it hath pleased your lordship to make choice of one such as was so likely to be welcome unto me, as indeed he shall be most heartily welcome. I am well recovered of my gout, I thank God, having felt no pain these three or four days, and now I doubt not but that these good news will set me on foot without delay.

And thus, with most humble thanks for your manifold favours, I commit your good lordship to the merciful protection of the Almighty.

From Fotheringay, the 13th of November, 1586.

Your lordship's to command,

A. POULET.

Addressed—To the right honourable my very good lord, the Lord of Burghley, Lord Treasurer of England.

Poulet to Walsingham.[2]

Sir,—Your several letters of the 13th of this present I received this day at nine in the morning, and now according to your direction Mr. Stallenge cometh unto you, who hath behaved himself here in good and honest sort, willing and ready to do his best endeavour to the furtherance of her Majesty's service, and yet to say truly unto you, having received no warrant for it, I have not

---

[1] Vol. xx., n. 27.   [2] Vol. xx., n. 28.

employed him in anything concerning this lady, neither hath he had access to her or any of her people but in my presence, not for any doubt I had of the gentleman, because he was sent unto me from her Majesty, but for that I had no commission to employ him in such like causes, whereof I thought good to advertise you for his discharge, doubting lest some greater report might be expected at his hands than he is able to make. Sir Drue Drury arrived here the 13th of this present, in the evening, by whose assistance I find myself so much strengthened, as I trust I may be bold to assure you that all things shall fall out here to the full discharge of his duty and mine. I have sent your letters to Sir Richard Dyer, trusting that your speedy resolution will abridge this trouble and charge, and indeed the gaining or losing of one day may be the gaining or losing of a kingdom. Sithence the writing of my last, I received these inclosed from Curle's wife, and will not fail to convey the letter received from you for her, as soon as I may.

And thus, with due commendations from Sir Drue Drury and myself, I commit you to the mercy of the Highest.

From Fotheringay, the 15th of November, 1586.

Your most assured poor friend,

A. POULET.

Queen Elizabeth to Poulet.[1]

Right trusty, &c.,—We have thought it very convenient for sundry respects to send our right trusty and well-beloved councillor the Lord of Buckhurst, and our servant Beale, to acquaint the Queen, your charge, as well with the proceedings of the Commissioners since their departure from our Castle of Fotheringay, as also what hath been lately done in Parliament. Upon communicating

[1] Vol. xx., n. 30.

unto them the said Commissioners' proceedings both at our said castle and since their return, as by their particular instructions you shall more at large understand, which we have willed them to impart unto you ; and therefore our pleasure is that you permit them to have access unto the said Queen, hoping in God that before their repair thither you will be restored to that good state of health, as you may be able to assist and join with them in the present service committed to their charge. And in case the said Queen shall desire to have any conference apart, upon pretence to reveal some secret matter to be communicated unto us, either with the Lord of Buckhurst, or with any one of our said servants above named, we are content to assent thereunto, if she shall earnestly request the same ; for that otherwise we could best like that you to whom the only charge of her is committed, should be present when any such speeches should be delivered.

Endorsed—The minute of a letter of her Majesty to Sir Amys Poulet.   November, 1586.

Poulet to Walsingham.[1]

Sir,—Your letters of the 19th came not to my hands until this present day at three after noon, wherein you may see the lewd negligence of the posts, who might have brought this letter inclosed to have been delivered to my Lord of Buckhurst before his departure from hence this present morning. My letters to her Majesty inclosed herein will be, I doubt not, imparted unto you, and although it pleaseth you to impute her Highness' intended liberality towards my servants and soldiers to the report of Mr. Stallenge, yet I am greatly persuaded that the same hath proceeded in the greater part, if not wholly, of your favour towards me and mine, wherein you have bound me very

---

[1] Vol. xx., n. 31'; Labanoff, tom. vii., p. 220.

much, and indeed I thank you for it as for a singular benefit.

And thus I leave to trouble you, beseeching God to bless all your actions to His glory.

From Fotheringay, the 21st of November, 1586.

Your most assured poor friend,

A. POULET.

I do not remember, and I think I may be bold to deny that I have at any time left this lady in her passionate speeches, but I confess that I have left her often in her superfluous and idle speeches. I have said to Mr. Stallenge, and it is very true, that in former time I have observed this course [to] have as little talk with her as I might, [but] now lately that, following your direction, I have given her full scope and time to say what she would, and yet at some times, finding no matter to come from her worthy of advertisement, I have departed from her, as otherwise she would never have left me, and I am deceived if my Lord of Buckhurst will not give the same testimony of her tediousness.

Poulet to Walsingham.[1]

Sir,—I perceive I was not much deceived in my conceit, upon the receipt of your late letter, mentioning the discharge of the trained soldiers appointed to be sent hither out of Huntingdonshire, and the same to be supplied by the like number to be taken out of .this shire of Northampton, which I took for an argument of the short continuance of this service, and that I should not be troubled with these soldiers at all. I am much confirmed in this opinion and hope, by the late repair hither of the Lord of Buckhurst, and now I trust the next messenger

[1] Vol. xx., n. 32.

will bring your last resolution, which God grant, to whose merciful protection I commit you.

From Fotheringay, the 21st of November, 1586.

Your most assured poor friend,

A. POULET.

Autograph postscript—I have requested this bearer, Mr. Beale, to pray your sign to a letter, wherein you shall do me friendly pleasure.

The "opinion and hope" expressed in the letter just given, pervades the last letter-book, to which we have now come. Poulet's eagerness for Mary's death grows upon him as he becomes personally more weary of the odious service in which he was engaged, and as delay brought with it a probability that her life would be spared. He looked forward with dread to the possibility of her becoming his Queen, and the expressions of his desire for her death are as strong as they well could be.

The value of this last letter-book consists in this, that with the exception of two letters that are in the Record Office, and one in the British Museum, its contents are unknown. As we approach the end of the tragedy, the letters increase in interest, and the letter-book fortunately supplies us with letters, the originals of which have been, we cannot doubt, purposely taken from the series in the State Papers.

The fragment with which the letter-book begins is a part of Poulet's letter to Queen Elizabeth, which was inclosed in the letter to Walsingham given above, dated the 21st of November.

. . . And this example so full of favour and bounty will move others to the like and greater fidelity upon like occasions occurring, as knoweth the Almighty, who always preserve your most excellent Majesty.

To my Lord of Buckhurst.

My very good Lord,—Your lordship hath bound me long sithence by your liberality towards myself, and now you have bound me again by your liberality extended towards my servants and soldiers, and as the same hath been greater than I would have wished, so my debt is thereby the more increased, which I do acknowledge with all thankfulness, and would make better satisfaction if I were able.

And thus, &c.

To Mr. Stallenge, eodem die.

Sir,—I have been informed by letters from Sir Francis Walsingham, of the friendly offices touching my servants and soldiers, wherein you have deserved more of them than they shall be able to acquite towards you ; and being not ignorant that I have great interest in any commandments that shall be made of them or their service, I acknowledge myself also to be beholden unto you herein, and will be always ready to acquite it in all that I may. And upon this promise, with my right hearty commendations, &c.

About this time Mary wrote several letters, which she intrusted to her servants to be delivered by them after her death.[1] In these she gives her own account of the manner in which her cloth of Estate or *dais* was taken down, and her account differs greatly from Poulet's. On Saturday, the 19th of November, O.S., Lord Buckhurst, and Beale, Clerk of the Council, were sent by Elizabeth to announce to Mary that sentence of death had been pronounced against her. On Monday the 21st, the day when Lord Buckhurst left Fotheringay,[2] Poulet and Drury told Mary that she was a dead woman without honour or dignity, and that therefore they must remove her cloth of Estate. Her own attendants refusing to touch it, they ordered in seven or eight of their servants, by whom it was taken down ; and then, sitting covered in her presence, Poulet ordered

---

[1] Her letter to Mendoza, dated November 23, 1586, O.S., was received by him October 15, 1587, N.S. (Labanoff, tom. vi., p. 461).

[2] Vol. xx., n. 31 ; *supra*, p. 310.

that her billiard table should be removed, as she had no further need of pastime. She answered that she had not used it since it was put up, and that she had other occupations. A sad office was in store for the cover of that billiard table. Immediately after the execution, when the headsman had despoiled Mary's corpse, it was carried into a room adjoining that in which her maids of honour were confined; and they looking through a crevice saw the body of their mistress half covered by a piece of rough woollen stuff, which had been hastily taken from the billiard table.[1] Mary said that all Poulet's insolence was brought upon her because she would not confess herself guilty and beg pardon of Elizabeth.[2]

After this, on the 23rd, some work was carried on in her dining-room, while she was writing to Mendoza, and she believed it to be the erection of a scaffold for her execution. On Thursday the 24th, she wrote to the Duke of Guise, that when Poulet and Drury visited her, "Je leur ay montré, au lieu de mes armes audit days, la croix de mon Sauveur." Poulet says very expressly that her servants took down the cloth of Estate, and not his, and he does not mention to Elizabeth his insolence in putting on his hat in Mary's presence.[3] Mary wrote[4] to Elizabeth about a month later, calling it a useless cruelty, and showing how keenly she felt the indignity. "Je pense que vous aurés bien sceu que, en vostre nom, on m'a faict abattre mon days, et après on m'a dict que ce n'estoit pas par votre commandement, mais par l'advis d'aucuns du Conseil. Je loue Dieu que telle cruaulté, ne servant qu'à exercer malice et m'affliger après me estre résolue à la mort, n'est venue de vous. Je crains que ainsi ne soit de beaucoup d'autres choses, pourquoy on ne m'a voulu permectre de vous escripre que après m'avoir eu, à tant qu'en eulx est, en forme dégradée de principaulté et noblesses, me disant que je n'estois qu'une simple femme morte, incapable de toute dignitez."

It would seem that it was from Poulet's own expression that he was "very curious and precise to be warranted in all his

---

[1] Brantosme; Jebb, vol. ii., p. 493.   [2] *Infra*, p. 327.

[3] Labanoff, tom. vi., pp. 459, 464, 469.   [4] *Ibid.*, p. 478.

proceedings," that Elizabeth drew the censure she passed upon him when he would not liberate her from her embarrassment, by the assassination of his prisoner.

To Mr. Secretary Davison, November 28, 1586.

Sir,—Finding by your letters of the 25th of this present that her Majesty doth not allow of my proceedings in two several things, I submit myself most humbly to her Highness' censure, with promise of all conformity to her better directions. And yet for my discharge at least in some little part of the blame imputed unto me, I am bold to trouble you with the true and plain circumstances of my doings herein, as one very willing to deserve no blame at all if it were possible, although my manifold infirmities of body and mind will not permit it in so weighty a charge.

Touching the matter and manner of the taking down of this lady's cloth of Estate. These are to advertise you that whereas I had been given to understand by a late letter from some friend about the Court, of her Majesty's mislike that this lady did enjoy her cloth of Estate, the truth is that I found her seized thereof, in her private dining-chamber, at my first entrance into this service, and had been informed by credible report that she had always enjoyed the same in the sight and view of many Councillors and others [nigh] unto her, and therefore I should never have been so bold to have taken [it] from her without direction from above, as one that ever hath been and shall be hereafter, very curious and precise to be warranted in all my proceedings. But finding her possessed at my first coming unto her, of one other cloth of Estate, set up in the chamber where I was to dine and sup, I thought it impertinent, and not meet to be tolerated by any English subject, and therefore caused it immediately to be taken down, to this lady's great discontentment.[1] And whereas

[1] See vol. xv., n. 74 ; *supra*, p. 11.

it is witnessed that this other cloth of Estate had been taken down in some morning before her coming into the place, or at some other time when she had been absent, I would gladly have done it in this sort, but by reason of the straitness of her bed-chamber and of the chamber adjoining, some of her gentlewomen are forced to take their lodging at night in the dining-chamber, where the said cloth of Estate was placed, so as I could have no access thither in the morning; and after noon she is very seldom out of her dining-chamber. And as I had no mean to know when she was retired into her bed-chamber; so if she had been there the same is so near adjoining, as I could not have done it without her privity. And you may believe that she would not have yielded unto it without conference with me. As likewise I have never had access unto her, but after knowledge given by one of her servants of my coming, and then I was always assured to find her [in her] dining-chamber under the cloth of Estate which was set over the chimney, and covered the place she was accustomed to sit at her dinner and supper, where I found her at this last doings, and prayed her to retire herself out of the chamber, which although she refused, yet she forsook her place and sat down on the other side of the chamber, and at my solicitation pretending that my servants could not take it down so well as her own servant who had set it up, she sent for the yeoman of her wardrobe and by him it was taken down in my presence, so as it was not done in such severe fashion as hath been supposed. And although my direction herein was delivered unto me by express words as from her Majesty, yet you may perceive by my last letters, that I used all possible moderation, saying only that "it was thought meet," without making mention of her Majesty or any other, so as, indeed, it might seem unto her, that I did it rather by order from Sir Francis Walsingham, or you, or from some other lords of the Council, than from her Highness.

Thus much for the matter and manner of the taking down of the said cloth of Estate. And now for some answer to the second fault in not entertaining this lady in the desire she had to write unto her Majesty, and that although she had not desired it of me sithence the departure from hence of the lords, yet I should have made offer thereof unto her, I must confess that I never made this offer, wherein if I have offended, the same deserveth grace in that I did it not maliciously, but of a settled opinion that without special direction, I ought not in duty to move her unto it until she had desired it, and in truth I was never willed and advised to do it by any Councillor whosoever. And in respect of my duty to her Majesty, I should never have done it without warrant. It seemed to me sufficient that I had signified to her once or twice, that if she had desired to write unto her Majesty it had been permitted, whereby she could not but understand that howsoever she had been restrained to write shortly after the taking away of her secretaries, yet now she might have done it, if she had been so disposed. And yet to [speak] truly unto you, I did advertise Mr. Secretary Walsingham of her desire to write, by two several letters, doubting lest the blame of the refusal should have lighted wholly upon myself, although I found it inconvenient in my simple judgment to give her that scope at that time without her Majesty's privity. This is all I can say for mine excuse in some part of those faults whereby I trust it will appear that the same have proceeded of ignorance, most humbly praying her Majesty's pardon.

Yesterday Sir Drue Drury and I took occasion to visit this lady after noon, whom we found in her dining-chamber sitting in her accustomed place ; and looking to the chimney she said unto me, that although I had taken down her cloth of Estate, which God and nature had given unto her, yet she trusted that I would not take those things from her which she had set up in the place thereof,

which were eight or ten pictures in paper of the Passion
of Christ, and of other like stuff fastened upon the hangings
over the chimney.   I answered that indeed it was not
thought meet by some of the lords of her Majesty's Council
that standing now convict in law, she should be used with
these respects and ceremonies which before were permitted
unto her.   She said she took it to have been so ordered
by her Majesty.   I told her she had no reason to take
it so, because I made no particular mention either of
her Majesty or of her Council, but said in general terms
it was thought meet to have it so done.   "Yea," saith she,
"many things are done by her Council which are not to be
imputed to her," affirming that for her part she did not
allow of the Council nor had to do with them.   And
staying at this speech, I declared unto her that the Lord
of Buckhurst had made report unto her Majesty of her
requests, and that she should receive answer therein within
a day or two. "My requests," said she, "are not so many but
they may be soon answered."   " Yet they are three or four
[in] number," quoth I, "[and] are so many as require some
consideration in the answer."   She said she moved them
to none other end than by taking order with her servants,
and settling her other things she might be the better
prepared towards God.   I told her that her purpose was
good, and no doubt she should receive answer very shortly,
adding that if she had been disposed to have advertised
by her letters to her Majesty, as well her requests, as
also such other matter as she delivered to the Lord of
Buckhurst in her private conference with him, I was very
well assured his lordship would not have refused it.   She
answered that because his lordship was sent hither unto
her from her Majesty, and as she heard did appertain
to her Highness, (whereby she meant some matter of
alliance, and after she did expound it) she thought it
sufficient to commit those things to his lordship's report.
I said there was no doubt but that his lordship would

make true report of all things, and that I had put her in remembrance of her writing for none other end than that she should know that she might have written by his lordship if she had desired it, and that if she continued in any disposition of writing I would not fail to convey her letters. She said that when all things were not so far past she was willing to have written, but now standing condemned, she was to think of other matters, and to prepare herself for a better life in another world. And hereupon she fell into a large discourse on the mercies of [God] towards her, and of her preparation towards Him, and into many other impertinent speeches not worthy to be recited ; as likewise I omit some other talk which passed between her and me, upon this ground tending only to the benefit of her soul, and the discharge of my conscience. And thus I departed from her, having endeavoured myself according to your direction, to salve the two faults mentioned in your letters in as clear manner as I could, without giving her cause to think that I came to her to that purpose.

And thus, &c.

Ad eundem eodem die.

Sir,—I have received your letters of the 25th of this present with great joy, because they give unto me not only assurance of her Majesty's safety (whom God in His mercy long preserve from the dangerous snares of this lady under my charge and her adherents), but also a most certain testimony of your good affection and favour towards me, which as I esteem very highly, so I will not be found unworthy thereof, if it may suffice to love you unfeignedly and to deal honestly and friendly with you. I am of this disposition, that where I owe much I would owe more, and therefore I pray you continue your good offices towards me, and to bind me more and more to be your thankful friend, and this is all you may expect of me. I, have delivered your commendations to Sir Drue Drury by the full view of your letters, and now both he and I return the like towards you in the best and heartiest manner we can devise, as knoweth the Almighty, &c.

To Sir Francis Walsingham, December 4, 1586.[1]

Sir,—I think the time very long sithence I heard from you or any other about the Court, and I should fear lest Fotheringay were forgotten, if I did not know that this lady under my charge has given great cause to be remembered by all true and faithful subjects ; whose dutiful care for her Majesty's subjects, the continuance of the Gospel, and the liberty and quiet of this realm, will not permit them to sleep soundly until the head and seed plat of all practices and conspiracies tending to the imminent subversion of Prince, realm, and people, be utterly extirped. I thank God I have conceived a most steadfast hope of a happy resolution, and yet the experience of former time doth teach us that opportunities neglected are very often accompanied with very dangerous. effects. God has the times and seasons in His hand, and His judgments cannot be prevented, but will appear in their due hour. The lady is said to be grieved in one of her knees, which is no new thing unto her, and is not likely to have any continuance. Thus you see that these few lines tend to none other end than to draw from you one or two, if your leisure will so permit.

And thus, &c.

To the Earl of Leicester, eodem die.

My very good Lord,—Being given to understand of your lordship's arrival at the Court, I would not fail to congratulate the same by these few lines, as also your happy success in your martial affairs, a principal mean of our happy quietness, which God continue, if it be His good pleasure. I trust to be so happy as to attend on your

[1] Vol. xx., n. 38.

lordship shortly at the Court, whereof I have the greater hope because the felicity of Queen and country consisteth especially next after God, in the sacrifice of justice to be duly executed upon this lady, my charge, the root and well-spring of all our calamities.

And thus I, &c.

Her Majesty's charges were increased now that there were two households to maintain instead of one, and the right chord to strike was to play on Elizabeth's parsimony. Poulet has done his best to play upon her fears.

To my Lord Treasurer, December 9, 1586.

My very good Lord,—Your lordship's letters of the 5th coming to my hands the 6th of this present, at nine in the night, I sent the next morning for Mrs. Bridget Digby, who coming to Mr. Cruse's house that day late in the evening, yesterday I conferred with her, and received such answer as may appear unto your lordship by this note inclosed, having taken order with Mr. Cruse according to your lordship's direction. I trust the Scottish household at Chartley is not forgotten, which no doubt is chargeable to her Majesty.

And thus, &c.

To Mr. Secretary Davison, December 11, 1586.

Sir,—Having not heard in many days from any friend about the Court, and upon that only ground written to Mr. Secretary Walsingham the 4th of this present, with request to receive somewhat again of him, your letters of the 6th of [the same] are come to my hands to my great satisfaction, partly for your liberal advertisement of home and foreign occurrents, for the which I most heartily thank you, but especially in that you are content in this time of expectation to remember your poor absent friend by your letters, without any cause touching Prince or State moving

V

you thereunto, wherein you have bound me greatly, and I pray you be not weary to bind me more and more, although I can yield nothing again but a thankful, friendly mind. I had written to my Lord of Leicester two days before the receipt of your letters mentioning his lordship's favourable remembrance of me.

These letters come unto you in a packet directed to my Lord Treasurer, containing the examination of a gentlewoman of [these] parts, taken before me by direction from his lordship.

And thus, &c.

Poulet's ingenuity is great in varying the phrases in which he expresses his vehement eagerness for Mary's death. A day or two ago it was "the sacrifice of justice" that was "to be duly executed upon this lady." Now it is a "gaol delivery" he is anxious for. Yet he had a strong dislike to the correlative title of gaoler.

To my Lord Treasurer, eodem die.

My very good Lord,—Captain Oliver has been here with me this day, with whom I have resolved upon all things touching the forty soldiers appointed for this service, which are promised to be brought hither on Monday next. I am so strongly persuaded of the honourable necessity of the cause as I will not take this new supply for an argument of a longer continuance of this service. I was not long sithence a suitor to your lordship for a new supply of powder, whereof surely there will be great need if the service have any little continuance, every harquebusier of my servants and soldiers having in store at my coming to this castle only one flask full of powder, whereof some part was spent the day of her Majesty's coronation. Although I have but thirty soldiers, yet I have more than fifty harquebusiers, it may please your lordship to relieve this household with a new supply of money, the 400*l.* which Mr. Darrell had last from your lordship being already

spent and 200*l.* more. The charges of this family will be
greatly increased by reason of the Scottish household at
Chartley and this new supply of soldiers, wherein there is
no other remedy than by a gaol delivery, which God will
send in due time.

And thus, &c.

The letter to Davison of this day's date had been despatched
before the arrival of this now acknowledged from Walsingham,
who had been long silent, and who did not write again, save a
few lines about Mary's accounts, until he signed with Davison
the assassination letter of February 1st. Poulet's fanatical hatred
to his prisoner quenches his natural feeling. He is mortally
afraid of anything that gives Mary the least chance of life; or
he could never, himself a father, have spoken, as he here speaks,
of the letter in which James pleads with Elizabeth for his
mother's life.

To Sir Francis Walsingham, eodem die.[1]

Sir,—I cannot thank you enough for your friendly
letters of the 7th of this present, and for your willing
favour to let me know upon every good occasion such
accidents as shall seem meet for me, which in this time
of expectation cannot but bring greater comfort, howsoever
things shall fall out, against all expectation. I should be
condemned for a busybody if I should write unto you all
that I think touching the copy of the Scottish King's
letters to Keith, not doubting but that her Majesty and
her most honourable Council will consider of it, in all
respect of honour to her Highness touching the manner,
and in all public and Christian judgment touching the
matter. Only I will say, that as I would be glad to
hear that her Majesty had not vouchsafed to read the
said letters at a second-hand, so I assure myself, that
having answered the French Ambassador (coming from
the mightiest Prince in Europe, and bringing a message of

[1] *Cotton. MSS.,* Caligula, C. ix., f. 561.

great temperance) in such round, princely, and majestical sort, as moved admiration in all the hearers; her Highness being now justly provoked many ways (if I do not mistake the copy), will not give place to the pride of so poor a neighbour, but repress the same in his first budding, a principal, or rather the only remedy, in such forward (I will not say) presumptuous attempts. I pray God the unthankfulness in the mother work not like effects in the son.

Captain Oliver has been here with me this day, and will bring hither the forty trained men on Monday next, being very glad of this supply in this dangerous and desperate time. And although I took the last delay thereof, for some argument of no long continuance of this service, yet I am so strongly persuaded of the honourable necessity of the cause (the rather upon the proclamation lately published), as these new forces cannot remove me from my former hope of a speedy discharge. I have been of late a suitor to my Lord Treasurer and you for a supply of powder, whereof in truth I shall have great need if the service have any little continuance. Every harquebusier of my servants and soldiers had only one flask full of powder remaining at my coming to this castle, whereof some part was spent the day of her Majesty's coronation. I have for the thirty soldiers allowed unto me only thirty calivers out of her Majesty's store, but I brought hither thirty calivers of my own store, which serve to furnish my household servants.

This letter cometh unto you in a packet sent to my Lord Treasurer, by the which I am a suitor to his lordship for a new supply of money, and also have put his lordship in remembrance of my former suit of powder.

And thus [I leave to trouble you, committing you to the mercy of the Highest.

From Fotheringay, the 9th of December, 1586.

Your most assured poor friend,

A. POULET.

Autograph postscript in the original—Sir Drue Drury hath seen your favourable remembrance of him in my letters and doth yield unto you all due thanks.]

On the 23rd of November, Mary wrote to Mendoza, "J'ai demandé un prêtre, je ne sais si je l'aurai; ils m'en ont offert un évêque des leurs. Je l'ai refusé tout à plat."

The tirade at the close of Poulet's letter, meant no doubt for Elizabeth's eye, reveals the writer's entire want of sympathy with what is noble and elevated in character. He puts as the climax of Mary's offences, that she makes no mention of desire for life.

To Sir Francis Walsingham, December 15, 1586.

Sir,—Having signified to this Queen that I was commanded to restore unto her the money which I took from her, and praying her to authorize some of her servants for the receipt thereof, she returned answer that as I had taken it from her, so she thought meet that I should render it unto herself: whereupon repaying unto her, accompanied with Sir Drue Drury and Mr. Darrell, I found her in her bed troubled with some weakness in one of [her] legs, but without grief as she said; where delivering unto her a particular note of the money which I received of her, together with the defrayments which I had made by her direction, she asked me for the two thousand crowns taken from Curle's wife. I told her that she was found seized of them, and that it was well known that they had been given unto her for her preferment in marriage. She said it was very true, but affirmed that the money was delivered here only by way of pawn or pledge, and that she had taken order with her officers in France for the payment of the like sum there to the use of Curle, and therefore prayed that order might be so taken for her discharge, as she might not pay the said sum both here and there. She said farther, that her chirurgeon, named Gervais, had delivered three hundred crowns or thereabouts to Nau upon hope to have received the same again in France. And that one of her gentle-women called Beauregard had delivered unto him six hundred crowns for like purpose, as likewise that Nau and Pasquier used her money at London for provision of divers things for themselves and their fellows, whereof yet no perfect account was made unto her. I answered that it was likely the certainty of all these things would appear in her papers or in Nau's papers, and that I knew very well nothing would be concealed that might concern any particular person in justice and equity. She prayed that it might be considered, and therewith asked me what answer I received to her other demands. I told her that her papers should be sent her very shortly, and that her servants should have free passport, to go into France or Scotland at their pleasure. "Yea," saith she, "but I cannot tell whether they shall have liberty to pass freely with such things as they shall have of me." I said that she had no cause to doubt of it. "I speak it," saith she, "for my movables, because I intend to send a bed to my son," saying that for such like causes she had prayed liberty to make her will, and asked me if I had received no answer therein. I told her no, and that it seemed to require no answer, because it was things that depended wholly of herself. Then she asked me what answer I had received touching her Priest. I told her it was intended that he should have access unto her shortly. This was the substance of her speech at that time. And so, after restitution made of the money, Sir Drue Drury and I departed from her.

I sent two of my servants for the Priest remaining with Mr. Thomas Gresley on Monday, and do look for their return this evening, or at the farthest this next morning, by the grace of God. This lady continueth in her former wilful and wicked disposition. No outward sign of repentance; no submission, no acknowledging of her fault, no

craving of pardon,[1] no mention of desire of life; so as it
may be feared lest as she hath lived, so she will die, and I
pray God that this Popish ignorant Priest be not admitted
unto her by His just judgment to increase her punish-
ment, being very likely that he will rather confirm her in
her stubbornness towards her Majesty, and in all her other
errors in matter of religion, than seek to reclaim her to a
better disposition. As knoweth the, &c.

Poulet represents to Burghley that Mary's almoner being
restored, "it may be repented of in policy," if she be not put
to death at once; but three days later he wrote to Davison
that the "inconvenience is not so great in matter of policy as
in conscience," as du Préau was of too "weak and slender a
judgment" to be dangerous.

To my Lord Treasurer, December 18, 1586.

My very good Lord,—Having long sithence received
express direction for the dismissing of the Scottish company now remaining at Chartley, within [the] five days
next following after the remove of this Queen from
thence towards this castle; and to that purpose, required
at that time to know what she would give them in reward,
and towards the charge of their journey; upon motion
made to her therein, I received her warrant under her sign
of certain sums of money to be delivered to every of them
for their travelling expences, referring them for their reward
to a farther consideration, which sums of money I left in
Mr. Richard Bagot's hands at my coming from Chartley,
to have been delivered by him to the Scottish train according to their several portions at their departure from thence,
which I had appointed to be within five days after the

---

[1] "On me menace si je ne demande pardon; mais je dis, Puisque jà ils
m'ont destinée à mourir, qu'ils passent outre en leur injustice, espérant que
Dieu m'en récompensera en l'autre monde." Mary to Mendoza, Nov. 23, O.S.
(Labanoff, tom. vi., p. 459).

remove, according to the order prescribed unto me in that behalf from above. And at that time did also deliver to Mr. Bagot passports for every of them, for their travel into France or Scotland according to their several desires, wherein also I was authorized by direction from above. These things being settled after this sort, in my way hitherward I received express commandment to stay them at Chartley until her Majesty's pleasure were further known. And now your lordship's letters of the 17th, coming to my hands this present day at five in the evening, I forbear to discharge the family until I hear again from your lordship, because you commanded me by your said letters to send unto your lordship a list of their names with the particular sums they are to have, that upon view thereof, order may be taken to pay and then to dismiss them, which are the very words of your lordship's conclusion upon the end of that article, by the which it appeareth that your lordship was not yet acquainted with the restitution made the last week to this Queen of all her money remaining in my hands by order from Mr. Secretary Walsingham. And therefore sending unto your lordship herewith the particular names of all the said family, together with the several sums given them by this Queen, I refer to your lordship's consideration if I shall acquaint her with their departure, or make any new motion of a further liberality towards them, and whether it shall be permitted unto them to make their repair to London in their way towards their several homes, which they desire and was granted unto them by their former passports, wherein I was also authorized from above.

Also I received direction by my last letter from Mr. Secretary Walsingham, to send for this Queen's Priest remaining with Mr. Gresley, and to permit him to have access unto her, who arrived here the 17th of this present; so as if the execution of this lady be delayed, it may be repented as well in policy as in Christianity that he hath so speedy access unto her, and thereby shall have so long continuance with her. Being desirous to be delivered of the household at Chartley for the diminishing of her Majesty's charges, and partly for mine own better discharge, being forced to commit that company to the order of one of my servants, I despatch these letters with the greater speed for your lordship's final resolution herein, intending very shortly to render unto your lordship Mr. Darrell's particular account of one month's charges in the state we live in here at this present.

And thus, &c.

The new form that Poulet's wish for Mary's death here assumes is almost comical. She is to be "removed," as the cause of "her Majesty's charges." There have not been many sovereigns to whom it could have been suggested, as a motive for putting to death a captive Queen, that it would be a good stroke of economy. What possible harm the restoration of Mary's money could do, or why Poulet should wish it had been delayed "until within a day or two before the execution," it is not easy to see. In truth, it is but another way of saying that he wishes that the execution might come within a day or two of the restoration of the money.

To my Lord Treasurer, December 19, 1586.

My very good Lord,—Having answered some part of your lordship's letters of the 17th by mine of yesterday, sent from hence this day at five in the morning, for your lordship's satisfaction in the residue I send inclosed herein an estimate of one week's expence of this family in diet, wages, and other incidents, wishing that her Majesty's charges herein might be lessened, whereof I see no reasonable mean, unless the cause were removed, which bringeth forth these chargeable effects, and without the special mercy of God may breed most lamentable and dangerous effects. As knoweth, &c.

For the little interest I have in this Scottish action by
reason of my charge in this castle, I trust it may be lawful
for me to wish without offence that this lady's money had
not been restored unto her until within a day or two before
the execution, and yet I doubt not to keep her fasting
from employing the same to any indirect or dangerous
uses.

There were two letters that about this time Mary addressed
to Elizabeth.   The first has no date, but is attributed to
November.   It asks of Elizabeth three favours, Christian burial,
a public execution, that no false rumours may be spread abroad
about the faith in which she would die, and free passage for her
servants, together with undisturbed possession of her gifts to
them.   The second, dated December 19, is longer, and as
there is nothing in the first letter that is not contained in the
second, and as Poulet's correspondence gives no trace of more
than one letter written at this time by Mary to Elizabeth, it
seems probable that the letter without date is a draft of that
dated December 19.[1]

Acting on Walsingham's instructions, Poulet, through the long
interview he here describes, was trying by insulting speeches to
exasperate Mary into rejoinders which might compromise her.
Iterating the instructions supplied to Lord Buckhurst, he tells
Mary that she had been tried by a commission composed of the
nobility as a great favour, that Elizabeth had long preserved her
life against the wish of the Scottish people and the desire of the
English Parliament, and that as a pretender to the crown she
had been well treated.   Poulet reproaches her with refusing to
give up her claim to the crown, save on condition that she
should be acknowledged heir presumptive, with fomenting rebellion, &c.   He speaks of " dangerous practices," but when Mary
rejoins that she was not accountable for what others have done,

---

[1] Prince Labanoff has printed the letter of December 19 (tom. vi., p. 474),
from a "minute avec corrections de M. de Châteauneuf," collated with the
copy in the Record Office (vol. xx., n. 40).   The letter having no date is
taken from *La vraye Histoire de Marie Stuart*, by N. Caussin, published at
Paris in 1624.

Poulet, instead of bringing home her share in Babington's conspiracy to her at once, reproaches her with keeping Morgan in her service. Had he not been, to say the least, doubtful of her guilt, he would have tried to wring some acknowledgment from her, if only to counteract the effect of her letter to Elizabeth. Lord Buckhurst, who probably did believe Mary guilty, had told her to her face, in Poulet's presence, that she "should die for the Queen's murder."[1] Why too does Poulet never mention the reputed crime in his letters?

To Mr. Secretary Davison, December 21, 1586.

Sir,—Although this Queen hath pretended with many shows of constancy neither to fear death, nor to desire life, yet being advertised in my last conference with her (as I doubt not you have heard by my letters of the 16th to Mr. Secretary Walsingham), that her Priest should have access unto her very shortly, whereof she will in reason make none other construction than that he was admitted for none other purpose then to satisfy her desire in her last tragical end, it seemeth by that which followeth that she is neither so mortified, as she is willing to die, neither doth think her case so desperate, but that some shift may be found to prolong her days.

Upon this opinion, if I be not deceived, she prayed me to repair unto her, which I did in the company of Sir Drue Drury, the 17th of this present, where she declared unto me that in time past she had been desirous to write to her Majesty, but sithence the advertisement of her conviction she prepared herself for another world. Nevertheless, she was willing, not for desire of life, but for the discharge of the rest of her conscience, and for her last farewell,—these were her very words,—to send a memorial of something concerning herself after her departure out of this world, and to remove from her Majesty all suspicion of danger in receiving the paper

[1] Labanoff, tom. vi., p. 467.

which should come from her, she said herself would take the assay thereof, and deliver it to me with her own hands. I asked her if she would not be also content to seal and inclose it in my presence, which she yielded unto, praying me to promise that it might be safely delivered; which being granted, she desired my further promise to procure certificate from above that the same was so delivered there. Sir Drue Drury told her that it was in our power to send but was beyond our power, and above us, to promise any certificate. She said she trusted that consideration would be had of her after her decease, as one proceeding from Henry VII., and according to the religion wherein she was born, and which she had professed all the days of her life, concluding that when her memorial was ready she would send for us, which we looked should have been the next day, but she did not send for us till yesterday, imputing the delay thereof to her lame hand, which would not permit her to write more speedily.

She took it in ill part that I had asked if she would be content to make up and seal her letter in my presence, which bewrayed my hard opinion of her. I told her that herself having proffered beside my expectation to take my first assay of the utter [outer] part of the letter, I was not ignorant that there might be as great danger within the letter as without, and therefore could not be blamed to concur with her in this jealousy, affirming that if herself had not moved it, Sir Drue Drury and I should not have thought it. Then [she] said she had moved it upon this occasion that having [been] accustomed in time past to send sometimes some tokens to her Majesty, and at one time sent certain clothes (so she called them), one standing by advised her Highness to be caused to be tried before she did touch them, which she said, she had sithence observed and had taken order with Nau at his last being at the Court to do the like to a furred counterpane which she sent at that time. I answered that

I thought her Majesty was at that time far from any
suspicion of such foul dealing, and wished that no just
cause had been sithence given, and then things had not
been as they now are. "Things are as they are," saith
she, "and I stand convicted and do not know how many
hours I shall live." "Madam," quoth I, "you shall live as
many hours as shall please God, but it may be said truly
that you have been convicted in very honourable and
favourable sort." "With what favour?" said she. I said
her cause had been examined by a number of the most
ancient nobility of the realm, where, by our laws she
should have been tried by twelve men as a common
person. "Your noblemen," saith she, "must be tried by
their peers." I told her all strangers of what quality soever
were in matter of crime tryable in the territories of other
Princes by the laws of that realm. "You have your laws,"
saith she, "but other Princes will think of it as they see
cause, and my son is now no more a child, but is come to
the state of a man, and he will think of these things."
Sir Drue told her that ingratitude was odious in all
persons, but especially in great personages, and that it
would not be denied but that her Majesty had deserved
greatly both of her and her son. "What shall I acknowledge?" saith she. "I am free from the world, and therefore
am not afraid to speak; I have had the favour to have
been kept here prisoner many years against my will."
"Madam," quoth I, "this was a great favour, and without
this favour you had not lived to see these days." "How so?"
saith she. I said her own subjects pursued her, and were
the stronger in her own country. "That is true," quoth
she, "because Mildmay (I think she did mean Sir Nicholas
Throckmorton) persuaded me to discharge my forces, and
then caused mine enemies to burn my friends' castles and
houses." I told her, however, it was great personages of
that country had made earnest suit to her Majesty to have
her delivered unto them, which her Highness refused to

their great dislike; and Sir Drue added that her Majesty
had saved her life seventeen years, and whereas she called
her Highness by name of sister, she had in [truth] dealt
most graciously with her in seeking to preserve both her
life and her honour. "Wherein?" said she. He answered,
in the commission of her causes sitten upon at York, which
was dissolved at the instance of her friends to save her
honour. "No," quoth she, "the cause of the dissolving of
the commission was, that my friends could not be heard to
inform against mine accusers." I told her that the Bishop
of Ross had written that it was dismissed in her favour,
and that his book was extant, and this was but one of many
favours which her Majesty had extended unto her. "It is
a great favour," said she, "to have kept me here many
years against my will." I said it was for her safety, and
that her countrymen sought her destruction, and to that
end required to have her delivered unto them, as was
before said. "Nay," saith she, "then I will speak. I am
not afraid. It was determined here I should not depart,
and my Lord Treasurer, when I was demanded by my
subjects, wrote in a packet to the Earl Murray (which was
intercepted and brought to me) that the devil was tied fast
in a chain, and that they could not keep her, but she should
be kept safely here." Sir Drue Drury told her that the
Earl Murray was a very honourable gentleman as ever he
knew bred in that country. She said the Earl Murray was
one of the worst men of the world; a common adulterer,
a spoiler, and a murderer. Sir Drue affirmed that he
remembered to have seen him here six weeks, and that he
governed himself very gravely, and carried the reputation
of a noble gentleman, neither did he ever hear him evil
spoken of till then. "Yea," quoth she, "my rebels are
honest men here, and have been maintained by the Queen."
I told her she did forget herself greatly to charge her
Majesty with so foul a fault, which she should be never
able to prove. "I pray you," saith she, "what did she with

the French at Newhaven?" "It appeared," quoth I, "that
you have conceived so hardly of the Queen my mistress,
that you interpret all her actions to the worst without
knowing the truth of the cause," but I could assure her that
her Majesty had just cause, as well in respect of Calais, as
other ways, to do as she did, and to have done more if it
had so pleased her. I told her this was great unthankfulness after so many great favours, whereof she would in no
ways acknowledge the least. I told her that her Majesty
had saved her life with the discontentment of her best
subjects in open Parliament, who craved justice against her
for matter of civil rebellion. She said she knew no such
matter, but knew very well that Sir Francis Walsingham,
after his last being in Scotland, had said that she should
rue his entertainment there. I told her she had not rued
it, but had been more honourably entreated then was ever
any competitor in any other realm, whereof some have
been kept close prisoners, others had been disfigured and
maimed, and some others had been murdered. "I was
no competitor," said she. "I required to be reputed as next
to the Crown." "Nay, madam," quoth I, "you went farther,
in giving the arms and style of England, as though our
Queen had been an usurper." She said her husband and
kinsmen had done what they thought good: she had
nothing to do with it. "Why, then," quoth I, "would you
not renounce your pretended claim herein, but with condition that you might be authorized next heir apparent to
the Crown." Whereunto she answered that she had made
great proffers at sundry times which could never be
accepted. I told her that it had been heretofore proved
unto her, that in the very instant of all her treaties and
offers of friendship, some dangerous practices were discovered. "You must think," saith she, "that I have some
friends, and if they have done anything, what is that to
me?" "Madam," quoth I, "it was somewhat to you (and
for your own sake I would you had forborne it), that after

advertisement given unto you of Morgan's devilish practice to have killed a sacred Queen, you would yet entertain him as your servant." She answered that she might do it with as good right, as that her Majesty entertained her rebels. Sir Drue told her the speech was very hard, and that the case differed greatly.

She fell from these discourses, and returned to the matter of her conviction, saying that she was condemned partially, and that the Commissioners knew, she being convicted, her son could have no right, and that her Majesty could have no children, whereby they might set up whom they liked. I told her that she did forget herself greatly to charge the nobility of the realm with two so foul and horrible faults, as first to take her life from her by partiality, and then to bestow the Crown where they liked. She said all was one to her, and that for her part she thanked God that she should die without regret (I use her own words) of anything that she had done. I prayed her to be sorry, at least for the great wrong she had done to the Queen my mistress. "Let others answer for themselves," saith she ; "I have nothing to do with it;" and then asked me if I had remembered her money matters, mentioned in her last conference with me, which I said was not forgotten. After this long discourse thus ended she took her letter sent herewith, which, notwithstanding her pretended lameness in her hand, could make up, seal and superscribe, without the help of any other, or outward show of ache or pain.[1] She had borne Sir Drue and me in hand (as is before remembered) that she would only send a memorial, but it appeared by the view of the paper, that this memorial was become a just letter. Sir Drue Drury and I might easily perceive that this lady doth not cease to carry a revenging mind

---

[1] Mary wrote to the Duke of Guise, "Ceste main droite, depuis ceste dernière venue, m'est si enflée et fait tant de mal qu' à peine puis-je tenir la plume, ny m'appaster" (Labanoff, tom. vi., p. 439).

towards her Majesty, her nobility and all her faithful subjects.

Thus you see what hath passed between this Queen and us, wherein to obey your direction I have not failed to do all that I might, to provoke her to utter her stomach, although I am persuaded her malice is so rooted as her Majesty shall make little profit thereof, and shall serve to none other purpose but to increase her·sin, whereof she hath enough otherways, as God best knoweth. You may believe that she hath been urged to all that she hath said, as otherways she would have used her late accustomed silence, and indeed her speeches have been very quiet sithence the taking away of her cloth of Estate. I have already by my late letters yielded to her Majesty, as I was most bound, my most humble and dutiful thanks for her intended liberality towards my servants and soldiers, and now it may please you to do the like to her Highness in my name for the performance thereof signified by your last letters, beseeching God to give His grace both to master and men to acknowledge this undeserved bounty with all dutiful thankfulness, and to live and die her Majesty's true and faithful subjects.

And thus, &c.

I had forgotten to signify unto you that this Queen, taking her letter in both her hands, and holding the leaves open, did wipe her face with every part of both the leaves; which no doubt she did in despite that I had told her there might be as great danger within the letter as without.

Clearly this second letter is not intended for Elizabeth's eye. It is a very important letter, showing that Poulet even took upon himself to delay the despatch of Mary's letter, for fear lest Elizabeth might be moved by it, and so recall any warrant issued for the execution. It may have been the knowledge of this cruelty and injustice on Poulet's par

W

that encouraged Walsingham to think him capable of a
still more grievous crime.   Poulet's motive for this delay
he himself explains.   He hoped that the warrant would be
signed before the Court went to Greenwich the week before
Christmas for the usual recess.   During the recess the warrant
would certainly not be signed.   He kept the letter till it was
too late to interfere with what might be done before the holiday
began.   In the subsequent letters, he expresses the greatest
relief that no harm had happened to Elizabeth that Christmas,
wishing it to be understood that to have spared Mary's life at
such a time was a singular peril to Elizabeth.

Ad eundem eodem die.

Sir,—We were not a little perplexed with this motion
of writing, and indeed did forbear to deliver our answer
until we had considered of the matter privately between
ourselves, wherein as we feared greatly to give any the
least cause of delay of the due examination [execution]
of the long desired justice, so having received lately her
Majesty's express commandment to make offer to this
lady to convey her letters, if she were disposed to write,
although she did not accept thereof at that time, yet
doubting lest our refusal to yield unto it at this present
might be offensive to her Highness, and perchance breed
some slander to the cause, we condescended to her desire,
beseeching God so to direct the sequel thereof, as the
same may redound to His glory and her Majesty's safety,
whereof there were no doubt, if we were as willing to take
the advantage of great and urgent occasions to further this
expected sacrifice, acceptable to God and man, as we are
easily diverted from it upon every sinister suggestion.   All
good and faithful subjects will be always careful of her
Majesty's safety, but especially in the time of Christmas
now at hand, which giveth occasion of many dangerous
assemblies.   We are content to be found faulty of this
pardonable jealousy.   Being not able to do any good in

this service, we should be very sorry and should think ourselves more than unhappy if anything should come from us that might do hurt. And, therefore, to be plain with you as with our very friend, we have used all convenient means to delay the receiving of this, to the end it might arrive at the Court too late to stay any action touching this lady that might be intended before Christmas, being strongly persuaded that the delay of the execution until after Christmas will give great cause to suspect an everlasting delay, either through her Majesty's too great inclination to mercy, or by reason of the danger of her person in the Christmas, a time subject to dangerous assemblies.

And thus, &c.

Post-scriptum inserendum in præcedenti epistola—I am very sorry that your letters of the 14th, received the 20th at nine in the morning, came not to my hands in time convenient for the stay of the Priest, who arriving here the 17th was immediately admitted to the presence of his mistress, according to the direction which I had before received in that behalf. The inconvenience whereof is not so great in matter of policy as in conscience, because, indeed, the Priest is [of] weak and slender judgment and can give neither counsel nor advice worthy of a young scholar. I feared lest he might have learned some bad news during his abode with Mr. Gresley, but having groped him the best I can, do find that he is a mere stranger almost to those things which are common to all men, which I impute to his want of our language, and to Mr. Gresley's absence from his house now many weeks by reason of his being at London, so that he hath had little other company then of his keeper. I might have doubted lest he had dissembled his knowledge in the occurrents of this time, but having searched his papers, do find two leaves of paper craftily (as he thought) inserted

W 2

in the midst of his philosophical exercises, wherein he hath set down a daily note of all that he heard spoken unto him, and likewise of his answers in all this time of his absence, the same being ridiculous as do bewray his great indiscretion. I would have been glad, for some Christian respects, that he should have had no access to this Queen until the night before her execution, and indeed having received direction to send for him, I took it for a strong argument that the time of her execution was near at hand.

The bounty mentioned in the following letter is the favour for which Poulet thanks Elizabeth in the letter, a fragment of which begins the first page of this letter-book. It is worthy of remark, how insignificant the two letters are, of which alone, amongst all the letters of this letter-book, the originals remain amongst the Public Records.

To Sir Francis Walsingham, January 2, 1586.[1]

Sir,—Whereas by your letters of the 26th of the last, you signified unto me that you had received a Privy Seal for a 100*l.*, bestowed by her Majesty in reward upon the soldiers serving in this castle, and that you reserve the same in your hands to be delivered to any such as I would appoint to take order for the receiving and conveying of it hither, it may please you to deliver the said Privy Seal to this bearer, my servant Thomas Knight, who is appointed to take order with one of his fellows remaining always in London to receive and convey the said money hither. I send the said bearer and three of his fellows to London at this present for none other cause than to bring hither 500*l.* in money for the use of her Majesty's household here. This country yields no means to receive it by exchange.

This lady findeth fault that her papers of account for this last year, which include all former years, are kept from

---

[1] Vol. xxi., n. 1.

her, as indeed I can say they are not sent, because I perused those which were sent before they were delivered, and the same may also appear by this copy inclosed of Nau's letters sent with the said papers. I have remaining in my hands some books of accounts found in Nau's chamber at the time of the search, and doubting lest they might concern these causes, I have without this Queen's privity perused them, and do find that they contain accounts of former years. I wish unto you all good means to increase your health, but it seemeth that the cold season of the year. had need of hot and earnest solicitors. The delay is fearful, God send it a good and happy issue.

And thus, &c.

[*Postscript in the original*—I thank you most heartily for Mr. Davison's letters, which I return unto you inclosed herein. Sir Drue Drury prayeth to be recommended to your good favour.]

Poulet is becoming uneasy at the long and unusual silence of Sir Francis Walsingham. The fact was that Walsingham had retired from the Court in dudgeon. The cause was no doubt, in the main, jealousy of Sir Christopher Hatton, and mortification that Elizabeth would not grant him Babington's forfeited estates,[1] yet probably vexation that his advice respecting Mary's speedy execution was not followed may have had some part in his resolution to withdraw from Elizabeth's presence. " I humbly beseech your lordship," he wrote[2] to Burghley from Barnes, December 16, " to pardon me in that I did not take my leave of you before my departure from the Court. Her Majesty's unkind dealing with me hath so wounded me as I could take no comfort to stay there. And yet if I saw any hope that my continuance there might either breed any good to the Church, or further-ance to the service of her Majesty or of the realm, the regard

---

[1] Sir Philip Sydney had died bankrupt, and Walsingham was surety for his debts. Babington's estates were given to Sir Walter Raleigh.

[2] *Domestic, Elizabeth*, vol. cxcv., n. 64. Holograph.

of my particular should not cause me to withdraw myself. But seeing the declining state we are coming into, and that men of best descent are least esteemed, I hold them happiest in this government that may be rather lookers-on than actors. I humbly therefore beseech your lordship, that as I do acknowledge myself infinitely bound unto you for your most honourable and friendly furtherance yielded unto me in my suit (which I will never forget), so you will be pleased to increase my bond towards you by forbearing any further to press her Majesty in the same, which I am fully resolved to give over. I do assure your lordship, whatsoever conceit her Majesty maketh either of me or of my [service], I would not spend so long time as I have done in that place, subject to so infinite toil and discomfort, not to be made Duke of Lancaster. My hope is, howsoever I am dealt withal by an earthly P[rince], I shall never lack the comfort of the P[rince] of Princes, to whose protection I commit your lordship, most humbly taking my leave."

And on the 5th of Jauuary he wrote[1] again, "I find your service in Court the more discomfortable for lack of resolution, and if I do not mistake it, her Majesty's great causes, both at home and abroad, are come to that period as they require present resolution. There are, as I am informed, most dangerous factions sprung up amongst the better sort of those of the United Provinces. The C[ount] Maurice, the C[ount] Hollocke, the C[ount] of Nuenor,[2] and the C[ount] William of Nassau are grown discontented with the English Government. And if the treaty of peace shall not be very warily handled, and some course taken for the contenting of those five noble persons, there will be a peace made without her Majesty, both to her peril and her dishonour. To serve all things upright, there is but one way (next after God), and that is, that her Majesty will be persuaded to preserve her safety before her treasure. The diseases of her Estate will not be cured with slight remedies, nor can long endure delay. I pray God, therefore, direct her Majesty's heart to do that which may be for her safety.

---

[1] *Domestic, Elizabeth,* vol. cxcvii., n. 5.   Holograph.
[2] Count Hohenlohe, and Count Nieuwenar, Stadtholder of Guelderland.

"For my own particular, I most humbly thank your lordship for your honourable care had of me therein. My stay in sending unto your lordship hath proceeded through the sickness of my servant Mills, in whose place I mean to substitute some other. If it were not for my promise made unto your lordship, whose advice I will both honour and follow, I would quite give over my suit. The grief of my mind hath thrown me into a dangerous disease, as by Mr. Dr. Bayly your lordship may understand."

To my Lord Treasurer, January 9, 1586.

My very good Lord,—The provision of wines for this household will be utterly spent within eighteen days at the farthest. And as I would not supply the same in this uncertain time without direction from your lordship, so being given to understand that the price of wine at this present is very excessive, as likewise that none are yet arrived in the ports of these parts, it may please your lordship to consider, if being resolved that a new provision of wine shall be made, it shall not be meet to have the same from London, whereby your lordship's good mean they may be taken at the Queen's price, whereby the long carriage,[1] and herein it may please your lordship to signify your pleasure unto me at your convenient leisure.

Although Mr. Cruse will never be weary of any guest committed unto him for her Majesty's service, yet I thought good to put your lordship in remembrance of Mrs. Bridget Digby, who remaineth yet under his keeping. I did forget in the late advertisement of the weekly expenses of this household, to make mention of the charges of the household at Chartley, which, although I did omit of forgetfulness, wherein I humbly pray your lordship's pardon, yet the truth is that the charges of that family stand upon a reckoning between Mr. Bagot and me, so as I am yet ignorant of what the same amounteth unto.

[1] A line has been missed here.

The poor prisoners of this castle, I mean Sir Drue Drury and myself, begin to faint for want of some comfortable matter from above, wherein we should find ourselves much refreshed, if we might hear any the least advertisement of the present state of things, having received no letter from the Court sithence the 20th of last month ; and therefore your lordship may [do] a deed of charity to bestow your alms of some trifling occurrents upon your poor languishing friends at Fotheringay. The truth is that I received this last week only five or six lines from Sir Francis Walsingham, making mention of the sending therewith of some papers of accounts for this Queen. Sir Drue and I cannot receive more comfortable matter from your lordship than to hear that her Majesty has passed this Christmas in good health. We beseech God long to preserve her Majesty, and to grant your lordship a happy New Year, and to live many years in all health and felicity.

From, &c.

Waad wrote[1] thus to Davison respecting Mary's books of accounts. "It may please your Honour,—Mr. Secretary Walsingham did let me understand her Majesty's pleasure for the seeking out the accounts of the Scottish Queen, which were amongst her writings : and because the coffers were left, as I take it, in her Majesty's gallery at Windsor, there is a messenger sent thither for to bring them to the Court by cart with a man of my own that assisted in the conveying of the same hither, and knoweth the chests. If they should happen to be rendered to any other room, which it may please your honour to let her Majesty understand. This day I have given my attendance here on the lords, otherwise would have waited on your honour. Thus leaving further to trouble [you], I rest most entirely at your commandment.

"From Cecil House, the 30th of November, 1586.

"Your Honour's in all duty and sincerity of good will,

"W. WAAD."

[1] Vol. xx., n. 34. Holograph.

And 'on the same subject Walsingham wrote to Phelippes, "After my hearty commendations, her Majesty, understanding that the coffer with the Queen of Scots' accounts are not yet sent down, is displeased therewith, and imputeth a fault of negligence in me. I pray you therefore to let me understand what hath been the cause of the stay thereof, for if I had known that you could not convey the same, I would have devised some means that it should have been sent before this time.

"And so I commit you to God. From Barnelmes the 18th of December, 1586.

"Your very loving friend,

"FRA. WALSINGHAM.

"*Autograph postscript*—Her Majesty doth find some fault that the original letters intercepted be not brought in unto her with the extract you promised to make."

To Sir Francis Walsingham, eodem die [Jan. 9].

Sir,—This Queen resteth not as yet satisfied for her books and papers of accounts, sending unto me after the delivery of those received with your letters of the 4th of this present, her master of household and physician, with a new request in that behalf, wherein she desireth that all other such books and papers which concern the estate of her payments of pensions and wages, with the accounts of her several officers in France, may be sent unto her, as likewise all such notes made by Nau of his receipts and payments, that he left behind him at Chartley at the time of his apprehension, saying that she cannot be satisfied with the new accounts made by him sithence his imprisonment; and further saith that all things are not clear betwixt her and Pasquier, whom she allegeth to have employed her money remaining in the French Ambassador's hands to the use of himself and his followers here for their necessaries, praying that his reckonings left by him at Chartley may be sent unto her, and that Cordaillot, the French Ambassador's secretary, who disbursed this money, may make a like reckoning of all employments made by him by direction from Nau and Pasquier. She also requireth Nau's answer touching the money supposed to have been committed to his custody by her gentlewoman, Beauregard, and her surgeon. And whereas I wrote unto you in my last letters that I had remaining in my hands some books of accounts left by Mr. Waad in Nau's chamber at Chartley, and doubting lest they might concern these causes, had, without this Queen's privity, perused them and did find that they contained accounts of former years, I have thought good to put you in remembrance of the said books, which I wish to be delivered unto her, to avoid further cavillation, whereunto this Queen is greatly inclined, and indeed they cannot serve to any other use. Thus for my better discharge I have delivered unto you the message which I received from this lady.

And now, referring these things to your better consideration, I commit you, &c.

Poulet, who is so precise that he will not give up to Mary her old accounts without special warrant, ventures, entirely on his own responsibility, first to keep back his prisoner's letter of December 19th, and afterwards to prevent her writing again, in the face of Elizabeth's orders to the contrary. It points to his dread lest her assertions of innocence should rouse Elizabeth's suspicions, an uneasiness which Walsingham's silence must have greatly strengthened.

To Mr. Secretary Davison, January 10, 1586.

Sir,—Although this Queen, my charge, hath received so many messages of death as might suffice to work true mortification in any good Christian soul, yet her froward flesh and crooked affection hath given sundry evident testimonies of want of charity, and many other wilful rebellions, notwithstanding that in many works [weeks] she expected from day to day the fatal stroke of her bloody deserts. And now it seemeth that still long delay of justice hath stirred her to hope of further mercy. Upon this ground, if I be not deceived, although with pretence to move me for some papers of accounts, she sends Melvin and her physician unto me, who after some talk touching the said papers, asked me in the name of their mistress if I had received any answer of her letter to her Majesty, which being denied, they said she was willing to write again, and when her letter was ready would send unto me to see the inclosing and sealing of it. Whereunto I answered that I would say nothing to that motion, forbearing either flatly to deny her, or to promise to convey her letters ; to be plain with you, being so well acquainted with her cunning, I would not wish that she might be permitted to write again to her Majesty, being assured that she will write nothing that shall be profitable to her Majesty's person or realm, and it may be feared lest her flattering and treacherous promises may incline the merciful disposition of our Queen to give better ear unto them than shall stand with her surety or with the quiet of her State, and therefore I thought it not agreeable with my duty to agree to the sending of a second letter with[out] special warrant, wherein it may please you to give your direction, having forborne to say to the messengers that I would write to this purpose, which shall be mine answer when she sendeth for me, whereby this -meantime may not hinder any good resolution that may come above.

And thus, &c.

Poulet manifests his bitter spirit against poor Mary by taking from her Melville, the faithful master of her household, and du Préau, her chaplain. It is singular that he should have selected the two men to whose inoffensiveness he has himself testified. He has spoken strongly in Melville's praise, saying that a strong hostility existed between him and Nau ;[1] and that

---

[1] *Supra*, p. 251.

no harm could possibly be worked by du Préau he has not long since written to Davison.[1] But Mary was attached to them, and therefore they are withdrawn from her. Melville she was allowed to see again on the morning of her execution, but not so the Priest, though she had earnestly begged for this last religious consolation. The sudden withdrawal of the Priest was an unexpected blow. To Elizabeth she had written, "L'on m'a dict que ne voulliez en rien forcer ma conscience ny ma religion, et que mesme vous m'avez concédé ung prebstre." On the eve of her death Mary wrote du Préau a letter[2] which begins, "J'ay esté combatue ce jour de ma religion et de recevoir la consolation des hérétiques." She calls her physician to witness her fidelity to her faith. "J'ay requis de vous avoir pour faire ma confession et recevoir mon sacrement, ce qui m'a esté cruellement refusé." She begs him to write instructions how she should spend her last night on earth, and she says that if she perceives him in the crowd in the morning, she will kneel before them all for his benediction. At two o'clock in the morning of the last day of her life she wrote[3] to Henry III., King of France, "La religion Catholique et le mantien du droit que Dieu m'a donné à ceste couronne sont les deux points de ma condemnation, et toutesfois ils ne me veulent permettre de dire que c'est pour la religion Catholique que je meurs, mais pour la crainte du change de la leur : et pour preuve, ils m'ont osté mon aumosnier, lequel, bien qu'il soit en la maison, je n'ay peu obtenir qu'il me vint confesser ny communier à ma mort ; mais m'ont fait grande instance de recevoir la consolation et doctrine de leur ministre amené pour ce fait. Ce porteur et sa compagnie, la pluspart de vos sujets, vous tesmoigneront mes déportemens en ce mien acte dernier."

Not only would Poulet deprive Mary of Melville and du Préau, but, writing too from his own sick bed, he betrays his wish to remove the medical attendants also, though his prisoner was in chronic ill health.

Drury's unwillingness to take Poulet's place as Mary's interrogator, irritating her that "in her heat" she might say something offensive to Elizabeth, is what we might have expected from

---

[1] *Supra*, p. 339. [2] Labanoff, tom. vi., p. 483. [3] *Ibid.*, p. 492.

him, whom Mary describes[1] as "ce Droury, plus modeste et gratieux de beaucoup."

To Mr. Secretary Davison, January 21, 1586.

Sir,—You write very truly that I thought myself utterly forgotten at the Court, in that I had not heard from thence in one whole month, saving that I received in that meantime four or five lines from Mr. Secretary Walsingham, which concerned only this lady's papers of accounts, and therefore you may believe that your letters of the 18th of this present were very welcome unto me, and I thank you most heartily for them, as likewise for your friendly advertisement of the state of things above at this present, whereby, although I can receive no great comfort by reason of the dangerous and most pitiful delay in [the] cause of all causes, and especially in these declining days, wherein Satan with his complices goeth roaring up and down with open throat, seeking by most horrible and execrable complots, as well domestical as foreign, how to devour our most gracious Queen, whom God in mercy long preserve ; yet it [is] some satisfaction to hear somewhat, and that there remaineth yet some hope that God in His wisdom hath decreed a day, which can neither be prevented nor disappointed. I do not marvel to hear that this lady's letters to her Majesty effected no good thing,[2] which agreeth with my former opinion therein, upon a full resolution in my simple conceit that she might do hurt by her writing, but good she would do none to Prince or State, and yet I have been blamed many times that I have not urged her to write, when I have had no commission for it. She

---

[1] Labanoff, tom. vi., p. 469.

[2] This refers to the impression made upon Elizabeth by Mary's letter dated December 19th, which we have seen Poulet so reluctant to forward. Leicester, writing to Walsingham on the 22nd, mentions it in these terms : "There is a letter from the Scottish Queen that hath wrought tears, but I trust shall do no further herein ; albeit the delay is too dangerous" (*Harl. MSS.*, 285 ; Ellis, vol. iii., p. 22).

delighteth in blood, mischief and slander, and other fruits come not from her.

Whereas her Majesty noteth want in me for permitting the whole retinue of this lady to resort as freely to her now as they were wont to do before her condemnation, which she would have somewhat restrained, referring the same to my discretion, I must confess to you that I am not sorry for this commission, having extended the same to the removing of Melvin and the Priest, who are the only two persons which this lady may best forbear, and have been esteemed unnecessary in former time, but have been restored to her lately sithence her coming to this castle by direction from above, and therefore she may spare them without any hindrance to her necessary service, as also they are lodged within the court adjoining to the inner gate, as they may take their meat and drink in this lady's pantry without resort to the hall. The physician, apothecary, and the surgeon have been so often allowed to this lady by her Majesty's order, that I may not take upon me to displace them without special warrant, referring the same to your better consideration. Those which remain take their meat and drink all together in a room at the foot of the stairs leading to this lady's dining-chamber, from whence they may have access to their mistress if they are disposed, because they are out of the view of my soldiers, which I have endured to avoid their eating and drinking in the hall among my servants and soldiers, having no other place in this castle for their assembly. Although divers of this number cannot be divided to have access to their mistress for her necessary service, yet for my better discharge, and to the end you may remove any other such as you think good from making their repair to their mistress, I have thought convenient to send unto you here inclosed a note of their particular names and functions.

You write that her Majesty wisheth I should resort often to this lady and give her cause to discover herself and her

affections as much as I can, because in her heat she is wont
to speak *ex abundantia cordis,* wherein if I have failed
during the little time of my health, after mine access unto
[her] signified by my former letters, it may please you to
excuse me, the same proceeding of no other cause than
that I looked daily to hear from you whether her Highness
continued in that disposition or no. And now lately, by
the space of fourteen days, I have been very sick of my
gout and have not departed from my bed, where I remain
as yet, not without great grief, I assure you, and do not
look to be recovered in few days. These are the fruits of
my long abode in Chartley House, a place environed with
naughty and corrupt waters, which have increased so much
my disease as I shall feel of it during the residue of my
short days. Being forbidden to repair to this lady by
reason of my sickness, and having acquainted Sir Drue
Drury with your letters, I have moved him to supply my
place, who prayeth to be excused herein, alleging many
reasons for his defence, whereof he supposeth this not to be
the least, that being a mere stranger to all her stratagems,
and not thoroughly acquainted with former proceedings,
he might perchance not urge her so aptly as might be
expected. He doth not doubt but that your good friendship (although by nothing else than by your silence) will
suffice to satisfy her Majesty in this trifle until God shall
restore me to better health. And yet if it shall be thought
meet to use his service herein, he will not fail to perform
her Majesty's direction. I cannot express unto you how
much I think myself bound to her Majesty in sending this
honest gentleman hither unto me, whose company hath
been no less com[fort unto] me in this late extremity of
sickness and sorrow, t[han] needful for her Majesty's
service, whereof he ta[keth the] whole burthen during
mine infirmity, and doth [bear it] with will and courage.

I trust the wicked conspiracies lately revealed wi[ll at
the] last open her Majesty's eyes, and incline her heart to

tak[e care] of the Church of God, herself, and her crown
and [realm, the] which are all assailed in her royal person.
Who is so [thoughtless], so void of reason, or so careless of
his duty [as not to sigh] and groan under this fearful delay,
and [we may fear] lest the old proverb be verified to our
utter [destruction, which] saith, "That so often goeth the
pot to the water, t[ill at last it] comes home broken," and
especially when God is tem[pted by over]security. You
and others placed about her Majesty's [person], do your
best endeavours, I doubt not, to prevent these [dangers] by
your actions, and I, a poor cripple, will assist you wi[th my]
hearty and humble prayers, and hereunto Sir Drue Drur[y,
my] yoke-fellow, saith, Amen.

And thus, &c.

This letter to Sir John Perrot ends with one of those quaint
sentences which served, according to the fashion of the time,
for a ring posy. The tone of affection throughout the letter
marks a natural sympathy between the gaoler, thirsting for the
blood of his helpless prisoner, and the Deputy who was
harrying and hanging the defenceless Irish by thousands.

To Sir John Parret [Perrot], January 26, 1586.

My good friend of old acquaintance,—I am very heartily
glad to understand by your letters to Sir Drue Drury, my
yoke-fellow in this heavy and unpleasant charge, that you
keep your health, and that among the broils of this tem-
pestuous world your Government standeth quiet, and as
the same was never more needful than at this present,
when all our neighbours on every side desire nothing more
than to disturb the happy peace of her Majesty's realms
and dominions, so it must be confessed that your desert is
the greater, and I wish it to be considered towards you, to
your satisfaction, and to the encouragement of others serving
in like place of trust and importance. I know you will look
for no new matter from a prisoner, wherein I must refer

you to the Court and courtiers, only I can tell you that we continue in our old security, and that our fearful delays threaten ruin to Prince and country. Love me still, I pray you, and I trust it shall not repent you.

And thus, &c.

It is noted in Rishton's "Diary of events in the Tower of London," that Edward Arden was executed December 23, 1583. The Arden, therefore, spoken of by Poulet in the next letter is probably Francis Arden, who was imprisoned in the Tower, according to Rishton, March 25, 1584. The injustice of his imprisonment is shown by one of the State Papers,[1] entitled "What course is meet to be held in the causes of certain prisoners remaining in the Tower," dated May 27, 1585, which says of him, "Francis Arden, indicted of treason, but the matter not full enough against him; to be removed to her Majesty's Bench." He probably was so removed and afterwards tried; and as in those days a verdict for high treason was easily obtained from a jury against a Catholic, even when the "matter" was not very "full," he was condemned and sent back to the Tower about the beginning of 1586; for in a subsequent list[2] of prisoners in the Tower, October 24, 1589, he is mentioned as "prisoner two years and three quarters, condemned of treason," and in the margin, "Referred to her Majesty." He was therefore under sentence of death when Poulet wrote. Nearly eleven years after this he escaped from the Tower in company with Father John Gerard.[3]

To Mr. Secretary Davison, January 27, 1586.

Sir,—I send unto you here inclosed a letter come to my hands from one of the justices of peace of the county of Huntingdon, which I answered forthwith, as may appear by this copy, whereof I thought good to advertise you without delay, to the end you may see that this dreadful

---

[1] *Domestic, Elizabeth,* vol. clxxviii., n. 74.
[2] *Ibid.,* vol. ccxxvii., n. 37.
[3] *Condition of Catholics under James I.,* p. cxv.

X

delay breedeth dread and danger of every side, and that every day bringeth forth his new mischief, whereof in reason and judgment there will be no end until the cause be removed, and that the wrath of God be appeased by the sweet-smelling sacrifice of justice executed upon this lady, whose life threateneth ruin both to Prince and people. There is also a great alarm in the county and in counties adjoining, upon the rumour of the escape of one Arden, a traitor.

And thus in haste.

In these letters Poulet has alluded to several of the stratagems that were adopted by the Government in order to hasten the execution of the Queen of Scots. By the "wicked conspiracies," mentioned in his letter[1] to Davison of the 21st, the discovery of which Poulet prays may put an end to the "fearful delay;" is doubtless intended the pretended plot of the younger Stafford, through which Destrappes, Châteauneuf's secretary, was thrown into the Tower. The spirit in which Poulet writes well illustrates the effect produced by the daily rumours set afloat, that London was fired by the Papists, that the Queen of Scots had escaped, that a Scotch army had crossed the Border, that a Northern rebellion had broken out, that Guise had landed in Sussex, that a Spanish fleet rode in Milford Haven; rumours all contrived to enlist the fears and the hatred of the nation against the Scottish Queen. Camden[2] represents these reports as expressly designed, "ad majores terrores Reginæ incutiendum," to terrify Elizabeth into signing the warrant.

Poulet, too blunt-minded to see that the hue and cry was a trick to hasten Mary's execution by spreading panic and arousing Elizabeth's fears, gives his "simple opinion" on "these seditious rumours" in a way that must have amused the more astute Secretaries of State. Among the Lansdowne Manuscripts[3] are two letters of the mayor and aldermen of Exeter, the first

---

[1] *Supra*, p. 351.

[2] *Annales*, p. 485.

[3] *Lansd. MSS.*, n. 51, f. 42 ; Wright's *Queen Elizabeth and her times,* vol. ii., p. 329.

written February 3, 158⁴⁄₇, to Lord Burghley, for instructions with regard to a precept of hue and cry for the Queen of Scots who was said to have made her escape; the other to the Privy Council, dated "the 4th of February, at the hour of one in the night," respecting another hue and cry received by them "that her Majesty's City of London by the enemies is set on fire," and commanding them to have their "men and armour in readiness upon pain of death." They are curious enough for insertion.

"Hue and Cry.

"These are to charge you in her Majesty's name upon pain of death, to make diligent search, and hue and cry for the Queen of Scots, who is fled, and to lay all highways, and stay all barks and shipping in your harbours, for that the direction came from Mr. Howard, Esquire; so you keep a standing watch day and night until you receive order to the contrary, and let this be done by the chief of your parish. This 2nd of February, anno 1586. Received into Honiton at 11 of the clock in the forenoon, this present Thursday.

"THOMAS WARD, Constable of Honiton.

"This hue and cry to go to the Mayor of Exeter, and so forth.

"Received by David Colles of Honiton the 2nd of February, about 1 of the clock in the afternoon, into Exon."

"Hue and Cry.

"These are in the Queen's Majesty's name to charge and command, immediately upon sight hereof, to send like precepts four manner of ways, from town to town, to make your armour and artillery in readiness, and that with all speed, upon pain of death, for London is set on fire. For Mr. Turlett of Anstenlewell brought this word from the Bell, the 1st of February. Send this to Exeter with all speed.

"WILLIAM BOWERMAN, Justice.

"This from Sampfield this 10th inst., Saturday, the 4th of February, 1586, at 8 of the clock in the evening.

X 2

"Received this by the hands of Robert Smythe of Collumpton, the 4th of February, at 10 of the clock in the night.

"WILLIAM MARSTON,
"WILLIAM KIRKHAM,
"EDWARD HATE.

"These are in her Majesty's name straitly to charge and command you that upon the sight hereof you send like precept two or three ways, from tithing to tithing, to set your men in armour with all speed upon pain of death, for London is on fire. Let this go to Exeter upon horseback. Haste! haste! haste!

"THOMAS WARD, Constable of Honiton.

"Received from Mr. Collins, this 4th day of February, about 8 of the clock at night.

"Received this by Philip Balston, of Honiton, victualler, betwixt the hours of 9 and 10,

"By me, ROGER CHANDON."

To Mr. Secretary Davison, January 30, 1586.

[Sir],—You may perceive by these letters inclosed, with mine [ans]wer to the same, that the report of the Scottish Queen's escape, or of her taking away, as it is now termed, carrieth such credit in these parts, as it [is] followed with hue and cry. And although, considering my late letters to like effect, I did not think needful to advertise you thereof with speed, yet I would not hide it from you, and therefore do send it by one of my servants repairing to London about his own business, not doubting but that the same will come as speedily to your hands as if it had been sent by the post. These seditious rumours are not to be neglected, in my simple opinion, and indeed there is not a more ready way to levy forces to the achieving of that which these lewd reporters pretend to fear. I cannot let them to flatter themselves with vain hope, but by the grace of God I will not lose this lady, my charge, without the loss of my life, neither shall it be possible for any force to take her out of my hands alive. And thus, &c.

To Mr. Secretary Davison, February 2, 1586.

Sir,—I pray you give me leave to deal plainly and openly with you, wherein I am the more bold because you carry the reputation to be round and sincere in all your proceedings. I may say truly, that I have been grieved and troubled in body and mind by the space of many weeks for the general, but now lately to increase my grief I have felt some disquietudes in particular. The cause is this: It pleased Sir Francis Walsingham not long before Christmas last, upon occasion of some intermission of writing at that time, to promise to take order that this charge should be more often remembered, as a thing very necessary and convenient, as he affirmed, sithence which time I have written many letters to you and others to several purposes, and for answer have received only one letter from you during the two months last past. It is far from me, as God best knoweth, to desire to be informed of secret causes, or of anything [beyond] that belonging in reason and necessity to the charge committed unto me ; but to hear nothing at all, I must confess that it breedeth in me some hard conceits against myself. I am occasioned many times, and sometimes directed to do things by discretion, and being now so well recovered, I thank God, of my . . .

It is greatly to be wished that here this volume might end. The new letters that we have undertaken to publish have been given in their integrity, together with many others taken from our Public Records. Once, it seems, there existed a narrative from Poulet's pen of the execution of the Queen of Scots, but it is now lost.[1] It was in the possession of his

[1] Mr. Ogle, the editor of Poulet's letters for the Roxburghe Club, in his Preface, mentions that "Hardinge, in his *Biographic Mirror* (vol. ii., p.74) quotes a passage from a letter to Burghley from Poulet before the latter left on his embassy to France, which he says is taken from a large collection of MSS. preserved among the family papers at Hinton St. George. The present Earl Poulett has kindly, at the editor's request, caused search to be made for these letters, but unhappily, neither they, nor any trace of such a collection, can be discovered" (p. 2, *note*).

descendants, together with other letter-books, which, at the beginning of the eighteenth century, were preserved among the family archives at Hinton St. George. Amongst these were the well known letters respecting the proposed assassination. We owe them to Hearne, by whom they were printed in the glossary to Robert of Gloucester.[1] They were transcribed and communicated to Hearne by Mr. Edward Prideaux Gwyn, gentleman commoner of Christ Church, and they are here printed from Hearne's manuscript Diary, which is preserved in the Bodleian Library.

Freebairn, in his *Life of Mary Queen of Scots,*[2] says that "a copy transcribed from the originals was sent to Dr. Mackenzie, by Mr. John Urry, of Christ Church, Oxford."

Another transcript exists in the British Museum, amongst the Harleian Manuscripts.[3] It is in the handwriting of Lord Oxford, and it is accompanied by the following letter from the Duke of Chandos.

"Cannons, Aug. 23, 1725.

"My Lord,—I ought long before this to have returned your lordship the inclosed, and made my acknowledgments to you for the liberty you gave me to take copies of 'em. They are a very valuable curiosity, and deserve well to be preserved.

"I am, my lord,

"Your lordship's obedient humble servant,

"Chandos."

Addressed—"To the right honourable the Earl of Oxford, at his house in Dover Street." On this correspondence Chalmers[4] remarks that "neither Lord Oxford nor the Duke seem to have known that those notorious epistles had been already published in 1722 by Dr. Mackenzie in his Life of Mary.[5] They were also published in 1725 in Jebb."[6]

Now, Queen Elizabeth had written[7] to Mary not quite two years before this about Sir Amias Poulet in these terms—"You need not to doubt that a man that reverenceth God, loveth his

---

[1] P. 673.　　[2] P. 270.　　[3] N. 6994, f. 50.　　[4] Vol. ii., p. 185, *note.*
[5] *Lives*, iii., 340.　　[6] App., viii.　　[7] Vol. xv., n. 57; *supra*, p. 6.

Prince, and is no less by calling honourable than by birth noble, will ever do anything unworthy of himself." This man, by calling honourable, by birth noble, reverencing his God and loving his Prince, was required by his sovereign, a Queen of England, to be the assassin of the helpless woman who was committed to his custody. Poulet had condescended to do much that was unworthy of himself during Mary's captivity. He had expressed himself as vehemently desirous of her death, and the words had been seen by Elizabeth, as the writer intended that they should be seen. But though Poulet thought in his fanaticism that to put Mary to death would be to do God service, he was not capable of the degradation to which Elizabeth urged him. We may feel certain that if he had obeyed the unworthy orders he received, Elizabeth would have left on him the full responsibility, and a worse fate than Davison's would have been his.

Once more we turn to Mr. Froude, and it is to draw from his pages this comment on the conduct of Queen Elizabeth. It "was not noble, but it was natural and pardonable."[1] *Natural!* Unhappily, it is quite possible that there have been some in whom even a mean and wicked endeavour to throw upon another the odium of the violent death of a kinswoman may be called in too true a sense *natural;* but God forbid that the day should ever come when an English writer unrebuked may say that such conduct is venial, *pardonable.*

To Sir Amias Poulet.[2]

After our hearty commendations, we find by speech lately uttered by her Majesty that she doth note in you both a lack of that care and zeal of her service that she looketh for at your hands, in that you have not in all this time of yourselves (without other provocation) found out some way to shorten the life of that Queen, considering the great peril she is subject unto hourly, so long as the said Queen shall live. Wherein, besides a kind of lack of love towards her, she noteth

---

[1] *History*, vol. xii., p. 241.
[2] Hearne's MS. Diary, vol. lxxxv., p. 89, from Gwyn's transcript.

greatly that you have not that care of your own particular safeties, or rather of the preservation of religion and the public good and prosperity of your country, that reason and policy commandeth, especially having so good a warrant and ground for the satisfaction of your consciences towards God and the discharge of your credit and reputation towards the world, as the oath of association which you both have so solemnly taken and vowed, and especially the matter wherewith she standeth charged being so clearly and manifestly proved against her. And therefore she taketh it most unkindly towards her, that men professing that love towards her that you do, should in any kind of sort, for lack of the discharge of your duties, cast the burthen upon her, knowing as you do her indisposition to shed blood, especially of one of that sex and quality, and so near to her in blood as the said Queen is. These respects we find do greatly trouble her Majesty, who, we assure you, has sundry times protested that if the regard of the danger of her good subjects and faithful servants did not more move her than her own peril, she would never be drawn to assent to the shedding of her blood. We thought it very meet to acquaint [you] with these speeches lately passed from her Majesty, referring the same to your good judgments. And so we commit you to the protection of the Almighty.

At London, February 1, 1586.

Your most assured friends,

FRANCIS WALSINGHAM,
WM. DAVISON.

This letter was received at Fotheringay the 2nd of February, at five in the afternoon.

An abstract of a letter from Mr. Secretary Davison, of the said 1st of February, 1586, as followeth—I pray let this and the inclosed be committed to the fire, which measure[1] shall be likewise mete to your answer, after it hath been communicated to her Majesty for her satisfaction.

A postscript in a letter from Mr. Secretary Davison, of the 3rd of February, 1586—I entreated you in my last to burn my letters sent unto you for the argument sake, which by your answer to Mr. Secretary (which I have seen) appeareth not to have been done. I pray you, let me entreat you to make heretics of the one and the other, as I mean to use yours, after her Majesty hath seen it.

In the end of the postscript—I pray you let me hear what you have done with my letters, because they are not fit to be kept, that I may satisfy her Majesty therein, who might otherwise take offence thereat, and if you entreat this postscript in the same manner, you shall not err a whit.

A. Poulet—D. Drury.

A copy of a letter to Sir Francis Walsingham, of the 2nd of February, 1586, *at six in the afternoon, being the answer to a letter from him, the said Sir Francis, of the 1st of February,* 1586, *received at Fotheringay the 2nd day of February, at five in the afternoon*—Your letters of yesterday coming to my hands this present day at five in the afternoon, I would not fail according to your directions to return my answer with all possible speed, which (*sic*) shall deliver unto you with great grief and bitterness of mind, in that I am so unhappy to have liven to see this unhappy day, in the which I am required by direction from my most gracious sovereign to do an act which God and the law forbiddeth. My good livings and life are at her Majesty's disposition, and am ready

---

[1] For *measure* Lord Oxford has read *we assure*.

to so lose them this next morrow if it shall so please
her, acknowledging that I hold them as of her mere
and most gracious favour, and do not desire them to
enjoy them, but with her Highness' good liking. But
God forbid that I should make so foul a shipwreck of
my conscience, or leave so great a blot to my poor
posterity, to shed blood without law or warrant. Trusting
that her Majesty, of her accustomed clemency, will take
this my dutiful answer in good part (and the rather by
your good mediation), as proceeding from one who will
never be inferior to any Christian subject living in duty,
honour, love, and obedience towards his sovereign.

And thus I commit you to the mercy of the Almighty.
From Fotheringay, the 2nd of February, 1586.

Your most assured poor friends,

A. POULET,
D. DRURY.

Your letters coming in the plural number seem to
be meant as to Sir. Drue Drury as to myself, and yet
because he is not named in them, neither the letter
directed unto him, he forbeareth to make any particular
answer, but subscribeth in heart to my opinion.

*I copied these letters in December, 1717, from a MS. folio
book of letters to and from Sir Amias Poulet, when the
Queen of Scots' governor at Fotheringay. This book is in
the hands of John Earl Poulett, his immediate descendant,
and in that book is likewise contained a particular account
of the trial and execution of the Queen of Scots, which seems
to be done by Sir Amias himself.*[1]

Poulet was too cautious to destroy the disgraceful letters
he had been dishonoured by receiving from the secretaries of
his sovereign. He carried the originals with him to London,

---

[1] With this note by Mr. Gwyn, Hearne's copy ends.

and there doubtless they were "made heretics of," as Davison had urged. But mindful of his own reputation, he left copies with his family, that, if necessary, it might be known in what terms he had repelled the base proposal.

Poulet to Davison.[1]

Sir,—The rule of charity commandeth to bear with the impatience of the afflicted, which Christian lesson you have learned, as I find by experience to my great contentment, in that you have been content to bear with my malapertness, wherein you bind me more and more to love you and to honour you, which I will do with all honest faithfulness.

If I should say that I have burned the papers you wot of, I cannot tell if everybody would believe me, and therefore I reserve them to be delivered to your own hands at my coming to London. God bless you and prosper all your actions to His glory.

From Fotheringay, the 8th of February, 1586.

Your most assuredly to my small power,

A. POULET.

Addressed—To the right honourable Mr. William Davison, esquire, one of her Majesty's principal secretaries.

Endorsed by Lord Burghley—February 8th, 1586, from Sir Amias Poulet to Mr. Secretary Davison.

We give two more letters, written by Poulet at Fotheringay, after the death of the Queen of Scots, and with them we bring the series to a close. By the time they reached London, Davison was in the Tower. They were received, as the endorsement shows, by Lord Burghley. If the mention of the usual straitness in money matters excites a smile, we are soon made serious again by Poulet's pious rejoicings over Mary's death, written on the day of her execution.

<hr>

[1] Vol. xxi., n. 13.

Poulet to Davison.[1]

Sir,—It may please you to let me know from you what shall become of the families of this castle and Chartley, and in what sort and for what places passports shall be made for the Scottish train when they shall be discharged, thinking, that considering the nearness of London, both the French and Scottish will desire to pass that way, which was so appointed long sithence by Mr. Secretary Walsingham for thóse remaining at Chartley, and their passports made to that effect, and left with Mr. Richard Bagot, because it was then intended that they should have been discharged within four or five days after the removing of this lady from thence.

It seemeth meet that some watch and ward be kept about this house during the continuance here of the Scottish company, which may be supplied by my thirty soldiers, if you shall like of it, and the forty soldiers taken out of Huntingdonshire may be discharged.

Although Mr. Darrell, master of her Majesty's household here, hath been destitute of money of late, yet I have forborne upon consideration of the uncertainty of our abode to trouble my Lord Treasurer therewith, and having no ready mean to bring money from London, I have supplied the want out of Nau's money remaining in my hands, which may be repaid hereafter at London, as shall be appointed by the lords of her Majesty's Council.

I trust I shall not need to put you in remembrance for order to be given touching her Majesty's plate and other household stuff here, as likewise for the coffers and trunks belonging to Nau and Curle.

Sir Drue Drury with his hearty due commendations unto you, prayeth your favourable mean for his revocation, which he would not desire (notwithstanding his great and urgent occasions) if the cause of his abode were not

[1] Vol. xxi., n. 12.

through the mercy and favour of our good God clearly removed, to the great comfort of himself and all other faithful Christian subjects. I will say nothing of his careful service in this place, because his zeal to religion, duty to his sovereign, and love to his country are very well known unto you.

The children of God have daily experience of His mercy and favour towards such as can be content to depend of His merciful providence, who doth not see as man seeth, but His times and seasons are always just and perfectly good. The same God make us all thankful for His late singular favours. And thus I leave to trouble you, wishing unto you all felicity in our Lord Jesus.

From Fotheringay, the 8th of February, 1586.

Your very assured friend to my small power,

A. POULET.

We may not forbear to signify unto you that these two Earls[1] have showed a very singular and faithful affection to her Majesty's service in this action, as you shall be informed more particularly by me, Robert Beale, at my return to the Court, which shall be shortly by the grace of God.

A. POULET.
D. DRURY.
ROBERT BEALE.

Addressed—To the right honourable Mr. William Davison, esquire, one of her Majesty's principal secretaries.

Endorsed in Lord Burghley's hand—8th February, 1586. Sir Amias Poulet, Sir D. Drury, to Mr. Secretary Davison.

---

[1] The Earls of Shrewsbury and Kent were the Commissioners to whom the warrant for the execution was addressed.

The following paper[1] is a list drawn up by Poulet with a view to the preparation of passports for those mentioned in it.

"Upon conference with the French and Scottish servants, they answer as followeth :

"Mr. Melvin, now remaining with Mr. Bagot, prayeth to take 'London in his way towards Scotland.

"I have not spoken with the Priest remaining with Mr. Gresley, but I find by a message received from him of late that he is willing to go directly into France.

"Bastian and his wife, with their two daughters and one son, are desirous to go to London, and from thence into France.

"Baltazar will go into France.

"Curle's servant is desirous to wait on his mistress.

"Nau's servant did once serve Mr. Pierrepont, and doth pray to return unto him.

"The cocher and the grooms of the stable are of Sheffield, in Derbyshire, and of the parts adjoining, and pray to return thither.

"Curle's wife prayeth to go to London.

"The three laundresses are of Derbyshire, and desire to return thither."

Poulet to Walsingham.[2]

Sir,—Following the direction of the lords of her Majesty's Council, signified by your letters of the 15th of this present, I have brought hither the Scottish household from Chartley, and have discharged all the soldiers, one porter and four soldiers only excepted which have the charge of the gate.

I send unto you herewith the inventory of her Majesty's plate, hangings, and other household stuff lately used in this castle, whereof the plate, the greater part of the hangings, and all the best stuff was removed from

---

[1] Vol. xxi., n. 21.   [2] Vol. xxi., n. 20.

hence yesterday under the conduct of some of my servants, praying you to signify forthwith to my servant Robert Hackshaw remaining in London, in what place there the said plate and other stuff shall be discharged, as likewise Mr. Darrell prayeth for the better clearing of his account, and doth think it so meet for her Majesty's better service that the said plate and other stuff may not be removed from the place where it shall be unladen, until his coming to London. One of the conductors of these carts is commanded to be at London four or five hours before the arrival of the carts to learn of my servant Hackshaw where the said carts shall be unladen.

The jewels, plate, and other goods belonging to the late Queen of Scots were already divided into many parts before the receipt of your letters, as may appear by the inventory thereof inclosed herein, the whole company (saving Kenethy [Kennedy] and Curle's sister, two of her gentlewomen) affirming that they have nothing to show for these things from their mistress in writing, and that all the smaller things were delivered by her own hands. I have, according to your direction, committed the custody of the said jewels, plate, and other stuff to Mr. Melvin, the physician, and Mrs. Kenethy, one of the gentlewomen.

The care of the embalming of the body of the late Queen was committed to the high sheriff of this county, who, no doubt, was very willing to have it well done, and used therein the advice of a physician dwelling at Stamford, with the help of two surgeons, and yet upon order given according to your direction for the body to be covered with lead, the physician hath thought good to add somewhat to his former doings, and doth now take upon him that it may continue for some reasonable time.

I purpose by the grace of God to depart from hence towards London on Monday next, the 27th of this present.

And thus I leave to trouble you, committing you to the mercy of the Almighty.

From Fotheringay, the 25th of February, 1586.

Your most assured poor friend,

A. POULET.

Addressed — To the right honourable Sir Francis Walsingham, knight, her Majesty's principal secretary. ˉˉ

Endorsed—25th February, 1586, from Sir Amias Poulet. Letters from Sir Amias Poulet, Mr. Somers, and Francis Mills, employed about the business with the Scottish Queen.

The inventory[1] of the property of the Queen of Scots, alluded to in the foregoing letter, is printed in Prince Labanoff's collection, in which it occupies more than twenty pages. Poulet compiled it by summoning Mary's servants before him, and requesting each of them to give him a written note of all that the Queen had given them.[2] A comparison of this inventory, made after Mary's death, with a former one, dated June . 13, 1586, which Prince Labanoff found amongst M. de Châteauneuf's papers[3] enables us to see that Mr. Froude has been led into a curious error respecting Mary Stuart's dress at the scaffold by the anonymous writer whose account he follows in preference to the narratives drawn up by responsible witnesses. It may seem to be of little importance, but as Mr. Froude has chosen to represent the last moments of Mary's life as "brilliant acting throughout," he should at least have been accurate in his details. He even goes so far as to say that she was deprived of the assistance of her chaplain for "fear of some religious melodrame." As to her dress, he says,[4] "She stood on the black scaffold with the black figures all around her, blood-red from head to foot. Her reasons for adopting so extraordinary a costume must be

---

[1] Vol. xxi., n. 20, I ; Labanoff, tom. vii., p. 254.
[2] Jebb, vol. ii., p. 649.
[3] Labanoff, tom. vii., p. 231.
[4] *History*, vol. xii., p. 254.

left to conjecture. It is only certain that it must have been carefully studied, and that the pictorial effect must have been appalling." And he quotes from the *Vray Rapport* the words, "Ainsy fut exécutée toute en rouge."

The *rouge* was not "blood-red," but a dark red brown. Blackwood says that she wore, with a pourpoint or bodice of black satin, "une juppe de vellours cramoisi brun," and the narrative called *La Mort de la Royne d'Escosse* says the same. There it is in the June inventory, "Une juppe de velloux cramoisy brun, bandée de passement noir, doublée de taffetas de couleur brune." In the inventory taken after her death it is wanting. As it happens, if she had wished to ·be "blood-red," she might have been so, for in the wardrobe there was "satin figuré incarnat," "escarlate," and "satin incarnate." These figure both in the June and February inventories. When she was dressed "le plus proprement qu'elle put et mieux que de coutume," she said to her maids of honour, "Mes amies, je vous eusse laissé plustost cet accoustrement que celui d'hier, sinon qu'il faut que j'aille à la mort un peu honnorablement, et que j'aye quelque chose plus que le commun." "La tragedie finie," continues Blackwood, "les pauvres damoiselles, soigneuses de l'honneur de leur maistresse s'adresserent à Paulet son gardien, et le prierent que le bourreau ne touchast plus au corps de sa Majesté, et qu'il leur fust permis de la despouiller, apres que le monde seroit retiré, afin qu'aucune indignité ne fust faitte au corps, promettant de luy rendre la despouille, et tout ce qu'il pourroit demander. Mais ce maudict et espouventable Cerbere les renvoya fort lourdement, leur commandant de sortir de la salle. Cependant le bourreau la dechausse, et la manie à sa discretion. Apres qu'il eust fait tout ce qu'il voulust, le corps fut porté en une chambre joignante celle de ces serviteurs, bien fermée de peur qu'ils n'y entrassent pour luy rendre leurs debvoirs. Ce qui augmenta grandement leur ennuy, ils la voyoient par le trou de la serrure demy couverte d'un morceau de drop de bure qu'on avoit arraché de la table du billard, dont nous avous parlé cy dessus, et prioyent Dieu à la porte, dont Paulet s'appercevant fist boucher le trou."[1]

[1] Jebb, vol. ii., pp. 306, 489, 640.

Y

The executioner snatched from her hand the little gold cross that she took from her neck. "Sa Majesté osta hors de son col une croix d'or, qu'elle vouloit bailler à une de ses filles, disant au maistre d'œuvres, Mon amy, cecy n'est pas à vostre usage, laissez la à cette damoiselle elle vous baillera en argent plus qu'elle ne vaut; il luy arracha d'entre les mains fort rudement, disant, C'est mon droit. C'eust esté merveille qu'elle eust trouvé courtoisie en un bourreau Anglois, qui ne l'avoit jamais sceu trouver entre les plus honestes du pais, sinon tant qu'ils en pouvoient tirer de profit." It was worthy of Poulet to insist that, even though everything Mary wore was to bê burnt and the headsman was to lose his perquisites lest he should sell them for relics, it was to be by his hands that they should be taken from the person of his victim.

Several narratives of the execution exist. The most complete, attributed to Bourgoin, is printed in Jebb.[1] Sir H. Ellis and Robertson print the official report of the Commissioners. Then there is Châteauneuf's Report to Henry III., February 27, 1587, N.S., in Teulet, and a narrative drawn up for Burghley by R. W. (Richard Wigmore). Blackwood also furnishes an interesting and trustworthy description. The anonymous *Vray Rapport* will be found in Teulet.[2] Mr. Froude appears to have selected it, partly because it was possible to expand the realistic description of the disseevered head, and in particular the inevitable contraction of the features, into the gross and pitiless caricature which he permits himself of the poor wreck of humanity; partly too, because the *Vray Rapport*, in direct contradiction to the other accounts, supports his assertion that Mary was "dreadfully agitated" on receiving the message of death from the two Earls. To convey the impression that the writer was bodily present on that occasion, Mr. Froude introduces him as "evidently an eye-witness, one of the Queen of Scots' own attendants, probably her surgeon." But the narrative shows us that the writer, whoever he was, could not have been one of Mary's attendants, nor even acquainted with them, for he designates the two ladies who assisted their mistress at the scaffold as "deux damoiselles, l'une Françoise nommée damoiselle

Ramete, et l'autre Escossoise, qui avait nom Ersex." There were no such names in Mary's household. The two ladies were both Scottish, Jane Kennedy and Elspeth Curle, Gilbert Curle's sister. Mr. Froude says, "Barbara Mowbray bound her eyes with a handkerchief." It was Jane Kennedy who performed for her this last service.

Poulet's inventory, amongst other things, contains the following entry: "Memorandum that the Priest claimeth as of the said late Queen's gift, a silver chalice with a cover, two silver cruets, four images, the one of our Lady in red coral, with divers other vestments and necessaries belonging to a Massing Priest." When the scaffold had been taken away, the Priest was allowed to leave his room and join the rest of the household. On the morning after the execution he said Mass for Mary's soul; but on the afternoon of that day Melville and Bourgoin were sent for by Poulet, who gave orders that the altar should be taken down, and demanded an oath that Mass should not be said again. Melville excused himself as he was a Protestant and not concerned; the physician stoutly refused. Poulet sent for the Priest, and required the coffer in which the vestments were kept to be brought to him. Du Préau, who was evidently a timid man, took the oath that Poulet insisted on, little thinking that he was pledging himself for six months. "Il jura sur la bible de ne faire aucune office de religion, craignant d'estre resserré en prison."[1]

The household of the late Queen were not allowed to depart as soon as Poulet expected. They were detained at Fotheringay, from motives of policy, till the 3rd of August, when the funeral of their mistress having been at last performed, they were set free. Some of them were taken to Peterborough to accompany the corpse and to be present at the funeral ceremonies on the 1st of August. Amongst them, in the order of the procession, it is surprising to find Mary's chaplain, "Monsieur du Préau, aumosnier, en long manteau, portant une croix d'argent en main." The account of the funeral from which this is taken, written by one of the late Queen's household, takes care to mention that when they

[1] Jebb, vol. ii., pp. 649, 656.

reached the choir of Peterborough Minster, and the choristers began "à chanter à leur façon en langage Anglois," they all, with the exception of Andrew Melville and Barbara Mowbray,[1] left the church and walked in the cloisters till the service was finished. "Si les Anglois," he says, "et principalement le Roy des heraux . . . estoit en extreme cholere, d'autant estoient joieux et contents les Catholiques."

Poulet left for London, and as long as Mary's servants were detained at Fotheringay, he seems to have retained jurisdiction over them. It was to him, therefore, that Melville and Bourgoin applied in March for leave to sell their horses and to write into France respecting the bequests made to them by the Queen of Scots; and to him that Darrell forwarded in June "the petition of the whole household and servants of the late Queen of Scotland remaining at Fotheringay,"[2] begging to be released from their prison and to be allowed to leave the country.

Poulet, as has already been said, was made Chancellor of the Garter in April, 1587, but he did not retain this preferment for a whole year. He continued in the Captaincy of Jersey up to his death, but he appears to have resided in and near London. In the British Museum are two letters[3] from him of small importance. One, addressed to the Lord High Admiral, is dated, "From my poor lodging in Fleet Street, the 14th of January, 1587," about "right of tenths in Jersey, belonging to the Government." The other, "From my little lodge at Twickenham, the 24th of April, 1588," "on behalf of Berry," whose divorce was referred by the Justices of the Common Pleas to four Doctors of the Civil Law, of whom Mr. Doctor Cæsar, Judge of the Admiralty, to whom the letter was written, was one.

His name also occurs in a letter from Walsingham to Burghley, dated May 23, 1587, while Elizabeth still kept up the farce of Burghley's disgrace for despatching Mary Stuart's death-warrant. "Touching the Chancellorship of the Duchy,

---

[1] Qy. Gillis. Barbara, her sister, was Curle's wife.
[2] Vol. xxi., nn. 30, 33, 34.
[3] *Additional MSS.*, n. 12507, f. 126; n. 12506, f. 261.

she told Sir Amias Poulet that in respect of her promise made unto me, she would not dispose of it otherwise. But yet hath he no power to deliver the seals unto me, though for that purpose the Attorney is commanded to attend him, who I suppose will be dismissed hence this day without any resolution." And on the 4th of January following, together with the other lords of the Council, he signed a letter addressed by the Privy Council to the Lord Admiral and to Lord Buckhurst, the Lieutenants of Sussex, against such Catholics as "most obstinately have refused to come to the church to prayers and divine service," requiring them to "cause the most obstinate and noted persons to be committed to such prisons as are fittest for their safe keeping: the rest that are of value, and not so obstinate, are to be referred to the custody of some ecclesiastical persons and other gentlemen well affected, to remain at the charges of the recusant, to be restrained in such sort as they may be forthcoming, and kept from intelligence with one another."[1] On the 26th of September, in the year in which this letter was written, 1588, Sir Amias Poulet died.

Poulet was buried in St. Martin-in-the-Fields, London. When that church was pulled down to be rebuilt, his remains, with the handsome monument erected over them, were removed to the parish church of Hinton St. George. After various panegyrics in Latin, French, and English inscribed on his monument, a quatrain, expressive apparently of royal favour, pays the following tribute to the service rendered by him to the State as Keeper of the Queen of Scots—

E. R.

Never shall cease to spread wise Poulet's fame;
These will speak, and men shall blush for shame:
Without offence to speak what I do know,
Great is the debt England to him doth owe.

---

[1] *Harl. MSS.*, n. 6994, f. 39; n. 703, f. 52; Wright's *Queen Elizabeth and her times*, vol. ii., pp. 338, 358. Mr. Wright is mistaken in stating (p. 255, note) that Poulet's Embassy in France was "at a later period," after he had the custody of the Queen of Scots.

ADDITIONAL NOTES.

Page 2.—In Lord Burghley's *Notes of Queen Elizabeth's Reign* (Murdin, p. 787), there occurs this entry. "February, 1587. The Chancellorship of the Garter by the death of Amyas Paulett granted to Mr. Secretary Walsingham." This must have been written by Burghley so long afterwards that he had forgotten the details. Poulet succeeded Walsingham in the Chancellorship, and was succeeded by Wolley, and though he died in 1588, he was not dead in the February of that year.

Page 21.—Lady Pope, mentioned by Morgan, was Elizabeth, eldest daughter of Walter Blount of Blount Hall, co. Stafford, who married first, Anthony Basford or Beresford of Bentley in Derbyshire; secondly, Sir Thomas Pope, whose third wife she was; and thirdly, Sir Hugh Poulet, father of Sir Amias. Sir Thomas Pope was the founder of Trinity College, Oxford, and his wife Elizabeth was a benefactor of the College. Her effigy is in the College chapel, beside that of Sir Thomas, and her picture is in the hall. The name of Lady Poulet appears in various lists of recusants. For instance, Justice Young wrote to Lord Keeper Puckering, February 25, 159⅔, that Thomas Hygate, a Priest, had been harboured, amongst other places, "at the Lady Pawlett's in Essex, with Mr. Southcote, who married her daughter" (*Domestic, Elizabeth*, vol. ccxliv., n. 48). And again, in May, 1587, in a list of "Common receivers, harbourers, and maintainers of Jesuits and Seminary Priests," we have, amongst other names, those of "The Lady Lovell, the Lady Paulet, the Lady Copley" (*Ibid.*, vol. cci., n. 53). She survived her third husband, and had issue only by Beresford, who left her a widow March 1, 1539. Sir T. Pope died Jan. 29, 155⁸⁄₉, and Sir H. Poulet in 1571. She died October 7, 1593, possessed of the estate of Tittenhanger, co. Herts., and was succeeded by her nephew, Sir Thomas Pope Blount, knight, son of her eldest brother, William Blount, which Thomas (her children by her first husband being then all dead) was not only her heir-at-law, but also great-nephew of her husband, Sir Thomas Pope, through his mother, Frances, daughter of Edward Love, Esq., by Alice, sister of Sir Thomas Pope (Clutterbuck's *Hertfordshire*; Burton's *Leicestershire*). Father Richard Blount, S.J., was the younger brother of Sir Thomas Pope Blount.

Page 85.—The *confitures seiches* had, as Poulet suspected, another meaning. It was Mary's secret supply of money, which was brought to her in a way that we should have thought could not possibly have escaped detection on arrival, if it escaped pillage on the road. Those through whose hands these boxes of *confitures* passed must have thought them singularly heavy.

In her letter to the Archbishop of Glasgow of July 17, 1586, Mary requests him to send to her four thousand crowns given to her by the King of Spain for the expenses of her escape. "Ce que vous pourrez aisément faire par mes nouveaulx serviteurs, s'ilz viennent en bref, ou dans deux cachettes secrètes aux deux boites d'un bahu, plain de boytes de confitures d'Italie et d'Espagne, le plus liegèrement remplis que pourrez. Car oultre que telles choses pour ma bouche sont plus respectées et moins maniées tant par les chemins que icy, ayant accoustumé d'en faire venir tous les ans, on se doubtera moins qu'il y aye rien de caché pardessoubs. Je vous envoyeray le mémoire de ces confitures par la voye ouverte, et en cas qu'il ne vous soit rendu en temps, ne laissez d'en choisir par précédentes mémoires des années passées" (Labanoff, tom. vi., p. 414).

Page 117.—The last we hear of Phelippes is in 1622, when he must have been an old man. He was then in the Marshalsea, "arrested upon an old quarrel between me and one Tyttyn," when he wrote two letters dated May 22, to Sir Robert Cotton, giving an account of a petition that he had presented to King James I. (_Cotton. MSS._, Julius, C. iii., f. 297). Perhaps the last thing we should have expected him to petition for would have been "some ecclesiastical dignity," even though "of the inferior sort." "Philips the decipherer hath been dealt with by such as take notice of his wants and oppressions, for to leave the realm, and to expect entertainment abroad to sell his skill. He was advised rather by others to have recourse to the King's bounty here, being also of himself loth to wander at these years, especially without leave of the State. He thereupon presented a petition to his Majesty, importing that he had been forced, since his Majesty's coming to this Crown, to part with a pension had for deciphering, towards satisfaction of a debt owing to the late Queen, which she was in mind to have pardoned. . . . His Majesty therefore may be moved—if not for his feat of deciphering, by the which, notwithstanding, England was sometime preserved to him, and sometime his Majesty to England, when he knew not of it—for these other abilities to bestow somewhat upon him for the present, for to pay his debts, till something may occur to repair his estate, and to entertain such a servant, which may be, perhaps, some ecclesiastical dignity of the inferior sort, whereof he is capable, pensions being burthensome to the Crown, and his estate and age not attending other casualties or inventions." It is hardly a conjecture to add that Phelippes must have sold to Sir Robert Cotton some of the documents in his collection, which could only have come through the hands of the old deceiver and decipherer.

Page 242.—The reader may be glad to have at hand the other letters in which Barnes is concerned. They are therefore given here.

Barnes to the Queen of Scots. (Vol. xviii., n. 6.)

"Madam,—The dutiful good mind I have always inwardly to your Highness borne hath been such as I have not only quietly lamented your undeserved estate, but have likewise sought by all means to me possible with as much as in me lay, I might any way yield you comfort in this your distressed case, or employ myself and that little I had to do you service, all which intentions of mine partly through my long imprisonment, and partly for divers other causes as hitherto could take no effect until of late, having conferred with a certain kinsman of mine about such affairs, he imparted to me this kind of service, which he could not so earnestly recommend unto me as I did willingly and affectuously accept of the same. And surely in this he hath satisfied me this far that I think not myself so much bound unto him in respect of our consanguinity, and I do acknowledge myself redevable and beholden to him for this his trust and courtesy. And, therefore, not only this way but howsoever it shall please your Highness to employ me, you shall find me ready according to my ability to perform as you shall upon occasions think convenient to command. I have here sent you a packet from France which you had received ere this if I had not in this strange country lighted in the hands of thieves, who having spoiled me of my horse and money, have enforced me to go on foot the best of my way. I expect your answer for the receipt as soon as may be, for that I would presently repair again to London to furnish myself of necessaries. I pray you send me a new alphabet, for that which I write by was worn out, because I had it of my cousin. Thus my humble duty to your Highness not forgotten, I commit you to God, whom I beseech long to preserve your Majesty in life, and shortly to deliver you out of the hands of your enemies.

"Dated this 10th of June.

"Deciphered by me, Gilbert Curle, 5th October, 1586.

"This is the copy of the true and only letter I sent to the Queen of Scots.

"By me, THOMAS BARNES."

Barnaby to Curle. (*Ibid.,* erroneously entered in the Calendar as with n. 26.)

"From Barnaby unto me.

"Sir,—In the way from London I met yours of the 20th May, according to the reformed calendar (which I will hereafter follow), which the bearer thereof delivered and is returned with this only letter. I was bold to pray the Ambassador to bestow an angel upon him, which would be a great encouragement to him being a foot boy to run it, being also the manner of our nation and a trifle in the whole year to her Majesty. Wherefore it may please you to give credit to this motion by your next to the said Ambassador, which was done in truth for her Majesty's better service. My brother desireth to be troubled as little as he may with waiting, but is content to bear any charges as I am any pains for her Majesty's good. Howbeit the alphabet in respect of any occasion that may happen in my absence is common between us, yet I shall not be long at any time so far off but your directions may be sent to myself. The 23rd of this present I will repair for answer. God have you in His keeping.

"Lichfield, 16th June, 1586.

"Deciphered by me, Gilbert Curle, 5th October, 1586."

Curle to Barnaby. (Vol. xviii., n. 10; Curle's draft, much corrected.)

"Sir,—At the seven night before my former, yours dated the 28th of April with your cousin and the whole mentioned therein, came safe to her Majesty's hands. So did on the 20th of this instant your other dated the 16th of the same conform to the reformed calendar, whereof before now I could not advertise you. Her Majesty thinketh herself not a little beholden to your said cousin for the finding out of you and your brother to pleasure her Majesty in this intercourse, nor less obliged unto yourselves for your so willing acceptance of the pain and travail that thereby you shall have, which her Majesty hath commanded me to signify unto you in her name, and withal to assure you of her goodwill and thankful mind to recognize the same in effect towards you and all yours whensoever occasion and means may offer thereunto. By any error or want of circumspection either in her Majesty's self, or any here about her person, you may be assured there hath no inconvenience happened unto any man whom her Majesty hath had intelligence withal, or employed as you are, having always kept that order and rule on her side for the surest, that never one almost should know of another dealing for her Majesty. But that which has overthrown many (to her Majesty's extreme great grief), hath been their own too great curiosity to know more than was requisite for their security, and jealousy one of another after their too liberal revealing amongst themselves of their goodwills in the cause, towards whom and their posterity, her Majesty notwithstanding esteemeth her and hers bound to acknowledge her obligation therein effectually, and will be no less careful in the meantime of your preservations every way than of her own, which her Majesty maketh not so much account of for any particular contentment she wisheth to herself as she doth for the maintenance of God's cause, and the common good of this isle, to which end her Majesty hath dedicated both her life and labour.

"On Monday last this bearer brought hither a letter written to her Majesty in [Gilbert Gifford] his alphabet without any name or sign who he may be that wrote it, except only that he asserted his kinsman imparted this way to him. The inclosed is for him, desiring to know his name, without the which her Majesty can ground no sure intelligence with him.

"For this day fortnight, which will be the 14th of July, her Majesty will have a packet finished to be sent unto the French Ambassador, wherefore desireth you for that time to hold your boy in readiness, and touching his encouragement, her Majesty shall let the Ambassador know her intention to your contentment. What correspondence I may give you for my own part in this trade, you shall be sure to have all also the pleasure and service my power can therewise do you, whom I pray God to preserve.

"Chartley this 29th day of June [N. S.].

"I have thought good to change the ciphered words added to this alphabet in other simple characters as are herein noted, which I pray you use in time coming, as I will to the end our ordinary writing in case of interception or loss of our letters be not discovered as might by the other, and so by consequence ourselves.

"From me to Barnabie at the Queen's Majesty my mistress' commandment,

"GILBERT CURLE.

"5th October, 1586.

"Whosoever you be that hath written a letter unto me in the alphabet hereof dated the 10th of this instant, whereunto before now I could not answer, I must thank you right heartily for the affection declared therein which you bear unto me, and the offer you make to let me effectually know the same. But I would more boldly accept thereof and employ you if I did know your particular intention therein, and what way you would pleasure me, and what is your name, omitted in your said letter, which by your next I pray you to utter. In the meanwhile, I do herewith send you a new alphabet conform to your desire, and pray God to preserve you. This 19th of June according to the new computation. [*Mr. Lemon adds*—A mistake, June 19, stylo veteri]."

Curle to Barnaby. (Vol. xviii., n. 16A.　*In cipher, with decipher in Phelippes'
handwriting, very illegible.*)

"On Sunday last I wrote unto you by this bearer, having received nothing
from you since your letter dated the 16th of this instant.　I hope to have her
Majesty's Ambassador's despatch mentioned in my foresaid ready for to-
morrow seven-night . . . appointment.　In the mean season her Majesty
prayeth you to send your footboy as closely as you can . . . two little [letters]
inclosed the one so mar[ked to] Anthoine Babington dwelling in Derbyshire
. · . . [ho]use of his own within two miles of . . . but you know for that in
this shire he hath both friends . . . or *super scriptum* to . . . in Nottingham
town unto neither of the said personages . . . with whom he shall have . . .
and what is given him . . . herself you will with all convenient diligence
. . . her Majesty desireth you would . . . occurrents as may for her Majesty's
knowledge . . . within or without the realm, and in particular what you understand of the Earl of Shrewsbury his going to Court . . . preserve you.

"Chartley, of July the 4th, on Saturday. [*Mr. Lemon's note.*　The day
of the month is the 5th, and according to the new style]."

Curle to Barnaby.　(Vol. xviii., n. 30.)

"The last of yours which came to my hands was dated the 17th of June,
since which have written to you twice, the one on this day was sennett,
and the other the 4th of this instant, but have had no word from you of the
receipt of either of the two.　Herewith is the packet mentioned in both, which
her Majesty prayeth you send by your boy or otherwise surely to the French
Ambassador.　So, expecting you will by the next commodity to communicate
to her Majesty such news as you hear, I pray God to preserve you.

"This Saturday at Chartley, the 12th of July. [*Mr. Lemon's note.*　This
according to the new style]."

Barnaby to Curle.　(Vol. xviii., n. 63.　*Draft in Phelippes' hand, much
corrected.*)

"Sir,—I have received your last of the 12th of July by my cousin Gilbert,
as also your other two therein . . . which in mine absence came to my
betters' hands, who took order for satisfaction of her Majesty touching the
contents, but . . . as a thing which he always desired he might not be charged
with.　The present packet is committed to my cousin Gilbert, to be by himself
delivered, who hath likewise signified as he tells. . . . this second messenger,
as I hold it needless to trouble you with anything myself touching that point
. . . delivery of the letters in cipher inclosed in yours of the 12th instant,
my brother at London despatched it accordingly thither . . . he received the
packet sent herewith, which Babington said required great haste, and therefore
the boy returned without staying for any despatch from the French Ambassador,
who attendeth letters he saith daily out of France.　I will take order for the
. . . letter myself.　I find the Earl of Shrewsbury he was greatly grieved with
a stay that the Queen of England made of a . . . punished by him about one
Babsthorpe, a gentleman, upon the statute of *scandalum magnatum*, for lewd
speeches uttered by the said Babsthorpe against the Earl.　Howbeit the Earl
since his going up hath prevailed so far with . . . the Queen of England is
content the law shall have course.　For other matters I refer to the next ; this
both sudden and speedy because of Mr. Babington's request.　I received your

alteration of the alphabet . . . the reason I wish for great expedition also in writing, that you would assign special characters for a number of the most common words. So God preserve you.

"The 20th of July."

Curle to Barnaby. (Vol. xviii., n. 42. *In cipher, with decipher in Phelippes' hand.*)

"Sir,—Yesternight your letter dated the 12th of this instant, with the inclosed to her Majesty received, who right thankfully at you which [?] diligence you show to pleasure her in all she desireth. I trust you have caused deliver her Majesty's answer to the second messenger, although (to say truly) her Majesty agreeth with your cousin Gilbert his advice, not much to employ the man, neither hath her Majesty been willing at any time unneedfully to this course for her part with any other than yourself, your brother, and your cousin Gilbert. If Mr. Babington be gone down to the country (for whom this character)-(shall serve in time coming), her Majesty·prayeth you to cause convey to him this inclosed, otherwise to stay it until you hear from her Majesty again. With my next I shall do of my best to satisfy you touching the other characters. God have you in protection.

"Of July the 22nd. CURLE, Chartley."

Curle to Barnaby. (Vol. xviii., n. 57. *In cipher, with decipher by Phelippes.*)

"Sir,—This afternoon, having received your letters of the 25th of this instant, and let her Majesty see the same wholly deciphered, which hath not a little augmented the good opinion she had conceived before of your affection towards God's cause and hers, she hath commanded me hereby to give you her right hearty thanks therefore, and to pray you in her name, until farther occasion shall be offered to employ you otherwise, that you will continue in occurrences as you promise and now have done, and to make this inclosed be surely delivered in the hands of Anthony Babington, if he be come down in the country. Otherwise that if it be kept still in yours or your brother's until Babington his arrival, or set an [?] ten days, within which time her Majesty intendeth to have a packet ready to be sent unto the French Ambassador by your boy, who by the same means may also carry the other to Babington at London, if he went down home. Herewith is the addition to this alphabet, and so I pray God to preserve you.

"Of July the 27th. CURLE."

Barnes was put into the Tower for a short time, but without any intention of bringing him to trial. The following letter it is hardly possible to look on in any other light than as written to hide the fact that he had been employed by Walsingham, and to justify his release from prison.

Barnes to Walsingham. (Vol. xxi., n. 26.)

"Right Honourable Sir,—Whereas upon a certain blind conceit of the late Queen of Scots' innocence in such matters as had or might have been imputed to her, and the opinion of her unjust imprisonment, with hope of doing myself good, both presently and in time to come, by doing her service in that distressed state, being withal thereunto persuaded and enticed by my cousin, Gilbert Gifford, I entered into this course of conveying letters unto her, I most humbly confess and acknowledge my fault committed therein, and crave pardon for the same. And as I protest before God that to be all and the very truth which hath passed that I have set down in writing, so if any way I may by my service for the repairing in some part of that fault committed serve your honour's turn by discovering or bringing to light any of their treacherous intents towards the State hereafter which be fugitives or traitors at home or abroad, I most humbly beseech your honour to accept of the same, and I will be right glad to be employed therein, promising you by the faith of a Christian, that I will truly, sincerely, and faithfully proceed therein according to such direction as I shall receive from your honour, and do renounce my part of Paradise if I do not discharge myself like an honest subject in that behalf. In witness whereof I give this my handwriting for a perpetual testimony against myself. Almighty God long preserve your honour in health, wealth, and prosperity.

"London, this 17th of March, 1587.

"Your honour's most humble orator,

"THOMAS BARNES.

"*Endorsed*—To the right honourable Sir Francis Walsingham, knight, principal secretary to her Majesty, and one of her Highness' most honourable Privy Council, give these."

Page 257.—The earliest record that we have of Gilbert Gifford is the entry in the Douay Diary, stating that he and his uncle, William Gifford, the Dr. Gifford of this correspondence, arrived at the College in 1582, the one to teach theology, the other logic. "Venerunt Roma hoc anno 1582 D. Gulielmus Giffordus ut S. Theologiam hic doceret, et cum illo Gilbertus Giffordus, qui logicam et philosophiam docere coepit."

It may be interesting to give some further extracts from the letter that Gifford wrote to Phelippes from Paris as soon as he received a cipher in which to write. The profanity of the letter is singular, and so is the reference to "men of my coat," or cloth, according to more modern phrase, of which, indeed, he was no ornament.

Gifford to Phelippes. (Vol. xx., n. 45. *In Phelippes' hand.*)

"I know not which way to turn me nor how to answer yours, but I perceive the ancient speech will be verified in me, that betwixt both I shall lose both, as commonly men of my coat do that deal, and bear sincere affection to our Prince. Pardon me if I speak boldly, for by God you touch me near, and though I should lose all the friends I have in the world, by God it is nothing in respect of that wherein most unjustly either you suspect or accuse me, wherein I defy all the world; and, by Jesus Christ, if there be any man alive accuseth me therein, I will be in England if I die a thousand times, either to purge myself before the world or to die ignominiously. . . .

"When Morgan examined me secretly touching the parties that conveyed letters, I was forced to name two, whereof Barnes was one, and for that purpose I dealt with Barnes, never thinking, as Christ Jesus save me, but to make him a colour for Emilio, and his writing once or twice would cause all blame to be removed from myself when things should be opened, which I knew must needs be shortly, and so in truth it is fallen forth, and otherwise it had been impossible to have continued, but as God is my witness, I thought to have withdrawn him after that Morgan fully perceived that the convoy was sure; and one thing I will tell you, if you handle the matter cunningly, Barnes may be the man to set up the convoy again for Paget, and Morgan be never

in rest inquiring for him. I have feigned as though the matter were irrecuperable, and therefore I have speculated upon the point.

"If you have Barnes, keep him close ; if you have him not, I would you
had him in your hands. However it be, either bring him by promise or fear
to write to Morgan, or if you have him not, feign his hand to me. His
name was Pietro Mariani. Write by the name of Pietro Mariani, discoursing
of the whole success, and that, as chance was, your name never came in
question, and that now is time to begin again, which they desire beyond
measure, and no doubt they will take hold of it, for they are about another
practice I assure you, and I pray you use Emilio no more. Let him be one
of those that were hanged, for before God they will suspect. After you have
written to me they will leap for joy. I cannot devise any better course, and
it is unpossible but it should hit. I know they burn. Paget hath written
to me twenty times. I show myself unwilling. But when you have written
I will stir them. Besides, if Cordaillot be there, tell him I left word with
you to send me two doublets and two pair of hose, which I left with him at
my departure, and a cloak and other little things. If he be not there speak
to Peter Francis and desire him to deliver them, and I pray you send them
to Thomas Evans, who is a good simple instrument.

". . . The greatest cause of my going away was that I feared to be
brought to witness some matters concerning the Scottish Queen face to face.
. . . Besides that I knew not what they had written of me to the Scottish
Queen. Perhaps they might have spoken to her some things in my commendation which might justly have bred jealousy in your head and yet I
nothing in fault. And if all this will not persuade you of my innocency, let
Mr. Secretary send for me in without any further warrant, and I will come
in, and howsoever it be, there is no man alive that knoweth my heart to her
Majesty and Mr. Secretary, and then God confound me when I leave to
honour him. And albeit he would command me silence, if I could by any
means pleasure or serve him otherwise, I would do it till death.

". . . I know Savage thought I had detected him, with whom I kept
company in truth only for that he was one of the best companions. . . .

"What as Morgan should say that D. Gifford meant not to deal sincerely
with Mr. Secretary. I never doubted it but that he would not, and so always
I told you, only in truth against those others they are and meant sincerely.
But I told you still that my credit could no otherwise have been kept but
by pursuing the matter. And as for Ballard, Christ confound me if ever
Gratley, Paget, Dr. Gifford, or Morgan, or any in the world, talked to me
of him on this side, and if ever I had any other acquaintance with him or
knew him otherwise than man I never saw. Wherefore I told them that they
failed, not to make me privy thereof. They told me it was for my safety, and
in truth Gratley and Morgan wrote to me expressly not to meddle with him,
which letters I sent to Mr. Secretary, and I think you saw them."

As the letters of Sir Edward Stafford, the Ambassador, to Walsingham
from Paris after the apprehension of Gifford throw great light on his relations
with Phelippes, it may be well in this place to extract more copiously from
them. The saddest revelation in these letters is the treachery of Sir Charles
Arundell, hitherto, as far as we are aware, unsuspected by the Catholics
(See, however, Murdin, p. 462). Cordaillot also, it seems, was no better than
Chérelles, and served as a means of communication, enabling Gifford in France

to send his letters to Walsingham or Phelippes in the French Ambassador's bag. "Besides as I hear that he hath accused Cordaillot for the convoy by the French Ambassador." Nau also was spoken of by Phelippes in a compromising manner. "I hear besides now that Nau entereth to be a party against him [Gifford] to clear himself of that which Phelippes writeth of him, so that I am afraid it will be a great broil, and that the knave will be instrument of whatsoever they will have him. And yet when they have all out of him that they desire, they will hang him if they can ; and I think they will put him to a hard plunge," &c. (*Domestic, Addenda, Elizabeth*, vol. xxx., n. 69, January 7, 158$\frac{7}{8}$).

The two letters (*Ibid.*, nn. 53, 55) from which the following extracts are taken were written a few days earlier than that last quoted. They are worth printing, for such a sentence as this speaks volumes—"I am promised if there be any means possible to get the letter of Phelippes, wherein the chief things be that may call anything in question. If I could get that, the chiefest things be in it ; if he were hanged for the rest it were not a halfpenny matter."

Sir Edward Stafford to Sir Francis Walsingham. Paris, Dec. $\frac{15}{25}$, 1587.

"I stayed this bearer hoping still to recover into my hands certain papers and coffers that have been taken in Gilbert Gifford's chamber, after he had been taken with an English quean . . . and with them also was taken one Cotton. . . . This was done upon Friday last, and I had warning of it by Charles Arundell that day, and that there are letters that Phelippes writ to him and a notable cipher that Phelippes sent him, and certain letters that they have intercepted any time this month or six weeks which he writ to Mr. Phelippes, which they have deciphered with the cipher. It is told me that things [are] discovered of the death of the Queen of Scots and the apprehension of the gentlemen that were executed, and things which they think to make their profit greatly of to her Majesty's dishonour. I have done what I can to have them into my hands, and Arundell laboured to get all, and assured [me] upon Friday I should have them the next day, or it should cost him his life." But Arundell fell ill and died. "So that now I cannot tell which way to go about it to have them, for, as I hear say, the Vicar-General of the Bishop of Paris [Rome *by error in the Calendar*], by these knaves means, hath laid his authority upon him because he is a Priest, which maketh me afraid that I shall not get them now, and that I shall hardly get him out, which I dare work all the means I can and will spare for nothing. And if I can and he will, I will find means to send him into England, for if he were away, what letters soever be taken there [could] be said to be counterfeit, but if he be here to avow them by constraint, they will make their profit of them greatly. They say they find that by Phelippes' mean he kept intelligence with her Majesty. I have set divers ways to have him spoken withal, to give him warning of the taking of his papers which he knoweth not yet, and to give him warning to keep his tongue, which is but too lavish, and not to bewray himself, and also to see if he can find any means to get out himself any way. I hope to-morrow some of them I have set about it will find some means to speak with him, for to-day is Christmas Day here, and is not possible to do it. If it had pleased God to send the poor gentleman [Charles Arundell], I could have done well enough, but I do not think he will live till to-morrow morning. Look sir, I pray you, whom you trust, for without doubt it hath been written

hither, and they that have writ it have writ that they had it from you, that
Arundell made a packet of Charles Paget's he brought to me, and that I
sent it you, and all that I writ to you of Paget's and Morgan's being in evil
predicament with the Spanish Ambassador, for it was shewed him written."

"Sir,—I writ to your honour the last day of the taking of the Priest
Gifford, for whom I have done what I could to help [him] any way out, I did
not care how, if that he had not discovered himself and me, thinking to save
himself and to get thereby favour and friendship in discovering that I offered
him favour and that he refused it. It may be I might have helped him, for
I would have spared nothing for that purpose, because his examination I am
afraid and his confession (for I see he will confess anything that is and more
than is) may give subject to the enemies of her Majesty to procure a
scandalous opinion to be conceived of her and of her Council, for they
mean to turn a letter or two, but especially one of Phelippes to him, to
prove that he was the setter on of the gentlemen that were executed for that
enterprise of the Queen of Scots, and then to discover them, and that he was
practised to this by you and Phelippes, and withal, they would fain have it,
with her Majesty's knowledge.

"They have made the Queen-Mother acquainted with this, and she hath
commanded the lieutenant-criminal to make the King acquainted with it, and
then she hath promised she will follow it, and the Bishop of Glasgow meaneth
to enter into it, and Madam Montpensier will put fire to it, who is the devil
of the world, so that as he hath now handled the matter, I know not in the
world how to deal in it, for they lie but at wait to find if any way I deal in
it, to take hold fast of it to make me a party, and to have as the Queen's
Minister intelligence with him in those causes to make the matter more odious.

"And in this time he hath showed himself the most notable double
treble villain that ever lived, for he hath played upon all the hands in the
world. I have sent you the copy of his answers, whereof I have the originals
with his own hand, whereby you may see how vilely he dealt with me, to say
that the billet was safe, and by word of mouth sent me word that it was burnt,
when it was shewed me by one that gave me warning of all, and gave me
warning afore his letter came to me, that I should receive such a letter from
him, to demand of me to send Grimston or somebody to him to get him a
procureur, which was a thing he was made to do of the nonce, that as soon as
ever any of mine came with a *procureur*, he should be seized upon to know
what interest I had in him and his cause, to have made me a party; which he
failed not to do to serve their turns as you may see by his letter to me, and
when he saw I could not be got to do that, but sent him word that I could
not deal that way, but sent him some money for God's sake that he might
not starve, and did offer to perform anything that he should promise to one
could help him to make a scape, he conferred that with them too, and then
they invented another way to take me withal, that he should send unto me
that if he could get caution he should be let out, and that he had found an
honest Catholic gentleman to avow the caution, because I should not be a
dealer in it; which, as by his letter you may see that he performed to catch
me in a trap; but as God would have it, I had warning of it and did it not,
and have therefore plainly given over dealing with him.

"It is a common saying, sir, that it is a simple thing that there is nothing
picked out of, nor an evil wind bloweth nobody good, as his knavish dealing

some would have served their turns of it to my affront and the discredit of her Majesty, so some others that loved me, thinking that I could not leave anything undone in respect what consequence his getting out was for the public service, and fearing lest I should do the public no good but myself for my own private harm, have, to incense me against him, thinking that would make me colder, found means to come by his letters he writ to Phelippes with his own hand, which I have seen with my eyes within these two days, the most villainous against me and all mine that could be in the world, whereof I am promised to have the copies, where in one of them are these words, ' I cannot directly (as I take it) answer you, but I am sure it is. I cannot directly say the Ambassador is a naughty man, but probably I can say it, for the haunting with Charles Arundell, the greatest traitor on this side the seas, is a proof. He speaketh evil, and all his men be naught,' and a great many things more which I do not remember. And withal I saw a copy of Phelippes' letter to him, whereby he eggeth him to write of me.

" Besides, the villain, to make them believe that he had done service with his dealing in England to the cause here, and to show that he went about to cozen her Majesty (for he braggeth he dealt with her directly by Phelippes' mean, and that you had most of things but by second hand) and to take away the credit that might be given to me or any [of] mine that might inform her from hence, he had so discredited me and mine that we were taken for worse or as bad as any that they counted traitors on this side the seas ; for having found commandment of you (for so he affirmeth it) and direction of Phelippes to inquire diligently of me and my actions, and finding that I was a shy child (for so, I thank him, he termed me) and that under colour of fair speeches and courteous usage of all men, I did nothing but draw wires out of their noses to know all and then to advertise it, to undo them on this side, and to hang as many as I could of the other side. . . .

" It shall be seen to my disgrace what a mistrust is made of me at home, what reputation I live in there and what credit I have, when such persons as Phelippes is, is countenanced to set such farther varlets as this is to look into my actions. I promise you I am so much grieved withal and so ashamed of my hard fortune, as with all my heart I rather wish to be dead than live. I do what I can to cover it the best that I can, both in the respect of mine own credit, but especially in respect of that which may touch her Majesty in opinion by these letters, for though I will do what I can to get as many of the originals as I can into my hands both of Phelippes' (if it be any way possible), and of the other knave's letters too ; both [but] to them that show them, I have and will affirm they be things counterfeit that they avow to be Phelippes', and the others to be letters written by consent and practice of knaves here, to have them to be surprised and to lean men's judgments [on] occasions to think amiss both of her Majesty and of all her Ministers, which is the best course that I know for me to take now that there is no remedy, and that I can deal no more to get the knave out ; because he hath betrayed me, thinking to help himself, but indeed he hath betrayed himself, for they will go near to make it cost him his life, for they have sent all copies of things to the Cardinal, and press him to make the Pope write to the King of it to use all extremity, and my Lord Paget and his brother, and others that he hath touched in his letters, follow it to the uttermost for their own credit. I am promised if there be any means possible to get the letter of Phelippes wherein the chief things be that may call anything in question. If I could get that, the chiefest things be in it; if he were hanged for the rest it were not a halfpenny matter. If Charles Arundell had either not fallen sick as he did, or had lived I had had all, though he say he be cause of this harm of his. I can assure you I had had them, and of him he is dead and gone, I will say to you in truth, and one day I will make you plainly see it, there was no man of this side served my turn as he did, for her Majesty's service, and never Spanish Ambassador nor his master were better handled. And if I do not make you see it and confess it one day, never give credit to anything I say to you again. I have had a great loss of him, for the certainest and quickest advertisements out of Spain I had of him, for the Spanish Ambassador had that credit in him as he hid nothing that was reasonable from him. He had continually letters from Sir Francis Englefield and Pridiox, whose letters I ever saw afore he deciphered them. And to tell you that I found him not dally with me was that the advertisements that he gave me were ever confirmed unto me in the same sort he gave them me, by those letters that come to the Venice Ambassador, and the advertisements that B. sent me as they came from their agent. For the rest it is not to be written of; you shall know it some day," &c.

The following extracts are taken from the letter of a Priest to Walsingham. The departure of Henry Cæsar from the College at Rheims is entered in the Second Douay Diary on the 12th of February, 1582. As to the book against Father Persons and the Society (*supra*, pp. 189, 219), the writer says that it was "the occasion of Gifford's trouble in Paris and of Gratley's in Rome." It was chiefly from Gratley's pen. One is sorry to see Gratley in such company as Gifford, as he is one of the Priests mentioned in the Life as well as in the indictment of Philip, Earl of Arundel (*Fourth Report of Deputy-Keeper of Public Records*, p. 279); but there was unhappily a suspicion among Catholics that he had some share in the betrayal of the Earl. He was accused also of retaining for his own use three thousand crowns sent through him to Cardinal Allen by the Countess of Arundel. For a time after the death of the Queen of Scots Gratley was an inmate of Cardinal Allen's household, but being the cause of disturbances there he was sent away. He betook himself to Padua, where, as a poor exiled Priest, he was kindly received by the Bishop; but his conduct again betraying him, he was by the Pope's command sent back to Rome, where he was imprisoned in the Holy Office for five years.

Henry Cæsar to Walsingham. Paris, Dec. 9, 1588. (*Domestic, Addenda, Elizabeth*, vol. xxx., n. 120).

"Right Honourable,—Having understood by Mr. Good that your honour was very desirous to understand the truth, as concerning Gilbert Gifford, Priest, which hath been now a year in prison in Paris, in the Bishop's prison. The truth is so, that to satisfy your honour I have taken pains therein to know the truth thereof; and did pen it down as it was told me by one of my own calling, by name William Nicolson, Priest, and greatest companion with Gifford, *qui mihi omnia verbatim retulit quæ hic sequuntur.* Gifford being a Priest, lived in Paris, and was apparelled as our disguised Priests are in England, whereat divers men were offended, and every man spake his pleasure, but in especially *miles Hispanicus ille*, Sir Charles Arundell, whom, indeed, Gifford did accuse to the Spanish Ambassador to be an espie for her Majesty of England; which thing Sir Charles Arundell (*ægre ferens*) never rested until such time as that he had brought the matter to that pass whereat it is.

"Lily, *alias* Ambodester, being very familiar with Gifford, also with Mr. Arundell, it was thought good by Sir Charles and his counsel, who were one Doctor Piers, *alias* Skinner, and one Birket, a Priest, to fee Lily, and so by his means to get at one time or another something to lay against Gifford, and prove him an espie, as he had accused the other to be. Lily being a fit man for the purpose, thought best to get that book that your honour had, which was made by Grackley [Gratley] and Gifford against the Jesuits, and as touching the authority of the Bishop of Rome, which book hath been the occasion of Gifford's trouble in Paris, and of Grackley's in Rome, the which book Phelippes, your man, did send unto Lily. . . .

"Gifford, a little before his taking, did write a book against Dr. Allen's book, which was made in the defence and maintenance of Sir William Stanley's fact, in delivering up of Daventry into the Spanish hands. The book Gifford delivered unto Lily, his trusty friend, to send unto your honour, yet afterwards mistrusting of him, he demanded for to have the book again. Lily did answer him that he had sent it unto your honour, whereas indeed he had delivered it to Sir Charles Arundell. A most wicked fact, and not only contented with this but adding to it, did intercept of packets of letters, the which Gifford did send unto your honour and others, being directed to Mr. Hugh Offley. All this aforesaid hath been the cause of Gifford's long imprisonment, although the occasion of his first taking was for that he was taken of a sudden in a suspected house."

There is some mention of Gilbert Gifford's imprisonment and examination in Paris in one of the Stonyhurst manuscripts, and as it has never before been published, it is subjoined. It contains some interesting details, and gives the feeling of all Catholics, both at the time and ever since, as to the true source of the Babington plot. The "Bishop of Armacan," mentioned in it was Richard Creagh, Archbishop of Armagh, of whom there is this testimony in the State Papers (*Domestic, Elizabeth*, vol. clxxviii., n. 74). "1585, May 27. Tower. Ri. Creaghe, a dangerous man to be among the Irish, for the reverence that is by that nation borne unto him, and therefore fit to be continued in prison."

"The matter of Babington was wholly of their plotting and forging, of purpose to make Catholics odious, and to cut off the Queen of Scots. The chief plotters were the Secretary, Leicester, and the Treasurer. Poley, the Secretary's man, was the chief actor in it here in England. Gilbert Gifford, by his own confession, their actor in it, both here and in France. Poley was for a fashion put in the Tower, but had what he would, and in the end, having there poisoned the Bishop of Armacan with a piece of cheese that he sent him, was let out, and is now in as great credit as ever, being as deeply to be touched in all things, and as much to be proved against him as any that were executed. He was continually with Ballard and Babington, he heard Mass, confessed, and in all things feigned to be a Catholic, and still learned his lesson of Mr. Secretary, whom they should draw into the plot, and what plot they should lay, and what course they should take, that might best serve the turn for which all this device was intended. He brought the copy of the letter penned by Mr. Secretary himself, or by his direction, that Babington writ to the Queen of Scots, and upon which she was afterwards condemned for having answered it as she did, Nau, her Secretary, and Curle, having been by the same Secretary hired with seven thousand pounds to betray their mistress, and it was found in a bill in his study after his decease, as hath been credibly reported. Poley now liveth like himself, a notorious spy, and either an atheist or an heretic.

"Also the same appeareth by Gilbert Gifford's letters to Philips the decipherer, and Philips' also to Gilbert Gifford, who purposely was made Priest, as he confessed, to play the Secretary's spy, and acknowledged he was his chief instrument in this plot, and Philips' letters having been taken unto him, wherein the same is most manifest. [*In the margin.* Inquire of this point of Gilbert's examiners.]

"Savage also being at the Court long before that any of the Council took notice of the matter, was by the Queen herself pointed at, and two pensioners commanded to have an eye unto him, that he should do her no harm, being known to be one of the agents, and yet permitted to go free, because they had not yet entrapped all they sought to bring in.

"Also, one of Poley's principles was, as appeared by the gentlemen's words and speeches at the bar, that none of the graver sort of Catholics, or those that were esteemed wise, should have any notice of their intents, because they doubtless would have smelled the fraud and train that was laid for them; but only young gentlemen, whose green heads and aspiring minds were easy to be deceived, and apt to be induced into any high attempt. Yea, they had so wrought Mr. Ballard, the Priest, that none of the same calling were acquainted with his intent, they fearing that if the graver Priests should have heard, they would have found the deceit, and hindered the course that was intended to all their undoings. As in truth it was easy for any that saw the raw device, and more than childish folly, and so lavish talk of it, that the Protestants knew it before Catholics, and the actors, long before their apprehension, pointed at in the streets of London, and yet not touched, until the matter was brought to that pass to which the Council would have it come.

"While Gilbert Gifford was in England he had continual access and intercourse with the Secretary Walsingham, and in being in danger of the laws, because he was deacon, went, nevertheless, at full liberty without fear; and when he went over, it was of purpose to set forward this action, and from thence he continually writ to Philips, and received letters from him; and I guess Ballard was by his means, and with his instructions, sent into England. [*In the margin.* Inquire of this point.]

"At the same time Mr. Martin Array, having been released and to go over sea, being by a round sum bought from the shambles, he desired of Mr. Secretary some twenty days to despatch his business. Whereat the Secretary pausing, 'No,' saith he, 'you shall have but fourteen; for within the time you require, the coasts would be too hot for you.' As in truth it fell out, for about that time was Babington's matter disclosed by the Council, watch and ward kept everywhere, and much fear showed where it was all prevented, and an ugly matter made against Catholics of a drift of their own devising. Which showeth who was the author of all this device, knowing it long before, and yet furthering it until their end was achieved, and all things ripe to reveal their own plot as the Catholics endeavour, who in truth were least acquainted with it.

Z 2

"Justice Young, and higher magistrates, as Tyrrell himself confessed under his hand and oath (for he most deeply avoweth it in his letter to the Queen), bade him say Mass, hear confessions, and minister Sacraments, so in the end he told them what, and to whom he had done it, so seeking to entrap folks, and making men to break their own laws of purpose to draw them into their penalties.

"Their spies, as namely, Burden, Baker, Vachel, have pretended themselves to be Catholics, and that by the warranties and advice of their superiors. They have heard Mass, confessed, and received, only of purpose to discover Catholics and to entrap them" (*Stonyhurst MSS.*, Angl. A., vol. i., n. 70, circ. 1592).

Since the foregoing sheet of *Notes* was printed, the Editor has, by the kindness of the Archbishop of Westminster, been permitted to examine the Douay Diaries, and in the Second the dates are entered with precision. They are here given, with some additional and interesting details.

Gifford's first admission into the College, which was then at Rheims, is thus noticed under the date of January, 1577, N.S. : "31° die Gilbertus Giffordus, clarus adolescens, prius ad aliquot menses in Collegio Aquicinctensi convictor, ad nostra communia est admissus."

He was sent to Rome in 1579 to the English College, where his name is the twenty-third in the list of the students. The name of Edward Gratley is not far from his. The Douay Diary incidentally mentions his being at Rome when recording the arrival at Rheims of his brother George, on the 24th March, 1580 : "Eodem die nuper ex Anglia commigrantes, Lutetia Parisiorum, duce Ric. Hargraves, ad hanc urbem advolarunt duo nobili genere oriundi adolescentes, viz., Georgius Giffordus, Gilberti frater, qui in Seminario Romæ vivit, et Jo. Wolsleius, qui ad mensam nostram statim admissi sunt."

We learn from the *Relatione del Collegio Inglese* (March 14, 1596) that Gifford's perversion was due to the influence of Solomon Aldred, a married man who was then in Rome, and who is doubtless the Aldred mentioned by Phelippes in his letter to Walsingham, March 19, 158⅚ (*supra*, p. 157). At first he earned his bread as a tailor, and at the intercession of Dr. Owen Lewis, afterwards Bishop of Cassano, obtained a pension of ten crowns from Pope Gregory XIII. He went to England, where he was taken into Walsingham's service, and passed to and fro between England and Rome, until on his third journey, having reached Bologna, he there learned that Cardinal Allen was at Rome, and if after this he revisited Rome, it was in secret. He was believed to have had secret service money placed at his disposal by Walsingham, and one of the first of the students of the English College whom he gained over was Gilbert Gifford.

The same paper informs us that one of Gilbert's first exploits in early life, before he came to Rome, was a challenge to a schoolfellow to fight a duel. The character given of him in the Roman College is just what we should have expected from his after conduct : "In hoc collegium admissus ut subdolo erat ingenio, egregia simulatione pudorem et modestiam primo mentitus est." Finding himself strongly supported by friends outside the College, he laid aside his modest demeanour, and soon brought upon himself a sentence of expulsion. From this dates his ill will to the Jesuits and to Cardinal Allen. In the sense of the narrative here given, the statement made in the body of this book (*supra*, p. 143) must be understood that "Gilbert Gifford had no Jesuit training, and that the Order never had anything to do with him."

After his ejection from the English College he lived for a time at Rome with the friends he had made ; and the next mention we have of him is that already quoted from the First Douay Diary, which tells us that he and William Gifford arrived at the College at Rheims in 1582, the one to teach theology, the other logic. The exact date is given us by the Second Diary, which says, "Junius, 1582 : 23° die Roma ad nos venerunt D. Guil. Giffordus, presbyter, et D. Gilbertus Giffordus alterius cognatus."

If there is no error in the dates or names this restless soul cannot have held his school of logic long, for the Second Douay Diary has the entry on September 13, 1583 : "Venerunt Roma D. Gib. Gifford et Ric. Bradshawe."

We next find his name in the Diary as ordained at Rheims, Subdeacon, on March 16, 1585, and Deacon on the Saturday before Passion Sunday, April 6, by the Cardinal of Guise in the Church of St. Remigius. His departure from the College is noted on the 8th of October in the same year. Apart from his hostility to the Jesuits, "on the business of which Order" Mr. Froude imagines Gifford to have "travelled" (*supra* p. 143), there was little time for such journeys, for Morgan's letter to the Queen of Scots, stating that "there was of late with him one Gilbert Gifford," is dated the 15th of that same month of October (*supra*, p. 112). The statement (*supra*, p. 144) requires correction that he was in Paris in the summer of 1585, for he was then at Rheims in the College.

The precise date of his ordination to the priesthood we learn from the Second Douay Diary, in the year 1587. "Post Dominicam *Lætare*, sabbato sequente, viz. 14 Martii, ad Presbyteratum evecti sunt D. Gilb. Gifford, diocesis Lichfeldensis," &c.

According to the *Relatione*, Gifford's plan was to return to Rome and to obtain a professorship in the schools of the Sapienza, and so form a position of influence to be able to watch and interfere with the students of the English College. Meanwhile he took to Walsingham the book written by Gratley and himself against the Jesuits, "pretending no other errand," as Phelippes wrote to Walsingham (*supra*, p. 219); and then on his return to Paris, the executions for the Babington conspiracy and the death of the Queen of Scots awakening suspicion against him, he was watched and apprehended under the disgraceful circumstances described by the English Ambassador. The same *Relatione* says that before his death he wrote to Cardinal Allen a full narrative of the harm done by him to the Cardinal and the Jesuits. It adds that in a letter to Walsingham, written and intercepted just before his arrest, he stated that he had obtained ordination that he might the better hide his dealings with Elizabeth's Minister.

Page 272.—John Savage in his confession said that the six conspirators who were to assassinate Elizabeth were "Robert Barnwell, Chideock Tichborne, Anthony Tychinor, Thomas Salisbury, as I think, and myself—Mr. Abington, I am not able to touch him."

The following passages in the same confession are interesting. Gifford considered that Savage thought that he had "detected," that is betrayed him.

"That there is one of the guards about the said Queen of Scots, a brewer by occupation, that is corrupted to convey letters unto her from whomsoever they come, and that by the means of Gilbert Gifford she had intelligence of the French Ambassador.

"*Item*, that there is one Thomas Barnes, a Warwickshire man, that Gilbert

Gifford left in his stead to take such letters as came to the French Ambassador's hands for the Queen of Scots, and carry them to the said brewer, to be delivered to the Queen, and to stay for the Queen's answer, which was transported by the Ambassador's means.

"*Item,* that Gilbert Gifford had often conference with Richard Gifford, brother to George Gifford, and that the said Richard was privy to this vowed attempt by his brother George against her Majesty, as Gilbert told me" (*Cotton. MSS.,* Caligula, C. ix., f. 374, 376).

The Queen's evidence against Gilbert Gifford, here given, induced his father, John Gifford, to write the following letter to Phelippes, which puts before us in lively colours the wretched state to which the Catholics were reduced, when a country gentleman was obliged to write in such terms to such an agent of the Government as Phelippes. Dodd introduces his Life of William Gifford, Archbishop of Rheims (*Church History,* vol. ii., p. 358), by this mention of the family: "The Giffords were Counts of Longueville in Normandy before the Conquest, and afterwards enjoyed the title of Earl of Buckingham, being persons of great note and very large possessions, in all the succeeding reigns. In the Conqueror's days Osbert Gifford was master of several lordships, but the chief seat of the family appears to have been at Brinsfield in Gloucestershire. A branch or the chief heir of the family, by marrying an heiress, obtained a plentiful estate at Chillington in Staffordshire." The position that Mr. Gifford of Chillington occupied in the county is shown by a commission from the Queen, dated October 27, 1570, addressed to Sir Thomas Cockayne, Sir George Blount, Richard Bagot, and John Gifford, to decide on a contention respecting a highway and a watercourse, between Lord Paget and William Gresley (*Domestic, Addenda, Elizabeth,* vol. xix., n. 18). His name is here associated with those with which, in the course of these letters, we have become familiar.

John Gifford to Phelippes. (Vol. xix., n. 101.)

"Sir,—I have written to my unfortunate son. I would God he had never been born. I may well say, Happy is the barren, that hath no child. I pray you peruse it, and pen it to your liking, and send it to me and I will write it up. I thank you for your letter, which did somewhat comfort me, but hearing by report of Savage his confession, how far he toucheth him in practice and generally at his names, I cannot but be very sorrowful. And in truth [it] hath cast me into [a] fit of an ague, but I heartily pray you to request Mr. Secretary for me that Savage and other moe [more] be examined whether they were privy of Gilbert's being left in London, whether he were in my company since his going from me before Easter, and what the cause was he kept himself secret from me; and further, as his honour shall think good, that either I may live in his honour's good favour, or be punished for mine offences. I beseech you that this may be before Savage die, unless their honours have searched so far before this time, and rest satisfied. Thus, resting upon your friendship, [I] do desire you to have consideration of me as you think best.

"Islington, this 14th of September.

"Your assured friend to his power,

"JOHN GIFFORD.

"I pray you have good consideration whether it be not dangerous for me
to write to him, standing indicted."

Addressed—"To his very good friend, Thomas Phelippes, Esq., these be
delivered with speed."

It will be seen that there is a concurrence of testimony between the
Stonyhurst paper, Châteauneuf's Memoir, the confession of Savage, and
the State Papers here given, that Gifford was a mover in Babington's conspiracy. His name was carefully kept out of the printed accounts, for
naturally enough Walsingham did not wish the part that he had taken to
be made known.

Page 305.—The Journals of the House of Lords give but scanty information respecting these Sessions, but enough is recorded to show us who the
four Bishops were, and also to let us see that no scruple was entertained by
the Lords Spiritual, who were willing to take part in petitioning for the
death of the Queen of Scots. It would appear that Elizabeth would not
allow them to do so. The Bishop of London was John Elmer ; of Winchester,
Thomas Couper ; of Durham, Richard Barnes ; and of Worcester, Edmund
Freak.

"On the 7th day of this instant month of November, while the Lords
were in consultation about the great matter of the Queen of Scots, the chief
and only cause of the summons of this Parliament, they of the Commons
House came up and desired conference with some of the Lords of this House,
what number it should please their lordships to appoint touching the said
great cause, which, as they affirmed, had been opened and declared unto
them ; whereupon the Lords made choice of these Lords following, viz. :
the Archbishops of Canterbury and York, the Lord Burghley, Lord Treasurer,
the Earl of Derby, Lord Steward, the Earls of Northumberland, Kent,
Rutland, and Sussex, the Bishops of London, Durham, Winchester, and
Worcester, the Lord Howard, Lord Admiral, the Lord Hunsdon, Lord
Chamberlain, the Lords Cobham, Gray, Lumley, Chandos, Buckhurst,
Delaware, and Norreys ; and to attend the said Lords, the Lord Chief
Justice of the Common Pleas, the Lord Chief Baron, and Justice Gawdie.
The place and time of their meeting was in the outer Parliament Chamber,
that afternoon, at two of the clock ; and after often meetings and long
conferences had, they agreed upon a form of petition, which by both the
Houses should be presented unto her Majesty, and that choice should be
made of a certain number of either House to prefer the same unto her
Highness ; which being reported to this House, the Lords liked very well
thereof, and thereupon made choice of these Lords following, *videl.* : the
Lord Chancellor, the Lord Treasurer, the Lord Great Chamberlain, the
Lord Steward, the Earls of Northumberland, Kent, Rutland, Sussex,
Pembroke, and Hertford, the Lord Admiral and Lord Chamberlain, the
Lords Abergavenny, Zouche, Morley, Cobham, Gray, Lumley, Chandos,
Buckhurst, Delaware, and Norreys ; and they of the Commons House
appointed their Speaker, and all such of that House as were of the Privy
Council, and so many others of that House as in all, with the said Privy
Council, made up the number of forty-two persons, to join with the said
Lords. And they altogether, understanding first her Majesty's pleasure for
the time of their repair to her Highness' presence, which was signified to

be on Saturday, the 12th day of November, on which day the Lord Chancellor, in the name of the Lords, and the Speaker, in the name of the Commons, declared unto her Majesty that both the Lords and Commons, after often conferences and long consultation, had concluded to be humble suitors unto her Majesty by way of petition ; the effect whereof was then at good length opened unto her Majesty by the Lord Chancellor and Speaker, and the petition thereupon delivered unto her Majesty in writing."

Queen Elizabeth's oracular answer to the petition is well known.

"If," said her Highness, "I should say unto you that I mean not to grant your petition, by my faith, I should say unto you more than perhaps I mean ; and if I should say unto you that I mean to grant your petition, I should then tell you more than is fit for you to know ; and thus I must deliver you an answer answerless" (*Journal of the House of Lords*, 28 Eliz., p. 123).

Page 320.—The Earl of Leicester, who had written from Holland to advise that Mary should be secretly removed by poison (Camden, *Annales*, p. 444), had now returned home to assist Elizabeth in her deliberations.

Page 335.—Mary's question, "What did she with the French at Newhaven?"—that is Havre de Grace—is in allusion to Elizabeth's interference in the civil war in France in 1562, when she had not only furnished money and troops to the Prince of Condé, but had occupied Havre with an English garrison. This was not the first time the question had been put to Poulet. Writing to Elizabeth from Paris, August 6, 1577, he describes a scene at Court, where he endeavours, very ineffectually, to screen Elizabeth's notorious aid to the Huguenots during the civil war then in progress. Catharine de Medicis cut short his protestations with the sharp rejoinder, "'Do you not remember what the Queen, your mistress, did at Newhaven?' I answered that I remembered well the time, but was ignorant of the occasions, which I doubted not were very sufficient."

ERRATA.

Page 4, line 2, *for* more than fifty letters not to be found in the Record Office, *read* nearly forty Letters not to be found in the Record Office or the British Museum. *See* p. vii.

Page 26, line 28, *for* bloodhounds *read* buckhounds. *See* p. 106, *note*.

Page 99, line 7, *for* father *read* grandfather. *See* p. 252, *note*.

Page 143, line 2, *for* the Order never had anything to do with him, *read* though he was for a time a student in the English College at Rome, which was under the charge of Jesuit Fathers, he was expelled by them from the College. *See* p. 388.

Page 144, line 13, *dele* Gifford. *See* p. 389.

The description of Sir Walter Aston's park at Standon has by error been applied to his park at Tixall in the footnote on page 249, which note should therefore be erased.

ALPHABETICAL· INDEX.

THE CONDITION OF CATHOLICS UNDER
JAMES I. Second Edition. London: Longmans, Green, and Co. 1872. *Demy 8vo, cloth,* 14s.

This work consists of two parts:

1. THE LIFE OF FATHER JOHN GERARD, S.J., chiefly translated from the narrative of his missionary career in England, written by him in Latin for his Superiors.

2. A NARRATIVE OF THE GUNPOWDER PLOT, written in English by Father Gerard, and now first published from the original Manuscript at Stonyhurst.

THE TROUBLES OF OUR CATHOLIC FORE-
FATHERS, related by themselves ; from hitherto unpublished Manuscripts. First Series. London: Burns and Oates. 1872. *Demy 8vo, cloth,* 10s. 6d.

Contents:

1. MOTHER MARGARET CLEMENT AND THE CARTHUSIAN MONKS.
2. THE IMPRISONMENT OF FRANCIS TREGIAN.
3. FATHER TESIMOND'S LANDING IN ENGLAND.
4. FATHER RICHARD BLOUNT AND SCOTNEY CASTLE.
5. THE BABTHORPES OF BABTHORPE.
6. ST. MONICA'S CONVENT IN WAR, PESTILENCE, AND POVERTY.
7. THE VENETIAN AMBASSADOR'S CHAPLAIN.
8. THE SOUTHCOTE FAMILY.
9. THE TICHBORNES OF TICHBORNE HOUSE.

A HUNDRED MEDITATIONS ON THE LOVE
OF GOD, by Father ROBERT SOUTHWELL, S.J., the Poet and Martyr. Now first published. London: Burns and Oates. 1873. *Fcap. 8vo, cloth,* 5s.

THE DEVOTIONS OF THE LADY LUCY HER-
BERT OF POWIS, formerly Prioress of the Augustinian Nuns at Bruges. London: Burns and Oates. 1873. *Fcap. 8vo, cloth,* 3s. 6d.

By the Woodbury or permanent process, 1s. each, or 7s. 6d. a dozen.

SIXTEEN PHOTOGRAPHS OF FATHERS OF THE SOCIETY OF JESUS, CHIEFLY MARTYRS,

FROM PICTURES IN HOUSES OF THE SOCIETY AT ROME.

From the Gesù.

FF. CAMPION, M.	FF. BRIANT, M.	FF. COTTAM, M.
GARNET, M.	WRIGHT, M.	WALPOLE, M.
OLDCORNE, M.	FILCOCK, M.	PERSONS.
HOLLAND, M.	CORNELIUS, M.	HAYWOOD.

From S. Andrea on Monte Cavallo.

FF. WESTON and DARBYSHIRE.

From the Roman College.

FF. PAGE and OGILVY, MM.

PHOTOGRAPHS OF PORTRAITS OR PRINTS OF ENGLISH MARTYRS FROM OTHER SOURCES.

SIR THOMAS MORE (from a beautiful picture in the Barberini Library at Rome).

CARDINAL FISHER.

ARCHBISHOP PLUNKET.

FF. WARD, DUCKETT, GREEN, *alias* BROOKE, TUNSTALL, GENINGS, Secular Priests.

F. BARLOW, O.S.B.

FF. BELL, BULLAKER, HEATH, WOODCOCK, and COLMAN (who died in prison), O.S.F.

FF. CAMPION, WHITBREAD, MORSE, WRIGHT, HOLLAND, CORBY, ARROWSMITH, BAKER, S.J.

RICHARD HERST, layman.

Of these, ten are taken from the Portraits that for two hundred years have been in the possession of the Teresian Nuns at Lanherne.

LONDON: BURNS AND OATES, 17 PORTMAN STREET.